Principles of Protocol Design

Robin Sharp

Principles of Protocol Design

 Springer

Robin Sharp
Technical University of Denmark
Informatics & Mathematical Modelling
Richard Petersens Plads Bldg. 321
2800 Kongens Lyngby
Denmark

ISBN 978-3-642-09628-0   e-ISBN 978-3-540-77541-6

Mathematics Subject Classification (2000): C.2.2, C.2.4

Cover design: KünkelLopka

Printed on acid-free paper

9 8 7 6 5 4 3 2 1

springer.com

Preface

This book introduces the reader to the principles used in the construction of a large range of modern data communication protocols. The approach we take is rather a formal one, primarily based on descriptions of protocols in the notation of CSP. This not only enables us to describe protocols in a concise manner, but also to reason about many of their interesting properties and formally to prove certain aspects of their correctness with respect to appropriate specifications. Only after considering the main principles do we go on to consider actual protocols where these principles are exploited.

This is a completely new edition of a book which was first published in 1994, where the main focus of many international efforts to develop data communication systems was on OSI – Open Systems Interconnection – the standardised architecture for communication systems developed within the International Organisation for Standardization, ISO. In the intervening 13 years, many of the specific protocols developed as part of the OSI initiative have fallen into disuse. However, the terms and concepts introduced in the OSI Reference Model are still essential for a systematic and consistent analysis of data communication systems, and OSI terms are therefore used throughout.

There are three significant changes in this second edition of the book which particularly reflect recent developments in computer networks and distributed systems. Firstly, the rise of the Internet has led to the development of large numbers of new protocols, particularly in the Application Layer, and a new chapter has been introduced focussing on some of the most important of these. These new protocols typically use new styles of encoding, particularly ASCII encodings such as MIME and XML, and rely on middleware solutions based on a variety of support protocols. Chapters 8 and 10 have therefore been extended to deal with these topics. Finally, there is today much more focus on security issues in networks. Chapter 6, which deals with the general concepts of security, has been heavily revised and brought up to date, while Chapters 8, 9, 10 and 11 now include sections discussing specific technologies such as IPsec, SSL/TLS, and secure protocols for e-mail and web-based applications.

The book has arisen from material used for teaching a course on *Distributed Systems* at the Technical University of Denmark. The exercises at the ends of Chapters 2 to 8 also originate in this course, either as weekly assignments or, in some cases, as examination questions. I hope you find them as interesting—and maybe even as challenging—as my students have done.

This text was originally written for third or fourth year students in Computer Science or Electrical Engineering, and is intended to be suitable for most final-year undergraduate or postgraduate courses on advanced data communications or computer networks. The reader is expected to have a software background, in particular including a basic knowledge of functional programming and parallel programming, combined with some knowledge of computer systems architecture and data transmission. Knowledge of formal methods, for example based on languages such as VDM or Z, is not essential, but to get the most out of the book you should know about the sort of discrete mathematics which is used in computer science, and be aware of the basic concepts of mathematical proof.

Many people deserve thanks for helping me in the task of preparing this text, and especially for reading and commenting on the various drafts which have seen the light of day. I would particularly like to thank my colleagues Hans-Henrik Løvengreen of this department, Arne Skou of Aalborg University, Klaus Hansen of the University of Copenhagen and Henrik Reif Andersen of the IT University in Copenhagen for their comments on important parts of the text. I also owe a great debt of thanks to my many students, who have been exposed to several provisional versions of this book, a fate which they have borne stoically. Their help in finding errors and pointing out the shakier parts of the presentation, where the arguments were weakest or the explanations most difficult to follow, has been invaluable.

Finally, I would like to thank my wife Lisbeth and daughter Melissa for continuing to be so tolerant about having an author in the house. The competition for the PC at home has at times been intense – and they have been really sweet about letting me win....

Technical University of Denmark,   *Robin Sharp*
October 2007.

Contents

Chapter 1
Introduction

Then a minstrel and loremaster stood up and named all the names of the Lords of the Mark in their order.... And when Théoden was named, Éomer drained the cup. Then Éowen bade those that served to fill the cups, and all there assembled rose and drank to the new king, crying: 'Hail, Éomer, King of the Mark!' "

"The Return of the King"
J. R. R. Tolkien.

A protocol is a set of rules which have to be followed in the course of some activity. Originally, the term was used solely of human activities, especially those of a somewhat formal kind, such as the state funeral for King Théoden described in the quotation at the start of this chapter. The *chef de protocole* for a Head of State sets formal rules for how activities take place according to the niceties of diplomatic practice. But protocols must also be followed in less elevated spheres, such as games of all kinds, the way in which conversations are conducted, and in fact all activities which are governed by custom and convention. If the protocol is not followed, the activity will not be successful.

In this book we shall consider *communication protocols*, and in particular those which regulate communication between computers. The characteristics of protocols mentioned above are equally evident in this case: A set of *formal rules* governs the exchange of information, and the communication activity *fails* if the protocol is not correctly followed.

1.1 What is a Protocol?

In the general sense, communication between computers takes place by the exchange of data – information encoded in some way which depends on the system concerned. We can consider this exchange as taking place in discrete steps, which we shall call *elementary communications*, in each of which a *message* is transferred. Again depending on the system, a message may be a single electronic signal, or a

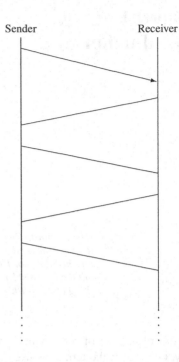

Fig. 1.1 Exchange of messages in a simple protocol.

larger amount of data. For generality, we shall use the term the *type* of the message
to cover both the general content and the detailed encoding.

A common definition of a communication protocol [133] is thus that it is a set of
rules for the order in which messages of particular types are exchanged. With our
definition of message type, this also implies a set of rules for the encoding of the
various types of message.

The exchange of data may take place between two or more parties. When there
are N parties to the exchange, we shall talk of *N-peer communication*, and speak of
the protocol as an *N-peer protocol*.

For each of the N parties to an N-peer communication, the protocol defines a
language, whose sentences are the legal sequences of messages received by that
party, and whose alphabet of symbols is the set of all possible messages. A machine
to obey the rules of the protocol must thus essentially be a recogniser for the protocol language. For simple protocols, this is a useful abstraction, as the language
is *regular* or at most *context-free*, and standard compiler techniques [124] can be
used to implement the machine as a finite state machine or push-down automaton
respectively.

A trivial example of a simple protocol described in this way is given below. It is a
type of *stop-and-wait protocol*. The sender requests the receiver to indicate when it
is ready to receive data, and waits for this indication. On receipt of the indication, the
sender sends the data and waits for an acknowledgment. The exchange of messages
is as shown in Figure 1.1. The languages to be recognised by the sender and receiver

respectively (and of course to be generated by the receiver and sender respectively) are defined by the BNF:

$sender$ ::= $readyindication\ acknowledge\ sender$
$receiver$ ::= $requesttoaccept\ data$ $receiver$

Each party must generate and recognise sentences of a regular language. This is a simple task for a finite state machine.

Unfortunately, there are some important objections to this language-oriented view of a protocol. The first is a practical objection: Simple languages generally do not correspond to protocols which can tolerate faults, such as missing or duplicated messages. Protocols which are fault-tolerant often require the use of state machines with enormous numbers of states, or they may define *context-dependent* languages.

A more radical objection is that classical analysis of the protocol language from a formal language point of view traditionally concerns itself with the problems of constructing a suitable recogniser, determining the internal states of the recogniser, and so on. This does not help us to *analyse* or *check* many of the properties which we may require the protocol to have, such as the properties of fault-tolerance mentioned above. To be able to investigate this we need analytical tools which can describe the parallel operation of all the parties which use the protocol to regulate their communication.

1.2 Protocols as Processes

A radically different way of looking at things has therefore gained prominence within recent years. This involves considering the protocol as being defined, not so much by the internal states of the protocol machine, but rather by the *observable external behaviour* of a *process*. The external behaviour is defined as the set of all possible *traces* – sequences of elementary communications in which the process takes part. The work of Hoare, Milner and others ([64], [128], [19], [94]) has shown how the behaviour of combinations of processes can be deduced from the behaviours of the individual component processes through the use of a calculus or algebra, and how it is possible to prove properties of processes starting from certain axioms about the behaviours of their component parts. Chapter 2 gives a short introduction to the method used in this book and the required notation.

This type of approach makes it possible to specify and analyse complex protocols. In particular, the rules for the composition of processes make it possible to analyse protocols which rely on the the use of other protocols in some layered manner, as is commonly the case in communication systems. A well-known example of this is seen in the OSI standard architecture for communication systems [133]. Some simple illustrations of the approach and an introduction to the OSI Reference

Model will be given in the Chapter 3, where we also consider the general properties which might be desirable for services in distributed systems.

1.3 Techniques for Actual Protocols

The central chapters of the book are devoted to a presentation of techniques for providing particular types of service by the use of appropriate protocols. This presentation is illustrated by theoretical analysis of some of the protocol techniques, and by a classification of some protocols used in practice today, according to the techniques on which they are based.

The presentation falls into four parts. In Chapter 4 we discuss a number of basic mechanisms for use in 2-peer point-to-point communication protocols, and the relation of these mechanisms to required properties of the service, particularly resilience to simple faults such as corruption or loss of messages.

Chapter 5 considers the problems associated with providing a service to more than two parties, and in particular the problem of getting several parties to agree in the presence of faults. Here we shall extend our repertoire of permitted faults to include arbitrary, possibly malicious faults – the so-called Byzantine errors.

In Chapter 6 we turn our attention to another form of malicious attack to which distributed systems are exposed – attempts by unauthorised persons to read or alter information to which they are not supposed to have access. This is the problem of computer security, whose solution, as we shall see, requires special protocols and a careful use of cryptographic methods.

Finally, in Chapter 7 we consider what techniques are available for locating an intended participant within a distributed system, and for organising transmission of messages so that they reach the recipient reliably and with a minimum of delay. This is the problem of naming, addressing and routing, which is interesting not only because it is a real, practical problem to be solved, but also because the solutions illustrate many of the strategic choices to be taken when decisions have to be made in distributed systems.

1.4 Real Protocols

After considering in a rather abstract manner the techniques available for constructing protocols with particular properties, the final chapters of the book will be devoted to looking at a selection of real protocols, and to analysing how the general techniques are deployed in them.

We start this part of the book by looking, in Chapter 8, at principles used for encoding the messages used in protocols. Then we go on to look at each of the layers of the OSI Reference Model in turn, presenting commonly used protocols, many of them internationally standardised, and classifying them according to the type of service which they support and the protocol mechanisms used in order to supply this service. Chapter 9 deals with the so-called OSI Lower Layers, which are the layers up to and including the Transport layer. Chapter 10 describes protocols in the OSI Upper Layers – the Session, Presentation and Application layers of the Reference Model – which provide general support for applications. And finally, Chapter 11 presents a number of important protocols associated with specific applications, including file transfer, mail transfer, transaction processing, document access via the World Wide Web and Web services.

This book is not a catalogue of standards, and many protocols of potential interest, particularly in the Application layer, have had to be left out. Even so, the bibliography at the end of the book contains references to more than 130 national and international standards, chosen because they illustrate interesting principles of design. On the other hand, we do not discuss any of the multitude of commercially available protocols from specific suppliers, nor do we enter into detailed presentations of particular protocols. For this kind of specific information, you will need to read the original descriptions of the protocols concerned.

1.5 Reader's Guide

This book deals with both theory and practice, and some readers may prefer to omit one or other of these subjects on the first reading. If you prefer to omit as much theory as possible, you can skip Sections:

- 2.1.2, which deals with process algebra,
- 2.2 and 2.3, which deal with the logic used to prove properties of systems of processes,
- 3.1, which gives an example of a proof that a protocol enjoys a particular property,
- 6.4.3, which deals with the logic used to prove the correctness of authentication protocols.

If on the other hand you prefer to think about the theory and are not much concerned with practice, then you can skip:

- Chapter 8, which deals with encoding of protocols, and
- Chapters 9, 10 and 11, which deal with real protocols used in the various layers of the OSI Reference Model.

Chapter 2
CSP Descriptions and Proof Rules

"There must be a mutual cooperating for the good of the whole."

"De Jure Regni"
in Buchanan's translation, 1689

In this book we shall describe protocols as systems of interacting processes, and we shall describe processes in a notation which, apart from minor deviations, is the notation of CSP in the form introduced by Hoare in his book "Communicating Sequential Processes" [64].

Two basic concepts lie behind the notation of CSP. Firstly, a system in which concurrent activities take place can be described as a sequential *process* which can take part in sequences of *events*. Secondly, that processes can be put together from component parts which are simpler processes. Thus the basic notation enables us to describe events, processes and ways of combining processes. For each construction the semantic rules of CSP then tell us what the *behaviour* of the corresponding process is.

In this chapter we present the CSP notation in the form in which we shall use it, and discuss ways of reasoning about the behaviour of processes described in CSP. As we shall see, there are two approaches to this reasoning. Firstly, we can define an *algebra* for processes. Such an algebra essentially expresses equalities between processes (where two processes are equal if they have the same behaviour) in terms of equalities between CSP expressions. Such equalities enable us to expand or reduce such expressions by algebraic manipulation, so that we can get them into a form where the behaviour of the process described becomes apparent.

Secondly, we can define a *logic* for reasoning about the properties of processes, and in particular for reasoning about whether they satisfy some predicate which we think of as a specification. This is a very valuable tool for analysis of protocols, as it enables us to give formal proofs that a protocol specified in CSP is correct, in the sense that it actually has some desired property, such as preserving the sequence of data communicated via the protocol. In the next chapter we shall present an extended example of a proof of correctness in this sense.

2.1 Processes and Process Synchronisation

Because one of the aims of CSP is to describe concurrent activities, one of the most important ways of combining processes is by setting them to run in parallel with one another. This is known as *parallel composition*. A characteristic of parallel composition in CSP is that when two processes P and Q run in parallel and are specified to take part in the same event, say a, then their activity can be *synchronised* at that event.

Synchronisation means that when one of them, say P, reaches a point where it could potentially take part in (say) a, then it cannot actually do so until its 'partner' Q also takes part in a. A common way of expressing this is to say that P makes an *offer* to take part in a, and that another process must *accept* this offer before P can continue. This is illustrated in Figure 2.1.

If P has reached a point where it can *only* take part in a, then it must wait until the partner is ready and willing to take part in just exactly the event a. If the partner never makes a suitable offer, then P will effectively be deadlocked. In many cases, however, there will be several events in which P could potentially take part, and it will be able to *choose* one of those events for which a partner is ready, or possibly an event for which no partner is required. Thereafter it will continue with whatever activities it can take part in after the chosen event.

The events which a process, say P, can take part in fall into two classes:

External events,   which are visible from outside P, and which other processes can synchronise with if they are combined with P by parallel composition.

Internal events,   which are not visible from outside P, and which other processes therefore cannot synchronise with. Evidently, no partner is needed for participation in internal events.

The set of externally visible events which a process P potentially can take part in is known as P's *alphabet*, which we shall denote αP. Note that it is not necessarily the case that a process actually *will* take part in all events in its alphabet; αP may in fact include events which P never offers to take part in. A simple example of this is a deadlocked process, which cannot take part in *any* of the events of its alphabet.

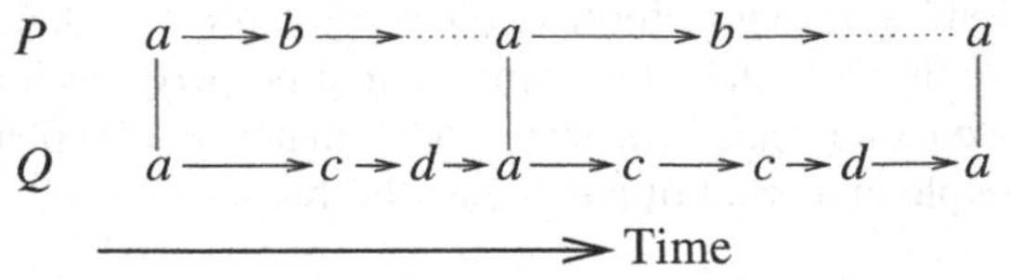

Fig. 2.1 Parallel execution of two processes with synchronisation.
P and Q are here required to be synchronised on every event a. The *thick vertical lines* indicate synchronised events in the two processes. The *dotted lines* indicate periods of time where P is willing to take part in an event a, but its partner Q is occupied with other activities.

P $a \longrightarrow b \longrightarrow \cdots\cdots a \longrightarrow b \longrightarrow \cdots\cdots a$

Q $a \longrightarrow c \rightarrow d \rightarrow a \longrightarrow c \longrightarrow c \rightarrow d \longrightarrow a$

$\longrightarrow$ Time

It is a feature of CSP that events from a process' alphabet can be explicitly *hidden*, i.e. made invisible to the external world. The hidden events are, by definition, removed from the alphabet. This feature is used to introduce abstraction in process descriptions. Otherwise, all events from all component processes in a complex process P would automatically be visible – and could be synchronised with, if another process were combined in parallel with P.

Effectively, every process runs within an *environment* made up of the totality of those processes with which it is running in parallel. However, this environment is never 'closed', and new processes can be added to it if desired. Because of the synchronisation rules, parallel composition of an existing process with a new process may of course affect which events the existing process will take part in. So we have to make clear to ourselves what environment we mean, when we are discussing what a process 'does'. In most of what follows, we shall suppose that processes run in an environment which enables them to take part in all the events which are not explicitly hidden.

2.1.1 Process Expressions

The basic notation for the definition of processes is by a set of *process equations*, each of them of the form:

$$p \stackrel{\text{def}}{=} \mathscr{P}$$
$$\text{or } p[i : \mathscr{D}] \stackrel{\text{def}}{=} \mathscr{P}$$

where p is a *process identifier*, possibly with one or more subscripts (parameters), i, in some domain $\mathscr{D}$, and $\mathscr{P}$ is a *process expression*, which may depend on p and i. To start with, we shall for generality define the syntactic class of process expressions, $\mathscr{P}$, by the grammar:

$$\mathscr{P} ::= STOP_A \mid p \mid p[e] \mid a \rightarrow \mathscr{P} \mid \mathscr{P} \sqcap \mathscr{P} \mid \mathscr{P} [\!] \mathscr{P} \mid$$
$$\mathscr{P} \parallel_A \mathscr{P} \mid \mathscr{P} \parallel\!\parallel \mathscr{P} \mid \mathscr{P}[d/c] \mid \mathscr{P} \backslash A$$

To avoid excessive use of brackets, we assume that $\rightarrow$ binds more tightly than $\sqcap$ or $[\!]$, so that for example $(a \rightarrow P[\!]Q)$ is to be understood as $((a \rightarrow P)[\!]Q)$.

The informal semantics of these expressions is as follows:

$STOP_A$ is a process which is unable to perform any action in the set A – the process is *deadlocked*. Often the set A will correspond to the alphabet of the process being defined, and in such cases we shall for notational convenience omit A.

p is a process identifier. The corresponding process must be defined by a definition of the form $p \stackrel{\text{def}}{=} \mathscr{P}$. The alphabet of p is then $\alpha\mathscr{P}$.

$p[e]$, where p is a process identifier and e is an expression of type $\mathscr{D}$, denotes a parameterised process whose definition is of the form $p[i : \mathscr{D}] \stackrel{\text{def}}{=} \mathscr{P}$, where each occurrence of i in $\mathscr{P}$ has been replaced by the value of e. In what follows we shall allow $\mathscr{D}$ if necessary to be a composite domain, so that i is in fact a sequence of parameters, and e correspondingly a sequence of values for these parameters. The actual notation which we use for denoting e and $\mathscr{D}$ is summarised in Appendix A; it follows the conventions of the specification language VDM. As in the case of non-parameterised processes, the alphabet of $p[e]$ is $\alpha\mathscr{P}$.

$a \rightarrow P$ is a process which must initially take part in the event a and then behaves like the process described by P. This syntactic construction is known as *prefixing*. Its alphabet is $(\alpha P \cup \{a\})$.

$P \sqcap Q$ is a process which behaves like P or Q, but the choice between them is non-deterministic and cannot be controlled from the environment in which $P \sqcap Q$ performs. This is known as *internal non-determinism*. From outside, it appears as though an arbitrary decision is made internally between the behaviour described by P and the behaviour described by Q. This is only defined if P and Q have the same alphabet, which thus becomes the alphabet of the combination.

Note that in CSP it is not assumed that this choice is *fair* – neither in the intuitive sense that there are equal probabilities of P and Q being chosen, nor even in the more restricted technical sense that if infinitely many attempts are made to perform $(P \sqcap Q)$, then each of the alternatives will eventually be observed. The choice really is an arbitrary one. If we want to assign probabilities to the alternatives, we must specify this separately, outside the process description itself.

$P \llbracket Q$ is a process which behaves like P or Q, but the environment 'decides' which of these possibilities will occur, by behaving in a way which enables P or Q to proceed, i.e. by accepting the offer of an event which is a prefix for P or Q respectively. If the environment enables *both* alternatives to proceed, the choice between them is arbitrary. This is known as *external non-determinism*. This is likewise only defined if P and Q have the same alphabet, which is also the alphabet of the combination.

$P \parallel_A Q$ is a process which behaves like P and like Q when they operate independently, except that all events in the event set A must be synchronised. This is known as *parallel composition*. Its alphabet is $\alpha P \cup \alpha Q$.

It is assumed that $A \subseteq (\alpha P \cup \alpha Q)$, i.e. that A is a subset of the combined alphabets of P and Q. For notational convenience we shall omit A if $A = (\alpha P \cap \alpha Q)$, i.e. if P and Q are synchronised over all events which they have in common. We write $P \parallel Q$ for the parallel composition in this case.

The case where $A = \{\}$ is special, as the two processes P and Q are then not synchronised with one another. To emphasise this, we shall use the following special notation:

$P \parallel\parallel\parallel Q$ denotes the process which behaves like P and Q running in parallel without mutual synchronisation. The meaning of parallel composition in this case is taken to be that the behaviour of $P \parallel\parallel\parallel Q$ is an *arbitrary interleaving* of the behaviours of P and Q. In other words, the sequence of events in which the composed process takes part is a member of the set of all possible interleavings of the sequences in which P can take part with those in which Q can take part.

Suppose for example that P can have the behaviour described by $(a \to b \to STOP)$, i.e. it can take part in an event a *and then* an event b before deadlocking, and that Q can have the behaviour given by $(a \to STOP \sqcap c \to STOP)$, i.e. can take part in an event a *or* an event c before deadlocking. Then the possible sequences of events which may be observed for $P \parallel\!\parallel Q$ are:

$$\langle a,a,b \rangle, \ \langle a,a,b \rangle, \ \langle a,b,a \rangle, \ \langle c,a,b \rangle, \ \langle a,c,b \rangle, \ \langle a,b,c \rangle$$

Similarly, if Q's behaviour is described instead by $(c \to d \to STOP)$, then the observable sequences of events for $P \parallel\!\parallel Q$ become:

$$\langle c,d,a,b \rangle, \ \langle c,a,d,b \rangle, \ \langle c,a,b,d \rangle, \ \langle a,c,d,b \rangle, \ \langle a,c,b,d \rangle, \ \langle a,b,c,d \rangle$$

$P[d/c]$ is a process which behaves like P with all occurrences of event c replaced by d. This is known as *renaming*. The alphabet after renaming is $(\alpha P) - \{c\} \cup \{d\}$.

$P \setminus A$ is a process which behaves like P except that all events in the event set A are invisible to the environment, and are therefore internal events. This is known as *hiding* or *restriction*. The alphabet after hiding is $(\alpha P) - A$.

Some simple examples of process definitions according to this grammar (partly taken from [64]) are given in Figure 2.3. These definitions describe a number of vending machines (*VMxxx*), a customer, and a small demon – as illustrated in Figure 2.2. The event *coin* represents the event in which a coin is put into the machine, while *choc* and *toffee* represent the events in which respectively a chocolate bar and a toffee bar are removed from the machine. Note that these events are in this style of description given in a very abstract manner, and that the 'direction' of the event cannot be seen in the process definition. We shall in Section 2.1.3 look at another style of description in which more details are included.

Note also that such events require the synchronised cooperation of two parties – here, for example, the machine and the customer or the machine and the demon. More generally, we assume that an event in one process can only take place if the process is composed with another process which has the same event in its alphabet.

VMBREAK0 is a process which can take part in a *coin* event and then deadlock. It thus describes a machine which breaks as soon as a coin is put into it, whereas *VMBREAK2* describes one which breaks after two coins have been put in and two chocolate bars have been taken out.

Fig. 2.2 The *Dramatis Personæ* described by the process expressions of Figure 2.3: A customer (left), a vending machine (center) and a demon (right).

$$VMBREAK0 \stackrel{\text{def}}{=} (coin \rightarrow STOP)$$

$$VMBREAK2 \stackrel{\text{def}}{=} (coin \rightarrow (choc \rightarrow (coin \rightarrow (choc \rightarrow STOP))))$$

$$VMCT \quad \stackrel{\text{def}}{=} (coin \rightarrow (choc \rightarrow VMCT \| toffee \rightarrow VMCT))$$

$$GRCUST \quad \stackrel{\text{def}}{=} (toffee \rightarrow GRCUST$$
$$\| choc \rightarrow GRCUST$$
$$\| coin \rightarrow (choc \rightarrow GRCUST))$$

$$GRCUSTVM \stackrel{\text{def}}{=} (GRCUST \|_{\{coin,choc,toffee\}} VMCT)$$

$$VMPOORM \stackrel{\text{def}}{=} (VMCT \sqcap VMBREAK0)$$

$$VMFAULTY \stackrel{\text{def}}{=} (coin \rightarrow (choc \rightarrow VMFAULTY$$
$$\| toffee \rightarrow VMFAULTY)$$
$$\sqcap VMBREAK0)$$

$$DEMON \quad \stackrel{\text{def}}{=} (choc \rightarrow DEMON)$$

$$VMDEMON \stackrel{\text{def}}{=} (DEMON \|_{\{choc\}} VMCT) \setminus \{choc\}$$

Fig. 2.3 CSP descriptions of some simple vending machines and their customers.

VMCT describes a machine which is prepared to accept a coin, and then either give out a chocolate bar or a toffee bar, depending on what the environment is prepared for. It then behaves like *VMCT*, i.e. it is prepared to accept a coin, and so on. This is an example of a recursive definition, where the behaviour being defined is referred to in the definition. This is the normal way to define repetitive behaviour in CSP.

GRCUST likewise describes a greedy customer, who is prepared to accept a toffee or a chocolate bar without paying, or to put a coin into the machine. If the greedy customer puts a coin in, then he (or she) is only prepared to accept a chocolate bar. The customer's greed is unlimited by internal factors: after accepting whatever the machine has to offer, the customer is ready to try again.

If, however, the environment in which *GRCUST* operates is a VMCT-machine, and there are no other (stupid) customers who put a coin in and forget to extract what they want, then he will have to pay every time. This is shown by the behaviour of *GRCUSTVM*, where the behaviours of *GRCUST* and *VMCT* are synchronised over the events $\{coin, choc, toffee\}$. Since the only common initial event for the two processes is *coin*, the only possible behaviour of *GRCUSTVM* is given by:

$$GRCUSTVM = (coin \rightarrow (choc \rightarrow GRCUSTVM))$$

in which both customer and machine indulge in an unlimited sequence of events in which the customer continually alternates between putting in a coin and taking out a chocolate bar.

The two machines *VMPOORM* and *VMFAULTY* are defective in different ways. *VMPOORM* is poorly manufactured, so when it is installed it may operate correctly (like *VMCT*) or it may not work at all (like *VMBREAK0*), whereas *VMFAULTY* behaves like *VMCT* until, quite at random, and determined by reasons internal to itself, it breaks by accepting a coin and then refusing to do anything more.

Finally, we consider the little demon, described by *DEMON*. Each time a chocolate bar appears, the demon removes it. The behaviour of the machine *VMDEMON*, in which the demon is included in the machine, can be rewritten as:

$$VMDEMON \stackrel{\text{def}}{=} (coin \rightarrow (toffee \rightarrow VMDEMON [\![\tau \rightarrow VMDEMON))$$

where τ represents some internal event which the customer, acting as external observer, cannot see. However, the customer notices the effect of the event, since if that path is chosen then the customer no longer has the option of extracting a toffee bar, but only of putting a new coin into the machine. In CSP, it is customary *only* to include externally visible behaviour in process expressions; if we follow this convention, then process expressions of the form:

$$(a \rightarrow P [\![\tau \rightarrow Q) \qquad \text{where } a \neq \tau$$

should be replaced by:

$$(Q \sqcap (Q [\![a \rightarrow P))$$

This expresses the fact that internal events appear to the external observer as internal non-determinism: the machine appears to make arbitrary decisions, which cannot be affected by the environment, about how to behave. In the case of *VMDEMON* we have:

$$VMDEMON = (coin \rightarrow (VMDEMON$$
$$\sqcap (VMDEMON [\![toffee \rightarrow VMDEMON)))$$

The proof of this is left as an exercise for the reader (Exercise 2.3).

2.1.2 Process Algebra

CSP processes can be analysed by use of a *process algebra*, which defines equivalences between process expressions. These equivalences can be used in order to simplify process expressions containing process operators, just as classical algebraic rules are used to reduce expressions containing arithmetic operators. Studying the equivalences can also give you more insight into the semantics of the process operators, so it is a good idea to look at them carefully, to see whether they correspond to your expectations. If they don't, you should try to clear up the misunderstanding. We consider the process operators in turn, as follows:

Internal non-deterministic choice, $\sqcap$

$$P \sqcap P = P \qquad\qquad\qquad (\sqcap 1)$$
$$P \sqcap Q = Q \sqcap P \qquad\qquad\qquad (\sqcap 2)$$
$$P \sqcap (Q \sqcap R) = (P \sqcap Q) \sqcap R \qquad\qquad\qquad (\sqcap 3)$$

In other words, $\sqcap$ is idempotent (1), commutative (2) and associative (3).

$$x \rightarrow (P \sqcap Q) = (x \rightarrow P \sqcap x \rightarrow Q) \qquad\qquad\qquad (\sqcap 4)$$

Thus $\rightarrow$ (and, as we shall see, $\|$, $[\![$, $\|\|$ and $\backslash$) distributes over internal choice. However, recursion does *not* distribute over $\sqcap$; a counter-example is:

1. $P \stackrel{\text{def}}{=} (a \rightarrow P) \sqcap (b \rightarrow P)$
   Here there is a choice between a and b for each iteration. The sequences of events in which P can take part (the *traces* of P) can thus contain mixtures of a's and b's, e.g. $\langle a, b, a, a, b \rangle$.
2. $Q \stackrel{\text{def}}{=} QA \sqcap QB$, where $QA \stackrel{\text{def}}{=} (a \rightarrow QA)$ and $QB \stackrel{\text{def}}{=} (b \rightarrow QB)$.
   Here there is a choice between a and b (i.e. between QA and QB) on the first step. The traces of Q can thus only be $\langle a, a, a, ... \rangle$ or $\langle b, b, b, ... \rangle$.

External non-deterministic choice, $[\!]$

$$P [\!] P = P \qquad\qquad\qquad ([\!] 1)$$
$$P [\!] Q = Q [\!] P \qquad\qquad\qquad ([\!] 2)$$
$$P [\!] (Q [\!] R) = (P [\!] Q) [\!] R \qquad\qquad\qquad ([\!] 3)$$
$$P [\!] STOP = P \qquad\qquad\qquad ([\!] 4)$$

In other words, $[\!]$ is idempotent (1), commutative (2) and associative (3), and has $STOP$ as neutral element. In addition it distributes over internal choice, $\sqcap$, and *vice versa*:

$$P [\!] (Q \sqcap R) = (P [\!] Q) \sqcap (P [\!] R) \qquad\qquad\qquad ([\!] 5)$$
$$(P [\!] Q) \sqcap R = (P \sqcap R) [\!] (Q \sqcap R) \qquad\qquad\qquad ([\!] 6)$$

This latter equality expresses the idea that internal choice and choices made by the environment are independent. You may find this rather surprising, so you should consider carefully why it is true.

Finally, we have a rule for combining multiple choices:

$$(x : A \rightarrow P[\![x]\!]) [\!] (y : B \rightarrow Q[\![y]\!]) = (z : (A \cup B) \rightarrow R[\![z]\!]) \qquad\qquad\qquad ([\!] 7)$$

where notations of the form $(v : \mathcal{E} \rightarrow S[\![v]\!])$ for a set of events $\mathcal{E} = \{e_1, e_2, ..., e_n\}$ are a shorthand for the multiple choice:

$$(e_1 \rightarrow S[\![e_1]\!]) [\!] (e_2 \rightarrow S[\![e_2]\!]) [\!] ... [\!] (e_n \rightarrow S[\![e_n]\!])$$

where $S[\![e_i]\!]$ describes the behaviour of S *after* initial event e_i. Then $R[\![z]\!]$ is given by:

$$R[\![z]\!] = \begin{cases} P[\![z]\!] & \text{if } z \in (A-B) \\ Q[\![z]\!] & \text{if } z \in (B-A) \\ P[\![z]\!] \sqcap Q[\![z]\!] & \text{if } z \in (A \cap B) \end{cases}$$

The two first possibilities here are obvious. The third possibility states that when an initial event may occur in two or more branches of a choice, then we cannot tell which of these branches will be chosen, so the overall behaviour appears like an internal choice. For example:

Given the definitions:

$X \stackrel{\text{def}}{=} (a \rightarrow b \rightarrow STOP$
$\quad\quad []b \rightarrow c \rightarrow STOP)$
$Y \stackrel{\text{def}}{=} (b \rightarrow d \rightarrow STOP$
$\quad\quad []e \rightarrow f \rightarrow STOP$
$\quad\quad []g \rightarrow b \rightarrow c \rightarrow STOP)$

Then $X[]Y$ has the form of the left-hand side in $[]7$, where:

$\quad A = \{a,b\}$
$P[\![a]\!] = b \rightarrow STOP$
$P[\![b]\!] = c \rightarrow STOP$
$\quad B = \{b,e,g\}$
$Q[\![b]\!] = d \rightarrow STOP$
$Q[\![e]\!] = f \rightarrow STOP$
$Q[\![g]\!] = b \rightarrow c \rightarrow STOP$

From this it follows that:

$A \cup B = \{a,b,e,g\}$
$R[\![a]\!] = \quad P[\![a]\!] \quad = b \rightarrow STOP$
$R[\![b]\!] = P[\![b]\!] \sqcap Q[\![b]\!] = (c \rightarrow STOP \sqcap d \rightarrow STOP)$
$R[\![e]\!] = \quad Q[\![e]\!] \quad = f \rightarrow STOP$
$R[\![g]\!] = \quad Q[\![g]\!] \quad = b \rightarrow c \rightarrow STOP$

and thus that:

$X[]Y = (a \rightarrow b \rightarrow STOP$
$\quad\quad []b \rightarrow (c \rightarrow STOP \sqcap d \rightarrow STOP)$
$\quad\quad []e \rightarrow f \rightarrow STOP$
$\quad\quad []g \rightarrow b \rightarrow c \rightarrow STOP)$

A simple but important special case of the equivalence $[]7$ is:

$$(a \rightarrow P[]a \rightarrow Q) = a \rightarrow (P \sqcap Q) \tag{$[]8$}$$

This corresponds to the rather obvious fact that if the environment offers to perform an event a, then either of the two branches $(a \to P)$ or $(a \to Q)$ in the left-hand process can be chosen. So seen from the outside, it appears as if the process internally decides whether to behave like P or Q after taking part in the event a.

Parallel composition with synchronisation, $\|$

The parallel operator, $\|$, is here specialised in the way that $(P \| Q)$ implies synchronisation on all events in P's and Q's common alphabet, $(\alpha P \cap \alpha Q)$. The equivalence rules are:

$$P \| P = P \tag{$\|$1}$$
$$P \| Q = Q \| P \tag{$\|$2}$$
$$P \| (Q \| R) = (P \| Q) \| R \tag{$\|$3}$$
$$P \| STOP_{\alpha P} = STOP_{\alpha P} \tag{$\|$4}$$
$$P \| (Q \sqcap R) = (P \| Q) \sqcap (P \| R) \tag{$\|$5}$$

In other words, $\|$ is idempotent (1), commutative (2) and associative (3), has $STOP$ as zero element (4), and distributes over $\sqcap$. In addition, assuming that

$$a \in (\alpha P - \alpha Q), \quad b \in (\alpha Q - \alpha P), \quad c,d \in (\alpha P \cap \alpha Q)$$

we have:

$$(c \to P) \| (c \to Q) = c \to (P \| Q) \tag{$\|$6}$$
$$(c \to P) \| (d \to Q) = STOP_{\alpha P \cup \alpha Q}, \quad c \neq d \tag{$\|$7}$$
$$(a \to P) \| (c \to Q) = a \to (P \| (c \to Q)) \tag{$\|$8}$$
$$(c \to P) \| (b \to Q) = b \to ((c \to P) \| Q) \tag{$\|$9}$$
$$(a \to P) \| (b \to Q) = (a \to (P \| (b \to Q)) \tag{$\|$10}$$
$$[\!] b \to ((a \to P) \| Q))$$

The more general case of parallel composition of processes with multiple choices of initial event is expressed by:

$$(x : A \to P[\![x]\!]) \| (y : B \to Q[\![y]\!]) = (z : C \to (P'[\![z]\!] \| Q'[\![z]\!])) \tag{$\|$11}$$

where we use the same notation for multiple choices as before. The set $C = (A \cap B) \cup (A - \alpha Q) \cup (B - \alpha P)$ is the set of possible initial events for the composed process. Events in $(A \cap B)$ require synchronisation between the two processes which are being composed, while events in $(A - \alpha Q)$ are initial events of the left-hand process which are not in the alphabet of the right-hand process, and which therefore do not need to be synchronised, and events in $(B - \alpha P)$ are correspondingly initial events of the right-hand process which are not in the alphabet of the left-hand process. To put this another way, the possible initial events are those which the two processes P and Q agree to offer, together with those events which either of them can perform without the cooperation of the other.

After taking part in an initial event z chosen from the set C, the composed process behaves like $P'[\![z]\!] \parallel Q'[\![z]\!]$, where:

$$P'[\![z]\!] = \begin{cases} P[\![z]\!] & \text{if } z \in A \\ (x : A \to P[\![x]\!]) & \text{if } z \notin A \end{cases}$$

$$Q'[\![z]\!] = \begin{cases} Q[\![z]\!] & \text{if } z \in B \\ (y : B \to Q[\![y]\!]) & \text{if } z \notin B \end{cases}$$

In other words, $P'[\![z]\!]$ and $Q'[\![z]\!]$ describe the behaviours of the component processes after taking part in the chosen initial event z. If the left-hand process cannot take part in z (because $z \notin A$), then it makes no progress. Correspondingly if the right-hand process cannot take part in z because $z \notin B$, then *it* makes no progess. For example:

Consider the process $X \parallel Y$, where X and Y are defined as on page 15 by:

$X \stackrel{\text{def}}{=} (a \to b \to STOP$
$\qquad [\![b \to c \to STOP)$
$Y \stackrel{\text{def}}{=} (b \to d \to STOP$
$\qquad [\![e \to f \to STOP$
$\qquad [\![g \to b \to c \to STOP)$

Then $X \parallel Y$ has the form of the left-hand side in $\parallel 11$, where:

$\quad A = \{a, b\}$
$P[\![a]\!] = b \to STOP$
$P[\![b]\!] = c \to STOP$
$\quad B = \{b, e, g\}$
$Q[\![b]\!] = d \to STOP$
$Q[\![e]\!] = f \to STOP$
$Q[\![g]\!] = b \to c \to STOP$
$\quad C = \{a, b, e, g\}$

where we here assume that $\alpha X = \{a, b, c\}$ and $\alpha Y = \{b, c, d, e, f, g\}$, which means that $A \cap B = \{b\}$, $A - \alpha Y = \{a\}$ and $B - \alpha X = \{e, g\}$. From this it follows that:

$P'[\![a]\!] = P[\![a]\!] \qquad\qquad = b \to STOP$
$P'[\![b]\!] = P[\![b]\!] \qquad\qquad = c \to STOP$
$P'[\![e]\!] = (x : A \to P[\![x]\!]) = X$
$P'[\![g]\!] = (x : A \to P[\![x]\!]) = X$
$Q'[\![a]\!] = (y : B \to Q[\![y]\!]) = Y$
$Q'[\![b]\!] = Q[\![b]\!] \qquad\qquad = d \to STOP$
$Q'[\![e]\!] = Q[\![e]\!] \qquad\qquad = f \to STOP$
$Q'[\![g]\!] = Q[\![g]\!] \qquad\qquad = b \to c \to STOP$

and rule $\|11$ then tells us that:

$$X \parallel Y = (a \rightarrow (b \rightarrow STOP \parallel Y)$$
$$[\!]b \rightarrow (c \rightarrow STOP \parallel d \rightarrow STOP)$$
$$[\!]e \rightarrow (X \parallel f \rightarrow STOP)$$
$$[\!]g \rightarrow (X \parallel b \rightarrow c \rightarrow STOP))$$

From this rule it also follows that parallel composition with synchronisation distributes over $[\!]$ in the sense that:

$$(a \rightarrow P[\!]b \rightarrow Q) \parallel_{\{a\}} (a \rightarrow R) = (a \rightarrow (P \parallel_{\{a\}} R) \tag{$\|12$}$$
$$[\!](b \rightarrow Q) \parallel_{\{a\}} (a \rightarrow R))$$

A large number of other useful derived rules can be demonstrated in a similar manner.

As a more interesting example, consider the process $GRCUSTVM$ of Figure 2.3, which we have previously discussed in an informal manner. It follows from the use of these rules that:

$$\begin{aligned}
GRCUSTVM &= (GRCUST \parallel VMCT) & Def. \\
&= (toffee \rightarrow GRCUST & Defs. \\
&\quad [\!]choc \rightarrow GRCUST \\
&\quad [\!]coin \rightarrow choc \rightarrow GRCUST) \\
&\quad \parallel (coin \rightarrow (choc \rightarrow VMCT \\
&\qquad\qquad [\!]toffee \rightarrow VMCT)) \\
&= coin \rightarrow ((choc \rightarrow GRCUST) \parallel (choc \rightarrow VMCT & \|11 \\
&\qquad\qquad\qquad\qquad [\!]toffee \rightarrow VMCT)) \\
&= coin \rightarrow choc \rightarrow (GRCUST \parallel VMCT) & \|11 \\
&= coin \rightarrow choc \rightarrow GRCUSTVM & Def.
\end{aligned}$$

This is the result which we presented above without proof. We note that the (only) possible initial event of $(GRCUST \parallel VMCT)$ is $coin$, and that after this $GRCUST$ behaves as $(choc \rightarrow GRCUST)$, while $VMCT$ behaves as $(choc \rightarrow VMCT[\!]toffee \rightarrow VMCT)$, according to rule $\|11$. The rest of the reduction is trivial.

Parallel composition with interleaving, $\|\|\|$

$$P \mathbin{\|\|\|} Q = Q \mathbin{\|\|\|} P \tag{$\|\|\|1$}$$
$$P \mathbin{\|\|\|} (Q \mathbin{\|\|\|} R) = (P \mathbin{\|\|\|} Q) \mathbin{\|\|\|} R \tag{$\|\|\|2$}$$
$$P \mathbin{\|\|\|} STOP_A = P, \qquad A \subseteq \alpha P \tag{$\|\|\|3$}$$
$$P \mathbin{\|\|\|} (Q \sqcap R) = (P \mathbin{\|\|\|} Q) \sqcap (P \mathbin{\|\|\|} R) \tag{$\|\|\|4$}$$

In other words, $\|\|\|$ is commutative (1) and associative (2), has $STOP$ as neutral element (3) and distributes over internal choice, $\sqcap$. Furthermore:

$$(x \rightarrow P) \,\|\|\, (y \rightarrow Q) = (x \rightarrow (P \,\|\|\, (y \rightarrow Q))$$
$$[\![y \rightarrow ((x \rightarrow P) \,\|\|\, Q)) \tag{$\|\|$5}$$

In other words, efter an initial event chosen from the left-hand or right-hand process, the 'rest' of the two processes continue to run in parallel. Or, to put it another way, the initial events of the two processes can occur in any order – a consequence of the fact that $\|\|$ gives in an interleaving of the behaviours of the two component processes. Using the notation for multiple choices from above, this rule can be generalised to:

$$(x : A \rightarrow P[\![x]\!]) \,\|\|\, (y : B \rightarrow Q[\![y]\!]) = (x : A \rightarrow (P[\![x]\!] \,\|\|\, (y : B \rightarrow Q[\![y]\!]))$$
$$[\![y : B \rightarrow ((x : A \rightarrow P[\![x]\!]) \,\|\|\, Q[\![y]\!])) \tag{$\|\|$6}$$

Note that, unlike $\|$, the interleaving operator $\|\|$ is *not* idempotent. As a simple example, consider the process P whose behaviour is given by $(a \rightarrow b \rightarrow STOP)$. Then the only possible sequence of observable events for P is $\langle a, b \rangle$, whereas for $P \,\|\|\, P$ the possible sequences are:

$$\{ \langle a, b, a, b \rangle, \langle a, a, b, b \rangle \}$$

i.e. the possible interleavings of the sequences from each of the two components.

Furthermore, $\|\|$ does *not* distribute over $[\!]$. A counter-example is:

---

1. $P \stackrel{\text{def}}{=} ((a \rightarrow STOP) \,\|\|\, (b \rightarrow R [\!] c \rightarrow S))$

   Only the left-hand process can here take part in the initial event a. After this, P behaves like $STOP \,\|\|\, (b \rightarrow R [\!] c \rightarrow S)$, which is identical to $(b \rightarrow R [\!] c \rightarrow S)$.

2. $Q \stackrel{\text{def}}{=} ((a \rightarrow STOP \,\|\|\, b \rightarrow R) [\!] (a \rightarrow STOP \,\|\|\, c \rightarrow S))$

   Either process can here take part in the initial event a. Since we cannot from the environment control which of the processes will be chosen, Q then behaves as $(STOP \,\|\|\, (b \rightarrow R)) \sqcap (STOP \,\|\|\, (c \rightarrow S))$, which (by Rule $\|\|$ 3) is identical to $(b \rightarrow R \sqcap c \rightarrow S)$.

Hiding, \

$$P \backslash \{\} = P \tag{$\backslash$1}$$

$$(P \backslash B) \backslash C = P \backslash (B \cup C) \tag{$\backslash$2}$$

$$(P \sqcap Q) \backslash C = (P \backslash C) \sqcap (Q \backslash C) \tag{$\backslash$3}$$

$$STOP_A \backslash C = STOP_{A-C} \tag{$\backslash$4}$$

$$P \backslash C = P, \qquad \qquad \text{if } C \notin \alpha P \tag{$\backslash$5}$$

$$(x \rightarrow P) \backslash C = \begin{cases} x \rightarrow (P \backslash C), & \text{if } x \notin C \\ (P \backslash C), & \text{if } x \in C \end{cases} \tag{$\backslash$6}$$

$$(x : B \rightarrow P[x]) \backslash C = x : B \rightarrow (P[x] \backslash C), \qquad \text{if } (B \cap C) = \{\} \tag{$\backslash$7}$$

$$(x \rightarrow P [\!] y \rightarrow Q) \backslash C = (P \backslash C) \sqcap ((P \backslash C) \qquad \text{if } x \in C, \, y \notin C \tag{$\backslash$8}$$
$$[\!] (y \rightarrow (Q \backslash C)))$$

Note that although $\setminus$ distributes over $\sqcap$ (Rule $\setminus 3$), it does *not* distribute over $[\!]$. A counter-example, which again illustrates the way in which the algebra can be used to reduce process expressions, is:

---

1. $P \overset{\text{def}}{=} (c \rightarrow STOP [\!] d \rightarrow STOP) \setminus \{c\}$
   This can be reduced as follows:

   $$\begin{aligned} P &= (STOP \setminus \{c\}) \sqcap ((STOP \setminus \{c\}) [\!] (d \rightarrow (STOP \setminus \{c\}))) && \text{Rule } \setminus 8 \\ &= STOP \sqcap (STOP [\!] d \rightarrow STOP) && \setminus 4 \\ &= STOP \sqcap (d \rightarrow STOP) && [\!] 4 \end{aligned}$$

2. $Q \overset{\text{def}}{=} ((c \rightarrow STOP) \setminus \{c\} [\!] (d \rightarrow STOP) \setminus \{c\})$
   This can be reduced as follows:

   $$\begin{aligned} Q &= ((STOP \setminus \{c\}) [\!] (d \rightarrow (STOP \setminus \{c\}))) && \text{Rule } \setminus 6 \\ &= (STOP [\!] d \rightarrow STOP) && \setminus 4 \\ &= (d \rightarrow STOP) && [\!] 4 \end{aligned}$$

Since neither P nor Q can be reduced further, we conclude that they are not equal – P can make an internal choice to deadlock immediately without taking part in any externally visible events, whereas Q must take part in a d event before deadlocking.

Renaming, /

$$P[x/x] = P \tag{/1}$$
$$\begin{aligned} P[x/y][v/w] &= P[v/w][x/y], && \text{if } x \neq w \wedge y \neq w \tag{/2} \\ &= P[x/y], && \text{if } y = w \\ &= P[v/y], && \text{if } x = w \end{aligned}$$

These rules state the rather obvious facts that renaming an event by itself has no effect (1), and that two consecutive renamings can be made in any order if they do not replace the same variables (2).

For analysis of communication protocols, the process algebra of CSP is particularly useful for reducing systems of cooperating procssses to simpler forms, whose properties can more easily be proved using the approach shown in Sections 2.2 and 2.3. We have seen an example of how this reduction can be done in the case of the process *GRCUSTVM*. More examples can be found in the exercises.

2.1.3 Process Expressions for Process Networks

The grammar of process expressions given above is based on a very general concept of events. For describing distributed systems, it is helpful to restrict it to deal with *communication events*, in which two processes synchronise their activity on passing a message from one to the other. Each such communication event corresponds to one of the elementary communications discussed in the first section of this chapter.

Our model of a distributed system will then be that of a *process network*: a set of uniquely named processes which communicate through a set of uniquely named *channels*. This is illustrated in Figure 2.4. In the figure, the channels with names $c1 \ldots c3$ are so-called *external channels* and $d1 \ldots d6$ are *internal channels*.

By analogy with the simple case discussed in section 2.1.1, we call the set of channels associated with process P the *channel alphabet* of P, denoted $\alpha_c P$. For example, in Figure 2.4:

$$\alpha_c P4 = \{c3, d2, d6\}$$

The full alphabet, αP, for a process P is as usual the set of externally visible events which P potentially can take part in. Simple (non-communication) events have, as before, no 'internal structure'. But each communication event needs to be described by two components: the channel and the value communicated. For channel c and value e we denote this $c.e$. Thus αP becomes the set of all combinations of a channel name with the values which can be passed on that channel. For example, if channel $c3$ can pass values in $\{1, 2, 4\}$, $d2$ can pass values in $\{true, false\}$, and $d6$ values in $\{0, 1\}$, then the full alphabet of process $P4$ in Figure 2.4 is:

$$\alpha P4 = \{c3.1, c3.2, c3.4, d2.true, d2.false, d6.0, d6.1\}$$

When dealing with process networks, we extend the grammar for process expressions $\mathscr{P}$ to:

$$
\boxed{
\begin{array}{l}
\mathscr{P} ::= STOP_A \mid p \mid p[e] \mid c!e \to \mathscr{P} \mid c?x : M \to \mathscr{P} \mid \\
\quad \mathscr{P} \sqcap \mathscr{P} \mid \mathscr{P} \,[\!]\, \mathscr{P} \mid \mathscr{P} \,\|_A\, \mathscr{P} \mid \mathscr{P} \,\|\!|\!|\, \mathscr{P} \mid \mathscr{P}[d/c] \mid \mathscr{P} \setminus L \mid \\
\text{(\textbf{if} } b \text{ \textbf{then} } \mathscr{P} \text{ \textbf{else} } \mathscr{P})
\end{array}
}
$$

Here e denotes a (non-process) expression, b a Boolean expression, $x{:}M$ a variable x of type M, c a channel, and A and L denote sets of channels. As before, we assume that $\to$ binds more tightly than $\sqcap$ or $[\!]$.

The informal semantics of these expressions is as follows:

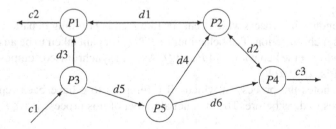

Fig. 2.4 A Process Network with five processes and nine channels

$STOP_A$ corresponds to *deadlock* for all communications over channels in the set
   A, as before.

p is a process identifier for a process whose definition is of the form $p \stackrel{\text{def}}{=} \mathcal{P}$,
   and $\alpha p = \alpha \mathcal{P}$, as before.

$p[e]$,   where p is an identifier and e is an expression of type $\mathcal{D}$, denotes a parame-
   terised process, whose definition is of the form $p[i : \mathcal{D}] \stackrel{\text{def}}{=} \mathcal{P}$, and $\alpha p = \alpha \mathcal{P}$,
   as before. The notation used for denoting e and $\mathcal{D}$ is given in Appendix A.

$c!e \to P$ denotes the process which first takes part in an communication event
   by *outputting* the value of e on channel c, and then behaves like P. When the
   processes associated with the channel are required to synchronise the events in
   which they take part via that channel, then the output event denoted by $c!e$ must
   be synchronised with an event in which *input* takes place. The alphabet of the
   process with prefixing is $\alpha P \cup \{c.e\}$.

$c?x : M \to P$ denotes the process which takes part in a communication event by
   inputting a value of type M to x via channel c, and then behaves like P. The
   variable x is a bound variable of the process, and will of course generally appear
   in P, where it takes on the input value. The alphabet in this case is $\alpha P \cup \{c.v | v \in$
   $M\}$

$P \sqcap Q$ **and** $P \,[\!]\, Q$ correspond to *internal* and *external non-determinism* respectively,
   as before. These are only defined when P and Q have the same alphabet, which
   is thus also the alphabet for the combination.

$P \,\|_A\, Q$ denotes *parallel composition* of P with Q, with synchronised communication over those channels which lie in the channel set A. It is assumed that
   $A \subseteq (\alpha_c P \cup \alpha_c Q)$, i.e. that A is a subset of the combined channel alphabets of
   P and Q. For notational convenience we shall omit A if it is the channels com-
   mon to the alphabets of P and Q, $(\alpha_c P \cap \alpha_c Q)$. We write $(P \,\|\, Q)$ for the parallel
   composition in this case. The alphabet of $P \,\|_A\, Q$ (or $P \,\|\, Q$) is $\alpha P \cup \alpha Q$.
   Note that if $\alpha_c P = \{a, b, c\}$, and $\alpha_c Q = \{b, c, d\}$, then $P \,\|\, Q$ denotes a network
   in which P and Q are connected to one another via the channels in $\{b, c\}$, and
   perform synchronised communication over them. P and Q are still free, however,
   to perform external communication over their external channels a and d, i.e. those
   channels which lie in $(\alpha_c P - \alpha_c Q)$ and $(\alpha_c Q - \alpha_c P)$ respectively.
   The case where $A = \{\}$ is special, as the two processes P and Q are then not
   synchronised with one another. To emphasise this, we shall again use the special
   notation:

$P \,|\!|\!|\, Q$ denotes the process which behaves like P and Q running in parallel without
   mutual synchronisation. The behaviour of $P \,|\!|\!|\, Q$ is again taken to be an *arbitrary
   interleaving* of the behaviours of P and Q. As with synchronised composition, the
   alphabet is $\alpha P \cup \alpha Q$.

$P[d/c]$ denotes the process in which all references to c have been replaced by
   references to d, as before. The channel alphabet of this process is $(\alpha_c P) - \{c\} \cup$
   $\{d\}$.

$P \setminus L$ denotes the process where all events taking place on (internal) channels in
   the set L within P are invisible. The channel alphabet of this process is $(\alpha_c P) - L$.

(**if** b **then** P **else** Q)   denotes the process which behaves like P if the Boolean expression b is true, and otherwise behaves like Q. This is only defined if P and Q have the same alphabet, which is then the alphabet of the combination.

Some simple examples of process descriptions using this notation are given in Figure 2.5. The process $VMCT'$ describes a component which first accepts a value of a coin on channel *slot*, and then either outputs a chocolate bar or a toffee on channel *drawer*. This is essentially the same as the vending machine $VMCT$ in Figure 2.3, but now described in terms of interactions where values are passed over channels. Note that we do not any more have to assume (or imagine) which direction the coins, chocolates and toffees move in. This information is explicitly given as part of the process description, which is therefore less abstract than before.

The process $BUF1$ describes a system component which continually inputs a non-negative integer from channel *left*, and outputs it again via channel *right*. This is a one-place buffer – a buffer with space for one number.

Processes $SENDER$ and $Q[x]$ are mutually recursive. $SENDER$ accepts input of a value for y (from some arbitrary domain of messages, $\mathcal{M}$) via channel *user* and then behaves like $Q[y]$. With parameter value y, Q outputs y via channel *wire* and is then prepared for input of a value in $\{\text{ACK}, \text{NACK}\}$ from the same channel. If the value received is ACK, then Q behaves like $SENDER$, otherwise it tries to send the message again. Note how parameters are used to describe *state components* of the process, i.e. values which need to be remembered from one recursive execution of the process to the next.

The process $TIMER$ represents a simple timer, which starts when it receives a value SET via channel *up*, and can then either accept a value RESET or send a value TIMEOUT. Once it has engaged in one of these events, it is ready to be started again.

Finally, the process QT represents an 'improved' version of Q, in which a SET message is sent via *up* every time a message received from the user has been sent via channel *wire*, and the user's message is retransmitted if a TIMEOUT message is received via *up*.

$$
\begin{aligned}
VMCT' &\stackrel{\text{def}}{=} (slot?c : Money \rightarrow &&(drawer!chocolate \rightarrow VMCT' \\
&&&[\!] drawer!toffee \rightarrow VMCT')) \\
BUF1 &\stackrel{\text{def}}{=} (left?x : \mathbb{N}_0 \rightarrow &&(right!x \rightarrow BUF1)) \\
SENDER &\stackrel{\text{def}}{=} (user?y : \mathcal{M} \rightarrow &&Q[y]) \\
Q[x : \mathcal{M}] &\stackrel{\text{def}}{=} (wire!x \rightarrow &&(wire?a : \{\text{ACK}\} \rightarrow SENDER \\
&&&[\!] wire?a : \{\text{NACK}\} \rightarrow Q[x])) \\
TIMER &\stackrel{\text{def}}{=} (up?s : \{\text{SET}\} \rightarrow &&(up?r : \{\text{RESET}\} \rightarrow TIMER \\
&&&[\!] up!\text{TIMEOUT} \rightarrow TIMER)) \\
\end{aligned}
$$

$QT[x : \mathcal{M}] \stackrel{\text{def}}{=} (wire!x \rightarrow (up!\text{SET} \rightarrow (wire?a : \{\text{ACK}\} \rightarrow (up!\text{RESET} \rightarrow SENDER)$
$[\!] wire?a : \{\text{NACK}\} \rightarrow (up!\text{RESET} \rightarrow QT[x])$
$[\!] up?t : \{\text{TIMEOUT}\} \rightarrow QT[x])))$

Fig. 2.5 CSP definitions of processes with communication

Process Algebra for Process Networks

With this extended syntax for process expressions, the process algebra for CSP needs to be modified slightly. Firstly, we have to remember that hiding and synchronised parallel composition now refer to sets of *channels* instead of sets of events. Secondly, the rule ($\|6$) for parallel composition with synchronisation becomes:

$$(c!e \to Q) \parallel (c?x : \mathscr{D} \to P[x]) = \begin{cases} c!e \to (Q \parallel P[e]) & \text{if } e \in \mathscr{D} \\ STOP_c & \text{otherwise} \end{cases} \qquad (\|6')$$

There are three important things to notice here. Firstly, an input and an output event of the same type on the same channel can be synchronised, and the value of the variable referred to in the input event takes on the value of the expression in the output event. Thus in $\|6'$, the variable x takes on the value of e. Secondly, if the input and output offers do not match with respect to type, the composed process deadlocks. And thirdly, when an input and output event are synchronised, the resulting event is presented as the *output*. This is a convention in CSP, reflecting physical reality. On a real physical channel, there can in general only be one party transmitting a signal at a given instant, whereas there can be many parties which receive the transmitted signal. Thus in CSP, an offer of output can be synchronised with multiple parallel offers of input. If the resulting event were represented by an *input* event, this could obviously be synchronised with another output, which does not make physical sense.

Rules $\|7$ to $\|10$ have to be modified in a similar way, but there are several variants of each, depending on whether the events which have to be synchronised are inputs or outputs. For example, under the assumption that:

$$a \in (\alpha P_c - \alpha Q_c), \ b \in (\alpha Q_c - \alpha P_c), \ c,d \in (\alpha P_c \cap \alpha Q_c)$$

we have

$$(a!e \to P) \parallel (c?x : \mathscr{M} \to Q[x]) = a!e \to (P \parallel (c?x : \mathscr{M} \to Q[x]) \qquad (\|7')$$

$$(c!e \to P) \parallel (b?x : \mathscr{M} \to Q[x]) = b?x : \mathscr{M} \to ((c!e \to P) \parallel Q[x]) \qquad (\|8')$$

whereas:

$$(a?x : \mathscr{M} \to P[x]) \parallel (c!e \to Q) = a?x : \mathscr{M} \to (P[x] \parallel (c!e \to Q) \qquad (\|8'')$$

$$(c?x : \mathscr{M} \to P[x]) \parallel (b!e \to Q) = b!e \to ((c?x : \mathscr{M} \to P[x]) \parallel Q) \qquad (\|9'')$$

Finally, the generalisation of these rules to rule ($\|11$) becomes:

$$(x : A \to P[\![x]\!]) \parallel (y : B \to Q[\![y]\!]) = z : C \to (P'[\![z]\!] \parallel Q'[\![z]\!]) \qquad (\|11')$$

where

$$P'[\![z]\!] = \begin{cases} P[\![\hat{z}]\!] & \text{if } z \in A \\ (x : A \to P[\![x]\!]) & \text{otherwise} \end{cases}$$

$$Q'[\![z]\!] = \begin{cases} Q[\![\hat{z}]\!] & \text{if } z \in B \\ (y : B \to Q[\![y]\!]) & \text{otherwise} \end{cases}$$

and $\hat{z}$ is the same as z if z is an output event or an unmatched input event (i.e. one where the parallel process does not offer a matching output), and is the *matching output event* if z is an input event for which the parallel process offers a matching output. For example:

Suppose our old friends X and Y are now defined by the process equations:

$$X = (a?t : \mathcal{M} \to b!t \to STOP$$
$$\quad \| b?u : \mathcal{M} \to c!u \to STOP)$$
$$Y = (b!v \to d?p : \mathcal{E} \to STOP$$
$$\quad \| e!v \to f?q : \mathcal{E} \to STOP$$
$$\quad \| g?r : \mathcal{R} \to b!r \to c?s : \mathcal{S} \to STOP)$$

Then $X \| Y$ has the form of the left-hand side in $\|11'$, where:

$$A = \alpha(a?t : \mathcal{M}) \cup \alpha(b?u : \mathcal{M})$$
$$= \{a.t | t \in \mathcal{M}\} \cup \{b.u | u \in \mathcal{M}\}$$
$$P[\![a?t : \mathcal{M}]\!] = b!t \to STOP$$
$$P[\![b?u : \mathcal{M}]\!] = c!u \to STOP$$
$$B = \alpha(b!v) \cup \alpha(e!v) \cup \alpha(g?r : \mathcal{R})$$
$$= \{b.v, \ e.v\} \cup \{g.r | r \in \mathcal{R}\}$$
$$Q[\![b!v]\!] = d?p : \mathcal{E} \to STOP$$
$$Q[\![e!v]\!] = f?q : \mathcal{E} \to STOP$$
$$Q[\![g?r : \mathcal{R}]\!] = b!r \to c?s : \mathcal{S} \to STOP$$
$$C = \alpha(a?t : \mathcal{M}) \cup \alpha(b!v) \cup \alpha(e!v) \cup \alpha(g?r : \mathcal{R})$$
$$= \{a.t | t \in \mathcal{M}\} \cup \{b.v, e.v\} \cup \{g.r | r \in \mathcal{R}\}$$

Here we assume that $\alpha X = \{a.t | t \in \mathcal{M}\} \cup \{b.u | u \in \mathcal{M}\} \cup \{c.u | u \in \mathcal{M}\}$ and $\alpha Y = \{e.v\} \cup \{b.r | r \in \mathcal{R}\} \cup \{c.s | s \in \mathcal{S}\} \cup \{d.p | p \in \mathcal{E}\} \cup \{f.q | q \in \mathcal{E}\} \cup \{g.r | r \in \mathcal{R}\}$, which means that $A \cap B = \{b.v\}$, $A - \alpha Y = \{a.t | t \in \mathcal{M}\}$ and $B - \alpha X = \{e.v\} \cup \{g.r | r \in \mathcal{R}\}$. From this it follows that:

$$P'[\![b!v]\!] = P[\![b?u : \mathcal{M}]\!] \quad = c!u \to STOP$$
$$P'[\![a?t : \mathcal{M}]\!] = P[\![a?t : \mathcal{M}]\!] \quad = b!t \to STOP$$
$$P'[\![e!v]\!] = (x : A \to P[\![x]\!]) \quad = X$$
$$P'[\![g?r : \mathcal{R}]\!] = (x : A \to P[\![x]\!]) \quad = X$$
$$Q'[\![b!v]\!] = Q[\![b!v]\!] \quad = d?p : \mathcal{E} \to STOP$$
$$Q'[\![a?t : \mathcal{M}]\!] = (x : A \to Q[\![x]\!]) \quad = Y$$
$$Q'[\![e!v]\!] = Q[\![e!v]\!] \quad = f?q : \mathcal{E} \to STOP$$
$$Q'[\![g?r : \mathcal{R}]\!] = Q[\![g?r : \mathcal{R}]\!] \quad = b!r \to c?s : \mathcal{S} \to STOP$$

and rule $\|11'$ then tells us that:

$$X \| Y = (a?t : \mathcal{M} \to (b!t \to STOP \| Y)$$
$$\quad \| b!v \to (c!u \to STOP \| d?p : \mathcal{E} \to STOP)$$
$$\quad \| e!v \to (X \| f?q : \mathcal{E} \to STOP)$$
$$\quad \| g?r : \mathcal{R} \to (X \| b!r \to c?s : \mathcal{S} \to STOP))$$

This may look complicated, but of course there are a lot of combinations of things which can happen when two processes are composed in parallel. Since this is a very common situation which you may need to analyse, it is important to make sure that you understand the rules involved here.

2.2 Channel History Semantics

The exact semantics of process expressions is given by a function which maps an arbitrary process expression onto its meaning. The 'meaning' of a process can be sensibly described in a number of ways, depending on which properties of the process we wish to take into account. In the first instance, we shall assume that the meaning is defined by the *set of all possible traces* – finite sequences of communications – of the process described by the process expression. The trace which has been observed on a particular channel at a particular moment is known as that channel's *history*, and the model is therefore often known as a *channel history model* for the semantics. Channel history models have been shown to be well-suited to describing the so-called *safety* properties of certain components of distributed systems, namely those components which are *buffer-like*, in the sense that what one process puts in at one end comes out again at the other [128]. A large number of communication protocols come into this class.

The safety of a system is roughly speaking the property that "bad things do not happen". In other words, if anything happens at all, then it is the 'right' things that happen. However, consideration of safety does not show that anything *will* in fact happen. To show this we need to consider the *liveness* properties of the system. These are only poorly described by semantic models based solely on traces, and a better model for discussing them will be introduced in the next section.

2.2.1 Transitions and Traces

The semantics will be described in terms of a *labelled transition system*:

$$\mathscr{T} = (\Gamma, A, \rightarrow)$$

where:

Γ is the domain of processes,

A is the domain of events, which includes externally observable communications but (in accordance with the previously mentioned conventions in CSP) excludes internal events, so that $A = (C \times M) \mid E$, where C is the domain of channel names, M is the domain of messages, and E is the domain of simple (non-communication) events. Here $\mid$ indicates an alternative, so each element of A either belongs to $(C \times M)$ or to E (see Appendix A). A trace will then lie in the domain A^* of all possible sequences of events.

$\longrightarrow: \Gamma \times A \times \Gamma$ is the domain of *transitions*. A transition is a ternary relation between (the behaviours of) two processes and an event.

Following standard conventions, we will write a transition in the form:

$$P \xrightarrow{a} Q$$

where P and Q are processes and a is an event, or by the shorthand

$$P \xRightarrow{s} Q$$

which really stands for a sequence of transitions:

$$P \xrightarrow{s_1} \xrightarrow{s_2} \dots \xrightarrow{s_n} Q$$

where $s = \langle s_1, s_2, \dots, s_n \rangle$ is a trace consisting of the sequence of n events $s_1, s_2, \dots, s_n$, in which s_1 is the first event to occur, and so on. These transitions are to be understood to mean that P can take part in the event a (or the trace s), and that P thereafter behaves like Q.

In order to discuss processes in terms of this formal system, a number of useful functions on processes can be introduced:

initials(P)   defined by:

$$initials(P) \stackrel{\text{def}}{=} \{a \in A \mid \exists Q \cdot P \xrightarrow{a} Q\}$$

where $\langle a \rangle$ is the sequence containing the single event a, defines the set of events in which P can engage in the very first step. For example:

$$
\begin{aligned}
initials(STOP) &= \{\} \\
initials(a \to P) &= \{a\} \\
initials(a \to P \| b \to Q) &= \{a, b\} \\
initials(c!e \to P) &= \{c.e\}
\end{aligned}
$$

traces(P)   defined by:

$$traces(P) \stackrel{\text{def}}{=} \{s \in A^* \mid \exists Q \cdot P \xRightarrow{s} Q\}$$

defines the set of all traces of P. It follows from this definition that:

$$
\begin{aligned}
\langle \rangle &\in traces(P) \\
s \hat{\ } t \in traces(P) &\Rightarrow s \in traces(P)
\end{aligned}
$$

where $\langle \rangle$ is the empty trace, and $s \hat{\ } t$ is the trace whose first elements are those of s and whose remaining elements are those of t. The operator $\hat{\ }$, of functionality $A^* \times A^* \to A^*$, is known as the *concatenation operator* on traces. As examples, we have:

$$
\begin{aligned}
traces(STOP) \quad &= \{\langle\rangle\} \\
traces(a \to P) \quad &= \{\langle\rangle\} \cup \{\langle a\rangle\hat{}\,t \mid t \in traces(P)\} \\
traces(a \to P \| b \to Q) &= \{\langle\rangle\} \cup \{\langle a\rangle\hat{}\,t \mid t \in traces(P)\} \\
&\quad\quad \cup \{\langle b\rangle\hat{}\,t \mid t \in traces(Q)\} \\
traces(c!e \to P) \quad &= \{\langle\rangle\} \cup \{\langle c.e\rangle\hat{}\,t \mid t \in traces(P)\}
\end{aligned}
$$

We then define the operations #, $\leqslant$ and $\upharpoonright$ on traces as follows:

Length, #,   of functionality $A^* \to \mathbb{N}_0$, such that #s is the length of (number of events in) the trace s. More formally:

$$
\begin{aligned}
\#\langle\rangle \quad &= 0 \\
\#\langle e\rangle\hat{}\,s &= 1 + \#s
\end{aligned}
$$

where e is an event and s is a trace.

Prefix, $\leqslant$,   of functionality $A^* \times A^* \to BOOL$, such that

$$
s \leqslant t \stackrel{\text{def}}{=} \exists u \in A^* \cdot s\hat{}\,u = t
$$

If $(s \leqslant t)$, then we say that s is a *prefix* of t. Note that $\leqslant$ defines a partial order, with least element $\langle\rangle$, since it obeys:

$$
\begin{aligned}
\langle\rangle \leqslant s \quad &\text{(least element)} \\
s \leqslant s \quad &\text{(reflexivity)} \\
s \leqslant t \wedge t \leqslant s \Rightarrow s = t \quad &\text{(antisymmetry)} \\
s \leqslant t \wedge t \leqslant u \Rightarrow s \leqslant u \quad &\text{(transitivity)}
\end{aligned}
$$

On the other hand, the prefixes of a sequence are totally ordered, since:

$$
s \leqslant u \wedge t \leqslant u \Rightarrow s \leqslant t \vee t \leqslant s
$$

Restriction, $\upharpoonright$,   of functionality $A^* \times A\text{-set} \to A^*$, such that $s \upharpoonright L$ denotes the trace s *restricted* to the events in the set L. For example,

$$
\langle a,b,b,a,c,a,b,d\rangle \upharpoonright \{a,c\} = \langle a,a,c,a\rangle
$$

For notational convenience, we shall allow ourselves to write the second operand of the restriction operator as a set of *channels*, with the meaning that the trace is to be restricted to all communication events over those channels.

In general, a function f, of functionality $A^* \times \ldots \to A^*$, is said to be *strict* if it maps the empty trace to the empty trace:

$$
f(\langle\rangle,\ldots) = \langle\rangle
$$

It is *distributive* if it distributes over concatenation of traces:

$$
f(s\hat{}\,t,\ldots) = f(s,\ldots)\hat{}\,f(t,\ldots)
$$

It is *monotonic* if it preserves prefixing:

$$(s \leqslant t) \Rightarrow (f(s,\ldots) \leqslant f(t,\ldots))$$

All distributive functions are strict and monotonic. Restriction, $\lceil$, is an example of a distributive function, so it is also strict and monotonic:

$$(s\widehat{\ }t) \lceil A = (s \lceil A)\widehat{\ }(t \lceil A)$$
$$\langle\rangle \lceil A \quad = \langle\rangle$$
$$s \leqslant t \quad \Rightarrow (s \lceil A) \leqslant (t \lceil A)$$

Finally, in discussing the behaviour of a process P, we will often find it useful to select the history for a particular channel, c, in the set of channels of P. For this purpose we define the function *past*, of functionality $C \rightarrow M^*$, such that for a given instant of time, $past(c)$ for a given channel $c \in C$ gives the sequence of *message values* observed on that channel up to that instant, i.e. the channel history for channel c. Suppose, for example, that the trace of P observed up to now is:

$$r = \langle a.1, c.0, c.0, a.0, c.1, a.2, c.0, b.\text{true}\rangle$$

then $r \lceil \{c\}$, the restriction of r to communication events over channel c, is:

$$s = \langle c.0, c.0, c.1, c.0\rangle$$

and $past(c)$ is:

$$t = \langle 0, 0, 1, 0\rangle$$

For notational convenience (and following [128]) we shall often omit the function name, and just write the channel name, say c, where it is clear from the context that the channel history $past(c)$ is intended.

2.2.2 Inference Rules for Specifications Based on Traces

For discussing the properties of communicating systems, we introduce the concept of a *specification*, which is a logical expression of the form:

P sat R

where P is a process expression, and R is an *assertion*, which in general will be a predicate involving the free variables of P and the channel names appearing in $\alpha_c P$, together with other variables, constants, logical operators and so on. The meaning of P sat R is that R is true before and after every communication event in which the process described by P can take part. In other words, R is an *invariant* of P. In particular, we expect that R will be true of all *traces* of P:

$$\forall s \cdot s \in traces(P) \Rightarrow R$$

If Γ and Δ are sets of predicates, possibly including specifications, then an *inference* is a formula of the form $\Gamma \vdash \Delta$, with the meaning that all predicates in Δ can validly be inferred from those in Γ. Typically, Γ will contain process definitions and other assumptions required to demonstrate the truth of Δ. An *inference rule* then has the form:

$$\frac{\Gamma 1 \vdash \Delta 1}{\Gamma 2 \vdash \Delta 2}$$

with the meaning that whenever the inference above the line is valid, then so is the inference below the line.

The inference rules for specifications based on traces are as follows:

1. ∀-introduction
$$\frac{\Gamma \vdash R}{\Gamma \vdash \forall x \in M \cdot R}$$

where x is not free in Γ. This and the three following rules are standard inference rules for natural deduction.

2. Triviality
$$\frac{\Gamma \vdash T}{\Gamma \vdash P \text{ sat } T}$$

If T is always true under assumptions Γ, then it is true before and after every communication of P.

3. Consequence
$$\frac{\Gamma \vdash P \text{ sat } R, R \Rightarrow S}{\Gamma \vdash P \text{ sat } S}$$

If R is an invariant of P, and R implies S, then S must also be an invariant of P.

4. Conjunction
$$\frac{\Gamma \vdash P \text{ sat } R, P \text{ sat } S}{\Gamma \vdash P \text{ sat } (R \wedge S)}$$

If R is an invariant of P and so is S, then so is $R \wedge S$.

The remaining rules are specific to the semantic model considered here. Let $R_{\langle\rangle}$ denote the assertion derived from R by replacing all channel histories by the empty trace, $\langle\rangle$. Then we can formulate the inference rule:

5. Emptiness
$$\frac{\Gamma \vdash R_{\langle\rangle}}{\Gamma \vdash STOP \text{ sat } R}$$

For example, given the process $BUF1$ defined above in section 2.1.3, we can take the definition of $BUF1$ as assumption Γ, and it is then true that $\Gamma \vdash R$, where the assertion R is $(right \leqslant left)$. The derived assertion $R_{\langle\rangle}$ is thus: $(\langle\rangle \leqslant \langle\rangle)$, and the inference rule enables us to infer the assertion:

$STOP$ **sat** $right \leqslant left$

Another way of looking at this is to say that if R is to be satisfied by $STOP$, then it must be true for all possible traces of $STOP$. As we have seen, $traces(STOP) = \{\langle\rangle\}$, so R must be true of the empty trace.

For the next rule, we introduce the notation that $R^c_{\langle e\rangle^\frown c}$ denotes the assertion derived from R by replacing c by $\langle e\rangle^\frown c$ (strictly, of course, replacing $past(c)$ by $\langle e\rangle^\frown past(c)$).

6. Output
$$\frac{\Gamma \vdash R_{\langle\rangle},\ P \text{ sat } R^c_{\langle e\rangle^\frown c}}{\Gamma \vdash (c!e \to P) \text{ sat } R}$$

As with the previous rule, this reflects the fact that if R is to be satisfied by $(c!e \to P)$, then it must be true for all possible traces of $(c!e \to P)$. Now, for communication events:

$$traces(c!e \to P) = \{\langle\rangle\} \cup \{\langle c.e\rangle^\frown t \mid t \in traces(P)\}$$

So R must be true of the empty trace, and if R is true of a trace, t, of P, then it must also be true of that same trace prefixed by the communication e on channel c.

Looking again at process $BUF1$, let us now suppose that it has the specification:

$$BUF1 \text{ sat } (right \leqslant left) \wedge (|\#left - \#right| \leq 1)$$

Then we wish to show that $(right!e \to BUF1)$ obeys the specification:

$$(right!e \to BUF1) \text{ sat } (right \leqslant \langle e\rangle^\frown left) \wedge (|\#\langle e\rangle^\frown left - \#right| \leq 1)$$

The right hand side of this is the assertion R. Then $R_{\langle\rangle}$ is:

$$(\langle\rangle \leqslant \langle e\rangle^\frown\langle\rangle) \wedge (|\#\langle e\rangle^\frown\langle\rangle - \#\langle\rangle| \leq 1)$$

which is trivially true, and the assertion $R^{right}_{\langle e\rangle^\frown right}$ is:

$$(\langle e\rangle^\frown right \leqslant \langle e\rangle^\frown left) \wedge (|\#\langle e\rangle^\frown left - \#\langle e\rangle^\frown right| \leq 1)$$

which follows directly from the assertion which we initially assumed held true of $BUF1$, and from the definition of a trace. Thus we have demonstrated the validity of both the required subsidiary inferences of the **Output** inference rule, and can thus infer that $(right!e \to BUF1)$ satisfies the specification given above.

The following rule applies correspondingly to input communications:

7. Input
$$\frac{\Gamma \vdash R_{\langle\rangle},\ \forall v \in M \cdot P[v/x] \text{ sat } R^c_{\langle v\rangle^\frown c}}{\Gamma \vdash (c?x : M \to P) \text{ sat } R}$$

(It is here assumed that v does not appear free in P, R or c.) For an input communication event to occur, the receiver must be prepared to receive *any* value in the domain M, so the invariant must be satisfied for all such values. In all other respects, the inference rule is the same as for output, as (successful) input and output both have the same effect in our current semantic model, in which we only consider the effects of operations on the channel histories. Both operations result in the transferred message being prefixed to the trace for the channel concerned.

Continuing to consider $BUF1$, we have shown above that:

$$\Gamma \vdash (right!e \rightarrow BUF1) \textbf{ sat } (right \leqslant \langle e \rangle ^\frown left) \wedge (|\#\langle e \rangle ^\frown left - \#right| \leq 1)$$

where Γ is the definition of $BUF1$. Since e is not free in Γ, we can use the inference rule $\forall$-**introduction** to deduce that:

$$\Gamma \vdash \forall v \in \mathbb{N}_0 \cdot ((right!v \rightarrow BUF1)$$
$$\textbf{sat } (right \leqslant \langle v \rangle ^\frown left) \wedge (|\#\langle v \rangle ^\frown left - \#right| \leq 1))$$

Taking the assertion on the right hand side of **sat** as $R^c_{\langle v \rangle ^\frown c}$, we find that the assertion $R_{\langle \rangle}$ is:

$$(\langle \rangle \leqslant \langle \rangle) \wedge (|\#\langle \rangle - \#\langle \rangle| \leq 1)$$

which is trivially true. We have therefore demonstrated the validity of the two subsidiary inferences of the **Input** inference rule, and can then infer that:

$$\Gamma \vdash (left?x : \mathbb{N}_0 \rightarrow (right!x \rightarrow BUF1))$$
$$\textbf{sat } (right \leqslant left) \wedge (|\#left - \#right| \leq 1)$$

The next two rules deal with alternatives:

8. Union
$$\frac{\Gamma \vdash P \textbf{ sat } R, \ Q \textbf{ sat } R}{\Gamma \vdash (P \sqcap Q) \textbf{ sat } R}$$

9. Alternative
$$\frac{\Gamma \vdash P \textbf{ sat } R, \ Q \textbf{ sat } R}{\Gamma \vdash (P [] Q) \textbf{ sat } R}$$

With our current semantic model, we are unable to distinguish between alternatives of type $(P \sqcap Q)$ and alternatives of type $(P [] Q)$. In both cases, the composed process can only satisfy an invariant if both component processes satisfy it.

For parallelism without channel synchronisation, we have the rule:

10. Interleaving
$$\frac{\Gamma \vdash P \textbf{ sat } R, \ Q \textbf{ sat } S}{\Gamma \vdash (P \ ||| \ Q) \textbf{ sat } (R \wedge S)}$$

The reasoning behind this rule is that if R is invariantly true of P, and S is invariantly true of Q, then when both P and Q run in parallel, both invariants must be true. For this rule to be sound, R and S must refer to disjoint sets of channels; this is ensured if $\alpha_c P \cap \alpha_c Q = \{\}$.

For parallelism with synchronisation over the events in common channels, we apply essentially the same rule as **Interleaving**. However, since there are now common channels in P and Q, the assertions R and S will contain common variables, reflecting the logical coupling between the behaviours of the two processes.

11. Parallelism
$$\frac{\Gamma \vdash P \text{ sat } R, \; Q \text{ sat } S}{\Gamma \vdash (P \parallel Q) \text{ sat } (R \land S)}$$

An example will be given below, when we have considered Renaming.

It is useful to consider process definitions as being parameterised with the channel names as parameters. By suitable renaming, we can then use the same definition (and suitably modified assertions) in a number of different situations. A good example of this appears when we wish to connect two processes together via a common channel. The channels to be joined together must then be renamed to have the same identity. The relevant inference rule is:

12. Renaming
$$\frac{\Gamma \vdash P \text{ sat } R_c^d}{\Gamma \vdash P[d/c] \text{ sat } R}$$

As an example, consider the two-place buffer defined by the expression:

$$BUF2 \overset{\text{def}}{=} (BUF1[c/right] \parallel_{\{c\}} BUF1[c/left])$$

This describes a buffer which behaves as two processes of type $BUF1$, connected so that the channel *right* in the left hand process becomes common with the channel *left* in the right hand process. The common channel is renamed c, as illustrated in Figure 2.6(b).

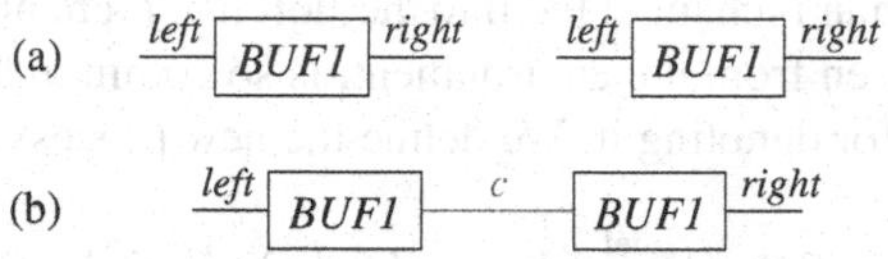

Fig. 2.6 Channel renaming

Let us first take the definition of $BUF1$ as our basic assumption, Γ. We can then use the inference rule **Renaming** to develop the inferences:

$$\Gamma \vdash BUF1[c/right] \text{ sat } (c \leqslant left) \land (|\#left - \#c| \leq 1)$$

and

$$\Gamma \vdash BUF1[c/left] \text{ sat } (right \leqslant c) \land (|\#c - \#right| \leq 1)$$

The rule **Parallelism** can then be used to deduce that:

$$\Gamma \vdash (BUF1[c/right] \parallel_{\{c\}} BUF1[c/left])$$
$$\text{sat } ((right \leqslant c) \land (|\#c - \#right| \leq 1)) \land$$
$$((c \leqslant left) \land (|\#left - \#c| \leq 1))$$

and this in turn can, by application of the rule **Consequence**, be shown to lead to:

$$\Gamma \vdash (BUF1[c/right] \parallel_{\{c\}} BUF1[c/left])$$
$$\text{sat } (right \leqslant left) \land (|\#left - \#right| \leq 2)$$

in accordance with our expectations of a two-place buffer!

Connection of two processes via a common channel does not automatically hide the activity on that channel, so if we wish to make it invisible to the environment, we need some rule for deducing what the externally observable behaviour becomes if a particular channel is hidden:

13. Hiding
$$\frac{\Gamma \vdash P \text{ sat } R}{\Gamma \vdash (P \backslash L) \text{ sat } \exists L \cdot R}$$

where L denotes a set of channels, say $\{c_1, c_2, \ldots, c_n\}$, whose communications are to be hidden, and $\exists LR$ means $\exists past(c_1), past(c_2), \ldots, past(c_n) \cdot R$, i.e. for each channel c_i in L, it is possible to find a channel history $past(c_i)$ such that R holds. A useful case is where R is independent of the hidden channels. For example, we see that the final assertion developed for the two-place buffer $BUF2$ above is independent of c, so it must also be true for the process $(BUF2 \backslash \{c\})$, illustrated in Figure 2.7.

Fig. 2.7 Channel hiding and piping

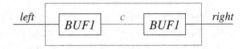

The type of system in which two processes are joined in series, with the 'right hand' channel fed into the 'left hand' channel of the next (as in $BUF2$) and then hidden from the environment, is so common that a special notation is often introduced for denoting it. We define the new process operator $\gg$ as follows:

$$P \gg Q \stackrel{\text{def}}{=} (P[t/right] \parallel Q[t/left]) \backslash \{t\}$$

This operator is usually known as the *piping* or *chaining* operator. It is an associative operator, which has important implications for its use in describing protocol systems, as we shall discuss in the next chapter. The proof rule for this operator is:

14. Piping
$$\frac{\Gamma \vdash P \text{ sat } R, \; Q \text{ sat } S}{\Gamma \vdash (P \gg Q) \text{ sat } \exists t \cdot R[t/right] \wedge S[t/left]}$$

To deal with processes whose behaviour depends on some Boolean condition we need the rule:

15. Condition
$$\frac{\Gamma \vdash P \text{ sat } (b \Rightarrow R); \; \Gamma \vdash Q \text{ sat } (\neg b \Rightarrow R)}{\Gamma \vdash (\textbf{if } b \textbf{ then } P \textbf{ else } Q) \text{ sat } R}$$

This expresses the obvious fact that the conditional (**if** b **then** P **else** Q) will have invariant R if the **then**-branch of the conditional has this invariant when b is true, and the **else**-branch of the conditional has this invariant when b is false.

The final inference rule which we shall consider is used to deal with recursively defined processes:

16. Recursion
$$\frac{\Gamma \vdash R_{\langle\rangle};\; \Gamma, (p \text{ sat } R) \vdash P \text{ sat } R}{\Gamma, (p \overset{\text{def}}{=} P) \vdash p \text{ sat } R}$$

where it is assumed that the process expression P is a function of p. Note that this rule requires the validity of two subsidiary inferences in order to demonstrate that p **sat** R. For a simple example, let us return to the one-place buffer. This is defined by $(BUF1 \overset{\text{def}}{=} P)$, where P is given by:

$$(left?x : \mathbb{N}_0 \to (right!x \to BUF1))$$

We wish to show that $BUF1$ **sat** R, where R is the assertion:

$$(right \leqslant left) \wedge (|\#left - \#right| \leq 1)$$

The first subsidiary inference requires the truth of $R_{\langle\rangle}$, which as we have seen before is trivially true. For the second subsidiary inference, we assume that $BUF1$ **sat** R – what we want to prove – and then need to show that P **sat** R. This has already been shown above, but to illustrate the style of a complete proof, we collect up all its steps and add annotations explaining the results and inference rules used in each step, as follows:

---

1. $\Rightarrow \{\text{Definitions of } \leqslant, \#\}$
   $\Gamma \vdash (\langle\rangle \leqslant \langle\rangle) \wedge (|\#\langle\rangle - \#\langle\rangle| \leq 1)$
2. $\Rightarrow \{\text{Assumption}\}$
   $\Gamma \vdash BUF1 \text{ sat } (right \leqslant left) \wedge (|\#left - \#right| \leq 1)$
3. $\Rightarrow \{2, \text{definitions of } \leqslant, \#\}$
   $\Gamma \vdash BUF1 \text{ sat } (\langle e\rangle^\frown right \leqslant \langle e\rangle^\frown left) \wedge (|\#\langle e\rangle^\frown left - \#\langle e\rangle^\frown right| \leq 1)$
4. $\Rightarrow \{1, 3, \text{Output}\}$
   $\Gamma \vdash (right!e \to BUF1) \text{ sat } (right \leqslant \langle e\rangle^\frown left) \wedge (|\#\langle e\rangle^\frown left - \#right| \leq 1)$
5. $\Rightarrow \{4, \forall\text{-introduction}\}$
   $\Gamma \vdash \forall v \in \mathbb{N}_0 \cdot ((right!v \to BUF1)$
   $\qquad\qquad \text{sat } (right \leqslant \langle v\rangle^\frown left) \wedge (|\#\langle v\rangle^\frown left - \#right| \leq 1))$
6. $\Rightarrow \{1, 5, \text{Input}\}$
   $\Gamma \vdash (left?x : \mathbb{N}_0 \to (right!x \to BUF1))$
   $\qquad\qquad \text{sat } (right \leqslant left) \wedge (|\#left - \#right| \leq 1))$
7. $\Rightarrow \{1, 6, \text{Recursion}\}$
   $\Gamma, (BUF1 \overset{\text{def}}{=} (left?x : \mathbb{N}_0 \to (right!x \to BUF1))) \vdash BUF1$
   $\qquad\qquad \text{sat } (right \leqslant left) \wedge (|\#left - \#right| \leq 1))$

Thus we can validly infer that $BUF1$ **sat** R, as required.

2.3 Failure Semantics

As previously noted, semantic models based solely on the use of channel histories do not deal successfully with many aspects of the behaviour of systems of processes.

A particular problem is that the process defined by $P \stackrel{\text{def}}{=} STOP$ satisfies the specification P **sat** R, for any R which is satisfiable for the empty trace, i.e. such that $R_{\langle\rangle}$ holds, since the history of the deadlocked process is $\langle\rangle$. This is, to put it mildly, inconvenient.

In order to be able to distinguish between useful solutions to a specification and deadlocked solutions, we need a more complex semantic model, in which we can not only express the idea that a process has a particular *channel history*, but also the idea that the process is *currently unable to take part* in certain communication events. This is often called a *failure model* for the semantics. Failure models can describe both *liveness* and *safety* properties of a system of processes, and are the basis of most recent work using CSP, including the very influential paper "A Theory of Communicating Sequential Processes" *(TCSP)* [19] and Hoare's 1985 version of CSP [64].

As in the case of the channel history semantics, we shall describe this model in terms of a set of inference rules which can be used to prove properties of systems. These rules are for process P now expressed in terms of *four* functions:

initials(P)   defined as before by:

$$initials(P) \stackrel{\text{def}}{=} \{a \in A \mid \exists Q \cdot P \stackrel{a}{\longrightarrow} Q\}$$

traces(P)   defined as before by:

$$traces(P) \stackrel{\text{def}}{=} \{s \in A^* \mid \exists Q \cdot P \stackrel{s}{\Longrightarrow} Q\}$$

refusals(P)   defined by:

$$refusals(P) \stackrel{\text{def}}{=} \{X \mid finite(X) \wedge X \subseteq \alpha P$$
$$\wedge \exists Q \cdot (P \stackrel{\langle\rangle}{\Longrightarrow} Q \wedge (X \cap initials(Q)) = \{\})\}$$

A *refusal set* of P is the set of events which P will *not* take part in when placed in a given environment. $refusals(P)$ is thus the set of all refusal sets of P. It follows from the definition that:

1. $\{\} \in refusals(P)$
2. $(X \cup Y) \in refusals(P) \Rightarrow X \in refusals(P)$
3. $X \in refusals(P) \Rightarrow (X \cup \{a\}) \in refusals(P) \vee a \in initials(P)$

This last property states that an event is either possible as an initial event or it must be in a refusal set for P. As examples of refusal sets, we have:

$$refusals(STOP_A) = \{X \mid X \subseteq A\}$$
$$refusals(a \rightarrow P) = \{X \mid X \subseteq (\alpha P - \{a\})\}$$
$$refusals(P[\!]Q) = refusals(P) \cap refusals(Q)$$
$$refusals(P \sqcap Q) = refusals(P) \cup refusals(Q)$$

failures(P)   defined by:

$$failures(P) \stackrel{\text{def}}{=} \{(s,X) \mid \exists Q \cdot P \stackrel{s}{\Longrightarrow} Q \wedge X \in refusals(Q)\}$$

In other words, a *failure* of P is a pair, (s,X), such that P can take part in the events of the trace s, and will then refuse the events in the refusal set X. It follows from this definition that, if $\mathscr{F} \stackrel{\text{def}}{=} failures(P)$:

1. $(\langle\rangle, \{\}) \in \mathscr{F}$
2. $(s\widehat{\ }t, X) \in \mathscr{F} \Rightarrow (s, \{\}) \in \mathscr{F}$
3. $(s, Y) \in \mathscr{F} \wedge X \subseteq Y \Rightarrow (s, X) \in \mathscr{F}$
4. $(s, X) \in \mathscr{F} \wedge a \in \alpha P \Rightarrow (s, X \cup \{a\}) \in \mathscr{F} \vee (s\widehat{\ }\langle a\rangle, \{\}) \in \mathscr{F}$

In this semantic model, a process is often identified with its failures; in other words, we say that a process 'is' its failure set, and that two processes with identical failure sets are identical.

As in the channel history model, a specification of the form

P sat R

means that R is true before and after every event in which the process described by P can take part. In particular, we expect R to be true of all *traces and refusals* of P. Thus R is in general a function of the traces and refusals of P, which we can denote $R(tr, ref)$, and it will be the case that:

$$\forall tr, ref \cdot tr \in traces(P) \wedge (\exists Q \cdot P \stackrel{tr}{\Longrightarrow} Q \wedge ref \in refusals(Q))$$
$$\Rightarrow R(tr, ref)$$

The inference rules for this model, which should be compared with those for 'pure' channel history semantics, are as follows. The first four rules are unchanged from before:

1. ∀-introduction
$$\frac{\Gamma \vdash R}{\Gamma \vdash \forall x \in M \cdot R}$$

where x is not free in Γ.

2. Triviality
$$\frac{\Gamma \vdash T}{\Gamma \vdash P \text{ sat } T}$$

3. Consequence
$$\frac{\Gamma \vdash P \text{ sat } R, R \Rightarrow S}{\Gamma \vdash P \text{ sat } S}$$

4. Conjunction
$$\frac{\Gamma \vdash P \text{ sat } R, P \text{ sat } S}{\Gamma \vdash P \text{ sat } (R \wedge S)}$$

Let $R_{\langle\rangle, B}$ denote an assertion derived from R by replacing each channel history by the empty trace, $\langle\rangle$, and each refusal set by the set B. Then we can formulate the inference rule:

5. Emptiness
$$\frac{\Gamma \vdash \forall B \subseteq A \cdot R_{\langle\rangle,B}}{\Gamma \vdash STOP_A \text{ sat } R}$$

We note that the process $STOP_A$ now only satisfies a specification if every subset of A will be refused when the channel histories are all empty. Since the subset can be chosen to be the entire alphabet A, the specification of $STOP$ is much stronger than before.

For the next two rules, we use the fact that communication of a value e on channel c can only occur if $refusals(P)$ does not contain $c.e$.

6. Output
$$\frac{\Gamma \vdash \forall B \subseteq \alpha P - \{c.e\} \cdot R_{\langle\rangle,B}, \ P \text{ sat } R^c_{\langle e\rangle^\frown c}}{\Gamma \vdash (c!e \rightarrow P) \text{ sat } R}$$

This follows from the results that:

$$traces(c!e \rightarrow P) \ \ = \{\langle\rangle\} \cup \{\langle c.e\rangle^\frown t \mid t \in traces(P)\}$$
$$refusals(c!e \rightarrow P) = \{X \mid X \subseteq (\alpha P - \{c.e\})\}$$

The following rule applies correspondingly to input communications:

7. Input
$$\frac{\Gamma \vdash \forall v \in M \cdot (\forall B \subseteq \alpha P - \{c.v\} \cdot R_{\langle\rangle,B}, \ P[v/x] \text{ sat } R^c_{\langle v\rangle^\frown c})}{\Gamma \vdash (c?x : M \rightarrow P) \text{ sat } R}$$

(It is here assumed that v does not appear free in P, R or c.)

The rule for internal non-determinism is unchanged from before:

8. Union
$$\frac{\Gamma \vdash P \text{ sat } R, \ Q \text{ sat } R}{\Gamma \vdash (P \sqcap Q) \text{ sat } R}$$

With our new semantic model, however, we are able to distinguish alternatives of type $(P \| Q)$ from alternatives of type $(P \sqcap Q)$. As pointed out in exercise 2, even a simple process of the type $(P \sqcap Q)$ can deadlock on its first step if placed in a suitable environment, whereas its sets of possible traces are indistinguishable from those of $(P \| Q)$. For external non-determinism, we now have the rule:

9. Alternative
$$\frac{\Gamma \vdash P \text{ sat } R, \ Q \text{ sat } R, (R_{\langle\rangle,X} \wedge R_{\langle\rangle,Y} \Rightarrow R_{\langle\rangle,X \cap Y})}{\Gamma \vdash (P \| Q) \text{ sat } R}$$

In this case, the composed process can only satisfy an invariant if both component processes satisfy it, and if their refusal sets match the invariant. In particular, before any communication has occurred (i.e. when their traces are empty), a set is refused by the composed process only if it is refused both by P and Q.

For parallelism without channel synchronisation, we still have the rule:

10. Interleaving
$$\frac{\Gamma \vdash P \text{ sat } R, \ Q \text{ sat } S}{\Gamma \vdash (P \ ||| \ Q) \text{ sat } (R \wedge S)}$$

The reasoning behind this rule is still that if R is invariantly true of P, and S is invariantly true of Q, then when both P and Q run in parallel, both invariants must be true. Again, R and S must refer to disjoint sets of channels, which is ensured if $\alpha_c P \cap \alpha_c Q = \{ \}$.

For parallelism with synchronisation over the events in common channels, however, we now have:

11. Parallelism

$$\frac{\Gamma \vdash P \text{ sat } R(tr, ref), \ Q \text{ sat } S(tr, ref)}{\Gamma \vdash (P \parallel Q) \text{ sat } \exists V, W \cdot (R(tr \upharpoonright \alpha P, V) \\ \land S(tr \upharpoonright \alpha Q, W) \\ \land (ref = V \cup W))}$$

This reflects the fact that the refusal set of the composed process is the union of the refusal sets of the two processes P and Q.

The rule for renaming is unaltered from before:

12. Renaming

$$\frac{\Gamma \vdash P \text{ sat } R_c^d}{\Gamma \vdash P[d/c] \text{ sat } R}$$

The rule for hiding, on the other hand, requires some thought, since a system of processes which are engaged in hidden internal communication is not deadlocked. However, such a system is not stable, in the sense of being able to offer a well-defined response to the environment. We can therefore not insist that it obeys a specification with respect to its externally observable behaviour. As an example, consider the process $BUF2$ defined on page 33. When its left-hand component process $BUF1$ has just accepted one message from the environment, $BUF2$ is only capable of internal communication (passing the message between the two $BUF1$ processes), and it obeys the assertion:

$$refusals(BUF2) = \{left, right\}$$

which is not in accordance with any reasonable specification for a buffer. We therefore require that the specification only has to be obeyed when the composed process is in a *stable state* – that is to say, when no internal communication can take place. This leads to the inference rule:

13. Hiding

$$\frac{\Gamma \vdash P \text{ sat } R(tr, ref)}{\Gamma \vdash (P \backslash L) \text{ sat } \exists s \cdot R(s, ref \cup L) \land s \upharpoonright (\alpha_c P - L) = tr}$$

where L denotes a set of channels whose communications are to be hidden. It can be shown that this rule leads to a contradiction if the internal communication never terminates, and a subsidiary condition for its use must thus be that this state of affairs (known as *livelock* or *divergence*) cannot occur. A more correct rule is thus:

13'. Hiding

$$\frac{\Gamma \vdash P \text{ sat } R(tr, ref) \land (\forall c \in L \cdot \#past(c) \leq f_c(past(d) \dots past(z)))}{\Gamma \vdash (P \backslash L) \text{ sat } \exists s \cdot R(s, ref \cup L) \land s \upharpoonright (\alpha_c P - L) = tr}$$

where channels $d \ldots z \notin L$, and f_c is some finite-valued function from channel sets to natural numbers. Further discussion of this point can be found in [63].

The rules for piping and for conditional constructions are unchanged from before:

14. Piping
$$\frac{\Gamma \vdash P \text{ sat } R, \ Q \text{ sat } S}{\Gamma \vdash (P \gg Q) \text{ sat } \exists t \cdot R[t/right] \wedge S[t/left]}$$

15. Condition
$$\frac{\Gamma \vdash P \text{ sat } (b \Rightarrow R); \ \Gamma \vdash Q \text{ sat } (\neg b \Rightarrow R)}{\Gamma \vdash (\text{if } b \text{ then } P \text{ else } Q) \text{ sat } R}$$

The inference rule for recursively defined processes is, however, considerably modified from before, for similar reasons to those presented in our discussion of hiding. The rule becomes:

16. Recursion
$$\frac{\Gamma \vdash R(0); \ \Gamma, \forall n \cdot (p \text{ sat } R(n)) \vdash P \text{ sat } R(n+1)}{\Gamma, (p \overset{\text{def}}{=} P) \vdash p \text{ sat } \forall n \cdot R(n)}$$

where it is assumed that the process expression P is a function of p, and the notation $R(n)$ is a predicate containing the variable n, which ranges over the natural numbers $0, 1, 2, \ldots$. Note that this rule again requires the validity of two subsidiary inferences in order to demonstrate that p **sat** R. To avoid livelock, it is a requirement that in the definition P, p is *externally guarded* (i.e. with a prefix which requires cooperation from the environment).

Further reading

The notation which we follow in these notes is as far as practicable that of Hoare in his 1985 book on CSP [64]. This represents the culmination of a line of development starting with Hoare's original presentation of CSP in his well-known paper from 1978 [62]. A channel history semantics for CSP first appeared in "Partial Correctness of Communicating Processes and Protocols" [128], where its use for proving correctness of protocols was demonstrated. Failure semantics were introduced in [63] and [19]. Note that these works all use slightly differing notations! Roscoe's book "The Theory and Practice of Concurrency" [111] gives a more modern presentation of CSP and its uses.

There are many other specification languages based on similar principles: description of systems as processes which interact by synchronised communication, and for which an algebra of processes can be defined. Two important examples are LOTOS [17, 156], which is a language developed within ISO for specification of cmmunication services and protocols, and CCS, originally proposed by Milner in his monograph "A Calculus of Communicating Systems" [94], and further developed in [95].

Failure semantics is an improvement on plain channel history semantics, in the sense that it enables us to distinguish between processes which have the same behaviour with respect to traces, but which differ with respect to refusals. However, both these semantic models are just two examples from a long series of models which could be applied to describing the behaviour of distributed systems. A more detailed and systematic discussion of further possibilities can be found in [102].

Exercises

2.1. Given the definitions on page 12, what is the alphabet of *VMCT*? of *DEMON*? of *VMDEMON*?

Describe the behaviour of the parallel composition of *GRCUST* with *VMDEMON* with synchronisation over the event set $\{coin, toffee, choc\}$.

2.2. Given the processes $P \stackrel{\text{def}}{=} (x \to P)$ and $Q \stackrel{\text{def}}{=} (y \to Q)$, describe the difference between:

$$(P [\!] Q) \parallel P \qquad \text{and} \qquad (P \sqcap Q) \parallel P$$

a) in terms of their possible traces and b) in terms of their deadlock behaviour.

2.3. Use the process algebra for CSP and the definitions on page 12 to demonstrate the result (previously stated without proof) that:

$$VMDEMON = (coin \to (VMDEMON \\ \sqcap (VMDEMON [\!] toffee \to VMDEMON)))$$

2.4. Describe the behaviour of $(S \parallel TIMER) \setminus \{up\}$, where:

$$S \qquad \stackrel{\text{def}}{=} (user?y : \mathcal{M} \to \qquad QT[y])$$
$$QT[x : \mathcal{M}] \stackrel{\text{def}}{=} (wire!x \to (up!\text{SET} \to (wire?a : \{\text{ACK}\} \to (up!\text{RESET} \to S) \\ [\!] wire?a : \{\text{NACK}\} \to (up!\text{RESET} \to QT[x]) \\ [\!] up?t : \{\text{TIMEOUT}\} \to QT[x])))$$

Assume that *TIMER* is as defined on page 23, that $\alpha_c S = \{up, wire, user\}$ and $\alpha_c TIMER = \{up\}$.

2.5. Process *VMCT'* in Figure 2.5 is a concretisation of process *VMCT* in Figure 2.3, in which the abstract events of process *VMCT* have been replaced by communication events which are more directly related to the informal description of the vending machine concerned. Give corresponding concretisations in terms of communication events of the processes *VMBREAK2*, *GRCUST*, *VMFAULTY* and *VMDEMON* from Figure 2.3.

2.6. Give the definition of a process E which inputs a stream of bits, and outputs them encoded in Manchester encoding, where each 1-bit is encoded as the sequence of values $\langle 1, 0 \rangle$, and each 0-bit is encoded as $\langle 0, 1 \rangle$. Then give a definition of a decoder process, D, which inputs a pair of values in $\{1, 0\}$, and outputs the bit value to which the pair corresponds. If the pair of values is not valid, the decoder stops.

2.7. Give the definition of a process $MULT$ which accepts on its input channel c a potentially endless series of digits of a natural number, C, in some (pre-defined) base $\mathcal{B}$, least-significant digit first, and outputs on channel d a series of digits which represent the product of C with a fixed multiplier digit, $M \in [0 \ldots (\mathcal{B} - 1)]$. The digits output via d are to be output with the least possible delay. You may assume that the processor which $MULT$ runs on is able to perform simple integer arithmetic in base $\mathcal{B}$.

(HINT: Try to parameterise the process using the carry from the previous multiplication of M with a digit of C as parameter.)

2.8. Develop your solution to the previous exercise further, so that you are able to multiply C by a multi-digit multiplier $M[1] \ldots M[n]$.

This requires n processes, which communicate the partial products to one another. (It also requires some thought!)

2.9. An alternative definition of a two-position buffer to the one given on page 33 is:

$$BUF2 \stackrel{\text{def}}{=} (BUF1 \gg BUF1)$$

Show by using the rule **Piping** that this satisfies the specification:

$$BUF2 \ \textbf{sat} \ (right \leqslant left) \wedge (|\#left - \#right| \leq 2)$$

2.10. An unbounded buffer is defined by:

$$BUF \stackrel{\text{def}}{=} (left?x : \mathbb{N}_0 \rightarrow (BUF[c/right] \parallel_{\{c\}} (right!x \rightarrow BUF1)[c/left]) \setminus \{c\})$$

Show that this obeys the specification $(BUF \ \textbf{sat} \ (right \leqslant left))$.

2.11. Which assertions does the process $TIMER$ defined on page 23 have as invariants? Formulate as many non-trivial ones as possible, and discuss their significance in relation to the supposed use of $TIMER$ to provide a timeout mechanism for other processes, such as QT.

2.12. Use the process algebra of CSP to demonstrate that the following rules apply to the piping operator, $\gg$:

$$P \gg (Q \gg R) = (P \gg Q) \gg R$$
$$(right!v \to P) \gg (left?y : M \to Q[y]) = P \gg Q[v]$$
$$(right!v \to P) \gg (right!w \to Q) = right!w \to ((right!v \to P) \gg Q)$$
$$(left?x : M \to P[x]) \gg (left?y : M \to Q[y]) = left?x : M \to (P[x] \gg (left?y : M \to Q[y]))$$
$$(left?x : M \to P[x]) \gg (right!w \to Q) = (left?x : M \to (P[x] \gg (right!w \to Q))$$
$$[\![right!w \to ((left?x : M \to P[x]) \gg Q))$$

where M is an arbitrary domain of messages.

Chapter 3
Protocols and Services

The concept of an elementary communication in CSP is an abstraction of a particular type of *interaction* between two processes. It is based on the idealisations that the processes only take part in synchronised communication, and that communication takes place over a perfect channel, which never loses or corrupts messages.

Real processes seldom, if ever, behave like this. So we need to be able to generalise the concept of an interaction to cover the non-ideal cases which turn up in practice. We shall do this by stepwise refinement. The first step is to introduce the concept of an *interaction point*. This is an abstraction of the 'point' at which a pair of processes appear to communicate, when we consider the totality of their communication with one another. In terms of their externally observable behaviour, we restrict our observations to that part of the behaviour which concerns exactly the two processes in question. This idea is illustrated in Figure 3.1.

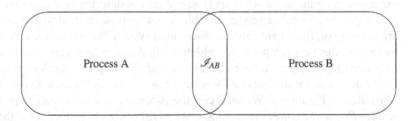

Fig. 3.1 Interaction point $\mathscr{I}_{AB}$ between processes A and B

This is a severe abstraction, and to introduce more realism into it, we can as our next step decompose the interaction point between the processes into a separate process, whose behaviour seen from each of the original processes is the same as the interaction point's. This new process describes the interaction between the processes in more detail, and is an abstraction of the *Service* offered to them by the real communication system. This idea is illustrated in Figure 3.2.

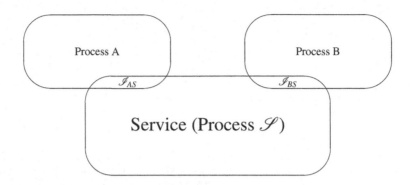

Fig. 3.2 Service between processes *A* and *B*

The processes *A* and *B* are commonly known as the *Service Users*. The interaction points between the Service Users and the service $\mathscr{S}$ are in OSI parlance known as *Service Access Points*, or *SAPs* for short. In Figure 3.2 they are denoted $\mathscr{I}_{AS}$ and $\mathscr{I}_{BS}$. To obtain a formal description and specification of the service, we shall model the service $\mathscr{S}$ as a CSP process (of arbitrary complexity), and each *SAP* as a set of CSP channels.

Note that in the figure only two users are shown – the simplest and commonest case. More generally, services may serve *N* users. For OSI and similar data communication services, *N* must of course be at least two, but for some models of distributed operating systems and the like it is convenient to describe services which are offered to a single user. The service is in such cases often denoted a *server*.

Whilst the concept of a service makes it possible to describe the interactions as experienced by the users of the service, it does not describe *how* these interactions actually come about. The service is a 'black box', whose internal workings the users are unaware of. But, at any rate in a distributed system, the service must be provided by interactions between processes which are in different locations. The interactions in which they take part in their effort to provide the required service are described by the *Protocol* for this service. A better view of the system as a whole is thus as illustrated in Figure 3.3. We shall call the processes which interact to provide the service *Protocol Entities* in accordance with OSI usage. Note that, as for the service users, we only show two protocol entities, *PA* and *PB*, whereas in general there may be a larger number of entities which cooperate to provide the service.

As the final step, we must recognise that the interaction $\mathscr{I}_{PA,PB}$ between the protocol entities will itself be based on a service. This produces the process picture illustrated in Figure 3.4.

For communication services, our formal description of this will be based on the abstraction that the original service, $\mathscr{S}$, between Process *A* and Process *B* is com-

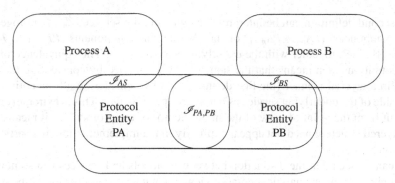

Fig. 3.3 Protocol to provide a service between A and B

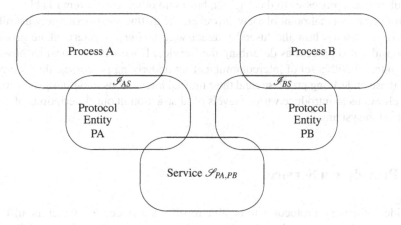

Fig. 3.4 Protocol based on a service

posed from the protocol entities and the underlying service $\mathscr{S}_{PA,PB}$ by piping:

$$\mathscr{S} \overset{\text{def}}{=} PA \gg \mathscr{S}_{PA,PB} \gg PB$$

In many cases, the service $\mathscr{S}_{PA,PB}$ will itself be composed from a set of protocol entities and an underlying service, and so on, in accordance with the usual structure of layered architectures. It is interesting to note that, since the operator $\gg$ is associative, then a service definition:

$$\mathscr{S}_n \overset{\text{def}}{=} (PA_n \gg (PA_{n-1} \gg \mathscr{S}_{n-2} \gg PB_{n-1}) \gg PB_n)$$

can be rewritten as:

$$\mathscr{S}_n \overset{\text{def}}{=} (PA_n \gg PA_{n-1}) \gg \mathscr{S}_{n-2} \gg (PB_{n-1} \gg PB_n)$$

This second definition can be interpreted as viewing the service $\mathscr{S}_n$ as put together from components $(PA_n \gg PA_{n-1})$ on the 'A-side' and components $(PB_{n-1} \gg PB_n)$ on the 'B-side', together with the underlying service $\mathscr{S}_{n-2}$. The equivalence of the two definitions then means that the same effect is obtained by considering the services in a layered manner (the first definition) as by considering all the entities on each side of the underlying service as being grouped together. This is extremely convenient from the point of view of the implementor of the protocol, as it means that the layered structure need not appear explicitly in the implementation in a particular location.

It can be seen that the distinction between protocols and services is a somewhat artificial one from an analytical point of view. Each new decomposition of the original interaction introduces one or more new processes, which from a CSP viewpoint are subordinate processes to the original, but in no other respect remarkable.

From a conceptual point of view, however, the distinction is extremely useful. If we wish to discuss how the 'users' interact with a *common* intermediate process, we consider this process as describing the Service. If we wish to consider how the users interact with a set of intercommunicating underlying processes, then we consider these underlying processes and their mutual interactions as defining a Protocol. This allows us to introduce various levels of abstraction in our descriptions of communication systems.

3.1 Providing a Service

The idea of using a protocol is to be able to offer a service, $\mathscr{S}'$, which is different in some way from the service, $\mathscr{S}$, which we have access to. Seen from a CSP viewpoint, this means that the externally observable behaviour of the process $\mathscr{S}'$ differs from that of $\mathscr{S}$. Usually it is 'better' in some sense, either because it is resilient to faults which may be produced by $\mathscr{S}$, or because it offers new facilities of some kind. Many people use the term *Value-Added Service* to describe this situation, particularly in relation to the standard services offered by public communication systems.

When we design a communication system to provide the service $\mathscr{S}'$, we can take either a top-down or a bottom-up approach. In the top-down approach, we produce a specification $Spec(\mathscr{S}')$ for $\mathscr{S}'$, and then develop a protocol using processes PA and PB, which we hope can offer this service. From $Spec(PA)$, $Spec(PB)$ and $Spec(\mathscr{S}')$ we then develop the required underlying service $\mathscr{S}$. The requirement is:

$$Spec(\mathscr{S}) \wedge Spec(PA) \wedge Spec(PB) \Rightarrow Spec(\mathscr{S}')$$

where

$$\mathscr{S}' \stackrel{\text{def}}{=} PA \gg \mathscr{S} \gg PB$$

$Sender \stackrel{\text{def}}{=} (SAPA?x : \mathcal{M} \to Q[x])$

$Q[x : \mathcal{M}] \stackrel{\text{def}}{=} (right!x \to \qquad (right?y : \{\text{ACK}\} \to Sender$
$\qquad\qquad\qquad\qquad [\![right?y : \{\text{NACK}\} \to Q[x]))$

$Receiver \stackrel{\text{def}}{=} (left?x : \mathcal{M} \to \quad left!\text{ACK} \to SAPB!x \to Receiver$
$\qquad\qquad\qquad [\![left?y : \mathcal{M}' \to \quad left!\text{NACK} \to Receiver)$

Fig. 3.5 Simple ACK/NACK protocol

True top-down development methodologies are not yet available for parallel systems, so in fact what we can do is determine the weakest specification – the so-called *weakest internal condition* – which must be satisfied by $\mathcal{S}$ in order for $Spec(\mathcal{S}')$ to be satisfied. Some examples of this technique can be found in [128]. It is especially useful if we wish to determine what minimum requirements the underlying service, $\mathcal{S}$, must satisfy, if we wish to use a certain protocol, $< PA, PB >$, to provide a certain service, $\mathcal{S}'$.

In the bottom-up method, we start with a given underlying service, $\mathcal{S}$, with specification $Spec(\mathcal{S})$, and try to develop a protocol which together with $\mathcal{S}$ can offer the desired service $\mathcal{S}'$. On the whole we shall follow this approach in this book. Let us consider an example.

Suppose we have a medium which can corrupt messages. However, each message sent via the medium contains a checksum, so that the process receiving the message can detect the corruption. On the basis of the service offered by this medium, we wish to build up a data transmission service which is correct in the sense that it transmits messages between pairs of users without loss, without corruption and with correct preservation of the order of the messages. A suitable specification is:

Specification 3.1 $\qquad \mathcal{S}'$ **sat** $right \leqslant left$

In other words, the sequence of messages received by the user on the right is an initial segment of the sequence sent off by the user on the left.

The service offered by the medium can be described by the CSP processes:

$Medium \stackrel{\text{def}}{=} (MM \,|||\, MA)$

$MM \qquad \stackrel{\text{def}}{=} (left?x : \mathcal{M} \to (\; right!x \to MM$
$\qquad\qquad\qquad\qquad\qquad \sqcap right!y \to MM))$

$MA \qquad \stackrel{\text{def}}{=} (right?a : K \to left!a \to MA)$

where $y \in \mathcal{M}'$ and $(\mathcal{M}' \cap \mathcal{M}) = \{\,\}$, where $\mathcal{M}$ is the domain of correct messages, while $K = \{\text{ACK}, \text{NACK}\}$ is the domain of acknowledgments, which, as we see, are in this example assumed never to get lost or corrupted.

The protocol which we shall use is the simple ACK/NACK protocol defined by the two processes *Sender* and *Receiver*, shown in Figure 3.5. In rough terms, the receiving protocol entity sends an ACK message back to the sending protocol entity if it receives a correct message, and passes the correct message on to the user (via the channel *SAPB*). If an incorrect message is received, the receiving entity sends a NACK back to the sender and does not pass any message on to the user.

3.1.1 Proving the Protocol Correct

The service offered by the combination of the two protocol entities and the underlying service, Medium, is then given by:

$$\mathscr{S}' \overset{\text{def}}{=} Sender \gg Medium \gg Receiver$$

A diagrammatic representation of this is shown in Figure 3.6. We then wish to prove

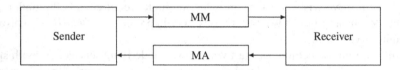

Fig. 3.6 Configuration of $\mathscr{S}'$.

that:

$$\mathscr{S}' \textbf{ sat } SAPB \leqslant SAPA$$

To take account of the possible retransmissions of data, we follow Zhou and Hoare [128] and introduce a filter function, f, of functionality $*(\mathscr{M} \cup \mathscr{M}' \cup K) \rightarrow *\mathscr{M}$, such that the value of $f(s)$ is obtained from s by cancelling all occurrences of ACK, and all consecutive pairs $\langle x, \text{NACK} \rangle$. For example:

$$f(\langle x, \text{NACK}, y, \text{ACK} \rangle) = \langle y \rangle$$

and, more generally:

$$
\begin{aligned}
f(\langle \rangle) \quad & = \langle \rangle \\
f(\langle x \rangle) \quad & = \langle x \rangle \\
f(\langle x \rangle \,\hat{}\, \langle \text{ACK} \rangle \,\hat{}\, c) \quad & = \langle x \rangle \,\hat{}\, f(c) \\
f(\langle x \rangle \,\hat{}\, \langle \text{NACK} \rangle \,\hat{}\, c) & = f(c)
\end{aligned}
$$

where c (strictly, $past(c)$) is a sequence of messages on channel c. Note that f is a *strict*, but not *distributive* function, in the sense defined in the previous chapter.

For the proof, we shall use Channel History semantics. We need to prove three subsidiary assertions:

$$Sender \ \textbf{sat} \ f(right) \leqslant SAPA \tag{1}$$

$$Receiver \ \textbf{sat} \ SAPB \leqslant f(left) \tag{2}$$

$$Medium \ \textbf{sat} \ left \upharpoonright K \leqslant right \upharpoonright K \tag{3}$$

where $c \upharpoonright K$ (strictly, $past(c) \upharpoonright K$) for a channel c means the channel history of c restricted to those messages which are in the domain K.

Let us start with the proof of assertion (2). We take as assumption $\Gamma 2$ the definition of *Receiver*, and we then wish to prove:

$$\Gamma 2 \vdash Receiver \ \textbf{sat} \ SAPB \leqslant f(left)$$

This requires the use of rule **Recursion**, where the assertion on the right of **sat** is R. We give the proof as a numbered sequence of annotated inferences. Each annotation indicates the assumptions for the proof step and the inference rule used to perform the inference. For example: $4. \Rightarrow \{2, 3, \text{Output}\}$ indicates that the conclusions of steps 2 and 3 were used with rule **Output** to infer the conclusion of this step, which is step 4. In this and the following proofs, the final conclusion is framed.

1. $\Rightarrow$ {Definitions of $\leqslant$, f}
    $\vdash \langle \rangle \leqslant f(\langle \rangle)$
2. $\Rightarrow$ {Assumption, Definition of $\leqslant$, f}
    $\Gamma 2 \vdash Receiver \ \textbf{sat} \ \langle x \rangle^\frown SAPB \leqslant f(\langle x \rangle^\frown \langle \text{ACK} \rangle^\frown left)$
3. $\Rightarrow$ {Definition of $\leqslant$, f}
    $\vdash \langle \rangle \leqslant f(\langle x \rangle^\frown \langle \text{ACK} \rangle^\frown \langle \rangle)$
4. $\Rightarrow$ {2, 3, Output}
    $\Gamma 2 \vdash (SAPB!x \to Receiver) \ \textbf{sat} \ SAPB \leqslant f(\langle x \rangle^\frown \langle \text{ACK} \rangle^\frown left)$
5. $\Rightarrow$ {Definition of $\leqslant$}
    $\vdash \langle \rangle \leqslant f(\langle x \rangle)$
6. $\Rightarrow$ {4, 5, Output}
    $\Gamma 2 \vdash (left!\text{ACK} \to SAPB!x \to Receiver) \ \textbf{sat} \ SAPB \leqslant f(\langle x \rangle^\frown left)$
7. $\Rightarrow$ {6, $\forall$-introduction}
    $\Gamma 2 \vdash \forall v \in \mathscr{M} \cdot (left!\text{ACK} \to SAPB!v \to Receiver)$
    $\qquad\qquad\qquad \textbf{sat} \ SAPB \leqslant f(\langle v \rangle^\frown left)$
8. $\Rightarrow$ {Definition of $\leqslant$, f}
    $\vdash \langle \rangle \leqslant f(\langle \rangle)$
9. $\Rightarrow$ {7, 8, Input}
    $\Gamma 2 \vdash (left?x : \mathscr{M} \to left!\text{ACK} \to SAPB!x \to Receiver)$
    $\qquad\qquad\qquad \textbf{sat} \ SAPB \leqslant f(left)$
10. $\Rightarrow$ {Assumption, definition of f}
    $\Gamma 2 \vdash Receiver \ \textbf{sat} \ SAPB \leqslant f(\langle x \rangle^\frown \langle \text{NACK} \rangle^\frown left)$
11. $\Rightarrow$ {Definitions of $\leqslant$, f}
    $\vdash \langle \rangle \leqslant f(\langle x \rangle^\frown \langle \rangle)$
12. $\Rightarrow$ {10, 11, Output}
    $\Gamma 2 \vdash (left!\text{NACK} \to Receiver) \ \textbf{sat} \ SAPB \leqslant f(\langle x \rangle^\frown left)$
13. $\Rightarrow$ {12, $\forall$-introduction}
    $\Gamma 2 \vdash \forall v \in \mathscr{M}' \cdot (left!\text{NACK} \to Receiver) \ \textbf{sat} \ SAPB \leqslant f(\langle v \rangle^\frown left)$

14. $\Rightarrow$ {Definitions of $\leqslant, f$}
$$\vdash \langle\rangle \leqslant f(\langle\rangle)$$
15. $\Rightarrow$ {13, 14, Input}
$$\Gamma2 \vdash (left?y : \mathscr{M}' \to left!\text{NACK} \to Receiver) \textbf{ sat } SAPB \leqslant f(left)$$
16. $\Rightarrow$ {9, 15, Alternative}
$$\Gamma2 \vdash \begin{array}{l} (left?x : \mathscr{M} \to left!\text{ACK} \to SAPB!x \to Receiver \\ [\![left?y : \mathscr{M}' \to left!\text{NACK} \to Receiver) \end{array}$$
$$\textbf{sat } SAPB \leqslant f(left)$$
17. $\Rightarrow$ {1, 16, Recursion}

$$\boxed{\Gamma2 \vdash Receiver \textbf{ sat } SAPB \leqslant f(left)}$$

The proof of assertion (1) is somewhat more complicated. We follow the procedure suggested in Zhou and Hoare's monograph, and take as assumption $\Gamma1$ the definitions of *Receiver* and *Q*. We then try to prove:

$$\Gamma1 \vdash Sender \textbf{ sat } f(right) \leqslant SAPA, \ \forall x \in \mathscr{M} \cdot (Q[x] \textbf{ sat } f(right) \leqslant \langle x\rangle\hat{}SAPA)$$

This consists of two subsidiary assertions, one for *Sender* and one for *Q*. The proof of each of these requires us to use the rule **Recursion**, where the assertion on the right of **sat** is *R*. The steps are as follows:

1. $\Rightarrow$ {Definitions of $\leqslant, f$}
$$\vdash \langle\rangle \leqslant f(\langle\rangle)$$
2. $\Rightarrow$ {Definitions of $\leqslant, f, \forall$-introduction}
$$\vdash \forall x \in \mathscr{M} \cdot (f(\langle\rangle) \leqslant \langle x\rangle\hat{}\langle\rangle))$$
3. $\Rightarrow$ {Definitions of $\leqslant, f$}
$$\vdash f(\langle\rangle) \leqslant \langle\rangle$$
4. $\Rightarrow$ {Assumption for Sender, 3, Input}
$$\Gamma1 \vdash (SAPA?x : \mathscr{M} \to Q[x]) \textbf{ sat } f(right) \leqslant SAPA$$
5. $\Rightarrow$ {Assumption for Q}
$$\Gamma1 \vdash x \in \mathscr{M} \Rightarrow Q[x] \textbf{ sat } f(right) \leqslant \langle x\rangle\hat{}SAPA$$
6. $\Rightarrow$ {5, Definition of Q}
$$\Gamma1 \vdash Q[x] \textbf{ sat } f(right) \leqslant \langle x\rangle\hat{}SAPA$$
7. $\Rightarrow$ {Assumption for Sender, definitions of $\leqslant, f$}
$$\Gamma1 \vdash Sender \textbf{ sat } f(\langle x\rangle\hat{}\langle\text{ACK}\rangle\hat{}right) \leqslant (\langle x\rangle\hat{}SAPA)$$
8. $\Rightarrow$ {7, $\forall$-introduction}
$$\Gamma1 \vdash \forall v \in \{\text{ACK}\} \cdot (Sender \textbf{ sat } f(\langle x\rangle\hat{}\langle v\rangle\hat{}right) \leqslant (\langle x\rangle\hat{}SAPA))$$
9. $\Rightarrow$ {6, definitions of $\leqslant, f$}
$$\Gamma1 \vdash Q[x] \textbf{ sat } f(\langle x\rangle\hat{}\langle\text{NACK}\rangle\hat{}right) \leqslant \langle x\rangle\hat{}SAPA$$
10. $\Rightarrow$ {9, $\forall$-introduction}
$$\Gamma1 \vdash \forall v \in \{\text{NACK}\} \cdot (Q[x] \textbf{ sat } f(\langle x\rangle\hat{}\langle v\rangle\hat{}right) \leqslant \langle x\rangle\hat{}SAPA$$
11. $\Rightarrow$ {8, definition f, Input}
$$\Gamma1 \vdash (right?y : \{\text{ACK}\} \to Sender) \textbf{ sat } f(\langle x\rangle\hat{}right) \leqslant \langle x\rangle\hat{}SAPA$$
12. $\Rightarrow$ {10, definition f, Input}
$$\Gamma1 \vdash (right?y : \{\text{NACK}\} \to Q[x]) \textbf{ sat } f(\langle x\rangle\hat{}right) \leqslant \langle x\rangle\hat{}SAPA$$

13. $\Rightarrow$ {11, 12, Alternative}
$$\Gamma 1 \vdash (right?y : \{\text{ACK}\} \rightarrow Sender \text{ sat } f(\langle x \rangle^\frown right) \leqslant \langle x \rangle^\frown SAPA$$
$$[\![right?y : \{\text{NACK}\} \rightarrow Q[x])$$

14. $\Rightarrow$ {Definitions of $\leqslant$, f}
$$\vdash f(\langle \rangle) \leqslant \langle x \rangle$$

15. $\Rightarrow$ {13, 14, Output}
$$\Gamma 1 \vdash (right!x \rightarrow (right?y : \{\text{ACK}\} \rightarrow Sender \text{ sat } f(right) \leqslant \langle x \rangle^\frown SAPA$$
$$[\![right?y : \{\text{NACK}\} \rightarrow Q[x]))$$

16. $\Rightarrow$ {15, $\forall$-introduction}
$$\Gamma 1 \vdash \forall x \in \mathcal{M} \cdot (right!x \rightarrow (right?y : \{\text{ACK}\} \rightarrow Sender \text{ sat } f(right) \leqslant \langle x \rangle^\frown SAPA)$$
$$[\![right?y : \{\text{NACK}\} \rightarrow Q[x])$$

17. $\Rightarrow$ {2, 16, Recursion}
$$\boxed{\Gamma 1 \vdash \forall x \in \mathcal{M} \cdot (Q[x] \text{ sat } f(right) \leqslant \langle x \rangle^\frown SAPA)}$$

18. $\Rightarrow$ {3, 4, Recursion}
$$\boxed{\Gamma 1 \vdash Sender \text{ sat } f(right) \leqslant SAPA}$$

The proof that the process *Medium* satisfies assertion (3) above is very simple, as we are only interested in considering the behaviour of the medium with respect to transmission of acknowledgments. (With respect to other messages, the only thing we can say is that the medium does not actually get messages to disappear, although they may be corrupted.) We proceed as follows:

Take as assumption $\Gamma 3$ the definition of *Medium*, with the subsidiary assumptions $\Gamma 4$ the definition of *MM*, and $\Gamma 5$ the definition of *MA*. Then we wish to prove:

$$\Gamma 3 \vdash (MM \, ||| \, MA) \text{ sat } (left \upharpoonright K \leqslant right \upharpoonright K)$$

We proceed as follows:

1. $\Rightarrow$ {Assumptions, definition of $\upharpoonright$}
$$\Gamma 4 \vdash (left \upharpoonright K = right \upharpoonright K = \langle \rangle)$$

2. $\Rightarrow$ {1, definition of $\leqslant$, Triviality}
$$\Gamma 4 \vdash MM \text{ sat } left \upharpoonright K \leqslant right \upharpoonright K$$

3. $\Rightarrow$ {Assumptions, definitions of $\leqslant$, $\upharpoonright$}
$$\Gamma 5 \vdash \langle \rangle \upharpoonright K \leqslant \langle \rangle \upharpoonright K$$

4. $\Rightarrow$ {Assumptions}
$$\Gamma 5 \vdash MA \text{ sat } left \upharpoonright K \leqslant right \upharpoonright K$$

5. $\Rightarrow$ {4, Definition of $\leqslant$}
$$\Gamma 5 \vdash MA \text{ sat } \langle a \rangle^\frown left \upharpoonright K \leqslant \langle a \rangle^\frown right \upharpoonright K$$

6. $\Rightarrow$ {Definition of $\leqslant$}
$$\vdash \langle \rangle \leqslant \langle a \rangle^\frown \langle \rangle$$

7. $\Rightarrow$ {5, 6, Output}
$$\Gamma 5 \vdash (left!a : K \rightarrow MA) \text{ sat } left \upharpoonright K \leqslant \langle a \rangle^\frown right \upharpoonright K$$

8. $\Rightarrow$ {7, $\forall$-introduction}
$$\Gamma 5 \vdash \forall v \in K \cdot (left!v \rightarrow MA) \text{ sat } left \upharpoonright K \leqslant \langle v \rangle^\frown right \upharpoonright K$$

9. $\Rightarrow$ {Definitions of $\leqslant$, $\upharpoonright$}
$$\vdash \langle \rangle \upharpoonright K \leqslant \langle \rangle \upharpoonright K$$

10. $\Rightarrow$ {8, 9, Input}

$\Gamma 5 \vdash (right?a : K \to left!a \to MA)$ **sat** $left \upharpoonright K \leqslant right \upharpoonright K$

11. $\Rightarrow$ {3, 10, Recursion}

$\Gamma 5 \vdash MA$ **sat** $left \upharpoonright K \leqslant right \upharpoonright K$

12. $\Rightarrow$ {2, 11, Interleaving}

$$\boxed{\Gamma 3 \vdash (MM \;\|\!|\; MA) \textbf{ sat } left \upharpoonright K \leqslant right \upharpoonright K}$$

Using the auxiliary assertions which we have now proved, we can prove the desired assertion about the composed service $\mathscr{S}'$. It follows from the proof rule **Piping** that:

$$(Sender \gg Medium \gg Receiver) \textbf{ sat } (\exists t \cdot (\exists s \cdot (f(s) \leqslant SAPA$$
$$\wedge (s \upharpoonright K \leqslant t \upharpoonright K))$$
$$\wedge SAPB \leqslant f(t)))$$

And it then follows from the definition of f that $SAPB \leqslant SAPA$, as required.

Interestingly enough, the only requirement of the medium in this case is that it does not lose acknowledgments. However, the proof is also based on the hidden assumptions that:

1. Messages do not get totally lost, and
2. Some correct messages do in fact arrive at the receiver.

If these assumptions are not satisfied, the process $\mathscr{S}'$ will in case 1 go into deadlock. In case 2 it will go into livelock and spend all its time sending incorrect messages one way and NACK responses the other way.

3.1.2 Structuring your Proof

Many people find it difficult at first to carry out proofs like the ones shown here, where there are many steps from the initial assumptions to the final conclusion. Experience, of course, is always the best teacher, and by the time you have done all the exercises in this book, you should be well on your way to understanding what to do. A good piece of advice for beginners is to inspect the *structure* of the process which you are trying to prove a property of. For example, if it is defined recursively, then you should be trying to apply the inference rule for Recursion. Try to identify the "variables" in the inference rule: What is R, what is P, what is p?

You may prefer to work backwards here, by a line of reasoning which goes something like "if I have to prove p **sat** R, and p is defined recursively via $p \stackrel{\text{def}}{=} P$, then I have to prove both $R_{\langle\rangle}$ and P **sat** R, where to prove the latter I am allowed to assume that p **sat** R." This shows you what you need to prove, and you can continue to work backwards, step by step, until you reach something which is either trivially true or is given by the definitions or assumptions. This proof strategy is often known as *backward proof*, as opposed to the *forward proof* of which we have just presented two large examples. Obviously, by presenting the steps in reverse order, starting from the definitions and assumptions, a backward proof can be presented as a forward one.

Likewise, if the process which you want to prove has the form of an internal or external choice, you will need to prove that the desired property holds for each of these components. If the process has the form of two processes composed in parallel, you can try to prove that each of them has the required property, say R, or you can try to find two properties, say R_1 and R_2, such that R_1 holds for one of the processes and R_2 for the other process, and where $R = R_1 \land R_2$. If the process whose property is to be proved starts with an input event, you will need to use the Input inference rule. If it starts with an output event, you will need to use the Output inference rule. And so on. The steps required in your proof are guided by the structure of the process being considered. Try now to work back through the proofs of the previous section, and see how this approach works.

3.2 Service Features

Let us at this stage consider what kinds of feature we might find desirable to introduce into a service. Generally speaking, service features fall into two classes. The first class is related to the kind of *logical assumptions* which we want to be able to make concerning the data which are transferred. An example of this might be the requirement that messages are always transferred to the receiver by the service provider in the same order as they were supplied to the service provider by the sender. If we cannot make this kind of assumption, many of our algorithms will be much more complicated. Try to imagine a message handling system in which the paragraphs of messages arrived in random order, for example! Luckily it is exactly this type of feature which can be dealt with using the formal methods and proof techniques which we have sketched in the previous section.

The other class of feature is more of a *technical or economic* nature, related to the price or capacity of the communication system. For example, there may be requirements for a particular throughput, a particular maximum time for transfer of a message, or more generally for transfer of data at the 'lowest possible' price. Typically, formal proof techniques ignore this aspect of services, and the tools available for analysing the properties of distributed systems in this respect come from the areas of graph theory and queueing theory.

In the very nature of things, it is impossible to produce a complete list of service features which might be required, but the following facilities are those used in the OSI Basic Reference Model [133] and its addenda, and are certainly among the most commonly found:

- Sequence preservation.
- Data Unit synchronisation
- Flow control.
- Freedom from error.

- Service reset.
- Connection establishment and release.
- Change of mode.
- Information about change of peer state.
- Expedited Data
- Security.

We shall look at these concepts in turn.

3.2.1 Sequence Preservation

This feature of a service corresponds to the property that the service provider delivers messages in the same order as they are sent off. As we have already seen, this property is susceptible to formal analysis, and corresponds to the simple specification:

Specification 3.2 $\mathcal{S}$ **sat** *received* $\leqslant$ *sent*

for the process $\mathcal{S}$ which represents the service.

3.2.2 Data Unit Synchronisation

In a service which offers this feature, there is a one-to-one correspondence between the messages passed to the service for transmission and the messages delivered to the receivers. In other words, each message supplied by a user for transmission will – if it arrives at all – be delivered to the intended receiver(s) as a unit. Sometimes such services are called *message oriented services* or *block oriented services*, as they deliver blocks of data in their entirety.

A common alternative is for the service to be *stream oriented*. This means that the boundaries between units of data supplied to the service are not necessarily preserved when the data are delivered to the receiver: Data are regarded as making up a (potentially endless) stream, which can be chopped up and delivered in units of any convenient size. This is illustrated in Figure 3.7.

3.2.3 Flow Control

A service which offers flow control ensures that messages are not delivered faster than the receiver can deal with them. This is equivalent to a requirement for synchronisation through a finite buffer, with the same specification as above.

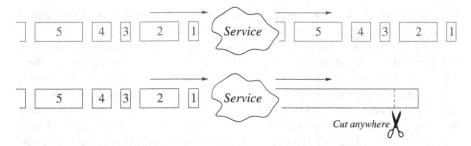

Fig. 3.7 A block-oriented service (above) and a stream-oriented service (below).

3.2.4 Freedom from Error

An error-free service delivers the same messages as those which are sent off, without corruption of any kind. The specification is the same as for sequence preservation.

When discussing errors, a simple classification scheme is useful. We base this on a the idea that we have two users, a sender U_s and a receiver U_r. The sender takes part in a communication event e_s, and the receiver takes part in a communication event e_r. Either of these events can (in a faulty system) be null, which we shall denote **nil**. The semantics of such a null event are empty, in the sense that it represents the idea that the process in question does *not* in fact take part in any event. The receiver's event results in his local message buffer, b_r, changing its contents from m_r to m'_r. There are four basic possibilities:

1. In a *fault-free* communication, $e_s = c_s!m_s$, $e_r = c_r?b_r$ and $m'_r = m_s$.
2. If a *message loss fault* occurs, $e_s = c_s!m_s$, $e_r = $ **nil**, and $m'_r = m_r$.
3. If a *spurious message fault* occurs, $e_s = $ **nil**, $e_r = c_r?b_r$ and $m'_r = ???$.
4. If a *message corruption fault* occurs, $e_s = c_s!m_s$, $e_r = c_r?b_r$ and $m'_r \neq m_s$.

All other faults, such as duplication of messages or misdelivery, can be expressed as combinations of these. Note that we use different channel names for the sender and receiver communication events, reflecting the idea that these are the channels through which the sender and receiver are connected to the possibly faulty *service*, rather than to one another.

This classification is the basis of the OSI concept of *residual error*. In OSI parlance, messages passed to the service by the service users for transfer to other service users are known as *Service Data Units* or *SDUs*. Given N_s SDUs sent off over a period of time by a user A for transfer to user B, let us suppose that N_a of these arrive correctly, that N_l are lost, and that N_c arrive corrupted. Let us also suppose that user B receives N_u spurious SDUs which have not been sent off by A (or anyone else?) at all. It is here assumed that none of these errors are detected (and indicated to the service user) by the service. The Residual Error Rate, RER, is then defined as

$$RER = \frac{N_l + N_c + N_u}{N_s + N_u}$$

Note that these quantitative features of the service, although important in practical situations, are not dealt with by our type of formal model.

The OSI concept of residual error is specifically restricted to those errors which the service user does *not* get told about. This is in contrast to *indicated errors*, where the service explicitly draws the user's attention to the fact that an error has occurred. This means that the user does not need to take special action (such as the introduction of redundancy into data) to detect such errors. Indicated errors are often related to service features which permit users to reset the service to some standard state (see next section). In general, the same classification of error types as above can be used, although in practice *message loss* faults are by far the most common types of indicated error.

3.2.5 Service Reset

Although well-behaved services operate indefinitely without ever stopping or being restarted, practical considerations may in fact dictate that the service needs to be set into a standard initial state from time to time. In OSI terms, this service feature is known as a *reset* feature. A well-known example of a service with this type of facility is the X.25 Packet Level (PLP) service.

Reset features are not pleasant to deal with from an analytical point of view, as they generally give rise to loss of arbitrary amounts of data – typically, all those messages which were in transit between service users at the time when the reset feature was invoked. This is also quite difficult to model: the service must be ready at all times to accept a *reset request* message from either user, and on receipt of this message must abandon all messages currently being transmitted. Essentially, reset features turn an otherwise reliable service into an unreliable one! A consequence of this is, as we shall see in the next chapter, that protocols based on services with reset facilities have to be constructed with special care.

3.2.6 Connection Establishment and Release

Many services require the users to establish a *connection* by setting up a logical or physical channel before 'real' exchange of data can take place. The channel is established by the exchange of particular types of message in a so-called *connection establishment phase* of communication, before the 'real' data are exchanged in a subsequent *data transfer phase*. This is illustrated in Figure 3.8.

The initial exchange enables the service users to establish their initial global state before they get down to serious business, so to speak. In particular, the connection establishment phase may be used to agree on some kind of parameters describing the data transfer phase, thus freeing the service users of the need to send all conceivable parameters with each individual data message. This can make the service

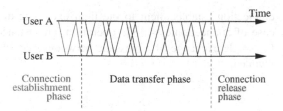

Fig. 3.8 Phases of operation
of a connection

more *efficient*, in the sense that repetitive transmission of this information can be avoided. Examples of what might be agreed on are the service facilities to be available in the data transfer phase, the identities of the service users, the syntax of data, the throughput and so on.

The values agreed for these parameters usually remain valid throughout the data transfer phase, until the connection is broken and the channel released in a final phase of the communication, known as the *connection release phase*. For an ideal service offering connection establishment and release facilities, connection release will always be voluntary (on the part of the users). An unreliable service may also produce involuntary forms of connection release, known in OSI parlance as *Provider Aborts*.

During the *lifetime* of the connection, which runs from the time when it is established to the time when it is released, it makes sense to speak of the ordering of messages sent from the source to the destination, as they pass along a single logical channel. Thus the properties of sequence preservation, error control and so on are only really meaningful in this mode of operation.

In OSI parlance this form of communication is known as *connection-mode* (or *connection-oriented*) *communication*, in contrast to *connectionless-mode* (or just *connectionless*) *communication*, where there is no logical relation expressed or implied between consecutive elementary communications between pairs of users. A number of other terms exist for the same thing, and are often found in the literature. In particular, connectionless-mode services are often known as *datagram* (or just *DG*) services, and connection-mode services as *virtual circuit* (or *VC*) services. Some people use the term 'virtual circuit service' in the special sense of an ideal, error-free, sequence preserving service. However, if we need this Utopian concept we shall call it a *perfect virtual circuit* service.

Obviously, a connectionless-mode service offers no facilities for connection establishment or release, and it is meaningless to consider sequence preservation or loss of data as features of the service. A connectionless-mode service has no memory of previous messages sent – it is *stateless* – so essentially, the service offers a facility for sending *individual* messages. A convenient model of this is that a new CSP channel is used for *every* message exchanged.

A useful concept in this context is that of an *instance of communication*, which is an OSI term defined as a logically related sequence of elementary communications. In the case of connection-mode operation, an instance of communication comprises all elementary communications from the initial exchange of messages to deal with connection establishment to the final exchange during the release phase[1]. In the case of connectionless-mode operation, an instance of communication comprises the single exchange of a message between users which occurs when the service is invoked.

3.2.7 Change of Mode

A service may offer a different mode of operation from the one offered by the service on which it is based. Confining ourselves to OSI modes of operation, the most important changes are those between:

- Connection and Connectionless modes.
- Point-to-point and Multi-peer modes.
- Simplex and Duplex modes.

Connection and Connectionless Modes

Given a connectionless-mode service, it is possible to build up a connection-mode service by introducing suitable facilities for correlating messages sent off independently of one another via what we can model as different logical channels. Details will be given in the next chapter. Similarly, if a connection exists, it is possible to consider the messages sent via it independently of one another, thus building a connectionless-mode service on a connection-mode one.

Point-to-point and Multi-peer Modes

In the point-to-point mode of operation, two service users communicate with one another through a physical or logical channel which connects them. In the multi-peer mode, several users communicate with one another.

Multi-peer mode services are often termed *broadcast* services if *all* available service users can receive a message sent by one of them, and *multicast* services if it is possible for a sender to select a particular sub-set of users to receive a particular message or messages. Occasionally the term *inverse broadcast* is used when a single receiver can receive simultaneously from all the other service users; nobody seems yet to have found a need for the term *inverse multicast*!

A great deal of confusion sometimes arises when multi-peer services are discussed because it is in practice clear that the sets of users involved in an instance of multi-peer communication may vary with time. It is therefore useful to distinguish between the following concepts:

---

[1] This assumes, of course, that connection establishment is successful. In the case of failure, the instance of communication ends when the attempt to establish the connection is aborted.

The invoked group   is that sub-set, $\mathscr{I}$, of users which a user initiating an instance of multi-peer communication wishes to communicate with. If $\mathscr{U}$ is the set of all users, and i is the initiating user, then a broadcast service is characterised by $\mathscr{I} = \mathscr{U} - \{i\}$ (or possibly $\mathscr{I} = \mathscr{U}$, if the service is reflexive), while a multicast service is characterised by $\mathscr{I} \subseteq \mathscr{U}$.

The active group   is that sub-set, $\mathscr{A}$, of users which a user actually communicates with. In general, $\mathscr{A} \subseteq \mathscr{I}$.

A static group   is a sub-set of users which does not alter with time during a single instance of multi-peer communication.

A dynamic group   is a sub-set of users which (can) alter with time during a single instance of multi-peer communication.

Group integrity   is a measure of the extent to which a group's composition satisfies some previously agreed criterion. Practical possibilities for such a criterion might, for example, be that particular members must be present, that a certain number of members must be present, and so on.

These terms are illustrated in Figure 3.9. Many of the terms can be used in com-

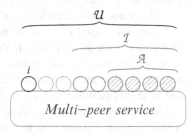

Fig. 3.9 Groups in a multi-peer service. The figure illustrates a single instance of communication, for which user i is the initiator.

bination. Thus it is meaningful to speak of a connection-mode multi-peer service supporting static invoked groups and dynamic active groups. This would mean that users, once the connection had been established, could leave and re-enter the active group. It must be assumed that the rules for group integrity have been agreed during connection establishment, and that the connection will be released if the minimum criterion cannot be met.

Not all combinations are meaningful, however. It makes no sense to talk about a connectionless-mode multi-peer service with dynamic active group, for example, as each instance of connectionless-mode communication only involves the transfer of a single message.

When a service offers a point-to-point service, a multi-peer service can be built up on top of it by using N separate transfers of messages to simulate a single transfer to N destinations. Similarly, a point-to-point service can be implemented using a multi-peer service by the introduction of suitable information to filter off the messages arriving at the (N-1) destinations which are not the intended ones. More details of mechanisms for this purpose can be found in Chapter 5.

Simplex and Duplex

By *simplex* operation, we understand a mode of operation in which transfer of messages only occurs in one direction through a logical or physical channel. In *duplex* operation, messages can pass in both directions. If they can pass in both directions at once, we speak of *full duplex* operation; if in one direction at a time, *half duplex* operation.

Plainly, two simplex-mode channels can be used to obtain the effect of duplex operation, while use of a duplex service can be restricted to a single direction to obtain a simplex mode of operation. More details of administrative mechanisms for ensuring the correct implementation of the change of mode will be discussed in the next chapter.

3.2.8 Information about Peer Change of State

A universal problem in distributed systems is that the processes in the system in general do not have knowledge of the *global state* of the system at any instant. To obtain some kind of view of the global state, they must deliberately exchange information with one another. If their local state changes in a significant manner (seen in relation to the task in hand), they may thus have a duty to inform others of this change. The service may provide facilities for passing information of this kind, independently of the stream of 'real' data.

Although they are usually treated separately, facilities for connection establishment and release come into this category, and so do flow control facilities. Less obvious examples include:

- The setting of marks in the stream of data to indicate particular points from which the stream may be retransmitted if this turns out to be necessary (for example, due to some error or due to lack of resources at the destination). In OSI parlance, such marks are known as *synchronisation points*.
- Indication that the following data in the stream of data represent the values of objects from some new *universe of discourse*, possibly with selection of a syntax suited to their representation. In OSI parlance, this is known as *context selection*.
- Indication of the start of a *commitment unit*, by which we understand a unit of data which must be transferred as a whole or not at all.

It is often convenient when the service offers this kind of feature if the exchange of information between the two parties is explicitly *confirmed*. That is to say, the party receiving the information explicitly sends some kind of acknowledgment back to the sender of the information. This means that the sender does not just have to rely on the reliability of the underlying service in order to be certain that those parties who need to know in fact *do* know about the change of state. Use of *confirmed services* for informing other parties about major changes of state is standard practice in OSI operation.

3.2.9 Expedited Data

Expedited data is an OSI term for data to be transferred with high priority. By definition, expedited data will arrive not later than 'ordinary' data sent subsequently to the same destination, and may arrive before ordinary data sent to the same destination at an earlier instant of time. Note that this is *not* a guarantee that they will arrive before ordinary data sent at the same time! The concept is illustrated in Figure 3.10.

Fig. 3.10 Expedited data arrives at least as fast as ordinary data sent at the same time to the same destination

To model this, we can model the service as containing a queue for the messages in transit, with the property that queue elements sent via the expedited data service can overtake those sent via the normal service. Obviously, this is in conflict with the concept of sequence preservation for messages sent between two service users, seen from a universal point of view. But the individual services (normal and expedited) may each possess the sequence preservation property when considered separately.

Although the OSI term is confined to a single high-priority service, the concept can be generalised to cover arbitrary numbers of priority levels. This type of service is commonly offered at the hardware level in Local Area Networks. Examples are the ISO/IEEE Token Bus [153], which offers four levels of priority, and the ISO/IEEE Token Ring [154], which offers eight levels.

3.2.10 Security

A *secure* service is one which prevents unauthorised persons from obtaining access to data transferred by it. This means that data cannot be read or altered by parties other than the intended sender and receiver(s). This is again not a concept which is susceptible to modelling in terms of message exchanges via CSP channels, as these are always secure in this sense. But it is a matter of extreme practical importance, and a great deal of effort has been expended on developing methods to protect data in transit from 'intruders'.

Various types of security can be identified. A common classification is the one given in Part 2 of the OSI Reference Model [134]:

Authentication: An authenticated service offers its users facilities for confirming that the party which they are communicating with actually *is* the party that they *believe* they are communicating with.

Data Confidentiality: A confidential service provides protection of data from unauthorised disclosure. This protection may, for example, cover:

1.   All data sent between users of the service,
2.   Particular fields within data (for example, fields containing passwords or keys),
3.   Information about the amount of data traffic being transmitted.

Data Integrity: A service offering integrity takes measures to withstand active attempts to modify data being passed via the service. As with confidentiality, all data may be protected, or only selected fields.

Non-repudiation: A service with non-repudiation offers undeniable proof that data have been sent or received by a particular service user. *Non-repudiation with proof of origin* prevents the sender from falsely denying that it has sent data; *non-repudiation with proof of delivery* prevents the receiver from falsely denying that it has received data.

Security specialists outside the world of communication systems usually add the property of *Availability* to this list. Availability refers to the ability of a service to be available to its authorised users to the promised extent. This is obviously a quantitative property of the service and therefore lies somewhat outside the scope of this book. Lack of availability shows itself via so-called *Denial of Service (DoS)* phenomena, where users are (to a greater or lesser degree) unable to use the service. This may be due to poor design or the efforts of evil-minded intruders or a combination of the two.

Mechanisms for ensuring that a service offers the desired type of security will be considered in Chapter 6.

3.3 OSI and Other Layered Architectures

The idea of using layered architectures, where each layer offers services for use by active objects in the layer above, is a common one in communication systems – and indeed in operating systems and other large system programs. The layered architecture described in the OSI Basic Reference Model [133] is a particular example of this, specifying which layers are conceptually to be found in a standard communication system, which services they conceptually offer, and which functions they are expected to be able to perform in order to offer these services. The model prescribes seven layers, arranged as shown in Figure 3.11.

It is important to understand that the model as such only concerns itself with the architecture of communication systems on the conceptual level: it describes an *abstract architecture*. In fact, the important features of the OSI Reference Model are the layering principle and the well-defined notation which it introduces. That,

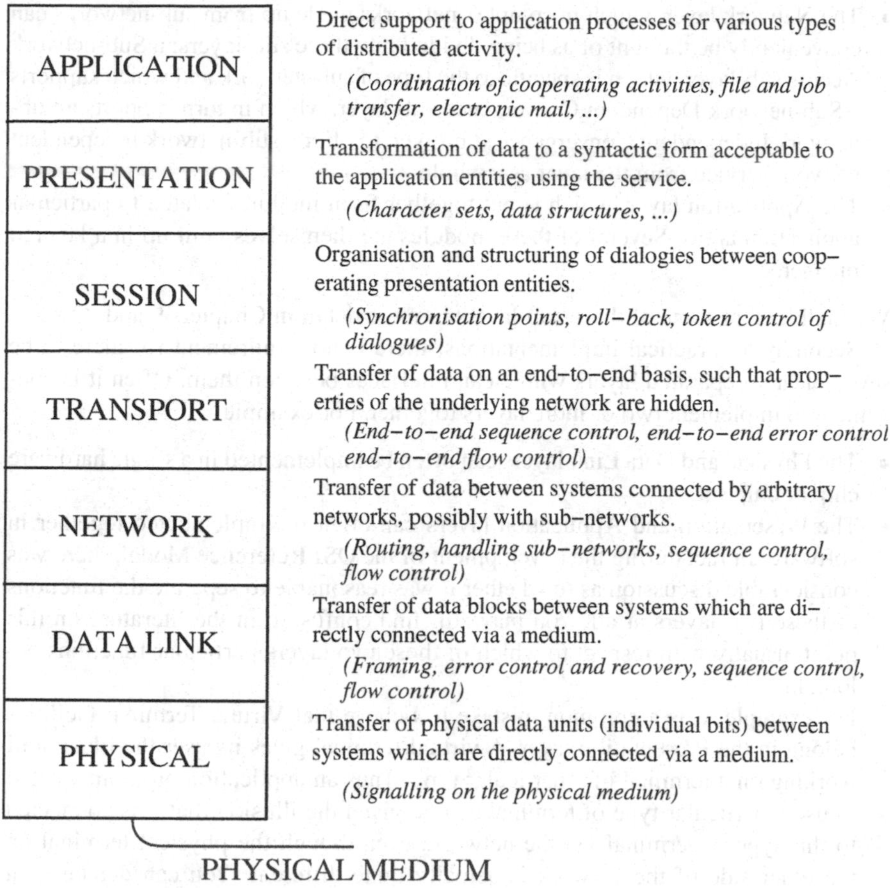

APPLICATION	Direct support to application processes for various types of distributed activity.
	(Coordination of cooperating activities, file and job transfer, electronic mail, ...)
PRESENTATION	Transformation of data to a syntactic form acceptable to the application entities using the service.
	(Character sets, data structures, ...)
SESSION	Organisation and structuring of dialogies between cooperating presentation entities.
	(Synchronisation points, roll–back, token control of dialogues)
TRANSPORT	Transfer of data on an end–to–end basis, such that properties of the underlying network are hidden.
	(End–to–end sequence control, end–to–end error control end–to–end flow control)
NETWORK	Transfer of data between systems connected by arbitrary networks, possibly with sub–networks.
	(Routing, handling sub–networks, sequence control, flow control)
DATA LINK	Transfer of data blocks between systems which are directly connected via a medium.
	(Framing, error control and recovery, sequence control, flow control)
PHYSICAL	Transfer of physical data units (individual bits) between systems which are directly connected via a medium.
	(Signalling on the physical medium)

PHYSICAL MEDIUM

Fig. 3.11 The OSI Reference Model's seven layers.

for example, there are seven layers is less important. Indeed, the explanations given for there being exactly seven layers are in general not serious technical reasons – two of the commonest ones are that seven has from ancient times been regarded as a mystical number, and that seven concepts are the most that the human brain can deal with at one time.

In practice, there are several deviations from the 7-layered scheme. Firstly, it is often convenient conceptually to divide some of the layers up into sub-layers. This is especially common in:

- The Data Link layer, which in Local Area Networks (LANs) is traditionally divided into two sub-layers: a Medium Access Control (MAC) sub-layer which is specific to the type of LAN technology concerned, and which supports a Logical Link Control (LLC) sub-layer to give a LAN-independent data link service from the layer as a whole.

- The Network layer, which in complex networks made up from sub-networks can conveniently be thought of as being divided into three sub-layers: a Sub-network Access sub-layer, which is specific to the type of sub-network and which supports a Sub-network Dependent Convergence sub-layer, which in turn supports a Sub-network Independent Convergence sub-layer, to offer a sub-network independent network service from the layer as a whole.
- The Application layer, which is put together from modules related to particular application areas. Several of these modules are themselves built up in a layered manner.

We shall look at some of these sub-layers in more detail in Chapters 9 and 10.

Secondly, in practical implementations, there is no requirement for there to be seven clearly separated layers with clean interfaces between them. Often it is convenient to implement two or more layers together. For example:

- The Physical and Data Link layers can often be implemented in a single hardware chip or chip set.
- The Presentation and Application layers can often be implemented together in software. In fact during the development of the OSI Reference Model, there was considerable discussion as to whether it was reasonable to separate the functions of these two layers at all. You may still find confusion in the literature on this point, usually with respect to which of these two layers particular functions belong in.

  For example, it is a common mistake to believe that Virtual Terminal facilities belong in the Presentation layer. A virtual terminal gives its user the illusion of working on a terminal of a particular type. Thus an application program written to use a particular type of terminal can be given the illusion that it is connected to this type of terminal via the network, even though the physical terminal on the other side of the network is actually quite different. You can debate with yourself whether this is just a matter of converting the character set and other data structures – in which case virtual terminals could be dealt with in the Presentation layer – or whether more functionality than this is required, so that they belong in the Application layer. The OSI answer is the Application layer.

Although the OSI Reference Model is a very general framework for describing communication systems, which could in principle be realised by any protocols which had the specified functionality, a particular set of standardised services and protocols have been designed for this purpose. These are known as OSI protocols, and originate from several standardisation organisations, particularly ISO, ITU-T (previously CCITT), IEC and IEEE (see Appendix B).

3.3.1 The Internet and Other Layered Architectures

The OSI Reference Model architecture is by no means the only layered architecture which you may meet in communication systems. A particularly common alternative arrangement is to consider the three upper layers as one unit, an 'Application-oriented layer' which depends directly on the Transport layer. A very well-known example of this approach is seen in the *Internet protocol suite*, originally introduced in the 1970's for use in the DARPA Internet[2] in USA, but now in almost universal use. Here, a whole series of application protocols – for example for file transfer (FTP), electronic mail (SMTP), and handling virtual terminals (TELNET) – run directly over the Transport layer, which in such systems is based on Internet standard protocols such as TCP or UDP. This architecture is illustrated in Figure 3.12.

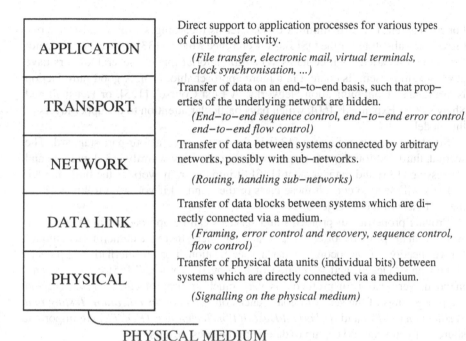

Fig. 3.12 The Internet layered architecture.

Several commercial manufacturers have also at various times developed products which are structured in a similar way, although the protocols used are not OSI protocols, and the layers do not always correspond exactly to the OSI ones, especially in the Session, Presentation and Application layers. Historically, IBM's SNA and Digital Equipment Corporation's DECNET were examples of this approach.

Finally, in modern telecommunication systems, a somewhat different layered architecture can be found in systems based on ATM (Asynchronous Transfer Mode), a technology for supporting high-speed transfer of data over a local area or wide area network. This architecture is described by the *Broadband ISDN Protocol Reference*

---

[2] DARPA = Defense Advanced Research Projects Agency, run by the U.S. Department of Defense. Several of the protocols have been standardised for military use, and they are therefore often known as *DoD protocols*. The DARPA Internet is also known as ARPANET.

Model (B-ISDN PRM) [255]. In this model, although the layers roughly correspond
to the OSI RM, there are several important technical differences, especially with respect to the way in which control and signalling information is transferred: In OSI,
it forms part of the ordinary data flow; in B-ISDN, it is transferred over a separate
connection.

Further reading

For a complete list of definitions of OSI terms regarding services and protocols,
there is no substitute for the OSI Basic Reference Model [133]. However, this is not
for the faint-hearted, as it contains very little tutorial matter. Several authors have
attempted to present its content in a more approachable form. A good introduction
is Walrand's "Communication Networks: A First Course" [125], or Henshall and
Shaw's "OSI Explained" [60], which pays particular attention to the upper layers of
the model.

Strictly speaking, reference [133] is the first part of a four-part standard. The
second, third and fourth parts respectively describe how security [134], naming and
addressing [135] and management [136] fit into the framework of the basic model,
and you will need to consult these parts of the standard if you want to know about
the OSI view of these subjects.

Proving properties of protocols and services can be approached in many ways.
Apart from the property-oriented approach used here, there are numerous techniques
for verification of protocols against a specification. For an alternative approach,
Holzmann's "Design and Validation of Computer Protocols" [65] can be recommended. Verification of protocols is very much an area of current research, and
the proceedings of the series of conferences on *Protocol Specification, Testing and
Verification (PSTV)* and on *Formal Description Techniques (FORTE)* are important
sources if you want to keep up to date with the latest results.

Exercises

3.1. Give descriptions in the form of CSP processes of services which respectively:

1. Introduce message loss faults into the stream of data which they are given to
   transmit.
2. Introduce spurious message faults into the stream of data which they are given to
   transmit.
3. Do not lose messages, but do not preserve the sequence of messages which they
   are given to transmit.

3.2. Use Failure Semantics to analyse the deadlock properties of the composed
process $\mathscr{S}'$ defined in Section 3.1.

3.3. The protocol entities in layer N of a layered system are described by the following pair of cooperating CSP processes, which describe a simple protocol which multiplexes data from two channels onto a single underlying service:

$$S \stackrel{\text{def}}{=} (SAPA[0]?x : \mathcal{M} \to right!(0,x) \to S$$
$$[\,]SAPA[1]?x : \mathcal{M} \to right!(1,x) \to S)$$

$$R \stackrel{\text{def}}{=} (left?(k : \{0,1\}, x : \mathcal{M}) \to SAPB[k]!x \to R)$$

where S is on the transmitting side and R on the receiving side. $\mathcal{M}$ is here an arbitrary domain of messages.

Using channel history semantics, prove that:

$$S \gg R \text{ sat } (SAPB[0] \leqslant SAPA[0]) \wedge (SAPB[1] \leqslant SAPA[1])$$

Hint: Introduce a filter function f, such that:

$$f(0, \langle\rangle) \quad = f(1, \langle\rangle) \quad = \langle\rangle$$
$$f(k, (k,x)\hat{\ }s) = x\hat{\ }f(k,s), \quad k = 0, 1$$
$$f(k, (l,x)\hat{\ }s) = f(k,s), \quad k = 0, 1; \, k \neq l$$

Then prove the following two lemmata:

$$S \text{ sat } (f(k, right) \leqslant SAPA[k]), \, k = 0, 1$$
$$R \text{ sat } (SAPB[k] \leqslant f(k, left)), \, k = 0, 1$$

and combine them to obtain the desired result.

3.4. Given two processes L and R, neither of which necessarily satisfies the buffer specification $right \leqslant left$, it is possible that their combination $L \gg R$ fulfils this specification. Show that this is in fact the case if it is true that:

$$(L \gg R) = (left?x : \mathcal{M} \to (L \gg (right!x \to R)))$$

where $\mathcal{M}$ is an arbitrary domain of messages.

3.5. Given two processes:

$$L \stackrel{\text{def}}{=} left?x : \{0,1\} \to right!x \to right!(1-x) \to L$$
$$R \stackrel{\text{def}}{=} left?x : \{0,1\} \to left?z : \{0,1\} \to (\textbf{if } x = z \textbf{ then } R \textbf{ else } (right!x \to R))$$

Use the process algebra of CSP to demonstrate that:

$$(L \gg R) = (left?x : \{0,1\} \to (L \gg (right!x \to R)))$$

and thus, as shown in Exercise 3.4, that $(L \gg R)$ fulfils the buffer specification $right \leqslant left$.

Chapter 4
Basic Protocol Mechanisms

"Thro' twenty posts of telegraph
They flashed a saucy message to and fro
Between the mimic stations."
"The Princess"
Alfred Lord Tennyson.

In the previous chapter we presented a number of general aspects of services, which it may be appropriate to provide in different contexts. Our view of a service as a 'black box', however, gave us no insight into how such so-called *facilities* might be provided. Mechanisms for this purpose within a layer are in OSI parlance known as *functions* of that layer.

In this chapter we shall look at those functions which are directly associated with protocols in the traditional sense, i.e. sets of rules governing the exchange of data between peer entities. A number of aspects of distributed systems are, however, not easily incorporated into a discussion of such protocols. In particular, quite basic questions, such as how the entities are identified and how the route to be followed from one entity to another is determined, are ignored. We shall return to these questions, and the functions associated with them, in Chapter 7.

The functions which we shall consider in this chapter are:

- Sequence control and error control.
- Flow control.
- Indication of change of peer state.
- Change of service mode.
- Multiplexing and splitting.
- Segmentation and reassembly.
- Prioritisation.

We shall consider them in as general manner as possible, and try to relate them to the OSI concepts of layer function to be found in the OSI Reference Model [133] and related documents. In the following chapters we shall return to the special problems associated with the provision of a multi-peer service and with the provision of a secure service.

71

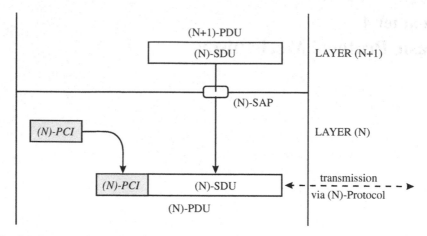

Fig. 4.1 Service and Protocol Data Units

OSI notation will be used as far as possible. Thus we shall relate our discussion to the *(N)-Service*, i.e. the service provided by the N'th layer in a layered architecture, and shall refer to the users of the service as *(N)-Service-Users* (or just *(N)-Users*), which of course lie in the (N+1)'st layer. The channels via which the (N)-Users interact with the (N)-Service will be referred to as *(N)-service-access-points* or *(N)-SAPs*, and the portions of data which these users send via the service as *(N)-service-data-units* or *(N)-SDUs*.

When the protocol entities within the (N)-layer communicate with one another with a view to providing the service, they will be said to exchange *(N)-Protocol-Data-Units*, (or just *(N)-PDUs*). In general, these PDUs may contain portions of data from zero, one or more (N)-SDUs, together with control information required for the execution of the protocol, *(N)-Protocol-Control-Information* (or just *(N)-PCI*). This is often illustrated by the diagram shown in Figure 4.1. This PCI (and indeed the entire working of the (N)-Protocol) is invisible to the users of the (N)-Service – although some components of it, such as addresses, may have to be provided by the user together with the SDU.

The figure shows a simple case where a single (N)-SDU is embedded into a single (N)-PDU for transmission. In more complex cases, several (N)-SDUs may be embedded into a single (N)-PDU (a technique known as *packing*), or a single (N)-SDU may be divided into several (N)-PDUs for transmission. This latter technique is known as *segmentation*. What happens at the receiver depends on the degree of data unit synchronisation required from the service. Standard OSI data transmission services are *block oriented*, which means that each (N)-SDU supplied by the sending (N)-user is delivered as a unit to the receiving (N)-user. In a service which is *stream oriented*, as is the case for many Internet services, the data can be delivered to the receiver in units of any convenient size, not necessarily related in any way to the sizes of the units supplied by the sender.

When discussing the interactions of the protocol entities, it will sometimes be convenient to distinguish between PDUs on the basis of their types. In particular, the principal function of some PDUs is to carry SDUs supplied by the service users; we shall denote these *data-PDUs*. Other PDUs carry only acknowledgments of receipt; we shall denote these *ack-PDUs* or just *acknowledgments*.

4.1 Sequence Control and Error Control

The purpose of these functions is to provide the service features of sequence preservation and freedom from error. Although mechanisms for sequence control do not necessarily ensure complete error control or *vice versa*, they are closely interrelated, and can conveniently be considered together.

The basic mechanism for sequence control is a numbering scheme for the messages passed along the logical channel between the users of the service. The numbers are, of course invisible to the user, and are part of the PCI. Consecutive natural numbers starting from some mutually agreed starting value are an obvious choice. The receiving (N)-entity must check that each (N)-PDU received bears the next number in the agreed sequence, and must take some suitable action if this is not the case.

A numbering scheme also enables the receiving entity to check for *lost* or *duplicated* PDUs, as well as those which arrive out of sequence. In fact, the entity cannot tell the difference between lost and out-of-sequence PDUs, since it cannot foresee whether the missing PDU will turn up later or not. (If it could, we wouldn't need the protocol!)

4.1.1 Corruption Control

Numbering schemes can not, however, protect against *corrupted* PDUs, and control of this type of error requires the use of another technique entirely. The traditional mechanism is to use a *checksum* or similar error-detecting code. The general principle is to add, say, $n - k$ bits of extra data (the 'checksum bits') to each block of, say, k bits of data (the 'message'), such that correct blocks of n bits satisfy a certain predicate, often called the *checksum relation*, whereas corrupt blocks in general do not satisfy this predicate.

How good the code is at distinguishing correct blocks from corrupt ones depends on the complexity of the predicate, and thus on the rule used to determine the $n - k$ checksum bits. However, even the most advanced codes in current use will fail if there are a sufficiently large number of errors in each block, as a block with sufficiently many bit errors can come to look like (another) correct block. The minimum number of bit errors required to transform a correct block into another apparently correct block is a property of the code known as its *minimum Hamming distance*.

Well-known error-detecting codes used in data transmission systems are the *polynomial block codes* (in this context also known as Cyclic Redundancy Check or *CRC* codes). Technically speaking, these are (n,k) *cyclic block codes*, i.e. codes with k data bits out of every block of n bits, and with the property that any cyclic permutation of the bits of a correct block gives another correct block. The cyclic property makes it easy to generate the checksum bits and to check the correctness of a received block by using simple shift register circuits with feedback connections.

The properties of such codes are most easily understood if we consider the binary encoding of the message as representing the coefficients of a polynomial, say $d(x)$, of degree $k-1$, with the least significant bit representing the coefficient of x^0, the next bit the coefficient of x^1 and so on. Technically, $d(x)$ is a polynomial over the finite field $\mathscr{GF}(2)$, i.e. it has coefficients in the subset of the integers $\mathbb{Z}_2 = \{0,1\}$, and all arithmetic on coefficients is to be done *modulo 2*. The checksum similarly represents a polynomial, say $c(x)$, of degree $n-k-1$ over $\mathscr{GF}(2)$, chosen so that the polynomial for the message with checksum appended:

$$u(x) = x^{n-k} \cdot d(x) + c(x)$$

is divisible by an agreed *generator polynomial*, say $g(x)$, of degree $n-k$. $c(x)$ is easily evaluated, since it is the remainder when $x^{n-k} \cdot d(x)$ is divided by $g(x)$. For example:

$$d(x) = x^9 + x^8 + x^6 + x^5 + x^4 + 1 \sim 01101110001$$
$$g(x) = x^4 + x^1 + 1 \qquad\qquad\qquad \sim 10011$$
$$c(x) = x^3 + 1 \qquad\qquad\qquad\quad \sim 1001$$
$$u(x) = x^4 \cdot d(x) + c(x) \qquad\qquad \sim 011011100011001$$

Remembering that in *modulo 2* arithmetic, addition, $\oplus$, and subtraction, $\ominus$, are the same, and that $0 \oplus 0 = 1 \oplus 1 = 0$ and $0 \oplus 1 = 1 \oplus 0 = 1$, you are encouraged to check that $c(x)$ has been correctly evaluated.

Suppose now that a block corresponding to a polynomial $r(x)$ is received. It is a property of cyclic codes that every multiple of $g(x)$ corresponds to a correct block, so it is only necessary to check whether $r(x)$ is such a multiple. In general:

$$r(x) = g(x) \cdot q(x) + s(x)$$

where $s(x)$, the remainder when the block is divided by $g(x)$, is a polynomial of degree $n-k$ or less. For every correct block, $s(x)$, often known as the *syndrome* for the block, is zero. A non-zero syndrome implies an error. Unfortunately, as indicated above, the opposite is not true – a block containing an error may in fact have a zero syndrome; the error will then remain undetected. If we suppose that the received block can be viewed as the polynomial sum of a correct block, $u(x)$, and an error polynomial, $e(x)$, then an undetected error evidently occurs if $e(x)$ is divisible by $g(x)$.

Any polynomial of degree $n-k$ which is a factor of $x^n + 1$ is a generating polynomial for an (n,k) cyclic code. For example, $x^4 + x^1 + 1$, as used above, is a factor of $x^{15}+1$, and generates a $(15,11)$ cyclic code. Since there may be many factors of x^n+1 for large n, the question arises how one should choose between them in order to leave as few errors as possible undetected. Analysis of this question relies on results in the algebra of finite fields. We can summarise them as follows:

1. If a single bit, say bit i, is in error, then $e(x)=x^i$. However, there are no factors of x^n+1 of the form $x^i \cdot p(x)$, for any n, so $e(x)$ cannot be divisible by $g(x)$. Thus no single-bit errors will go undetected.
2. If two bits, say i,j where $i>j$, are in error, then $e(x)=x^j \cdot (x^{i-j}+1)$. Since x^j is not divisible by $g(x)$, $e(x)$ will only be divisible if x^m+1, where $m=i-j$ (and thus $m<n$) is. For polynomials over the finite field $\mathcal{GF}(2)$, there is a smallest value $m \leq 2^{n-k}-1$, for which x^m+1 is a multiple of a polynomial of order $n-k$, such as $g(x)$. However, if $g(x)$ is a so-called *primitive polynomial* over the field[1], then the smallest value of m is just exactly $2^{n-k}-1$. So if $g(x)$ is primitive, and n is restricted to be less than or equal to $2^{n-k}-1$, then no double bit errors will go undetected.
3. If there is a burst of errors – i.e. a consecutive sequence of say b bits are in error – then $e(x)=x^j \cdot (x^{b-1}+\ldots+1)$, where j gives the position of the burst of errors within the block. Since x^j is not divisible by $g(x)$, $e(x)$ is only divisible if $(x^{b-1}+\ldots+1)$ is. Since $g(x)$ is of degree $n-k$, this is not possible if $b-1 < n-k$. So no bursts shorter than the length of the checksum will go undetected.
4. If there are an odd number of errors, then $e(x)$ has an odd number of non-zero coefficients. However, for polynomials over $\mathcal{GF}(2)$, there are no multiples of $x+1$ which have an odd number of non-zero coefficients. Thus, if $g(x)$ contains $x+1$ as a factor, no cases where a block contains an odd number of errors will go undetected.

A common practice is therefore to let $g(x)$ be the product of a primitive polynomial of degree $(h-1)$ with $x+1$. This gives a code with minimum Hamming distance at least 4, and the ability to detect error bursts of length up to h, in blocks of length up to 2^h-1. Standard choices for $g(x)$ are:

$$
\begin{aligned}
CRC\text{-}12 &= x^{12}+x^{11}+x^3+x^2+x^1+1 \\
CRC\text{-}16 &= x^{16}+x^{15}+x^2+1 \\
CRC\text{-}CCITT &= x^{16}+x^{12}+x^5+1 \\
CRC\text{-}32 &= x^{32}+x^{26}+x^{23}+x^{22}+x^{16}+x^{12}+x^{11}+x^{10} \\
&\quad +x^8+x^7+x^5+x^4+x^2+x^1+1
\end{aligned}
$$

CRC-32 is a primitive polynomial of degree 32, while the other three are products of primitive polynomials with $x+1$. A more detailed analysis of error-detecting codes of this type can be found in [87].

---

[1] A polynomial $g(x)$ of degree n over a field is primitive if it is *irreducible* (has no factors other than unity which are polynomials over the field), and is a *generator* for the polynomials over the field. This means that the powers of x evaluated modulo $g(x)$ give all the non-zero polynomials of order less than n over the field. You can check for yourself that, for example, x^4+x^1+1 is a primitive polynomial of degree 4.

Evaluation and checking of the checksums required for polynomial block codes is most commonly performed by use of suitable hardware. If you want a little programming challenge, then try to write a program to do it!

4.1.2 Simple ACK/NACK protocols

In the previous chapter we analysed a protocol for use over a service which corrupted data, and where we assumed that a checksum mechanism could be used to detect the corruptions. In this case it was sufficient to allow the receiver to respond to correct data-PDUs by sending a *positive acknowledgment* (ACK), and to respond to corrupt data-PDUs by sending a *negative acknowledgment* (NACK). For ease of reference, we repeat the protocol here as **Protocol 1**.

Protocol 1

$Sender \overset{\text{def}}{=} (SAPA?x : \mathcal{M} \to Q[x])$

$Q[x : \mathcal{M}] \overset{\text{def}}{=} (right!x \to \quad (right?y : \{\text{ACK}\} \to Sender$
$\qquad\qquad\qquad\qquad\qquad [\!]right?y : \{\text{NACK}\} \to Q[x]))$

$Receiver \overset{\text{def}}{=} (left?x : \mathcal{M} \to \quad left!\text{ACK} \to SAPB!x \to Receiver$
$\qquad\qquad\quad [\!]left?y : \mathcal{M}' \to left!\text{NACK} \to Receiver)$

Fig. 4.2 Simple ACK/NACK protocol. Here, $(\mathcal{M}' \cap \mathcal{M}) = \{\,\}$, where $\mathcal{M}$ is the domain of correct data-PDUs.

The system configuration for this protocol is shown in Figure 4.3. This corresponds to the definition that the service offered by the combination of the two protocol entities and the underlying service, $\mathcal{S}$, is given by:

$$\mathcal{S}' \overset{\text{def}}{=} Sender \gg \mathcal{S} \gg Receiver$$

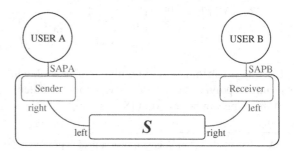

Fig. 4.3 System configuration
for **Protocol 1**

where we remember that the piping construction $P \gg Q$ expresses the idea that the right hand channel of P is joined to the left hand channel of Q, as shown in the figure.

If the service $\mathscr{S}$ can *lose* or *duplicate* PDUs, this protocol is inadequate. We can analyse its behaviour in these cases as follows:

1. A PDU passed from the *right* channel of *Sender* to $\mathscr{S}$ gets lost before it reaches the *left* channel of *Receiver*. In this case the protocol deadlocks, as the receiver never receives a data-PDU, and so never generates either an ACK or NACK. If the sender receives no acknowledgment, it sends no further data-PDUs.
2. An acknowledgment (either positive or negative) gets lost on its way back from *Receiver* to *Sender*. The protocol deadlocks, as in (1).
3. The service $\mathscr{S}$ generates spurious or duplicated PDUs at the left channel of *Receiver*. These will be mistaken for PDUs received from *Sender*, and an ACK or NACK will be sent back via the service $\mathscr{S}$. Next time *Sender* is ready to accept an acknowledgment from its right channel, it will receive this spurious acknowledgment, with ill-defined results. Depending on whether a false ACK or NACK was delivered, and on what happens to the next genuine data-PDU sent by *Sender*, the receiver may thus lose correct SDUs from the stream of data to be passed to the user, insert spurious SDUs in the stream or any combination of the two.

This may make the protocol sound quite useless, but this is not really the case. The protocol is simple and easily implemented, and there do exist systems where the underlying service (or the medium) for all practical purposes does not lose or duplicate messages. In such systems, the protocol would be an ideal choice.

4.1.3 Simple Polling Protocols

In the simple ACK/NACK protocol, it is the sender who takes the initiative for sending a data-PDU, and the receiver merely responds to this. Effectively, this obliges the receiver to be able to receive data at any time after it has sent an acknowledgment. An alternative strategy is for the *receiver* to have the initiative, and for it explicitly to *request* data when it is able to receive them. This is known as *polling*. A simple protocol of this type is shown in Figure 4.4 as **Protocol 2**. As in **Protocol 1**, $\mathcal{M}$ is the domain of correct data-PDUs, and $\mathcal{M}'$ the domain of corrupted messages, where $(\mathcal{M}' \cap \mathcal{M}) = \{\,\}$. The message a, which is the initial value for S's parameter, is arbitrary. The protocol works in the way that the receiver first sends a POLL-PDU to the sender. If it receives a correct data-PDU, it polls for the next data-PDU; if it receives a corrupted data-PDU, it sends a REPT-PDU to request retransmission of the most recent data-PDU. This version of a simple polling protocol has been chosen to correspond as closely as possible to **Protocol 1**, with POLL corresponding to ACK, and REPT to NACK.

Apart from the question of where the initiative for sending a data-PDU lies, **Protocol 2** has very similar properties to **Protocol 1**. If any type of PDU gets lost, the protocol deadlocks. If the underlying service generates spurious or duplicated PDUs, they may easily be accepted as genuine. You are invited to investigate the protocol more closely in exercise 4.3.

4.1.4 ACK/NACK Protocols with Timeout

If the underlying service loses messages, the simplest cure is to introduce a rule for retransmission by the sender after a suitable period of time without an acknowledgment. Our analysis of the effects of loss on the simple ACK/NACK protocol above showed that the sender waits permanently if either the data-PDU or its acknowledgment get lost by the service $\mathscr{S}$. Thus reactivation of the sender should be a cure for either fault. The protocol is given in **Protocol 3**, where we note that the sending entity now incorporates an internal timer, so that the system configuration is as shown in Figure 4.5.

Unfortunately, this protocol is not much better than **Protocol 1**. Consider the situation where the receiver receives a data-PDU with a correct checksum via its channel *left*, and then sends a positive acknowledgment. Suppose the acknowledgment gets lost. The sender will eventually time out, and retransmit the *same* message in the next PDU, so the receiver receives the message twice and passes it on to the user (via *SAPB*) twice. Thus it will not be true that $\mathscr{S}$ **sat** $SAPB \leq SAPA$. The situation where the underlying service produces spurious or duplicate PDUs is likewise

Protocol 2

$Sender \quad \overset{\text{def}}{=} \quad S[a]$

$S[x : \mathscr{M}] \quad \overset{\text{def}}{=} \quad (right?y : \{\text{POLL}\} \rightarrow SAPA?x : \mathscr{M} \rightarrow right!x \rightarrow S[x]$
$\qquad\qquad\quad [\![right?y : \{\text{REPT}\} \rightarrow right!x \rightarrow S[x]\!])$

$Receiver \quad \overset{\text{def}}{=} \quad (left!\text{POLL} \rightarrow R)$

$R \qquad\quad \overset{\text{def}}{=} \quad (left?x : \mathscr{M} \rightarrow SAPB!x \rightarrow Receiver$
$\qquad\qquad\quad [\![left?y : \mathscr{M}' \rightarrow left!\text{REPT} \rightarrow R)$

Fig. 4.4 Simple polling protocol.

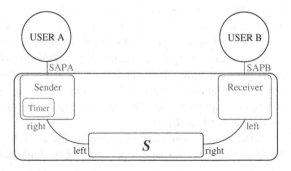

Fig. 4.5 System configuration
for **Protocol 3**

Protocol 3

$Sender \overset{\text{def}}{=} (S \parallel Timer) \setminus \{up\}$

$S \overset{\text{def}}{=} (SAPA?x : \mathcal{M} \to \qquad QT[x])$

$QT[x : \mathcal{M}] \overset{\text{def}}{=} (right!x \to (up!\text{SET} \to (right?y : \{\text{ACK}\} \to up!\text{RESET} \to S$
$[\![right?y : \{\text{NACK}\} \to up!\text{RESET} \to QT[x]$
$[\![up?t : \{\text{TIMEOUT}\} \to QT[x])))$

$Receiver \overset{\text{def}}{=} (left?x : \mathcal{M} \to \qquad left!\text{ACK} \to SAPB!x \to Receiver$
$[\![left?y : \mathcal{M}' \to \qquad left!\text{NACK} \to Receiver)$

$Timer \overset{\text{def}}{=} (up?s : \{\text{SET}\} \to \qquad (up?r : \{\text{RESET}\} \to Timer$
$[\![up!\text{TIMEOUT} \to Timer))$

Fig. 4.6 ACK/NACK protocol with timeout.

Protocol 4

$Sender \overset{\text{def}}{=} (S[1] \parallel Timer) \setminus \{up\}$

$S[n : \mathbb{N}_0] \overset{\text{def}}{=} (SAPA?x : \mathcal{M} \to \qquad QT[n,x])$

$QT[n : \mathbb{N}_0, x : \mathcal{M}]$
$\overset{\text{def}}{=} (right!(n,x) \to (up!\text{SET} \to (right?y : \{\text{ACK}\} \to up!\text{RESET} \to S[succ(n)]$
$[\![up?t : \{\text{TIMEOUT}\} \to QT[n,x])))$

$Receiver \overset{\text{def}}{=} R[0]$

$R[n : \mathbb{N}_0] \overset{\text{def}}{=} (left?(i : \mathbb{N}_0, x : \mathcal{M}) \to \qquad (\textbf{if } (i = succ(n))$
$\textbf{then } left!\text{ACK} \to SAPB!x \to R[succ(n)]$
$\textbf{elseif } (i = n)$
$\textbf{then } left!\text{ACK} \to R[n]$
$\textbf{else } R[n])$
$[\![left?(i : \mathbb{N}_0, y : \mathcal{M}') \to \qquad R[n])$

$Timer \overset{\text{def}}{=} (up?s : \{\text{SET}\} \to \qquad (up?r : \{\text{RESET}\} \to Timer$
$[\![up!\text{TIMEOUT} \to Timer))$

Fig. 4.7 PAR protocol with sequence numbers and timeout.
Here, notations of the form $c!(n,x)$ indicate an offer to output, via channel c, the value of the composed object whose first component is n and second component x, and similarly for input.

not treated properly. In relation to **Protocol 1**, the protocol with timeout is only an improvement with respect to what happens if an 'outgoing' PDU gets lost. Loss or corruption of PDUs carrying acknowledgments, or duplication of PDUs, cause the protocol to misbehave in a different way from **Protocol 1**, but the result is barely more acceptable.

The only reasonable cure for this is, as suggested previously, to introduce a numbering scheme for the PDUs, so that duplicated PDUs can be filtered off by the receiving protocol entity before their SDU content is passed to the receiving user. A protocol of this type is shown as **Protocol 4**. The system configuration is once again as in Figure 4.5. This protocol is also slightly simplified in relation to **Protocol 3**, as the NACK type of acknowledgment has been removed. It should be clear that, when a timeout mechanism is used, negative acknowledgments only have an effect on the response time of the protocol, since they can be used to provoke retransmission before the timeout period runs out. They do not affect the logical properties of the protocol in any way. Such protocols, with only positive acknowledgments, and using a timeout mechanism to control retransmission, are often called *Positive Acknowledge and Retransmission* (*PAR*) protocols.

This is evidently an improvement, as it can deal with lost, corrupted and many types of spurious data-PDUs. The data-PDU received by *Receiver* is only passed on to the user if its sequence number is the successor to the previously accepted PDU's sequence number. If the sequence number is the same as before, the acknowledgment is repeated (thus guarding against lost acknowledgments), whereas in all other cases the PDU is ignored. *Sender* continues to repeat the same data-PDU until it receives a positive acknowledgment for it, using the timeout mechanism to decide when to retransmit the PDU.

Unfortunately, this protocol also has several ways in which it may fail. Firstly, if $\mathscr{S}$ introduces duplicates of correct PDUs (simple example: $\mathscr{S}$ repeats all messages twice!), the receiver will acknowledge them all, assuming that the sender has not received the acknowledgments. Suppose *Sender* sends PDU number 3, and $\mathscr{S}$ duplicates it. *Receiver* will then send two acknowledgments, the first of which will cause *Sender* to send PDU number 4, and the second PDU number 5. Suppose now PDU number 4 gets lost by $\mathscr{S}$. *Receiver* is in a state where it expects to receive PDU number 4 (or at the very least, a repeat of number 3). Instead it receives number 5. The sender believes that the receiver has acknowledged number 4, and continues to send number 5. The protocol is livelocked.

A similar situation arises if the timeout period is too short. Then the acknowledgment may in fact already have been sent, and be on its way via the service $\mathscr{S}$, when the timeout causes the sender to retransmit the latest data-PDU. The retransmission will of course also be acknowledged, and so the sender, as in the previous example, receives two acknowledgments for the same data, with the same possibilities for livelock as before.

Polling protocols can be constructed in a similar manner with sequence numbers and timeout. In this case, the timeout function would most naturally be incorporated in the *receiver*, which would poll the sender again if it did not receive a data-PDU within a suitable period of time. This would make the protocol able to deal with lost PDUs, just like **Protocol 4**. However, it would also suffer from the same faults as **Protocol 4**, as you can convince yourself if you do Exercise 4.4.

4.1.5 The Alternating Bit Protocol

The real problem with **Protocol 3** and **Protocol 4** is that they rely on the use of anonymous acknowledgments. If it were possible for the sender to see what is being acknowledged, a more suitable reaction could be arranged for. The related polling

Protocol 5

$Sender \quad \overset{\text{def}}{=} (S[1] \parallel Timer) \setminus \{up\}$

$S[n : \mathbb{N}_0] \quad \overset{\text{def}}{=} (SAPA?x : \mathcal{M} \to \qquad\qquad QT[n,x])$

$QT[n : \mathbb{N}_0, x : \mathcal{M}]$

$\qquad \overset{\text{def}}{=} (right!(n,x) \to (up!\text{SET} \to (right?a : \mathbb{N}_0 \to$

$$(\textbf{if } (a = n)$$
$$\textbf{then } up!\text{RESET} \to S[succ(n)]$$
$$\textbf{else } QT[n,x])$$
$$[\!] right?a : E \to QT[n,x]$$
$$[\!] up?t : \{\text{TIMEOUT}\} \to QT[n,x])))$$

$Receiver \quad \overset{\text{def}}{=} R[0]$

$R[n : \mathbb{N}_0] \quad \overset{\text{def}}{=} (left?(i : \mathbb{N}_0, x : \mathcal{M}) \to \quad (\textbf{if } (i = succ(n))$

$$\textbf{then } left!i \to SAPB!x \to R[succ(n)]$$
$$\textbf{else } left!n \to R[n])$$
$$[\!] left?(i : \mathbb{N}_0, y : \mathcal{M}') \to \quad R[n] \ )$$

$Timer \quad \overset{\text{def}}{=} (up?s : \{\text{SET}\} \to \qquad (up?r : \{\text{RESET}\} \to Timer$

$$[\!] up!\text{TIMEOUT} \to Timer))$$

Fig. 4.8 PAR protocol with sequence numbers in data and acknowledgments.
Here, E represents the domain of acknowledgment PDUs with erroneous checksums.

protocols fail similarly because they rely on anonymous polling requests (either POLL or REPT).

This reflects a general problem in distributed systems: namely, that the cooperating parties do not in general know what their collective *global state* is, and therefore have to make decisions on the basis of whatever information they locally have available, or which their cooperators have sent them. In this case the information ACK just tells the sender that the other party has received a data-PDU which came in the right order. The user has no means of knowing exactly which data-PDU is referred to. By assuming that it was the latest data-PDU sent, the sender will be right most of the time, but in special cases will make a mistake which, as we have seen, will cause the protocol to fail.

The only cure for this is to include yet more PCI in the PDUs, so that the sender and receiver can build up a more complete picture of one another's state. The necessary PCI here is an identification on the acknowledgments, indicating the sequence number of the latest correctly received data-PDU. This leads us to **Protocol 5**, which again assumes the system configuration shown in Figure 4.5.

In this case, *Sender* repeats PDU number n until it receives an acknowledgment explicitly denoting n, and with correct checksum. *Receiver* replies to each incoming data-PDU (regardless of whether it was correct or not) with an acknowledgment which includes the sequence number of the *last correctly received PDU* – which, of course, may be the PDU just received or a previous one.

This protocol is resilient to all the types of error which we have considered up to now: Loss, corruption or duplication of data-PDUs, and loss, corruption or duplication of acknowledgments. The class of error which it is not resilient to is *masquerading*, i.e. introduction by the service $\mathscr{S}$ of false PDUs which look as though they are correct ones, because they have correct checksums and appropriate sequence numbers. We shall look at some ways in which this can occur in Section 4.1.6 below.

Although the use of a segment of the natural numbers for the sequence numbers is an obvious one, it is not a very practical one in a real system, where the PCI has to be encoded into a finite number of bits! At some stage one runs out of numbers which can be uniquely represented. However, with the protocol shown, the sender has at any time at most one data-PDU for which it has not received an acknowledgment – it does not try to send PDU number $succ(n)$ before it receives an acknowledgment for PDU number n. Thus no ambiguity can arise in the numbering scheme if we count *modulo* some small natural number, S_{mod}, and define the successor function *succ* accordingly by:

$$succ(n) \stackrel{\text{def}}{=} (n+1) \bmod S_{mod}$$

In particular, we can count *modulo 2*. If this is done, the protocol is known as an *Alternating Bit Protocol*, as the sequence numbers lie in $\{0,1\}$, and can be represented by a single bit which alternately takes on the values 0 and 1 in PDUs derived from consecutive SDUs.

This is a protocol of great antiquity, which in this case means it originates from the late 1960s. It took some years before its properties were generally realised (see [5]). But in later years, in a variety of variations, it has become one of the most investigated protocols of all time, especially by theoreticians wishing to demonstrate the merits of their methods. For examples, see [16,57,76].

Many modern protocols use a rather larger sequence number space than just $\{0,1\}$. However, the real advantage of allowing a greater sequence number space is that it permits several PDUs to be outstanding (unacknowledged by the receiver) at one time. Since this implies something about how much data the receiver is willing to accumulate before sending an acknowledgment, it will be treated under the subject of *Flow Control* in Section 4.2 below.

Table 4.1 summarises the techniques which we have looked at and the types of error which they are resilient to. The table only considers acknowledgment protocols; for the corresponding polling protocols, the same results apply if we consider polling requests rather than acknowledgments.

4.1.6 The Case of the Floating Corpses

Although it is normally true, when the sender waits for acknowledgment of each PDU before going on to send the next one, that counting sequence numbers *modulo*

Table 4.1 Error control mechanisms and error resilience

Mechanisms					Resilience to error type					
					data-PDU			ack-PDU		
check sum	time out	plain ACK	seq.nos. in data	seq.nos. in ack.	loss	corruption	duplication	loss	corruption	duplication
+		+				+				
+	+	+			+	+				
+	+	+	+		+	+				
+	+		+	+	+	+	+	+	+	+

some relatively small integer will give no ambiguity, ambiguities can arise in certain special circumstances.

Imagine a system where PDUs can get lost for a considerable period of time. The sender eventually times out, declares the PDUs 'dead', and retransmits them. The receiver accepts the retransmitted PDUs. All seems well. So much time goes by that the same sequence numbers start to be re-used again. And at this moment, just as in some detective story, the corpses come floating up to the top of the service, as it were, and arrive at the receiver. Total confusion arises, as most protocols are unable to counteract this form for *masquerading*.

This kind of situation occurs unpleasantly often in practice. In large networks, in particular, there may be several routes which can be followed between any pair of systems. If one of these routes becomes impassable due to some error, PDUs which are being sent along this route cannot get through to their destination, and 'get stuck' somewhere on the way. At some stage the sender times out, and retransmits the PDUs, which (see Chapter 7) are sent by one of the alternative routes to avoid the blockage. When the blockage is cleared, the PDUs which were held up continue on their way, and arrive, after a possibly enormous delay, at their destination.

The theoretical solution to this problem is simple: Never re-use sequence numbers! A practical approximation to this might be to count, say, *modulo* 2^{48}, which with a PDU sent every millisecond (quite an achievement in most communication systems) would mean that the system could have a lifetime of the order of 10^4 years before we ran out of sequence numbers. Unfortunately, it is most unlikely that a system can run for so long without ever 'crashing', and after a crash it may be extremely difficult to guarantee that we can remember where we got to in the sequence number sequence.

Alternative solutions are usually based on some scheme for explicitly limiting the time during which a PDU with a particular sequence number is allowed to wander round in the network without reaching its destination. The time limit is usually called the *maximum PDU lifetime*, traditionally denoted L. There are several factors which can affect L, including:

- The maximum time for the physical transfer of a PDU between different systems, which we shall denote M.
- The number of times which the sender is willing to retransmit a PDU with a given sequence number, which we shall denote R_{max}.

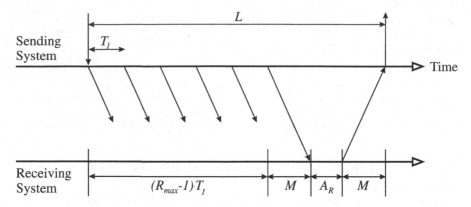

Fig. 4.9 Components of the maximum PDU lifetime, L.
Here T_1 is the sender's timeout time, R_{max} the maximum number of retransmissions, M the maximum transfer time between the systems, and A_R the response time in the receiving system.

- The time for generating some kind of response in the receiving system, which we shall denote A_R.

It may seem odd to include the receiver's characteristics in this list, but this is necessary if the sender is to be quite certain that the receiver has finished dealing with the PDU before it risks sending another one with the same number. The composition of L is shown in Figure 4.9.

The maximum transfer time, M (and thus also L), can be limited by a number of techniques, including:

1. **Careful design** of the routing and congestion control algorithms (which will be discussed in Chapter 7), so that PDUs cannot go round in loops. This prevents potentially infinite delays, but does not put any specific limit on the transfer time.
2. **Use of 'hop counters'** as part of the PDU's PCI. On each direct transfer between one physical system and another, the counter is decremented by one. If it reaches zero, and the PDU is not by then at its destination, the PDU is discarded (i.e. thrown away). This sets an implicit limit on the maximum transfer time. To determine M exactly, it is necessary to know what the maximum time for transfer between directly connected systems is, and to have an estimate of how many 'hops' between directly connected systems are required to reach an arbitrary destination across the network. A reasonable estimate of the number of hops is the graph-theoretic diameter of the network.
3. **Use of timestamps** as part of the PCI. The sender includes the time at which the PDU was first transmitted. If any system receives a PDU which is older than the agreed maximum, it discards it. Obviously the method only works if all systems agree to use the same time scale. We shall discuss some ways of achieving this in Section 5.5.

In practice, combinations of these techniques are often used. For example, the Internet Protocol (IP) used in the Network layer of the Internet protocol suite, uses a '*time-to-live*' *counter* in each PDU. This is initially set to an estimate of the time (in seconds) which it will take to reach the destination. At each intermediate system through which the PDU passes, the counter is decremented by an estimate of how many seconds it has taken to handle the PDU in this system, with the restriction that if this estimate is less than one second, the counter must be decremented by one. If the counter reaches zero, the PDU is discarded. This is a combination of the hop counter and timestamp based techniques.

If a reasonable estimate of L can be determined, then the general strategy for avoiding the floating corpses is simply to wait a time L before re-using any sequence number over the same logical channel. This can be done in a number of more or less intelligent (and efficient) ways, depending on the way in which the initial sequence number is chosen when the logical channel is set up.

1. **Channel freezing.** Every time a particular logical channel is set up, sequence numbering is restarted from 0. When use of the logical channel is terminated (the connection is broken), its re-use is forbidden for a time L, and the channel is said to be 'frozen' in this period. The period during which the channel is frozen is often referred to as the *quiet time*.

2. **Continuation.** Every time a logical channel is set up, sequence numbering on that channel is restarted from wherever it got to last time the channel was used. Compared to channel freezing, this reduces the risk of running out of channels, which may be a scarce resource in a practical system. However, it only works if all systems can remember where they got to, so after a system crash it is necessary to wait during a quiet time L before continuing.

3. **Time-based initialisation.** In this method, originally suggested by Tomlinson [123], the initial sequence number for each use of a particular logical channel is a representation of the time of day, TD_0. At any given instant, we know that all sequence numbers generated within the previous period L may be valid. In order to avoid confusion between numbers generated in one use of the channel and those generated in the next use of the channel, we must at all times avoid using sequence numbers for a period L before they could potentially be used as initial sequence numbers (in the next use of the channel). This means that we must avoid:

   • Using numbers which are greater than the current time of day, TD. If we wished to open the channel again, these numbers would apparently lie in the valid interval for the new use of the channel.

   • Using numbers which are less than $TD - L$ (mod S_{mod}), where S_{mod} is the modulus of the sequence number arithmetic. These would also apparently lie in the acceptable interval if we opened the channel again.

Figure 4.10 illustrates these rules. If the sender detects that it is about to enter the forbidden sequence number zone with respect to the current time of day, it must either wait until TD 'catches up' with the chosen sequence number (if the number is too large) or wait an interval L, until TD (mod S_{mod}) 'catches up' with the number (if the number is too small).

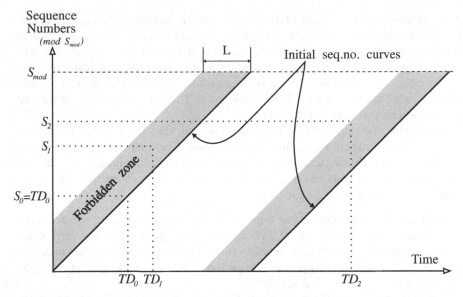

Fig. 4.10 Selection of unambiguous sequence numbers based on time of day.
At time TD_0, the channel is opened with initial sequence number S_0 $(= TD_0)$. At time TD_1, sequence number S_1 is too large, and the sender must wait until time S_1 before using it. At time TD_2, sequence number S_2 is too small, and the sender must wait until $(TD_2 + L)$ before using it.

This method is interesting because of the way in which time is used to introduce a form of universal ordering in the distributed system, so that a unique sequence of identification numbers can be generated on the basis of this ordering. The principle is quite simple, although it may appear complicated due to the need to avoid the extra ambiguities which arise from the use of modulus arithmetic. Unfortunately, these types of complication appear in many other contexts in 'real-life' systems, where modulus arithmetic has to be used because of limitations on the size of the number representation. We shall see some more examples in the next section.

4. **Randomised initialisation.** All three of the above methods are *deterministic*, which means that anyone monitoring the traffic in the network can predict which initial sequence numbers will be chosen next time two given parties, say A and B, try to set up a connection. So although the methods effectively solve the problem of avoiding *outdated* messages, they do not protect A and B against malicious intruders who *deliberately* insert fake messages into the stream of data. This is a security risk: A malicious intruder M can pretend to be A or B, and can effectively insert messages with suitable sequence numbers into the stream of PDUs. To avoid this problem, Bellovin [8] proposed that the initial sequence number should be computed as the sum of the "time of day" (as proposed by Tomlinson) and a random number. Bellovin's specific recommendation was to compute this number as the cryptographic checksum (see Section 6.2) of the addresses of the two parties who are trying to communicate, together with a secret not known to

others. Good secrets could, for example, be generated by a genuine (electronic) random number generator or by using internal system information such as the setting of the system clock when the system was last booted.

4.2 Flow Control

The purpose of the Flow Control function is to prevent the receiver from being flooded with more data than it has resources to deal with. This is obviously particularly important when the sender and receiver operate at different speeds. This aim is easy to achieve in polling protocols, as the receiver explicitly controls the flow of data via the polling mehanism. But in fact all the acknowledgment protocols which we have considered have implicitly contained a flow control function, as they all have the property (as long as we avoid their failure modes) that the sender will not send a new PDU until the previous PDU has been acknowledged. This corresponds to the intended specification:

Specification 4.1 $\mathscr{S}'$ **sat** $(SAPB \leq SAPA) \wedge (|\#SAPB - \#SAPA| \leq 1)$

for the composed service

$$\mathscr{S}' \stackrel{\text{def}}{=} Sender \gg \mathscr{S} \gg Receiver$$

This specification will in fact be satisfied, again as long as the underlying service, $\mathscr{S}$, only introduces those types of error which the protocol can deal with correctly.

Acknowledgement protocols which satisfy the specification above are often known as *Stop-and-wait* protocols. Their advantage is that they are easy to implement, and the receiver can control the flow to a certain extent (within the limits set by the sender's timeout period) by introducing a delay before it sends the acknowledgment. Their obvious disadvantage is that at most one data-PDU is passed from sender to receiver for each 'round trip' time, that is to say, the time it takes for a PDU to be transmitted via the underlying service from sender to receiver, plus the time the receiver takes to evaluate its response, plus the time the acknowledgment takes to return to the sender.

If this round trip time is much larger than the time it takes to transmit (i.e. physically send the bits of) the single data-PDU, then it is clear that the system's throughput will only be a small fraction of the transmission rate. In many systems, this is unacceptable. Particularly extreme cases are systems using satellite communication channels, where the round trip time is of the order of 500 milliseconds, and the transmission rate is of the order of 10^6–10^9 bit/s. A PDU of size 10^4 bits (which is rather large for many applications) only takes of the order 0.01–10 ms. to transmit. Use of a stop-and-wait protocol means that only one such PDU can be transmitted per 500 ms., so despite the large bandwidth of the satellite channel, the average throughput over a longer period of time is of the order of 2×10^4 bit/s, and the sender spends most of its time waiting for acknowledgments.

4.2.1 Fixed Window Protocols

The next development to improve the throughput, of course at the expense of potentially requiring more resources in the receiver, is to allow more than one data-PDU
to be outstanding – i.e. sent but not yet acknowledged. The specification for the
protocol then becomes:

Specification 4.2 $\mathscr{S}'$ sat $(SAPB \leq SAPA) \wedge (|\#SAPA - \#SAPB| \leq W_s)$

where W_s is some constant for the service $\mathscr{S}'$, known as the *send window size*.
Evidently, for stop-and-wait protocols $W_s = 1$.

The simplest implementation of this specification is to allow the sending protocol
entity, when in the state where it has sent and received acknowledgments for PDUs
with sequence numbers from 0 to n_s, to send those with numbers from $n_s + 1$ up to
$n_s + W_s$, (where all arithmetic is done modulo S_{mod}, the modulus of the sequence
number arithmetic). This interval of sequence numbers is known as the *send window*. At any time, the send window describes the set of PDUs which are allowed
to be sent but not acknowledged. In a *fixed window* system, W_s is a constant, and
(depending on the circumstances) may at any instant be larger or smaller than the
number of PDUs which the sender actually has available to send. If the window size
is larger, then we say that the send window is not *full*. The filled portion of the send
window corresponds to those PDUs which in fact have been sent, but for which no
acknowledgments have been received. This is illustrated in Figure 4.11.

The receiver must always acknowledge the PDU with the largest number which
it has received correctly, and by convention this implicitly acknowledges all PDUs
with smaller numbers. 'Correctly' means here that the PDU arrives without checksum error, and *that the receiver has accepted all preceding PDUs in the sequence*.
Thus if the receiver has already accepted PDUs with numbers:

   $0, 1, 2, 3, 5, 6$

and receives PDU number 7, then it acknowledges number 3, whereas if it receives
number 4, then it acknowledges number 6.

Note the careful choice of words in the previous paragraph. The acknowledgment
only applies to those PDUs which the receiver has *accepted*. The number of PDUs
which it is prepared to accept while there are some previous PDUs missing is known
as the *receive window size* for the protocol, often denoted W_r. If the receiver has
correctly received and acknowledged all PDUs with sequence numbers from 0 to
n_r, then its *receive window* is the sequence number interval $\{n_r + 1, \ldots, n_r + W_r\}$
(mod S_{mod}). If $W_r = 1$, then no 'holes' are allowed in the received sequence, and
the receiver will ignore all PDUs except *exactly* the one with number $n_r + 1$, which
is the next one it expects to receive. In stop-and-wait protocols, $W_r = W_s = 1$.

If $W_r > 1$, then any PDUs with numbers in the window can be accepted. Evidently, in the example above, W_r must be at least 3. Note that the receive window
does not in general need to be full – it defines the *maximum* number of PDUs which
the receiver is willing to collect up while waiting for a missing one in the sequence.

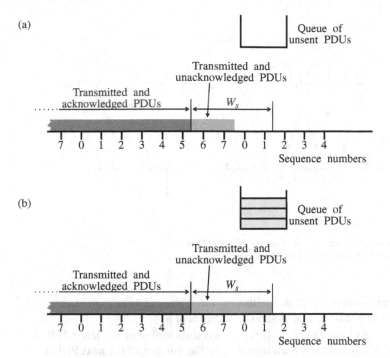

Fig. 4.11 Functioning of a window protocol.
(a) Send window with $W_s = 4$ not full. Two PDUs have been sent but not yet acknowledged.
(b) Send window with $W_s = 4$ full. Four PDUs have been sent but not yet acknowledged. Further PDUs to be transmitted have to wait in a queue until there is room in the window.

If no out-of-sequence PDUs arrive, if the receiving service user is able to accept SDUs as fast as the service provider can generate them from PDUs, and if each SDU is generated from a single PDU, then the window need never contain more than one PDU, regardless of W_r.

Protocols with $W_r = 1$ and those with $W_r > 1$ have rather different properties in a number of respects. The most important differences are in the available strategies for *retransmission after error*, and in the permissible range of *send window sizes*. We shall consider each class of protocol in turn.

4.2.2 Protocols with Receive Window Size 1

Since protocols with $W_r = 1$ have the property that the receiver will refuse to accept any PDU except the one with number $n_r + 1$, it follows that the sender must retransmit *all* unacknowledged PDUs if it detects an error – that is, if it times out due to not receiving an acknowledgment. It must assume that the receiver has never received the PDU it was waiting for, and that any subsequent PDUs in the send window have

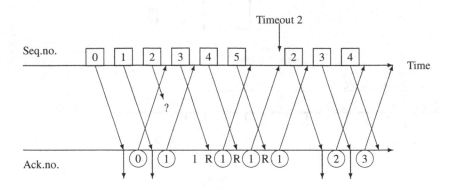

Fig. 4.12 Retransmission strategy with Receive Window Size 1.
R indicates PDUs which are rejected by the receiver.

therefore also been lost or rejected. An illustration of this can be seen in Figure 4.12, and a protocol using this scheme is shown as **Protocol 6**.

In the definition of the sender, $acks$ represents the number of the latest PDU for which an acknowledgment has been received, n_s the number of the next PDU to be sent, and ml the list of PDUs which have been sent but not acknowledged. On receipt of an acknowledgment for PDU number a, PDUs with numbers from $succ(ack_s)$ up to a are removed from the list, and ack_s is adjusted accordingly (process QA).

Note that a timer is required for each value of n_s, but when a timer runs out, it is assumed to be for the 'oldest' unacknowledged PDU, with number $succ(ack_s)$, and all PDUs with numbers from $succ(ack_s)$ up to n_s are retransmitted (process QR).

This retransmission strategy, often known as a *go back n* strategy, is quite simple to administer, but can obviously cause significant overhead if the send window is large, so that there can be many unacknowledged PDUs outstanding. It is therefore most suitable for use in systems where the error rate is reasonably low.

A rather less obvious property of protocols with $W_r = 1$ is that the send window size must not exceed $S_{mod} - 1$, where S_{mod} is the modulus of the sequence number arithmetic. In other words W_s is limited to *one less than* the maximum number of distinguishable sequence numbers. To see why this is so, consider a scenario where this rule is *not* enforced:

1. The sender sends a sequence of S_{mod} PDUs with sequence numbers $0, \dots, S_{mod} - 1$.
2. The sender receives an acknowledgment for the PDU with the sequence number $S_{mod} - 1$.
3. The sender sends S_{mod} new PDUs with sequence numbers $0, \dots, S_{mod} - 1$.
4. The sender receives another acknowledgment for a PDU with sequence number $S_{mod} - 1$.

Evidently, the sender is then unable to tell whether the latest acknowledgment is for the last PDU in the second sequence of PDUs which it has sent, or whether the

Protocol 6

$Sender \overset{\text{def}}{=} (S[0,1,[\,]] \parallel Timer[0,0]) \quad \backslash\{up\}$

$S[ack_s, n_s : \mathbb{Z}_{S_{mod}}, ml : \mathscr{M}^*]$
$$\overset{\text{def}}{=} (SAPA?x : \mathscr{M} \to right!(n_s, x) \to (up!\text{SET} \to S[ack_s, succ(n_s), ml\hat{\ }x])$$

$\quad\quad [\!]\, right?a : \mathbb{Z}_{S_{mod}} \to \quad\quad QA[ack_s, a, n_s, ml]$

$\quad\quad [\!]\, right?a : E \to \quad\quad\quad S[ack_s, n_s, ml]$

$\quad\quad [\!]\, up?t : \{\text{TIMEOUT}\} \to \quad QR[ack_s, ack_s, n_s, ml, ml])$

$QA[ack_s, a, n_s : \mathbb{Z}_{S_{mod}}, ml : \mathscr{M}^*]$
$$\overset{\text{def}}{=} (\textbf{if } (ack_s < a < n_s)$$

$\quad\quad \textbf{then } up!\text{RESET} \to \quad\quad QA[succ(ack_s), a, n_s, \text{tl}\,ml]$

$\quad\quad \textbf{else } S[ack_s, n_s, ml]\,)$

$QR[ack_s, a, n_s : \mathbb{Z}_{S_{mod}}, ml, ml' : \mathscr{M}^*]$
$$\overset{\text{def}}{=} (\textbf{if } (succ(a) < n_s)$$

$\quad\quad \textbf{then } right!(succ(a), \text{hd}\,ml) \to up!\text{RESTART} \to$

$\quad\quad\quad\quad\quad\quad\quad QR[ack_s, succ(a), n_s, \text{tl}\,ml, ml']$

$\quad\quad \textbf{else } S[ack_s, n_s, ml']\,)$

$Receiver \overset{\text{def}}{=} R[0]$

$R[n : \mathbb{Z}_{S_{mod}}] \overset{\text{def}}{=} (left?(i : \mathbb{Z}_{S_{mod}}, x : \mathscr{M}) \to (\textbf{if } (i = succ(n))$

$\quad\quad\quad\quad\quad\quad\quad\quad\quad \textbf{then } left!i \to SAPB!x \to R[succ(n)]$

$\quad\quad\quad\quad\quad\quad\quad\quad\quad \textbf{else } R[n]\,)$

$\quad\quad [\!]\, left?(i : \mathbb{Z}_{S_{mod}}, y : \mathscr{M}') \to R[n]\,)$

$Timer[ack_s, n_s : \mathbb{Z}_{S_{mod}}]$
$$\overset{\text{def}}{=} (up?s : \{\text{SET}\} \to \quad\quad Timer[ack_s, succ(n_s)]$$

$\quad\quad [\!]\, up?r : \{\text{RESET}\} \to \quad\quad Timer[succ(ack_s), n_s]$

$\quad\quad [\!]\, up?r : \{\text{RESTART}\} \to \quad Timer[ack_s, n_s]$

$\quad\quad [\!]\, up!\text{TIMEOUT} \to \quad\quad\quad Timer[ack_s, n_s]\,)$

Fig. 4.13 Window protocol with $W_s > 1$ and $W_r = 1$.
Here, $\mathbb{Z}_{S_{mod}}$ is the domain of integers modulo S_{mod}, E represents the domain of acknowledgment
PDUs with erroneous checksums, and $\mathscr{M}^*$ the domain of sequences of messages.

PDU with number 0 in this sequence got lost, with the result that all subsequent
PDUs in the sequence were rejected by the receiver, so that the acknowledgment
is really for the last PDU in the *first* sequence of S_{mod} PDUs. If the sender is at
most allowed to send $S_{mod} - 1$ PDUs without receiving an acknowledgment, then
this type of ambiguity cannot arise. Stop-and-wait protocols, where W_s is restricted
to 1, can clearly obey this rule for any value of S_{mod} greater than or equal to 2; thus
the Alternating Bit Protocol is safe from error in this respect.

This reflects a general problem in distributed systems: What exactly can one party
deduce about the other party on the basis of the information available? In this case,
what can the sender deduce when it receives an acknowledgment for a PDU with
sequence number N? It can deduce that the receiver has received just exactly the
PDU with that number, since $W_r = 1$. But it also needs to be able to deduce whether
N lies within the current send window (in which case it is a 'new' acknowledgment,

and the send window can be moved to cover a new interval) or whether it lies outside the current send window (in which case it is an acknowledgment for an 'old' PDU, which implies that none of the PDUs in the current send window have yet been accepted). The sender can only distinguish between these two cases if it knows that the send window and receive window do not overlap until the receiver in fact has received all PDUs before the current send window. This implies that the send and receive windows must not be so large that they cannot form disjoint intervals in the sequence number space. A minimum condition for this, when $W_r = 1$, is that $W_s \leq S_{mod} - 1$.

4.2.3 Protocols with Receive Window Size Greater than 1

When the receive window size exceeds one, the receiver is willing to accept PDUs which arrive out of sequence, leaving 'holes' in the sequence which have to be filled in later. Assuming that the service is to offer sequence preservation, the protocol must incorporate some strategy for retransmitting the missing PDUs, preferably without retransmitting those PDUs which in fact have been accepted out of sequence by the receiver.

The simplest strategy is just to use a timeout mechanism at the sender, in the usual way. Suppose the receiver has acknowledged PDUs with sequence numbers up to n_r, is missing the PDU with number $n_r + 1$, and has accepted (but neither acknowledged nor passed on to the service user) PDUs with numbers from $n_r + 2$ to $n_r + m$, where of course $m < W_r$ and all arithmetic is performed modulo S_{mod}. The receiver continues to acknowledge receipt of PDU number n_r, until it receives PDU number $n_r + 1$ as a result of retransmission by the sender following timeout. The receiver then acknowledges receipt of PDU $n_r + m$, thus implicitly acknowledging receipt of all the preceding PDUs, derives SDUs from all PDUs with numbers $n_r + 1$ to $n_r + m$, and passes them on to the user in correct sequence number order. This is illustrated in Figure 4.14.

Unfortunately, although this strategy is logically correct, it is difficult to organise it properly in practice. The reason for this is that it takes some time for an acknowledgment to arrive back at the sender after a retransmission. During this time, several other timeout periods may have expired – for PDUs with numbers $n_r + 2, n_r + 3$ and so on – so that a whole series of PDUs will in fact be retransmitted. This is exactly what we wanted to avoid. A common way to prevent this is to allow the receiver explicitly to request any PDUs which appear to be missing, *before* the sender starts to time out. This is commonly called a *selective repeat* (or *selective reject*) mechanism. A well-known protocol which incorporates such a mechanism is HDLC [131].

Since we have seen that the maximum permissible size of send window is related to the modulus of the sequence number arithmetic in a particular way when $W_r = 1$, it is natural to ask what the relation might be when $W_r > 1$. Once again, we want to make it impossible for the sender to misinterpret the acknowledgment. Let us again assume that the sender knows how big W_r is. When the sender receives an acknowl-

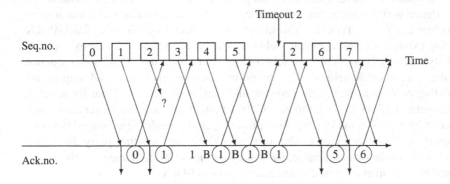

Fig. 4.14 Retransmission strategy with Receive Window Size >1.
B indicates out-of-sequence PDUs which are buffered by the receiver until the missing PDU is
received.

edgment for PDU number N, it then knows that the receiver has received one or more
PDUs with sequence numbers in the interval $\{N - W_r + 1, \ldots, N\}$ (mod S_{mod}). To
avoid ambiguity, it must be possible to decide whether this interval lies inside or
outside the current send window. Thus a minimum requirement in this case is that
$(W_s + W_r) \leq S_{mod}$. A common arrangement is to choose $W_s = W_r$, in which case the
limit for each of them is $S_{mod}/2$.

4.2.4 Dynamic Window Systems and the Concept of Credit

A clear requirement for the implementation of a protocol with send window size W_s
is that there be W_s buffers available at the sender to keep the unacknowledged PDUs
in until the acknowledgments for them arrive. Likewise, when the receive window
size is W_r, there must be W_r buffers available at the receiver to keep out of sequence
PDUs in until all preceding PDUs in the sequence have arrived.

There is therefore in general a balance to be sought between using large windows (which can improve the throughput of the system) and limiting the amount of
buffer space required. This is particularly important in systems which maintain large
numbers of active logical channels at the same time. This is for example a common
situation in implementations of the upper OSI layers (from the Transport Layer and
up). A useful strategy in such systems is to use dynamic buffer allocation according
to the current needs of each logical channel, and dynamically to modify the window
sizes accordingly.

The most usual mechanism for this purpose is the so-called *credit* mechanism,
whereby each party using a logical channel informs the other(s) from time to time
how many buffers it is prepared to offer for receiving data. 'From time to time'

usually means whenever there is a change in the number of buffers available, in accordance with the usual practice of keeping peer entities informed about important changes of state. Typically, this information is transferred in special ack-PDUs bearing explicit acknowledgments and the current credit value. Thus for example an OSI style ack-PDU might bear an acknowledgment for the data-PDU with sequence number n_r, and credit value C. This would tell the other party that PDUs up to and including number n_r had been received, and that credit was available for sending PDUs with numbers $n_r + 1$ up to $n_r + C$. In a system offering stream services, such as a service based on the Internet TCP protocol, credit would be measured in octets rather than PDUs, so a credit value of C would inform the other party that space for C octets of data was available; the sender would be left to decide whether these should be sent all at once or divided among several PDUs.

4.3 Indication of Change of Peer State

A change in the state of one of the users of a service can in principle be indicated to the other user(s) by the transfer of a single PDU. In simple cases, this may be enough. As an example, consider a service which enables users to tell one another how much data they are prepared to accept. This information could be carried in a single ack-PDU bearing credit information, as described in the previous section.

In more critical cases, however, this would not be satisfactory, and a more complex exchange of PDUs is required. Firstly, because of the possibility of error, and secondly, in order to allow the *users* to exchange data, in order to establish their global state. In many cases, it may indeed be a service requirement that such exchanges take place as *atomic actions*, so that the desired updating of state information takes place for all users at the same time, uninterrupted by other activities. If the exchange takes place atomically, we shall call it an *atomic exchange*.

4.3.1 Two-way Exchanges

Simple protocols which allow two service users to exchange data usually follow a scheme something like that given as **Protocol 7**. Such protocols are usually known as *two way exchange* or *(two-way) handshake* protocols. The particular example here is based on a number of ISO protocols for connection establishment.

In OSI parlance, as discussed in Chapter 2, the users of a service interact with the service at Service Access Points by taking part in interactions known as *service primitives*. In **Protocol 7**, the Service Access Points are modelled by CSP channels *SAPA* and *SAPB*, as in the previous examples of this chapter. The protocol is initiated when the user at *SAPA*, known as the *initiating user*, interacts with the service provider in a *request* service primitive, here abstracted as a CSP message in the domain *req*. The protocol entity on the initiating side (*Sender*) then transmits

Protocol 7

$Sender \overset{\text{def}}{=} (S \parallel Timer) \setminus \{up\}$

$S \overset{\text{def}}{=} (SAPA?r : req \to right!r \to \qquad up!\text{SET} \to SR)$

$SR \overset{\text{def}}{=} (right?c : accept \to up!\text{RESET} \to \quad SAPA!c \to (\ldots)$
$\quad [\!] right?a : refuse \to up!\text{RESET} \to \quad SAPA!a \to S$
$\quad [\!] up?t : \{\text{TIMEOUT}\} \to \qquad\qquad SAPA!ref \to S)$

$Receiver \overset{\text{def}}{=} (R \parallel Timer) \setminus \{up\}$

$R \overset{\text{def}}{=} (left?r : req \to SAPB!r \to \qquad up!\text{SET} \to RR)$

$RR \overset{\text{def}}{=} (SAPB?c : accept \to up!\text{RESET} \to \quad left!c \to (\ldots)$
$\quad [\!] SAPB?a : refuse \to up!\text{RESET} \to \quad left!a \to R$
$\quad [\!] up?t : \{\text{TIMEOUT}\} \to SAPB!ref \to left!ref \to R)$

$Timer \overset{\text{def}}{=} (up?s : \{\text{SET}\} \to \qquad\qquad (up?r : \{\text{RESET}\} \to Timer$
$\qquad\qquad\qquad\qquad\qquad\qquad\qquad\quad [\!] up!\text{TIMEOUT} \to Timer))$

Fig. 4.15 Basic protocol for providing confirmed service.
Here, *ref:refuse* denotes an internally generated message to indicate that the attempt to terminate the protocol normally has been abandoned.

a *request-PDU*, whose information content is essentially the same as that of the request primitive.

On receipt of such a request-PDU, the protocol entity *Receiver*, in this context often known as the *responding entity*, interacts with the user attached at *SAPB* via an *indication* primitive, derived from the same information. The user is then expected to reply by taking part in a *response* primitive. The response can here be either positive (in domain *accept*) or negative (in domain *refuse*), and causes the responding entity to transmit a corresponding PDU back to the initiating entity, which then interacts with the initiating user via a *confirm* primitive, which bears essentially the same information as the responding user included in its response. This style of service, in which the responding user must respond explicitly to the receipt of information from the initiating user by sending a reply, is known as a *user-confirmed service*. It gives an effective guarantee that the user has in fact received the information. Another style of confirmed service, in which the provider issues a *confirm* as soon as the information is delivered on the responding side, without requiring the responding user to react, is found in some systems. This is known as a *provider-confirmed service*. Evidently it does not give as convincing a guarantee that the information has been received.

The interactions between the users and the service are in OSI literature often described by so-called *time-sequence diagrams*, which show the temporal relationships between the service primitives in diagram form. For user-confirmed services, such as the one provided by **Protocol 7**, the diagram is as shown in Figure 4.16.

In time-sequence diagrams, time is assumed to run from top to bottom. This diagram states that the request primitive precedes and leads to the indication primitive,

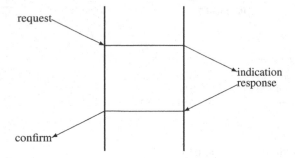

Fig. 4.16 Time-sequence diagram for a user-confirmed service.

and that the response primitive precedes and leads to the confirm primitive, while the indication primitive precedes, but does not directly lead to, the response.

If the protocol succeeds, in the sense of terminating with a positive confirm at the initiating user, the next phase of operation is started. This is indicated in **Protocol 7** by (...). If the protocol is in fact a connection establishment protocol, this phase would be the data transfer phase.

4.3.2 Atomic Two-way Exchanges

In the very nature of things, connection establishment protocols give atomic exchanges, since in connection-mode operation it is meaningless to do anything else before the connection is established. In other situations this is not necessarily the case. In order to ensure that the exchange is atomic, it may then be necessary for the protocol entities to delay, ignore, or refuse to carry out requests from the service users until the protocol has terminated. Alternatively, and less satisfactorily, a strict discipline could be imposed on the service users, ensuring that *they* do not do anything which might prejudice the atomicity of their exchange.

An example of a case where atomicity is important is the setting up of a *synchronisation point* in the stream of data passing between two users of a service, so as to be able to return to this point after an error or for other reasons. The setting of the point must clearly not be interrupted by further data transfers, as otherwise there would be doubt about where exactly in the data stream the point was placed. The ISO OSI Session Service [139] contains a facility of this type, with rules specifying that, except in the case of genuine failure of a user, primitives not related to the synchronisation point facility will not be accepted:

1. On the initiator side, between the occurrence of the request and confirm primitives.
2. On the responder side, between the occurrence of the indication and confirm primitives.

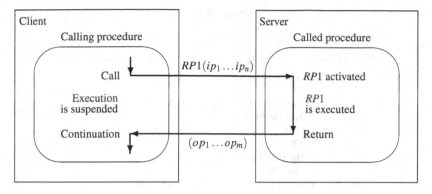

Fig. 4.17 Remote Procedure Call of procedure $RP1$ with calling parameters $ip_1 \ldots ip_n$ and return parameters $op_1 \ldots op_m$.

This is most easily understood with reference to Figure 4.16.

Atomicity of exchanges is also desirable because it makes it easy to implement a number of structuring concepts which are useful in system design. A well-known example of this is the *Remote Procedure Call (RPC)* convention illustrated in Figure 4.17. Here all interactions between systems on different sites are expected to appear like procedure calls executed by the initiating party, which in this context is usually known as the *Client*. The outgoing part of the exchange carries 'call parameters' to the remote system, often called the *Server*, and the returning part of the exchange carries 'return parameters' back to the Client. To give the desired atomicity, the client's activity is *suspended* while the remote procedure is being executed. This is a generally accepted extension to distributed systems of the 'send message/wait answer' system call convention well-known from many operating systems.

4.3.3 Exchanges in the Presence of Errors

In **Protocol 7**, the initiating protocol entity simply gives up the exchange if it receives no PDU from the responding entity within a certain period of time. Likewise, the responding entity gives up (and generates a negative 'reply') if it does not receive any response from the responding user within a suitable time. It follows from the general discussion earlier in the chapter that this is not necessarily a safe procedure in the presence of errors.

It is obviously particularly dangerous to rely on a simple protocol for *connection establishment* when errors may occur, as the protocol is intended to make it possible for the service users to establish their initial global state. If this is wrong from the very start, almost anything might happen later!

A simple modification to **Protocol 7** would of course be for *Sender* to retransmit the initial request-PDU, r, several times instead of giving up after one failed

Protocol 8

$$
\begin{array}{lll}
\mathit{Sender} & \stackrel{\text{def}}{=} (S \parallel \mathit{Timer}) \setminus \{up\} & \\
S & \stackrel{\text{def}}{=} (\mathit{SAPA}?r : req \rightarrow right!(x,r) \rightarrow & up!\text{SET} \rightarrow \mathit{SR}[x]) \\
\mathit{SR}[x : \mathsf{tok}] & \stackrel{\text{def}}{=} (right?(p,q : \mathsf{tok}, c : accept) \rightarrow & up!\text{RESET} \rightarrow \\
 & \quad (\textbf{if } (p = x) & \\
 & \quad \textbf{then } (right!(p,q,check) \rightarrow & \mathit{SAPA}!c \rightarrow \ldots) \\
 & \quad \textbf{else } (\mathit{SAPA}!ref \rightarrow S)\ ) & \\
 & [\!]\, right?(p,q : \mathsf{tok}, a : refuse) \rightarrow & up!\text{RESET} \rightarrow \\
 & \quad (\textbf{if } (p = x) & \\
 & \quad \textbf{then } (\mathit{SAPA}!a \rightarrow S) & \\
 & \quad \textbf{else } \mathit{SR}[x]\ ) & \\
 & [\!]\, up?t : \{\text{TIMEOUT}\} \rightarrow & \mathit{SAPA}!ref \rightarrow S\ )
\end{array}
$$

$$
\begin{array}{lll}
\mathit{Receiver} & \stackrel{\text{def}}{=} (R \parallel \mathit{Timer}) \setminus \{up\} & \\
R & \stackrel{\text{def}}{=} (left?(x : \mathsf{tok}, r : req) \rightarrow \mathit{SAPB}!r \rightarrow & up!\text{SET} \rightarrow \mathit{RR}[x]) \\
\mathit{RR}[x : \mathsf{tok}] & \stackrel{\text{def}}{=} (\mathit{SAPB}?c : accept \rightarrow left!(x,y,c) \rightarrow & \mathit{RC}[x,y] \\
 & [\!]\, \mathit{SAPB}?a : refuse \rightarrow left!(x,y,a) \rightarrow & R \\
 & [\!]\, up?t : \{\text{TIMEOUT}\} \rightarrow left!(x,y,ref) \rightarrow & \mathit{SAPB}!ref \rightarrow R\ ) \\
\mathit{RC}[x,y : \mathsf{tok}] & \stackrel{\text{def}}{=} (left?(p,q : \mathsf{tok}, c : check) \rightarrow & \\
 & \quad (\textbf{if } (p = x) \wedge (q = y) & \\
 & \quad \textbf{then } (up!\text{RESET} \rightarrow \ldots) & \\
 & \quad \textbf{else } \mathit{RC}[x,y]\ ) & \\
 & [\!]\, up?t : \{\text{TIMEOUT}\} \rightarrow & \mathit{SAPB}!ref \rightarrow R\ )
\end{array}
$$

$$
\begin{array}{lll}
\mathit{Timer} & \stackrel{\text{def}}{=} (up?s : \{\text{SET}\} \rightarrow & (up?r : \{\text{RESET}\} \rightarrow \mathit{Timer} \\
 & & [\!]\, up!\text{TIMEOUT} \rightarrow \mathit{Timer})\ )
\end{array}
$$

Fig. 4.18 Three-way Handshake protocol.
Here, *ref:refuse* denotes an internally generated message to indicate that the attempt to terminate the protocol normally has been abandoned, and *x* and *y* denote values generated by the initiator and responder respectively, in order to identify the exchange.

attempt to establish the connection. The organisation of the protocol would then be analogous to the data transfer protocols presented in the early part of the chapter: *Sender* would retransmit the request-PDU after a certain time without a response, and *Receiver* would retransmit the refuse- or accept-PDU if it received a duplicate copy of the request-PDU. By including a checksum in the PDUs, we could ensure that the protocol was as least as resilient to errors as **Protocol 5**.

One particularly nasty problem would, however, remain: How to avoid the 'floating corpses'. It lies in the nature of things that the PDUs of an establishment protocol cannot themselves usefully bear sequence numbers – the initial sequence number for data-PDUs is one of the components of the global state which we wish to establish. So we must find some other information which can be exchanged and which will enable us to distinguish false PDUs from genuine ones during connection establishment.

$(a)\,A$ B

$\rightarrow\ <req,\quad ourref = x>$ $\rightarrow$ A initiates.

$\leftarrow\ <accept,\ ourref = y,\quad yourref = x>\ \leftarrow$ B responds.

$\rightarrow\ <check,\quad ourref = x,\quad yourref = y>\ \rightarrow$ A confirms.

$(b)\,A$ B

$\ldots\ <req,\quad ourref = x>$ $\rightarrow$ delayed req-PDU

$\leftarrow\ <accept,\ ourref = y,\quad yourref = x>\ \leftarrow$ B responds.

                                             A gives up.

                                         (B times out.)

$(c)\,A$ B

$\ldots\ <req,\quad ourref = x>$ $\rightarrow$ delayed req-PDU

$\leftarrow\ <accept,\ ourref = y,\quad yourref = x>\ \leftarrow$ B responds.

$\ldots\ <check,\quad ourref = x,\quad yourref = z>\ \rightarrow$ Delayed check-PDU

                                         A and B give up.

Fig. 4.19 Operation of three-way handshake protocol.
(a) Normal operation, (b) Delayed request-PDU, (c) Delayed request-PDU and check-PDU.

A widely accepted method is the so-called *Three-Way Handshake* protocol, first proposed by Tomlinson [123]. As the name implies, this involves a *three-way* exchange. The general scheme of this is given as **Protocol 8**. Essentially, the initiating protocol entity sends a request-PDU carrying an arbitrary value, x, the responding entity replies with a response-PDU bearing (x,y), and the initiating entity repeats this in a check-PDU as an extra confirmation. An analogy is the use of 'our reference' and 'your reference' fields in an exchange of letters: if you get a letter with an unknown reference on it, you throw it straight in the wastebin. The normal operation of the protocol is illustrated in Figure 4.19(a).

What happens if 'floating corpses' do in fact turn up when this protocol is used is illustrated in Figure 4.19(b) and (c). In (b), B responds to a false request-PDU, but A is unable to match B's reference x to any exchange in which it (A) is currently taking part. A gives up and (in our version of the protocol) B subsequently times out and therefore also gives up. In (c), B responds to a false request-PDU, but when it receives the false check-PDU it finds an incorrect reference, z, instead of the value y which it itself had generated. In this case, both A and B give up without timeout.

The protocol will in fact survive receipt of out-dated request-, response- and check-PDUs, assuming that the references used do not by some horrible chance get re-used again *in both systems* just at that moment when the delayed PDUs turn up again. With normal error rates, this may reasonably be considered a very rare possibility indeed.

In Tomlinson's original version of this protocol, the two references were the initial sequence numbers for use during transmission from initiator to responder and vice-versa. More recently, the scheme has been used for the connection establishment phase of the Internet/DoD TCP Transport layer protocol [212], and the ISO Class 4 Transport Protocol [138], two protocols specifically designed for use over relatively unreliable underlying services, including connectionless-mode Network services. While TCP uses Tomlinson's scheme unaltered, the references in the ISO protocol are arbitrary values used for identifying the connection under establishment. More generally, the three-way handshake protocol finds uses in all situations where a confirmed service is required over an unreliable underlying service.

4.4 Change of Service Mode

It should be clear from the techniques already presented that offering a different mode of service from that offered by the underlying service is not so difficult as might be imagined at first sight. Many of the techniques are relatively independent of the mode of the underlying service, and are thus readily modified for use over a different mode. However, there are a few central ideas which it can pay to look at more closely.

4.4.1 Connection-mode and Connectionless-mode

To provide a connectionless-mode service over a connection-mode one, we essentially have to hide the fact that the connection-mode service requires the user to perform some administrative tasks to establish the logical channel before sending data, and to release it again afterwards. A simple-minded implementation might be to establish a new connection *every* time a connectionless-mode SDU is to be sent, but this would in many practical cases be excessively expensive – both in time and money, since public networks often charge an initial sum every time a connection is set up.

A more attractive alternative, at least in cases where non-trivial amounts of data are to be sent, is to set up the underlying connection when the user requests transmission of the first connectionless-mode SDU, and then to keep it set up for as long as a 'reasonable' data flow is maintained. This can be estimated by the time which elapses between consecutive transmission requests from the user, in the way that a long period without data causes the connection to be released. This type of approach is, for example, suggested in Part 3 of ISO Standard 8473 [143], which deals with the specific problem of operating ISO's Connectionless-mode Network protocol over (amongst other possibilities) a Connection-mode X.25 service.

To produce a connection-mode service from a connectionless one, the PDUs required for the operation of the protocol which provides the connection-mode service must be sent via the connectionless-mode one. This gives the obvious problem that there is no guarantee that the PDUs arrive in correct sequence, or even that they arrive at all. The solution is just as obvious – choose protocol mechanisms which are resilient to these phenomena. A typical example can be seen in the ISO Class 4 Transport Protocol, which is intended for use in these circumstances. This protocol makes use of 3-way handshake for connection establishment, and offers the possibility of using a large receive window during data transfer.

4.4.2 Point-to-point and Multi-peer

Generally speaking, the transformation between a multi-peer and a point-to-point ('two-peer') service is not so much a protocol question as a matter of efficiency. A point-to-point service is a special case of a multi-peer service, and protocols which make it possible to offer a service to several users at the same time can generally operate quite satisfactorily if there are only two users. If problems arise, it is usually because multi-peer services may involve considerable administrative overhead, which would be wasted in a situation where there are only two users. Some multi-peer services – for example, the connectionless-mode broadcast services offered by some local area networks – essentially cost nothing, and only require the presence of suitable addressing mechanisms, in order to be able to offer a point-to-point transmission service.

The transformation from a point-to-point to a multi-peer service, on the other hand, in general involves a good deal of new administration. There are several reasons for this. Firstly, the simple-minded serial realisation of a multi-peer service by using a point-to-point service to transmit sequentially to each of the other parties causes greater delays. This can be inconvenient in two ways:

- The system will have to wait, resources will have to be retained, and so on, for a long time.
- There is a greater risk of an error occurring before the transmission to all parties is completed.

Thus more efficient ways of *distributing* the message to the parties involved are worth looking for. What can be done here will depend on the *topology* of the communication network, which determines which parties can send directly to which others. Secondly, the protocol must take into account the possibility that the slaves operate at *different speeds*, so that any timeout periods must be set to suit the slowest of the slaves. And finally, the protocol may need to allow for the *failure* of one or more of the parties, while still performing correctly for the others. We shall discuss these problems and some solutions for them in more detail in Chapter 5.

4.4.3 Simplex and Duplex

It requires no special effort to offer a simplex data transfer service on the basis of a duplex underlying service. All you have to do (at least in principle) is not send data in both directions! In fact, all the data transfer protocols which we have looked at up to now have offered a *simplex* data transfer service, but have essentially been based on a duplex underlying service, since data-PDUs and acknowledgments flow in opposite directions. (To offer a duplex service, our protocols would need to be modified to carry data in both directions.)

To obtain slightly more formal control over the use of a duplex service, the standard technique is to use a so-called *token* mechanism. A token is in this context a conceptual object which gives its owner the right to perform certain functions – for example, to send data. If there is only one token, then there can only be one service user at a time who can send data, so the service essentially becomes a simplex service (if the token is permanently owned by one party) or a half-duplex service (if the token can be passed from one party to the other). More generally, tokens can be used to offer multiplexing so that a channel can be shared among a group of N users, of which only one has the right to send at any time. This technique is, for example, used in local area networks which are based on token ring technology [154, 171].

More complex use of tokens can also be relevant in certain types of system. A well-known example is the ISO OSI Connection-mode Session Service and its corresponding protocol [139, 140]. Here, the presence or absence of four tokens is agreed at the time when the connection is established. One of these is a Data Token. If present, this enables its current owner to send data, thus offering a half-duplex data transfer service. (Note: The Session Service is assumed to be based on the ISO Connection-mode Transport Service [137], which is always full duplex.) If the data token is absent, a full duplex data transfer service is offered. The other tokens, if present, are used to regulate the *control flow* in the service, enabling their owners to set (two sorts of) synchronisation points, and to refuse to release the connection, respectively.

4.5 Multiplexing and Splitting

4.5.1 Multiplexing

A service whose provider performs a *multiplexing* function internally combines the streams of messages which the users regard as being sent via several logical channels (for example, to different destinations) and sends them via a single logical or physical channel, after which it separates the streams again and directs them to their individual destinations. This reverse function is known as *de-multiplexing*. A figurative illustration of these concepts can be seen in Figure 4.20.

Conceptually, this makes no difference to the formal specification of the service as seen by the individual user. In practice it will usually reduce the *cost* of using the service, as the price of running a service is normally based on the number of channels which are kept open. Other things being equal, the utilisation of the channel will also be increased, which may likewise be expected to reduce the cost per user.

Technically speaking, channel multiplexing can be performed in a vast number of different ways, but from an analytical point of view only the so-called *time-division*

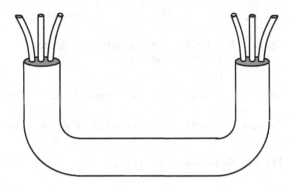

Fig. 4.20 A communication system with multiplexing.

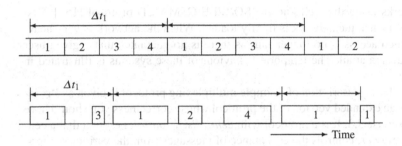

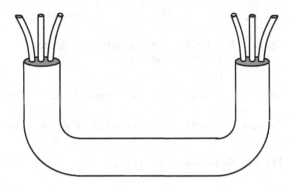

Fig. 4.21 Time-division multiplexing.
Above: Deterministic, classical TDM system for four users. Users have opportunities to send with fixed intervals, here illustrated for user 1.
Below: Non-deterministic multiplexing. The interval between successive opportunities to send varies randomly, usually as a function of the load on the system. The intervals for user 1 are illustrated in the figure

multiplexing (TDM) is of real interest. Here, each user of the multiplexed channel is offered access to the channel during certain periods of time, which may be long or short according to the type of system and the technique used. The access may be characterised in a number of ways, of which the most important are:

1. **Fairness.** If access is fair, all users who have something to send have an equally good chance of obtaining access to the channel. This has the corollary that a user who attempts to obtain access infinitely often will sooner or later obtain it.
2. **Determinism.** If access is deterministic, then the interval between successive offers of access by the service to a given user is a deterministic function of the load on the service. In extreme cases the 'function' may, of course, be a constant!

An example of a fair, deterministic system is a classical TDM system, in which time is divided into cycles of, say, N_{max} time frames of equal length, and each user is allocated one frame in each cycle. An example of a fair, non-deterministic system is a local area network with access to the medium controlled by a CSMA/CD algorithm

Protocol 9

$Sender \overset{\text{def}}{=} (SAPA[0]?x : \mathcal{M} \to right!(0,x) \to Sender$
$\quad\quad\quad [\![SAPA[1]?x : \mathcal{M} \to right!(1,x) \to Sender$

$\quad\quad\quad \vdots$

$\quad\quad\quad [\![SAPA[N-1]?x : \mathcal{M} \to right!(N-1,x) \to Sender)$

$Receiver \overset{\text{def}}{=} (left?(k : \mathbb{Z}_N, x : \mathcal{M}) \to SAPB[k]!x \to Receiver)$

Fig. 4.22 Simple multiplexing protocol.

(as in networks using the well-known ISO/IEEE CSMA/CD protocol [152][2] discussed below) when the network is lightly loaded. When the network is very heavily loaded, then access is no longer fair, as there is no guarantee that a given user will obtain access at all. The temporal behaviour of these systems is illustrated in Figure 4.21.

A process-based description of a simple multiplexing protocol is given as **Protocol 9**. This is an extended version of the protocol whose correctness you should have proved in Exercise 3.3. It is a protocol with *centralised control*, i.e. such that a central process, *Sender*, controls the acceptance of messages from the various senders. The messages (in domain $\mathcal{M}$) received via the access points $SAPA[0] \ldots SAPA[N-1]$ are all passed via the same channel to the protocol entity *Receiver*. To permit their separation, messages passed via $SAPA[k]$ are marked with a tag k. This tag identifies the logical channel connecting the sender and receiver. In practical systems, it might for example be an *address* identifying the intended recipient, or a *reference* identifying the conversation concerned; this latter possibility would make it possible to have several simultaneous conversations going between the same two parties.

With this definition, the sending users appear to be able to obtain access to the service at random times, and the capacity of the shared service is divided out among then in a statistical manner, as in a so-called *statistical multiplexer*. Unfortunately, the protocol as it stands is very impractical except in very special circumstances. If the user at $SAPA[k]$ obtains access to the channel, then the user at $SAPB[k]$ must be ready to accept the message, otherwise the whole system hangs up! For the protocol to work at all, the receiving users must be coordinated with the sending users in some way – which is not included in the protocol as defined here.

There are several cures for this disease. One is to insist on a strictly *synchronous* system, with the sending and receiving sides controlled by identical clocks, and where the SAPs are treated in cyclic order, for example as illustrated in **Protocol 10**. This is the classical TDM case mentioned above. Another technique is for the receiver to *poll* each of the potential senders in turn, as it becomes able to receive a message. This is particularly popular in the Data Link layer of the OSI model; a well-known example is the Normal Response mode of operation of the HDLC

---

[2] and its commercial implementations, such as Ethernet, thinwire Ethernet, Cheapernet etc.

Protocol 10

$Sender \overset{\text{def}}{=} S[0]$

$S[i : \mathbb{Z}_N] \overset{\text{def}}{=} (SAPA[i]?x : \mathscr{M} \rightarrow right!(i,x) \rightarrow S[succ(i)])$

$Receiver \overset{\text{def}}{=} (left?(k : \mathbb{Z}_N, x : \mathscr{M}) \rightarrow SAPB[k]!x \rightarrow Receiver)$

Fig. 4.23 Multiplexing protocol using classical TDM.
Here $succ(i)$ is assumed to have the value of $(i + 1) \bmod N$, where N is the number of senders whose traffic is to be multiplexed.

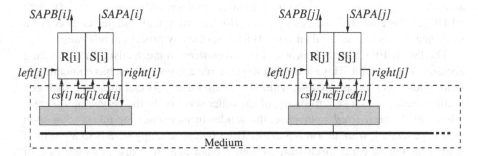

Fig. 4.24 Physical arrangement of senders and receivers in a cable-based CSMA/CD system.
Sender $S[i]$ and receiver $R[i]$ are bundled together and connected to the physical medium via a transceiver *(filled box)*. The *dashed box* delimits the system components which together provide the Physical layer service.

protocol [131]. Another important possibility is to introduce *independent flow control* via an acknowledgment and/or credit mechanism on each 'sub-channel', k, a technique commonly preferred in the middle OSI layers. This type of control is the subject of Exercise 4.9. These techniques both enable us to avoid loss of data and 'hang ups'. A fourth possibility is to discard data if the receiving user is not ready – a surprisingly common solution in practice. If this solution is adopted, the assumption is that the loss will be detected by the users and corrected by *their* protocol.

A typical example of a multiplexing protocol where data are discarded if the receiver is not ready to receive is the ISO/IEEE Carrier Sense Multiple Access (CSMA/CD) protocol mentioned above, and described by **Protocol 11**. This protocol illustrates a number of interesting principles. Firstly, we notice that the sender and receiver are each described by a set of N_{max} unsynchronised parallel processes. This reflects the idea that there are actually N_{max} independent senders and receivers *distributed* over a system. In a physical system which uses the CSMA/CD protocol, the senders and receivers are in fact distributed along a coaxial transmission cable, to which they are attached by so-called *transceivers*, which are circuits for sending and receiving physical signals. The medium together with the transceivers offers a Physical layer service for transmitting individual bits, and it is this service to which access is to be multiplexed.

Unlike the multiplexing protocols considered previously, the CSMA/CD protocol does not have any centralised form for control over access to the shared service – we say it is a multiplexing protocol with *distributed control*. Thus each of the senders $S[i]$ tries to decide for itself whether it is allowed to transmit via the shared medium. In **Protocol 11**, each sender is modelled by a pair of cooperating processes, $SUI[i]$ and $SMA[i]$. Process $SUI[i]$ describes the user interface for the sender and $SMA[i]$ the actual protocol for obtaining access to the medium. The user interface process accepts one message at a time from the user via a service access point (modelled by the channel $SAPA[i]$), passes it on to $SMA[i]$ via channel *right*, and then waits for a positive (ACK) or negative (ABORT) response. The medium access control process assembles the message, x, and the source and destination addresses, *src* and *dst*, into a PDU, in this context known as a *frame*, which to all intents and purposes is just a sequence of bits. These are then sent off as described by process *SendFrame*.

The ISO/IEEE CSMA/CD protocol uses a *contention* mechanism for controlling access to the medium. This means that in principle a sender which has something to send sends it as soon as possible, without waiting for any special message, such as a polling request or a token, from any of the other senders. In the very simplest case, often called *unrestricted contention*, the sender in fact sends the message as soon as it is generated, without waiting at all. The obvious analogy here is to a group of people having an eager discussion without a chairman. And just as in the case of such a discussion, if several senders send at the same time then all their transmissions will get garbled. We say that a *collision* has taken place. In a contention-based protocol, the attitude to this is that each sender will sooner or later discover that its transmission failed due to a collision, and will, after waiting a while, try to re-transmit its message. After a number of attempts, the message will presumably get through, unless of course the system is overloaded or one of the senders has a defect and never stops transmitting[3].

Contention protocols offer a form of what is known as *statistical multiplexing*, where the capacity of the multiplexed service is divided out among the senders in a non-deterministic manner. Their analysis (see, for example, Chapter 4 in [11]) is usually based on the theory of discrete-time Markov chains, which we shall not consider in detail here. In the case of unrestricted contention protocols, this analysis yields the intuitively obvious result that unless the generated traffic (number of new messages generated per unit time) is very moderate, then unrestricted contention is not a very effective method, leading to many collisions and long delays before a given message in fact gets through. Most modern contention protocols therefore require the senders to follow a more disciplined scheme of behaviour. One clear improvement is to insist that each sender listens to find out whether another sender is busy transmitting, before itself starting a transmission. If the medium is occupied, then the sender must wait until the medium becomes free. This is known as the *Carrier Sense Multiple Access (CSMA)* principle.

However, even if each sender waits for the medium to be free before starting to send, it is still possible for several senders to start at approximately the same time.

---

[3] Most of us have a colleague who can suffer from this defect during discussions, too.

Protocol 11

$Sender$ $\overset{\text{def}}{=} (S[1] \;|||\; S[2] \;|||\; \dots \;|||\; S[N_{max}])$

$S[i : \mathbb{N}_1]$ $\overset{\text{def}}{=} (SUI[i] \gg SMA[i])$

$SUI[i : \mathbb{N}_1]$ $\overset{\text{def}}{=} (SAPA[i]?(dst : \mathbb{N}_1, x : \mathcal{M}) \to right!(i, dst, x) \to$
$$(right?a : \{\text{ACK}\} \to S[i]$$
$$[\![right?a : \{\text{ABORT}\} \to S[i]))$$

$SMA[i : \mathbb{N}_1]$ $\overset{\text{def}}{=} (left?(src : \mathbb{N}_1, dst : \mathbb{N}_1, x : \mathcal{M}) \to nc[i] \to$
$$SendFrame[i, [\,], enframe(src, dst, x), 0])$$

$SendFrame[i : \mathbb{N}_1, sent, rest : \text{bit}^*, retry : \mathbb{N}_0]$
$\overset{\text{def}}{=} (\textbf{if } rest = [\,]$
   $\textbf{then } left!\text{ACK}$
   $\textbf{else } (right!(\text{hd } rest) \to SendFrame[i, sent\,\widehat{}\,(\text{hd } rest), \text{tl } rest, retry]$
   $[\![cd[i] \to SCD[i, \text{JAM}, sent\,\widehat{}\,rest, retry]))$

$SCD[i : \mathbb{N}_1, jam, f : \text{bit}^*, retry : \mathbb{N}_0]$
$\overset{\text{def}}{=} (\textbf{if } jam = [\,]$
   $\textbf{then } SRA[i, f, retry]$
   $\textbf{else } right!(\text{hd } jam) \to SCD[i, \text{tl } jam, f, retry])$

$SRA[i : \mathbb{N}_1, f : \text{bit}^*, retry : \mathbb{N}_0]$
$\overset{\text{def}}{=} (\textbf{if } retry < R_{max}$
   $\textbf{then } wait(rand(2^{retry}) \cdot t_0[i]) \to nc[i] \to$
   $$SendFrame[i, [\,], f, succ(retry)]$$
   $\textbf{else } left!\text{ABORT} \to SMA[i])$

$Receiver$ $\overset{\text{def}}{=} (R[1] \;|||\; R[2] \;|||\; \dots \;|||\; R[N_{max}])$

$R[i : \mathbb{N}_1]$ $\overset{\text{def}}{=} (SAPB[i]?s : \{\text{SETUP}\} \to GetFrame[i])$
$[\![cs[i] \to SkipFrame[i])$

$GetFrame[i : \mathbb{N}_1]$ $\overset{\text{def}}{=} (cs[i] \to left?b : \text{bit} \to AccFrame[i, \langle b \rangle]$
$[\![nc[i] \to GetFrame[i])$

$AccFrame[i : \mathbb{N}_1, f : \text{bit}^*]$
$\overset{\text{def}}{=} (cs[i] \to left?b : \text{bit} \to AccFrame[i, f\,\widehat{}\,\langle b \rangle]$
$[\![nc[i] \to (\textbf{if } dest(f) = i$
   $\textbf{then } SAPB[i]!deframe(f) \to R[i]$
   $\textbf{else } GetFrame[i]))$

$SkipFrame[i : \mathbb{N}_1]$ $\overset{\text{def}}{=} (cs[i] \to left?b : \text{bit} \to SkipFrame[i]$
$[\![nc[i] \to R[i])$

Fig. 4.25 CSMA/CD multiplexing protocol.

In particular, this can happen because in a real network the senders are separated by a finite distance, and the physical signals therefore take a finite time to propagate between them. Those senders which have not yet been reached by the transmitted signal continue to believe that the medium is free, and may therefore themselves start to transmit. This phenomenon is illustrated in Figure 4.26, which shows the progress of the signals in space and time for two senders who both have something to send. In the more effective CSMA/CD protocols, the CSMA mechanism is therefore supplemented by *Collision Detection* (hence the CD in the name), which leads to the

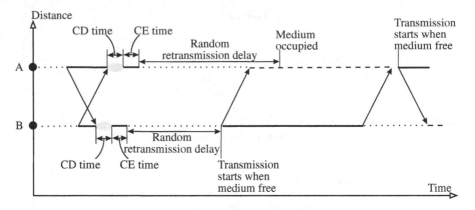

Fig. 4.26 Operation of the ISO/IEEE CSMA/CD Medium Access protocol.
For a given sender (A or B), *full lines* indicate periods during which the sender is transmitting, *dashed lines* periods during which it observes that another sender is transmitting, and *dotted lines* periods during which it detects no activity in the medium. The *skew arrows* indicate how the signals propagate along the medium.
CD time is the time required for collision detection. CE time is the time required for collision enforcement (jamming).

transmission being broken off as soon as possible, if the sender detects that another sender is transmitting at the same time as itself.

These mechanisms are described by the process *SendFrame*[$i, \ldots$] of **Protocol 11**. The progress of this process is controlled by two events, $nc[i]$ and $cd[i]$, which in reality are signals generated by the transceiver which joins the sender $S[i]$ to the medium. Event $nc[i]$, for No Carrier[4], indicates that signals transmitted by another sender are not currently passing through the medium under the sender in question. When $nc[i]$ occurs, transmission of the frame by $S[i]$ is allowed to start.

Likewise, $cd[i]$ indicates that the transceiver in system i has detected a *collision*. As discussed above, this happens if several senders independently react to *nc* signals from their respective transceivers, and begin to transmit a frame at about the same time. If $cd[i]$ occurs, transmission of the current frame is broken off as soon as possible, a standard bit sequence known as a jamming sequence is transmitted so that all parties are made aware that a collision has taken place (process *SCD*), and retransmission is attempted. If neither $nc[i]$ nor $cd[i]$ is present, another sender is busy, and *SendFrame*[$i, \ldots$] waits. The Physical layer is constructed in such a way that it is not possible for *both* $nc[i]$ and $cd[i]$ to occur at the same time.

Retransmission, described by process *SRA*[$i, f, retry$], is unusual in the CSMA/CD protocol because it follows a stochastic algorithm. Here we have to extend the notational conventions of CSP somewhat in order to describe what happens: the event *wait*(t) is assumed to correspond to a delay of t time units, and the function *rand*(d)

---

[4] In the actual ISO/IEEE CSMA/CD protocol, it is the *absence* of the signal *cs* (Carrier Sense) which indicates that the medium is free.

to a value chosen randomly in the interval $[0; d[$. Thus $SRA[i, f, retry]$ waits a time chosen randomly in the interval $[0; 2^{retry}[\cdot t_0[i]$, where $t_0[i]$ is some arbitrary time characteristic for $S[i]$. When this randomly chosen *retransmission delay* has passed, a new attempt to send the frame is made as soon as the medium again appears free. If this attempt also ends in a collision, a new waiting period starts, with the re-transmission delay chosen randomly from an interval twice as large as before. This procedure continues until either the whole frame is sent, in which case a positive response is sent back to the user interface, or until R_{max} attempts have been made, in which case a negative response is sent back.

The reason for doubling the average retransmission delay on each failed attempt merits some discussion. Random selection of the retransmission delay from some fixed interval, say $[0; t_0[$, makes it highly improbable that two senders who are in-volved in a collision will both try to retransmit at the same instant on their next attempts. However, when the system is very busy, there may be *many* senders trying to send frames. So even if a sender manages to avoid colliding with exactly the same sender as last time, it may collide with one of the others. Analysis of this situation (see for example Chapter 4 in [11]) shows that when the (new) traffic generated by the users exceeds a certain value, then the retransmissions themselves cause so many extra collisions that the throughput of the system actually begins to fall as the load of new traffic rises further. This leads to instability in the system, which can only be avoided by *reducing the rate of retransmission* as the load increases. Doubling the average retransmission delay for each failed attempt is a simple way of doing this. The technical term for this is *Binary Exponential Backoff (BEB)*; or, if the doubling process terminates after a certain maximum number of attempts, as in the case of the ISO/IEEE CSMA/CD protocol, *truncated BEB*.

The receiver processes, described by $R[i]$ are much simpler. These are controlled by the signals $cs[i]$, which indicates the presence of an arriving transmission, and $nc[i]$, which indicate the absence of such a transmission. These signals are mutually exclusive. An SDU is only accepted, and passed to the user via channel $SAPB[i]$, if the user has indicated by sending a SETUP message that it is willing to accept one. On receiving such a message, the receiver begins to accumulate bits from the Physical layer as soon as this is possible (indicated by signal $cs[i]$), and continues until the transmission stops. If the accumulated bits, f, represent a PDU intended for this receiver $(dest(f) = i)$, the contents of the PDU are passed on to the user; otherwise the receiver waits until a new transmission begins, and tries again. If the user has not indicated that it can accept an SDU, or if the PDU is intended for another destination, then it is ignored. As can be seen, this scheme of operation relies on all the receivers receiving all transmissions, and filtering off those which do not concern them. This is typical of multiplexing techniques based on distributed control.

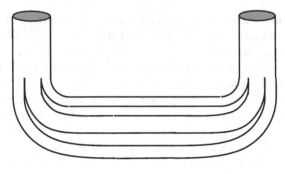

Fig. 4.27 A communication
system with splitting.

Protocol 12

$Sender \stackrel{\text{def}}{=} S[0]$

$S[i : \mathbb{Z}_N] \stackrel{\text{def}}{=} (SAPA?x : \mathcal{M} \rightarrow right[i]!x \rightarrow S[succ(i)])$

$Receiver \stackrel{\text{def}}{=} R[0]$

$R[i : \mathbb{Z}_N] \stackrel{\text{def}}{=} (left[i]?x : \mathcal{M} \rightarrow SAPB!x \rightarrow R[succ(i)])$

Fig. 4.28 Simple splitting protocol. Here $succ(i)$ is assumed to have the value of $(i+1) \bmod N$, where N is the number of channels among which the traffic is split.

4.5.2 Splitting

A service which offers *splitting* does the 'opposite' of one which offers multiplex-ing: It internally divides the messages to a single destination among several logical or physical channels, and *recombines* them at the destination to produce a single stream of messages to be passed to the service user. This is sometimes known as *striping* or *downward multiplexing*, while 'ordinary' multiplexing is known as *up-ward multiplexing*. Splitting is illustrated in Figure 4.27. As with multiplexing, split-ting makes no difference to the logical properties of the service, but in practice it is used to increase the *throughput* or the *reliability* available from the service. Splitting may also reduce the *costs* of providing a given service, since it may be significantly cheaper, for example, to buy (or hire) N pieces of equipment, each giving bandwidth B, than to buy (or hire) one piece of equipment providing bandwidth $N \cdot B$.

A simple example of a protocol for this purpose is given as **Protocol 12**. In this example, the channels of the underlying service are implicitly assumed to have the same capacity, and are used cyclically. This is often denoted *Round Robin (RR)* striping. RR striping makes it easy for the service to deliver the data in FIFO order, since the next SDU arrives in the PDU on the (cyclically) next channel. However, in practical systems it may also be important to provide *fair load sharing* among the channels, in the sense that (measured over a long period) all channels carry the same proportion of their capacity. Two simple strategies which ensure this are:

Protocol 13

Sender $\overset{\text{def}}{=} S[0,[q,0,0,\ldots,0]]$

$S[i : \mathbb{Z}_N, DC : \mathbb{Z}^*] \overset{\text{def}}{=} (SAPA?x : \mathcal{M} \to right[i]!x \to$
$$(\textbf{if } size(x) < DC(i)$$
$$\textbf{then } S[i, DC \dagger [i \mapsto DC(i) - size(x)]]$$
$$\textbf{else } S[succ(i), DC \dagger [i \mapsto DC(i) - size(x),$$
$$succ(i) \mapsto DC(succ(i)) + q]]))$$

Receiver $\overset{\text{def}}{=} R[0,[q,0,0,\ldots,0]]$

$R[i : \mathbb{Z}_N, DC : \mathbb{Z}^*] \overset{\text{def}}{=} (left[i]?x : \mathcal{M} \to SAPB!x \to$
$$(\textbf{if } size(x) < DC(i)$$
$$\textbf{then } R[i, DC \dagger [i \mapsto DC(i) - size(x)]]$$
$$\textbf{else } R[succ(i), DC \dagger [i \mapsto DC(i) - size(x),$$
$$succ(i) \mapsto DC(succ(i)) + q]]))$$

Fig. 4.29 Fair splitting protocol using SRR strategy. Here q is the size of the data quantum added to each channel in each round, and $size(x)$ is the size of the message x.

Random Stripe Selection (RSS): Random selection of which channel to use next ensures a statistically fair distribution of load on the N channels.

Shortest Queue First (SQF): A queue is maintained for each channel, and the next SDU supplied by the user is added to the shortest queue. Large SDUs take a long time to transmit, and so cause a queue to build up on the relevant channel, so this strategy maintains equal loads on all channels in a self-regulating fashion.

Unfortunately, neither of these strategies maintains FIFO ordering, so if sequence preservation is required, then it will be necessary to add sequence numbers to the PDUs and to introduce (possibly substantial) buffering in the receiver. In some types of network, such as ATM networks where PDUs have a fixed size and cannot be expanded to contain additional PCI, this is not acceptable.

To avoid this problem, Adiseshu et al. proposed the *Surplus Round Robin (SRR)* strategy [1], based on a *fair queuing* algorithm known as *Deficit Round Robin* [116]. The basic SRR protocol is shown as **Protocol 13** in Figure 4.29. In this protocol, the state of the sender and receiver are described by the number of the channel currently in use, i, and the free capacities of the N channels, DC. In each round of operation, during which the sender cycles through all N channels, the free capacity of every channel is increased by a *data quantum*, q, corresponding to the desired average load. It is assumed that q is at least as big as the size of the largest PDUs. When a PDU of size s is sent on a given channel, the free capacity of that channel is reduced by s. If the free capacity of the channel is still positive, the next PDU is sent on the same channel; otherwise, the next channel is used. The receiver follows the same algorithm, so as to maintain correct sequencing in the final data stream produced at SAPB.

As can be seen, this strategy requires no PCI to be added to the PDUs, and works well as long as no data-PDUs get lost. To avoid loss of ordering due to loss of a

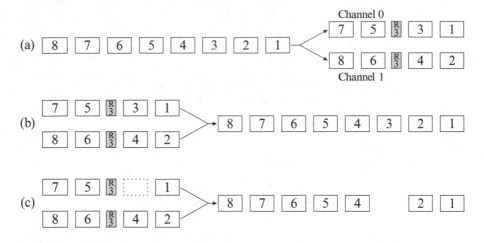

Fig. 4.30 Resynchronisation after a lost data-PDU in the SRR protocol.
(a) Normal transmission. The stream of PDUs is divided among the two channels. For illustration purposes, the PDUs are all assumed to be the same size. The mark-PDUs are shaded.
(b) Normal receipt. The incoming streams of data-PDUs on the two channels are merged and the mark-PDUs are discarded.
(c) Resynchronisation after data loss. When data-PDU no. 3 is lost, the receiver receives the mark-PDU announcing the start of round 3 on channel 0 during round 2. Instead of delivering the next data-PDU (no. 5) to arrive on channel 0, it proceeds directly to channel 1.

data-PDU on one of the channels, synchronisation marks (mark-PDUs) are inserted on all channels at regular intervals, for example at the start of every m rounds of operation. Each mark-PDU contains the number of the current round. If a mark-PDU announcing round $r + 1$ arrives on channel i when the receiver expects a PDU from round r, then a data-PDU on that channel must have been lost, and the next data-PDU on that channel is therefore not delivered until the following round of transmission. This technique, illustrated in Figure 4.30, is sometimes called *implicit numbering*, as the sequence numbers needed to ensure synchronisation are sent separately from the data-PDUs. Note that the technique does not include retransmission, so missing data-PDUs are never recovered. Obviously, this is only suitable for providing a connectionless-mode service.

4.6 Segmentation and Reassembly

When a service provider uses the *segmentation* function, the sending protocol entity divides the SDUs passed to it by the service user into smaller portions for transmission via the underlying service. The receiving protocol entity then performs the *reassembly* function, to produce the SDUs originally generated by the sending user, before these are passed to the receiving user, as illustrated in Figure 4.31. All this is

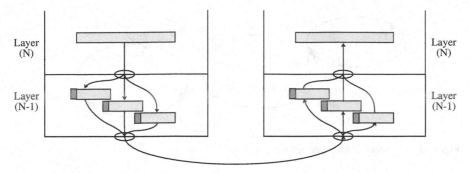

Fig. 4.31 A system with segmentation and reassembly. An $(N-1)$-SDU passed down from layer N is divided into three $(N-1)$-PDUs, each with their own $(N-1)$-PCI *(dark shading)*. On receipt by the receiving system, the PCI is removed, and the data are reassembled to form the received $(N-1)$-SDU which is passed to the receiving user in layer N.

invisible to the users of the service, whose logical properties are unaffected. These functions are essentially practical tricks to avoid having to send very long PDUs. There are three reasons why we might want to do this:

1. Long PDUs offer a greater risk of the PDU being struck by errors, since error probabilities are usually more or less proportional to the length. If errors do occur, long PDUs also give a greater overhead on retransmission.
2. The protocol may implement a form of multiplexing where the transmission of long PDUs on one of the multiplexed channels would prevent transmission on the other channels.
3. The underlying service via which the PDUs are transmitted may have restrictions on the size of SDU *it* is willing to accept. (Remember that PDUs in one layer appear as SDUs to the layer underneath!) This is because the underlying service must buffer each SDU until all of it has been passed to the remote service user, and there will be practical limits on how much buffer space is available.

The modifications to **Protocols 1** to **6** in order to permit segmentation and reassembly are basically very simple. When the sending protocol entity accepts an SDU via *SAPA*, it divides it into segments, before sending each of them in a numbered PDU. The receiver checks the incoming PDUs for sequence preservation as usual, but does not pass their SDU content to the user via *SAPB* until a whole SDU has arrived. For this to work satisfactorily, each PDU must contain an indication of whether it is the *last* PDU in an SDU. This information is part of the PCI.

A more complicated situation arises when segmentation has to be performed over a network which is composed of a number of interconnected sub-networks, as in Figure 4.32. This is, for example, the case in so-called *internet protocols*, such as the ISO connectionless internet protocol [142] and the Internet/DoD IP protocol [210], where the aim is to transfer data across such a composite network. In general, as illustrated in the figure, the individual sub-networks may have different restrictions on maximum PDU size.

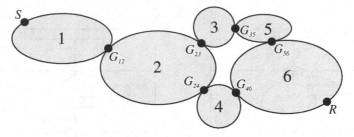

Fig. 4.32 A system of interconnected sub-networks.

The figure shows six sub-networks which in the examples in the text are assumed to permit the following maximum PDU sizes (in octets):

Sub-network	Max. PDU size	Sub-network	Max. PDU size
1	1536	2	512
3	1000	4	256
5	1450	6	1784

Systems G_{ij} are *gateways* on the boundaries between sub-networks.

Two strategies are then available for segmentation. In the first of these, the original sender must segment all SDUs to the *smallest maximum size* of PDU permitted by the sub-networks through which they may pass. In general this means either that the original sender must know the route which the PDUs will follow through the network, or that all SDUs must be segmented into the smallest size permitted by *any* of the sub-networks in the network. In the network in Figure 4.32, this would for example mean that an SDU to be sent from S to R would be segmented into PDUs not bigger than 512 octets if S knew that all PDUs to R would be routed via sub-networks 1, 2, 3, 5 and 6 (in this instance not the most direct route!), or into PDUs not bigger than 256 octets if the route were unknown.

In the alternative strategy, PDUs are divided up into even smaller pieces when they reach the boundary of a sub-network which only permits smaller PDUs to be transmitted. This subdivision takes place in the so-called *gateway* systems, which lie on the boundaries and are responsible for transferring data between sub-networks with possibly different properties. This strategy, known as *resegmentation*, means that the original sender only needs to know the requirements of the sub-network to which it is itself connected. But it carries the risk that the original SDUs may be fragmented into many small pieces if they pass through a series of sub-networks which permit smaller and smaller maximum PDU sizes, unless these sizes are convenient multiples of one another. Suppose, for example, that an SDU of size 2000 octets is to be sent from S to R, and that the PCI added to each segment of the SDU is always of length 64 octets. Then the SDU would be fragmented as shown in Figure 4.33(a), if it were sent via sub-networks 1, 2, 3, 5 and 6 using this strategy.

(a)

S	Sub-network					R
	1	2	3	5	6	
2000	1472	936	448	448	448	2000
			448	448	448	
			40	40	40	
		536	448	448	448	
			88	88	88	
		528	448	448	448	
			80	80	80	

Fig. 4.33 Fragmentation of SDUs due to resegmentation. The figure shows the sizes in octets of the fragments of an SDU of size 2000 octets transmitted from R to S via sub-networks 1, 2, 3, 5 and 6 of Figure 4.32.
(a) Simple resegmentation on passing to a network where smaller PDUs are required.
(b) Resegmentation combined with partial reassembly on passing to a network where larger PDUs are permitted.

(b)

S	Sub-network					R
	1	2	3	5	6	
2000	1472	936	448	1384	1384	2000
			448			
			40			
		536	448			
			88	616	616	
		528	448			
			80			

Note that sub-network 3 could carry the 2000 octets of SDU in five PDUs (four with the maximum segment size of 448 octets and one with 208 octets), but that seven are in fact used. A common way to counteract this fragmentation is to perform partial or complete reassembly on reaching the boundary of each sub-network which again permits larger SDUs to be transmitted. This can be done in several ways. One simple style of partial reassembly is illustrated in Figure 4.33(b): as many complete PDUs as possible are reassembled into a single PDU on the boundary between sub-networks 3 and 5 (and in principle again between 5 and 6).

Although this technique alleviates the problem, fragmentation may still occur if the sizes of the PDUs and SDUs do not 'match' one another. Minimal fragmentation can only be achieved by completely reassembling the original SDU on each sub-network boundary, and then re-segmenting it for further transmission. This can easily lead to much duplication of effort, with each SDU being segmented and re-assembled several times as it passes through the network. Moreover, for this to be possible at all, all the gateways between networks must be capable of reassembling the entire original SDU. From the very nature of things, this is rather unlikely.

In systems with dynamic buffer allocation, reassembly offers an interesting possibility for deadlock. Imagine a situation where we have N buffers allocated between M logical channels (with $N > M$). Then suppose we receive N PDUs, *none of which makes it possible to pass a SDU to a user.* Perhaps we are missing exactly the last PDU needed to complete one of the SDUs. But now we have nowhere to put it if it arrives. We are obliged to discard it, and the system is deadlocked. Not very surprisingly, this is known as *reassembly deadlock*. The only way out is to throw away one of the incompletely reassembled SDUs, so as to release some buffers; however, the PDUs in these buffers will normally have been acknowledged, so evidently we can only escape from the deadlock by losing data.

Prioritised Queue.

$$PQueue \quad \stackrel{\text{def}}{=} \quad (left?x : LD \rightarrow (PQueue \gg Lcell[x])$$
$$[\![left?y : HD \rightarrow (PQueue \gg Hcell[y]))$$

$$Lcell[x : LD] \quad \stackrel{\text{def}}{=} \quad (right!x \rightarrow B1$$
$$[\![left!x \rightarrow left?y : HD \rightarrow Hcell[y])$$

$$Hcell[y : HD] \quad \stackrel{\text{def}}{=} \quad (right!y \rightarrow B1$$
$$[\![right?x : LD \rightarrow right!y \rightarrow Lcell[x])$$

$$B1 \quad \stackrel{\text{def}}{=} \quad (left?x : LD \rightarrow Lcell[x]$$
$$[\![left?y : HD \rightarrow Hcell[y])$$

Fig. 4.34 A prioritised queue with two levels of priority. Here *LD* is the domain of low priority messages, and *HD* the domain of high priority messages.

Since *recovery* from reassembly deadlock in general causes data loss, it is normally preferable to use a strategy of deadlock *avoidance*. It is exactly for this reason that many services limit the size of SDUs which they are willing to handle. If we know what this maximum size is, then we can choose our buffer allocation algorithm so that it will always give each channel at least this maximum size, or else nothing at all. Allocation of buffer amounts between zero and the maximum SDU size is dangerous and should be avoided. Better to have no buffers at all – then at least we can refuse incoming SDUs from the very first PDU in the SDU, so that we do not risk having to discard acknowledged PDUs later.

4.7 Prioritisation

The idea of having a prioritised service is to allow some data streams to be dealt with more quickly than others. In most of our previous examples of protocols, this has been a 'non-problem', since our process descriptions have implicitly assumed that we only have one stream of data passing along our logical channel, and that all PDUs can be accepted by the underlying service (according to our convention, at channel *left*) without having to be buffered by the protocol entity. We have therefore no concept of *waiting to send*, and therefore no concept of priority. Likewise, at the receiver, we only consider one stream of data, and assume that the receiving user is ready to accept whatever comes. To introduce the idea of waiting, we need to introduce a *queue* between the service access points for the user and the underlying service.

Some examples of simple, non-prioritised queues (disguised as sequential, sequence-preserving buffers) have been given in Chapter 2. A two-level priority queue, as for example would be required for modelling the OSI concepts of Normal and Expedited data, is shown in Figure 4.34. For each value accepted at the *left* (input) channel of the queue, a new queue element is created, which behaves like *Lcell* if the value is in *LD*, the domain of low priority messages, and like *Hcell* if the value is in *HD*, the domain of high priority messages. If an *Hcell* process is on the left of an *Lcell* process, they swap contents, and the *Hcell* process continues like an *Lcell* process and *vice versa*. Thus the high priority messages work their way forward in the queue.

Further reading

The protocol mechanisms described in this chapter are the ones defined in an abstract manner in the OSI Basic Reference Model [133], and further information can be sought in the same references as given in Chapter 3. At this stage, you might also like to look at some real protocols, in order to find out for yourself what mechanisms are used. A good place to start is the ISO OSI Transport Protocol [138], which (since it includes 5 variants) uses a particularly large selection of mechanisms: Start with the short introduction given in Chapter 9 of this book, and go on to the actual text of the ISO standard. Other ISO OSI protocols are described in references [131]– [205].

ISO is, of course, by no means the only source of information about protocols. Telecommunication systems run by Telecom operators follow ITU-T (formerly CCITT) recommendations (ITU terminology for 'standards'). Those in the so-called *X-series* are particularly relevant to this chapter. This series includes the well-known X.25 network protocol [129], and the series from X.211 to X.229, which are technically identical to some of the ISO OSI protocols. Yet other sources of common protocols are the Internet community, and the UNIX™ community, who make extensive use of Remote Procedure Call (RPC, or Client-Server) protocols for performing operations remotely in a network. Appendix B gives an overview of the standardisation situation. There are also a considerable number of 'industry standards', promoted by individual companies or consortia. Many of these have general interest and turn into international standards if they achieve sufficiently broad acceptance.

Another line of approach is the historical one. For example, you might like to pursue all the references to the Alternating Bit Protocol in the literature, starting with the ones given in connection with **Protocol 5**. This will lead you into the area of other proof techniques for protocols, as well as illustrating how new mechanisms develop as time goes by.

Finally, you might like to investigate quantitative properties of some protocols, such as their throughput and delay in the presence of varying loads of traffic. Generally speaking, this requires a knowledge of queueing theory and the theory of stochastic processes. This is not a subject which we pay more than passing attention to in this book. However, some protocols, especially multiplexing protocols, have been the subject of intensive investigation from this point of view. Good discussions of the general theory required are found in [73], while [11] relates the theory more explicitly to the analysis of network protocols.

Exercises

4.1. A point-to-point protocol uses a (16,12) cyclic block code to detect transmission errors. The code uses the generator polynomial $g(x) = x^4 + x^3 + x^2 + 1$. Two blocks of data:

    1011011100011000
    1000001110001101

(where the leftmost bit in each block corresponds to the highest power of x) arrive at the receiver. Do these blocks contain errors which are detectable by this code?

4.2. The time taken to send an SDU of size L bits between two systems physically separated by a data link of length D, through which data can be passed at B bits/unit time, can be expressed as:

$$t_s = A + D/C + L/B$$

where A is the time required to obtain access to the data link via the service in use, including all delays before transmission starts, and C is the signal velocity in the medium used to provide the data link.

How large a send window size is required to maintain an average data flow of 2Mbit/s in the cases where:

1. The data link is a geosynchronous satellite data link, offering a transmission rate of 10Mbit/s, the average access time is 100ms, and the SDUs are of size 1000 bits.
2. The data link is a 140Mbit/s fiber optic point-to-point link over a distance of 100m, the average access time is 10μs, and the SDUs are of size 100 bits.

Assume that the link is error-free, and ignore (or make an estimate of) the time taken in the receiving system to produce an acknowledgment.

4.3. Prove that the simple polling protocol given as **Protocol 2** satisfies the specification $SAPB \leq SAPA$ if used over a medium which may corrupt (but not lose or duplicate) data-PDUs, and which always delivers polling requests without loss or corruption. Then discuss the ways in which the protocol can fail.

4.4. Give a description in the form of a set of interacting CSP processes of a polling protocol with timeout analogous to **Protocol 4**. (Remember that in a polling protocol, it is the receiver which has to be controlled by the timeout mechanism.) Then analyse your proposal to see how it behaves if the timeout period is too short, so that the receiver polls the sender again when the sender has already sent a PDU in response to the previous POLL-PDU.

4.5. In **Protocol 6**, the process QA, which deals with tidying up acknowledged PDUs contains a test $(ack_s < a < n_s)$. What would be the effect on the protocol if the first $<$ were changed to $\leq$? What if the second $<$ were changed to $\leq$?

4.6. Discuss the nature of the processes *Timer* which are used in **Protocol 3** and in **Protocol 6**. Are they realistic descriptions of what you intuitively understand by a timer for controlling a timeout mechanism? If not, can you make them more realistic? (Explain what you mean by 'realistic'!)

4.7. Prove that the Alternating Bit Protocol given as **Protocol 5** satisfies the specification *right* $\leq$ *left* if it is used over a service $\mathscr{S}$ which may corrupt or lose data or acknowledgments.

Note: This is quite a challenging problem. You may find it easiest first to use process algebra to reduce the process *Sender* to:

$$
\begin{aligned}
&Sender \;\overset{\text{def}}{=} S'[1] \\
&S'[n : \mathbb{Z}_2] \overset{\text{def}}{=} (SAPA?x : \mathcal{M} \to QB[n,x]) \\
&QB[n : \mathbb{Z}_2, x : \mathcal{M}] \\
&\qquad \overset{\text{def}}{=} (right!(n,x) \to \; (QB[n,x] \\
&\qquad\qquad\qquad\qquad\qquad \sqcap (QB[n,x] \\
&\qquad\qquad\qquad\qquad\qquad [\![right?a : \mathbb{Z}_2 \to \\
&\qquad\qquad\qquad\qquad\qquad\qquad (\textbf{if } (a = n) \textbf{ then } S'[n \oplus 1] \textbf{ else } QB[n,x]) \\
&\qquad\qquad\qquad\qquad\qquad [\![right?a : E \to QB[n,x]) \,) \,)
\end{aligned}
$$

where $\oplus$ represents addition *modulo 2*. Then introduce an appropriate filter function, in order to prove the desired result.

4.8. Develop a more fault-tolerant version of **Protocol 7** on the lines suggested in the main text. It should be resilient to loss and corruption of PDUs (but not necessarily floating corpses). Consider carefully what a good strategy might be for informing the user of the service what has happened if there are errors, and build your strategy into the protocol.

4.9. Develop a CSP process description of a protocol system in which **Protocol 9** has been modified to give individual flow control on each sub-channel. (Concentrate on the problem as given – don't make things complicated by introducing timeout or other error control facilities!)

4.10. A token ring local area network essentially offers a service to all its users by use of a multiplexing protocol. The protocol is controlled by passing a token between the protocol entities. At any given moment, only the entity which has the token has permission to transmit. At the end of its transmission (or if it has nothing to transmit), it passes the token to the next protocol entity in cyclic order round the (physical) ring. Develop a CSP process description of a simple token ring of this type.

First, try to solve this problem without considering whether the receiving entity actually can receive the data and pass them to its associated user (i.e. under the same assumptions as lie behind **Protocol 9**). Then, when you feel you have managed this, add flow control, so that the current receiving entity can send a positive acknowledgment back to the entity which is currently sending, if it could accept the PDU, and can send a negative acknowledgment if the PDU was refused. Ignore retransmission – it is not normally used in token rings.

Chapter 5
Multi-peer Consensus

"Behold how good and joyful a thing it is,
brethren, to dwell together in unity!"
Psalm 133, Book of Common Prayer.

In a multi-peer service, a number of special complications arise from the need to guarantee that *all* active users of the service have the same picture of their common global state. The general problem is usually said to be one of reaching *agreement* or *consensus* on a value or set of values. This can arise in a number of somewhat different ways:

1. One party may need to distribute a given value or set of values to a group of others. This is the problem of achieving a *multicast* or *broadcast* service already touched upon in previous chapters.
2. Several parties may need to agree on which one of them is to take over a particular rôle, say as the master or supervisory agent, in a subsequent protocol. This is generally known as *election*.
3. Several parties may need to agree on an action to take, for example whether to save some changes to a database or not. This is generally known as the problem of deciding on *commitment* to the action.
4. Several parties may need to agree on a value for some common variable, such as the time of day.

Obtaining consensus among several parties is particularly difficult because the individual parties may behave in different ways, offer different values or even fail completely during the course of trying to reach agreement. As we shall see, this makes multi-peer protocols for these purposes comparatively complicated.

Because any of the above forms of consensus will require some sort of exchange of messages between $n > 2$ parties, the combinatorial nature of the task also merits attention. Simple strategies, such as directly sending messages to all the other participants, require a network topology which is a complete graph. Exchange of messages between all participants requires $O(n^2)$ messages. It is therefore important to analyse multi-peer protocols in order to discover their inherent complexity, and to attempt to reduce these requirements by the design of more elegant protocols.

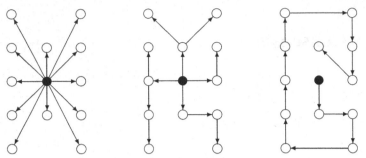

Fig. 5.1 Broadcast strategies.   **Left:** Rooted bush in a fully connected network; **Centre:** Spanning tree; **Right:** Degenerate tree (chain)

5.1 Reliable Broadcasts

The problem with broadcasting (which in what follows we shall use as a general term, thus including multicasting) is to make it *reliable* in the presence of faults, so that at least all correctly functioning members of the invoked group receive the message. Many simple systems (in particular local area networks), provide a broadcast service which only works correctly if the members of the invoked group in fact are unoccupied with other activities. The broadcast fails to reach a member if, for example:

- Its buffer for receiving messages is full,
- Its physical interface to the network fails to respond to the arrival of the message,
- In a contention network, an undetected collision occurs.

In CSMA/CD-type networks, the sender would be unaware that these faults had occurred.

If the underlying service is a point-to-point one, the broadcast must, as previously mentioned, be simulated by a series of transmissions to the intended recipients. If the network is fully connected, this is simple: the originator sends directly to each member of the invoked group in turn. In more restricted topologies (and indeed for efficiency reasons in a fully connected network), it will usually be necessary to use a strategy in which the message is sent down the branches of a more general spanning tree for the network, with the originator at the root. In extreme cases, this tree may reduce to a chain passing through all the destination nodes in turn. These cases are illustrated in Figure 5.1. Note that with a tree of depth > 1, failure of a node will require the other nodes to take action so that successors to the failed node in the tree still receive the message. Essentially this requires the reconfiguration of the spanning tree. All successful protocols for reliable broadcast allow for this.

The protocol which we shall consider in detail is due to Schneider, Gries and Schlichting [112], and is presented in Figure 5.2 as **Protocol 14**. The protocol is intended to provide a reliable broadcast, in the sense that if any functioning process receives a copy of message m then all functioning processes receive a copy of message m, under the following assumptions:

1. The underlying communication system is error-free and sequence preserving.
2. Any process can send a message to any other process which has not failed.
3. Processes which fail cease to do anything. This is known as the *fail-stop* failure mode.
4. When a process fails, the functioning processes will sooner or later get to know about this failure.

Following the discussion in the previous chapter, we must suppose that the first assumption is reasonable for all practical purposes. The second assumption implies that the topology of the communication network is such that communication can be maintained even if some of the nodes fail. If we postulate, for the sake of example, that up to t nodes may fail, then the network must provide at least $t + 1$ direct or indirect connections between each pair of processes. The third assumption is perhaps a simplification; we shall return to more complicated modes of failure later in this chapter. Finally, the fourth assumption is unavoidable if we are to be able to react to the failure of a process.

In **Protocol 14**, the process B describes the originator, and $R[i,\dots]$ the i'th receiver. A receiver can play two *rôles*, which in the figure are indicated by the value of its parameter *role*: If *role* = i, the receiver plays its normal rôle, while if *role* = b, where $b \neq i$ identifies the current originator, then the receiver has taken over the rôle of originator for the current broadcast, as a result of being told that B has failed.

In this protocol, the originator is assumed to be connected to its associated service user through the channel *SAPA*, and to the underlying service via the set of $n - 1$ channels *right*[i], where $i \in \{1,\dots,n\}$. For simplicity, we denote the set $\{1,\dots,n\}$ by *NS*. Each of the $n - 1$ receivers is likewise connected to the underlying service via a channel *left*[i], in such a way that messages passing through *right*[i] reach *left*[i] and vice-versa. How the service in fact connects the channels up to one another is, as indicated above, unimportant here.

In **Protocol 14**, notations of the form $\coprod_{i \in D} right[i]!x \to P$ are used as shorthand for the process which makes multiple offers of output via the channels *right*[i] for all $i \in D$, and then proceeds as process P. Likewise, $right[i \in D]?a : \mathcal{M} \to P$ is used as shorthand for the process which accepts input of a value in the domain $\mathcal{M}$ on *any* of the channels *right*[i] for $i \in D$, and then proceeds as process P.

The processes use a number of set-valued arguments to describe the progress of the broadcast:

sendto The set of processes to which the current message has yet to be sent.

ackfrom The set of processes from which acknowledgments for the current message are being awaited.

ackto The set of participating processes that all sent the current message, and to which acknowledgments must be returned. Note that the originator does not have any such processes, so this argument is not required. On the other hand, for the receivers, there can be several processes in this set if a failure occurs, since the process which takes over the function of the failed process will send the latest message again to all the failed process' successors.

Protocol 14

$B[b:NS,n:\mathbb{N}_0]$
$\qquad \overset{\text{def}}{=} (SAPA?x:\mathcal{M} \rightarrow$
$\qquad\qquad \coprod_{j \in sset(b)} right[j]!(x,succ(n),b) \rightarrow S[b,\{\},sset(b),x,succ(n),b])$
$S[b:NS,sendto,ackfrom:NS\text{-set},x:\mathcal{M},n:\mathbb{N}_0,s:NS]$
$\qquad \overset{\text{def}}{=} (left[k \in NS]?(n':\mathbb{N}_0,s':NS) \rightarrow$
$\qquad\qquad (\textbf{if } n'=n$
$\qquad\qquad \textbf{then } (\textbf{if } ackfrom = \{s'\}$
$\qquad\qquad\qquad \textbf{then } B[b,n]$
$\qquad\qquad\qquad \textbf{else } S[b,sendto,ackfrom - \{s'\},x,n,s])$
$\qquad\qquad \textbf{else } S[b,sendto,ackfrom,x,n,s])$
$\qquad \| left[k \in NS]?f:NS \rightarrow$
$\qquad\qquad (\textbf{if } f \in ackfrom$
$\qquad\qquad \textbf{then } \coprod_{j \in sset(f)} right[j]!(x,n,s) \rightarrow$
$\qquad\qquad\qquad\qquad\qquad\qquad S[b,\{\},ackfrom - \{f\} \cup sset(f),x,n,s]$
$\qquad\qquad \textbf{else } S[b,sendto,ackfrom,x,n,s]))$

$R[i,b,role:NS,sendto,ackfrom,ackto:NS\text{-set},x:\mathcal{M},n:\mathbb{N}_0,s:NS]$
$\qquad \overset{\text{def}}{=} (left[k \in NS]?(x':\mathcal{M},n':\mathbb{N}_0,s':NS) \rightarrow$
$\qquad\qquad (\textbf{if } n' < n$
$\qquad\qquad \textbf{then } right[k]!(n',s') \rightarrow R[i,b,role,sendto,ackfrom,ackto,x,n,s]$
$\qquad\qquad \textbf{elseif } n' = n$
$\qquad\qquad \textbf{then } (\textbf{if } role = b \vee (sendto = \{\} \wedge ackfrom = \{\})$
$\qquad\qquad\qquad \textbf{then } right[s']!(n,s) \rightarrow R[i,b,role,sendto,ackfrom,ackto,x,n,s]$
$\qquad\qquad\qquad \textbf{else } R[i,b,role,sendto,ackfrom,ackto,x,n,s])$
$\qquad\qquad \textbf{else } \coprod_{j \in ackto} right[j]!(n,s) \rightarrow SAPB[i]!x' \rightarrow$
$\qquad\qquad\qquad\qquad\qquad \coprod_{j \in sset(i)} right[j]!(x',n',s') \rightarrow$
$\qquad\qquad\qquad\qquad\qquad\qquad\qquad R[i,b,i,\{\},sset(i),\{s'\},x',n',s'])$
$\qquad \| left[k \in NS]?(n':\mathbb{N}_0,s':NS) \rightarrow$
$\qquad\qquad (\textbf{if } n' = n$
$\qquad\qquad \textbf{then } (\textbf{if } ackto \neq \{\} \wedge (role = b \vee (sendto = \{\} \wedge ackfrom = \{s'\}))$
$\qquad\qquad\qquad \textbf{then } \coprod_{j \in ackto} right[j]!(n,s) \rightarrow$
$\qquad\qquad\qquad\qquad\qquad\qquad R[i,b,role,sendto,ackfrom - \{s'\},\{\},x,n,s]$
$\qquad\qquad\qquad \textbf{else } R[i,b,role,sendto,ackfrom - \{s'\},ackto,x,n,s])$
$\qquad\qquad \textbf{else } R[i,b,role,sendto,ackfrom,ackto,x,n,s])$
$\qquad \| left[k \in NS]?f:NS \rightarrow$
$\qquad\qquad (\textbf{if } f \in ackfrom$
$\qquad\qquad \textbf{then } \coprod_{j \in sset(f)} right[j]!(x,n,s) \rightarrow$
$\qquad\qquad\qquad\qquad\qquad R[i,b,role,\{\},ackfrom - \{f\} \cup sset(f),ackto,x,n,s]$
$\qquad\qquad \textbf{elseif } f = b \wedge role \neq b \wedge sendto = \{\} \wedge ackfrom = \{\}$
$\qquad\qquad \textbf{then } \coprod_{j \in sset(f)} right[j]!(x,n,s) \rightarrow$
$\qquad\qquad\qquad\qquad\qquad R[i,b,b,\{\},ackfrom - \{f\} \cup sset(f),ackto,x,n,s]$
$\qquad\qquad \textbf{else } R[i,b,role,sendto,ackfrom,ackto,x,n,s]))$

Fig. 5.2 Fault-tolerant broadcast protocol

The current message is described by the arguments x, which is the 'text' of the message, n, the sequence number, and s, the source of the message.

The originator, described by B, is very simple to understand. On receiving a message from a user (assumed attached via channel $SAPA$), it sends it to all its successors in the tree – the function $sset(b)$ is assumed to give the set of identifiers of these successors, as illustrated in Figure 5.3 – and awaits all their acknowledgments. This waiting is described by process S, which has two possible types of initial event. Firstly,

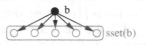

Fig. 5.3 The successor nodes to b in the tree of processes

it may receive an *acknowledgment*, (n', s') for message number n' from process s'. If n' is the sequence number of the current broadcast, then s' is removed from the set of processes from which acknowledgments are being awaited. Acknowledgments for anything except the current broadcast are ignored. When all the acknowledgments have been received, *ackfrom* becomes empty, and the originator goes back to behaving like process B, where it can again accept a new message from the user.

Secondly, the originator (in process S) may receive information that a *failure* has occurred in process f. If f identifies one of the processes from which the receiver expects an acknowledgment, the receiver must take over the function of f. Just in case f's successors have never received the message (the exact time of f's 'death' is unknown), the receiver therefore sends the current message to all of them again, and expects them to acknowledge it. This is illustrated in Figure 5.4.

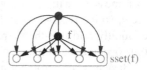

Fig. 5.4 Reaction to failure in node f in the tree of processes

The receivers are somewhat more complicated. The differences arise for two reasons:

1. The receivers can receive *messages* from the other receivers. This means that they have to keep track of a set *ackto* of processes to which they have to send acknowledgments.
2. The receivers not only have to react to failure of arbitrary receivers, but also to failure of the originator. If the originator fails, they must take on a special rôle.

For the receivers, there are therefore three initial events which may occur. Firstly, the receiver may receive a *message*, (x', n', s'). If the sequence number, n' is 'before' the number of the current message, then an acknowledgment is sent at once. If the number is the same, then the message is a repeat, and must have been sent out as a reaction to a failure. The receiver must not send the acknowledgment for this until it has actually completed sending the current message to all its successors in the tree and has successfully received their acknowledgments. So an acknowledgment is only sent if this condition is already satisfied. Finally, if the number is 'after' the number of the current message, the incoming message must be from a new broadcast; the receiver will first complete any outstanding acknowledgments for the current message, and then go on to distribute the new message to its successors in the tree.

Secondly, the receiver may receive an *acknowledgment*, (n', s'), for the message with number n' sent to process s'. If this completes all the acknowledgments expected for the current message, n, then the receiver will in turn send acknowledgments to all those processes from which it received the current message. It also does this if it is playing the rôle of b when an acknowledgment arrives.

Thirdly, the receiver may receive information that a *failure* has occurred in process f. If f identifies one of the processes from which the receiver expects an acknowledgment, the receiver must, as in the case of the originator, take over the function of f, send the current message to all f's successors again, and expect them to acknowledge it. If, on the other hand, the failed process is the actual originator of the broadcast, b, then a more complicated action is required. Not only must the receiver send the current message to all the successors of b, it must also take over the rôle of b for the rest of the current broadcast. Finally, if the failed process is neither b nor in *ackfrom*, then the failure is ignored.

It is a feature of the protocol that new requests from the user will *not* be accepted until the current broadcast is completed. In fact, the receivers exploit this fact in order to deal with new messages in an efficient manner. If it were not the case, receipt of a message with $n' > n$ would not necessarily mean that broadcast n was complete, so the receiver would need to keep copies of all outstanding messages until explicitly told that the corresponding broadcast was finished. The protocol would thus become much more complex.

Basically, the protocol uses a so-called *diffusing computation*, a method originally introduced by Dijkstra [33], in which the message is passed down the tree in a 'wave' propagated from the root, and the wave of acknowledgments is passed back up it. In the absence of failures, this requires $2 \cdot (n - 1)$ steps for n processes, where a 'step' is the transmission of a message or acknowledgment. If a failure occurs, say in process f, then the predecessor of f in the tree will re-send the message to all f's successors. If there are a number of successive failures, it is reasonably easy to see that this can at worst result in each process sending the message once to every other process and receiving at most one acknowledgment from each of them, which takes at most $2n \cdot (n - 1)$ steps. For this price, the protocol ensures that the message will be distributed to all functioning processes as long as *at least one functioning process succeeds in receiving the message from the originator*.

5.2 Election

Broadcasting is a very one-sided form of consensus in which one process tells the others which value they are to agree on. In more interesting forms of consensus, all parties must exchange information with a view to reaching a mutually acceptable agreement. The simplest example of this is *election*, where the aim is to choose one of the processes from the set to perform some particular function, such as to be master or coordinator.

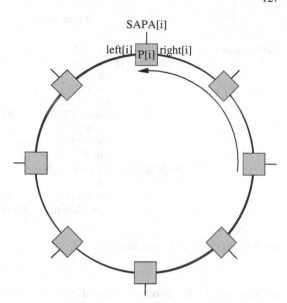

Fig. 5.5 Message passing in a
Unidirectional Ring

Most protocols for election assume that there is a total ordering among the processes, and are actually distributed algorithms for finding an extremum of a set. Typically, the ordering is achieved simply by giving the processes unique numbers. An efficient algorithm for finding the maximum element of the set of numbers can then be attained by organising the processes in a logical or physical *ring*, and sending messages round this ring. Such algorithms are in the literature often known as algorithms for finding *circular extrema*.

A simple protocol for this purpose is the one due to Chang and Roberts [24] given as **Protocol 15** in Figure 5.6. This protocol assumes that the ring is *unidirectional*. The process with number i in the ordering is described by $P[i, active]$. It receives messages on channel $right[i]$ and sends messages on channel $left[i]$, as illustrated in Figure 5.5. We do not make any assumptions about what order the processes are connected up in – indeed, if we knew this we wouldn't need the protocol! The parameter *active* of process P indicates whether the process is actively taking part in an election or not.

Elections are started by a user, here assumed attached to $P[i, ...]$ via the channel $SAPA[i]$, making a request for an election. This results in the i'th process actively joining the election, and sending an ELECTION message with its own number off round the ring.

If process i receives an ELECTION message, $(ELECTION, j)$, from a process j, three cases can be distinguished: If $j > i$, process j has priority over i, so i will pass the message on. If $j < i$, then i should be elected rather than j. There are then two cases: either i is already actively taking part in the election, in which case it just ignores j's bid, or i is not yet active. In the latter case i enters the election, taking over j's bid and replacing it with one of its own. Finally, if $j = i$, i's bid has been all

Protocol 15

$P[i : \mathbb{N}_0, active : \mathbb{B}] \stackrel{\text{def}}{=} (SAPA[i]?r : request \to left[i]!(\text{ELECTION}, i) \to P[i, \text{true}]$
$\quad\quad [\![right[i]?(e : \{\text{ELECTION}\}, j : \mathbb{N}_0) \to$
$\quad\quad\quad\quad\quad (\text{if } j > i$
$\quad\quad\quad\quad\quad \text{then } left[i]!(e, j) \to P[i, \text{true}]$
$\quad\quad\quad\quad\quad \text{elseif } j < i \wedge \neg active$
$\quad\quad\quad\quad\quad \text{then } left[i]!(e, i) \to P[i, \text{true}]$
$\quad\quad\quad\quad\quad \text{elseif } j = i$
$\quad\quad\quad\quad\quad \text{then } left[i]!(\text{ELECTED}, i) \to P[i, active]$
$\quad\quad\quad\quad\quad \text{else } P[i, active])$
$\quad\quad [\![right[i]?(e : \{\text{ELECTED}\}, j : \mathbb{N}_0) \to$
$\quad\quad\quad\quad\quad (\text{if } j \neq i$
$\quad\quad\quad\quad\quad \text{then } left[i]!(e, j) \to SAPA[i]!j \to P[i, \text{false}]$
$\quad\quad\quad\quad\quad \text{else } SAPA[i]!j \to P[i, \text{false}]) \,)$

Fig. 5.6 Election in a Unidirectional Ring.

the way round without being 'overbid' by one of the other processes, so i must have the largest value of all the processes in the ring, and has therefore won the election. It communicates this result to the other participants by sending an ELECTION message.

Receipt of an ELECTED message, $(\text{ELECTED}, j)$, indicates that the election has been won by process j. If $j \neq i$ then the winner is not the current process; the result is sent to the local user at $SAPA[i]$, the message is passed on round the ring, and the current process ceases to participate in the current election. If $j = i$, an ELECTED message sent by the current process has been all the way round the ring. The result is communicated to the local user, and the current election terminates completely.

If only the user attached to the process with the largest number, say m, requests an election, the protocol terminates after two rounds of the ring. In the first round, the $(\text{ELECTION}, m)$ message circulates and, since m is the maximum value, it returns to its sender without being overbid. In the second round, m circulates an $(\text{ELECTED}, m)$ message, indicating that it has won the election. Since each full trip round a ring containing n processes requires n message transfers, the total number of transfers in this case is $2n$.

If only the user attached to process number k, where $k < m$, requests an election, then the election terminates after at most three rounds. First, $(\text{ELECTION}, k)$ is sent off by k. As this passes processes with larger and larger numbers, they replace the number k with their own numbers, until finally the ELECTION message carries the number m. In the worst case (when m is just on the 'right-hand' side of k), this takes a whole round. m's $(\text{ELECTION}, m)$ message and the subsequent $(\text{ELECTED}, m)$ message must then circulate right round the ring, giving two more rounds before the election procedure is completed. The total number of message transfers in this case becomes $(3n - 1)$.

More complicated cases arise if several users request an election at more or less the same time. The best case is when the processes are arranged round the ring in increasing order. If all processes initiate an election at the same time, each of them –

except the process with the maximum number – sends an ELECTION message to its neighbour, who ignores it because it has a lower number than the neighbour's own. The message from process m, on the other hand, is passed all the way round. Thus $(2n - 1)$ ELECTION messages are sent. These are followed by the circulation of the ELECTED message, making $(3n - 1)$ messages in all.

The worst case is when the processes are arranged in decreasing order round the ring. An $(\text{ELECTION}, j)$ message then has to go j steps before reaching a process which ignores it and refuses to pass it on. Although the election still only takes three rounds, $(n + \sum_{j=1}^{n} j)$ messages are sent, making $O(n^2)$ messages in total. However, Chang and Roberts show that in the *average* case, only $O(n \ln n)$ messages are required.

Several protocols which improve the worst-case behaviour of Chang and Roberts' protocol have been given in the literature. Hirschberg and Sinclair [61] present a protocol which only requires $O(n \ln n)$ messages in the worst case, but which is based on a *bidirectional* ring, while Dolev, Klawe and Rodeh [34] give a protocol which requires $O(n \ln n)$ messages in the worst case on a unidirectional ring. It is not possible to improve on this behaviour: It has been formally proved that the lower bound for both the maximum and the average numbers of messages needed for election in a ring is $O(n \ln n)$ [20, 104].

Practical examples of election appear in many distributed systems. One of the best known is the selection of the station which is to function as a *monitor* in local area networks such as the ISO/IEEE Token Bus [153], and Token Ring [154]. This station is responsible for monitoring the ring, to ensure that the access control token is continually present. In the Token Bus, the physical topology of the network is a bus or tree, so a logical ring is used , while in the Token Ring, the fact that the physical topology is a ring is exploited directly. The Token Ring uses a protocol which is essentially the same as Chang and Roberts', where the ELECTION messages are called *Claim Token frames* and the ELECTED messages are called *Purge frames*.

5.3 Commitment

In many types of distributed application, the parties involved need at some stage to be certain that they have all carried out a particular sequence of exchanges, in order to ensure *consistency* of data. The classic example is of a database describing a number of bank accounts, where the exchanges of data between service users describe bank transactions on these accounts, i.e. the transfer of money between them. Obviously, the data are only consistent when a complete transaction has been carried out, whereas the situation where, say, a sum x has been debited from one account but not yet credited to another account is *inconsistent*. Amongst other things, it is only meaningful to set *synchronisation points* (or, of course, to return to them after an error) when the data are in a consistent state.

The general problem here is to create agreement between a possibly large number of parties as to whether a particular change or set of changes in their global state is to be carried out as a whole or not at all. Such a set of changes is often known as the *commitment unit* for the transaction. Of course, the problem also arises when there are only two users of a service, but can then usually be solved in a simple manner by the use of confirmed services (possibly implemented using three-way handshake) to ensure agreement on the beginning and end of the commitment unit, and on whether the changes are to be carried out (*committed*) or given up (*aborted*).

In multi-peer services, the end of the commitment unit is not so easily recognised, since in principle the various users of the service may respond in different ways, some of them agreeing to perform the changes, while others propose that the changes should be aborted. Some of them may even fail completely during the execution of the protocol. Thus there are many ways in which we may potentially arrive in a situation where it would be unclear what the fate of the commitment unit had been.

The simplest protocol for dealing with this problem is the so-called *two-phase commit* protocol, originally suggested by Gray [54], and subsequently refined by several others [81, 82, 96]. In the original version, which is strictly speaking a *centralised* (or *central site*) two-phase commit protocol, one of the participants acts as *coordinator*, and the others as *slaves*. A variety of more distributed versions are discussed by Skeen [117]. The basic protocol is presented as **Protocol 16** in Figure 5.7.

In this protocol, the Coordinator protocol entity is assumed to be connected to its associated service user through the channel *SAPA*, and to the underlying service via the set of n channels $right[i]$, where $i \in \{1, \ldots, n\}$. Each of the n slave protocol entities, $Slave[i]$, is likewise connected to the underlying service via a channel $left[i]$, in such a way that messages passing through $right[i]$ reach $left[i]$ and vice-versa. The system configuration is shown diagrammatically in Figure 5.8. Whether the underlying service connects the channels up pairwise or whether it supplies a multi-peer service to the $n+1$ protocol entities is unimportant here.

As in **Protocol 14**, the notation $\coprod_{i \in rs} right[i]!x \to P$ is used as shorthand for the process which makes multiple, parallel offers of output via the channels $right[i]$ for all $i \in rs$, and then proceeds as process P. Likewise, $right[i \in rs]?a : \mathcal{M} \to P$ is used as shorthand for the process which accepts input of a value in the domain $\mathcal{M}$ on *any* of the channels $right[i]$ for $i \in rs$, and then proceeds as process P.

In the coordinator process, the sets of indices rs, cs and as describe the complete set of slave processes, the sub-set which have replied that they are willing to carry out the transaction, and the sub-set which have replied that they wish to abort the transaction, respectively. In the first phase of the algorithm, the Coordinator receives a request from the user to commit the transaction, passes this request to all the slaves (process *Phase1*), and collects their responses (process *MR*). If all the responses are positive ('COMMIT'), the coordinator will, in the second phase of the algorithm, order all the slaves simultaneously to perform the changes associated with the commitment unit (process *Phase2C*). If any of the responses are negative ('ABORT'), or if some slaves do not reply at all, so that timeout occurs, the coordinator will instead

Protocol 16

$Coordinator \quad \stackrel{\text{def}}{=} (C \parallel Timer) \setminus \{up\}$

$C \qquad\qquad \stackrel{\text{def}}{=} (SAPA?r : request \rightarrow \qquad Phase1[\{1,\ldots,n\},\{\},\{\},r])$

$Phase1[rs,cs,as : \mathbb{N}_0\text{-set}, r : request]$

$\qquad\qquad \stackrel{\text{def}}{=} ((\coprod_{i \in rs} right[i]!r) \rightarrow \qquad up!set \rightarrow MR[rs,cs,as])$

$MR[rs,cs,as : \mathbb{N}_0\text{-set}]$

$\qquad\qquad \stackrel{\text{def}}{=} (right[i \in rs]?a : \{\text{ABORT}\} \rightarrow$
$\qquad\qquad\qquad\qquad (\textbf{if } (cs \cup as \cup \{i\}) = rs$
$\qquad\qquad\qquad\qquad \textbf{then } up!\text{RESET} \rightarrow Phase2A[cs]$
$\qquad\qquad\qquad\qquad \textbf{else } MR[rs,cs,as \cup \{i\}])$
$\qquad\qquad\quad [\!] right[i \in rs]?c : \{\text{COMMIT}\} \rightarrow$
$\qquad\qquad\qquad\qquad (\textbf{if } (cs \cup \{i\}) = rs$
$\qquad\qquad\qquad\qquad \textbf{then } up!\text{RESET} \rightarrow SN \rightarrow Phase2C[rs]$
$\qquad\qquad\qquad\qquad \textbf{elseif } (cs \cup as \cup \{i\}) = rs$
$\qquad\qquad\qquad\qquad \textbf{then } up!\text{RESET} \rightarrow Phase2A[cs \cup \{i\}]$
$\qquad\qquad\qquad\qquad \textbf{else } MR[rs,cs \cup \{i\},as])$
$\qquad\qquad\quad [\!] up?t : \{\text{TIMEOUT}\} \rightarrow \qquad Phase2A[cs])$

$Phase2C[cs : \mathbb{N}_0\text{-set}]$

$\qquad\qquad \stackrel{\text{def}}{=} ((\coprod_{i \in cs} right[i]!\text{COMMIT}) \rightarrow SC \rightarrow Coordinator)$

$Phase2A[cs : \mathbb{N}_0\text{-set}]$

$\qquad\qquad \stackrel{\text{def}}{=} ((\coprod_{i \in cs} right[i]!\text{ABORT}) \rightarrow \quad SA \rightarrow Coordinator)$

$Slave[i : \mathbb{N}_0] \quad \stackrel{\text{def}}{=} (left[i]?r : request \rightarrow \qquad SAPB[i]!r \rightarrow SR[i])$

$SR[i : \mathbb{N}_0] \quad \stackrel{\text{def}}{=} (SAPB[i]?a : \{\text{ABORT}\} \rightarrow \quad SA \rightarrow left[i]!a \rightarrow Slave[i]$
$\qquad\qquad\qquad [\!] SAPB[i]?c : \{\text{COMMIT}\} \rightarrow \quad SN \rightarrow left[i]!c \rightarrow SPhase2[i])$

$SPhase2[i : \mathbb{N}_0] \stackrel{\text{def}}{=} (left[i]?a : \{\text{ABORT}\} \rightarrow \quad SA \rightarrow Slave[i]$
$\qquad\qquad\qquad [\!] left[i]?c : \{\text{COMMIT}\} \rightarrow \quad SC \rightarrow Slave[i])$

$Timer \qquad \stackrel{\text{def}}{=} (up?s : \{\text{SET}\} \rightarrow \qquad\qquad (up?r : \{\text{RESET}\} \rightarrow Timer$
$\qquad\qquad\qquad\qquad\qquad\qquad\qquad\qquad [\!] up!\text{TIMEOUT} \rightarrow Timer))$

Fig. 5.7 Basic Two-phase Commit protocol.

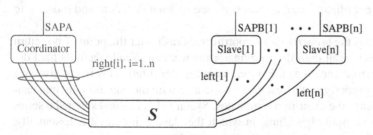

Fig. 5.8 System configuration for the basic 2-Phase Commit protocol

order all slaves who have voted COMMIT to abort rather than complete the transaction (process *Phase*2A). In other words, a single negative or missing vote from any slave will cause the commitment unit to be abandoned.

The slaves have a much simpler task. On receipt of a request to commit the commitment unit, they pass the request on to their associated user, and await its reply. This reply is then sent back to the coordinator (process *SR*). If the reply was negative, the slave can abort the local part of the transaction immediately. This is imagined to take place in process *SA*. The details of this process depend critically on the nature of the changes involved in the transaction, but in general will involve deleting any changes which would have been made, releasing any resources reserved for the transaction and so on.

If the slave's user's reply was positive, the slave must note that this was the case (process *SN*), and then wait for the final decision from the coordinator (process *Sphase*2). If this is negative, the transaction is abandoned as above. If it is positive, the changes associated with the commitment unit are carried out (process *SC*).

Although not shown in detail here, the process *SN* is in some ways the most critical in the whole algorithm. For the algorithm to work successfully even in the presence of 'crashes', it is essential that the coordinator and the slaves agree on a *point of no return*, in the sense that they cannot back out of the transaction after this point. Process *SN* involves noting, in some form of storage whose contents will *not* be destroyed by a crash, sufficient details of the transaction for it to be possible to carry it out even if a crash occurs. However, the changes involved in the transaction are not in fact carried out until the final confirmation arrives from the coordinator.

If faults occur, either in the underlying service or in any of the processes involved, before the point of no return is reached, the algorithm will simply result in the transaction being aborted. If a fault occurs between the execution of process *SN* and the termination of the algorithm, a recovery mechanism is assumed to exist which can 'see' from the information noted during execution of *SN* what the state of the transaction is. For example, if a slave crashes, it can on recovery see that it had a non-terminated transaction involving a particular coordinator, and it is then expected to ask the coordinator what the fate of the commitment unit became. Likewise, a crashed coordinator can, on recovery, see its final decision, and repeat it to the slaves.

Protocol 16 has the property that a coordinator crash after the point of no return causes the slaves to wait until the coordinator recovers and sends them its final decision. It is therefore known as a *blocking* commit algorithm. This is not always a very convenient property, as the resources associated with the commitment unit cannot be released until the algorithm terminates. Skeen [117] has investigated a series of *non-blocking* commit algorithms, in which the slave can continue. Essentially, these are more fault-tolerant, in the sense that all functioning processes complete the protocol correctly, even if some of the participants fail by stopping.

The key property of a blocking commit protocol is that a participant has one or more states in which it itself is willing to commit the transaction, but where it cannot infer whether the other participants will vote (or already have voted) COMMIT or ABORT. If the coordinator crashes while the participant is in such a state, then the participant has no means of discovering whether the transaction should be committed or aborted. Such a state exists for the slaves in **Protocol 16** at the beginning of process $Sphase2$. Depending on the exact timing of the messages and the crash, other slaves may have received:

- COMMIT messages. They must then be in states where they will definitely complete (or already have completed) their part of the transaction – so-called *commit states*.
- ABORT messages. They must then be in states where they will definitely abort (or already have aborted) their part of the transaction – so-called *abort states*.
- No final message from the coordinator at all, in which case they are still in the state at the start of *SPhase2*.

We say that the *concurrency set* of this state (i.e. the set of states which the participants can be in when a given participant is in the state) contains both *abort* and *commit* states. This is the dangerous situation where the participant cannot be certain of the outcome.

Skeen then describes the requirements on a non-blocking protocol by the following theorem:

Theorem 5.1. Fundamental non-blocking theorem
A protocol is non-blocking if and only if it satisfies both of the following conditions for every participant:

1. *There exists no local state of the participant such that its concurrency set contains both an* abort *and a* commit *state.*
2. *All states whose concurrency set contains a commit state are* committable *states.*

A *committable* state is one in which the participant knows with certainty that all the other participants have committed or will do so.

The major states of **Protocol 16** can be illustrated by the finite-state machines shown in Figure 5.9(a). The concurrency set of the state w_c in the FSM for the coordinator is $\bigcup_i \{q_i, w_i, a_i\}$, while the concurrency set of the states w_i in the FSMs for the slaves is $\{w_c, a_c, c_c\} \bigcup_{j \neq i} \{q_j, w_j, a_j, c_j\}$, so the states w fail to fulfil either of the conditions of Theorem 5.1. Thus **Protocol 16** is a blocking protocol. The simplest way to create a non-blocking protocol is then to introduce an extra round of message exchange: After receiving only votes for COMMIT from the slaves, the coordinator sends a PREPARE, rather than a COMMIT, message to all of them. On receipt of this, each functioning slave replies with an acknowledgment. On receipt of all the acknowledgments, the coordinator finally sends a COMMIT message to all the slaves, who then complete the transaction. This gives a *Three-phase Commit* protocol, with the FSM shown in Figure 5.9(b). There is now a state p between w and c in each participant. The state p_i has $\bigcup_{j \neq i} \{p_j, c_j\}$ as its concurrency set, and is therefore committable, while the state w_i, which is still not committable, has concurrency set $\bigcup_{j \neq i} \{w_j, a_j, p_j\}$. Thus the requirements for a non-blocking protocol are now fulfilled.

It is very easy to see that the simple 2-Phase Commit protocol **Protocol 16** uses at most $3 \cdot (n-1)$ messages, where there are n participants in total, including the

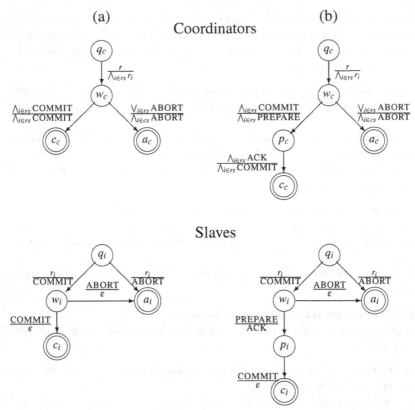

Fig. 5.9 FSM representation of major states of commit protocols.
(a) Two-phase blocking protocol (**Protocol 16**), **(b)** Three-phase non-blocking protocol.
FSM state changes marked $\frac{i}{o}$ are triggered by receipt of input message i and cause transmission of output message o. The symbol ε represents the empty message, and $\wedge$ and $\vee$ signify respectively the conjunction and disjunction of receipt or transmission of messages.

coordinator, and that the simple 3-Phase non-blocking protocol sketched above uses $5 \cdot (n-1)$ messages. Analysis of commit protocols by Dwork and Skeen [38] has shown that the absolute lower bound for commit protocols of either type is $2 \cdot (n-1)$ messages. However, to achieve this lower bound for a non-blocking protocol requires a good deal of ingenuity – for details of the resulting protocol, see [38].

There is a wealth of examples of the practical use of commitment protocols, as the literature on the topic demonstrates. All distributed databases use commitment in one form or another. Within ISO, a 2-phase commit protocol essentially the same as **Protocol 16** with the addition of recovery facilities, has been standardised as part of the so-called *CCR (Commitment, Concurrency and Recovery)* protocol for use in the Application Layer of OSI systems [189, 190]. In OSI systems, this is specifically used by the Job Transfer and Manipulation protocol to ensure that groups of remotely running tasks are completed as a whole or not at all [162, 163], and by the Distributed Transaction Processing protocol for handling distributed transactions [195–197]. We shall look at both OSI CCR and Distributed Transaction Processing in more detail in Chapter 10.

5.4 Byzantine Agreement

Although many of the protocols described in this chapter are resilient to processes stopping – the so-called fail-stop failure mode – all the protocols considered in this book up to now have the property that they fail if presented with *false* messages. As we have seen in Chapter 4, a great deal of effort goes into ensuring that such false messages cannot arrive due to poor protocol design with respect to PDU lifetimes. However, in an error-prone system, anything might happen, and the generation of completely false messages cannot be excluded.

Avoidance of arbitrary false messages (or, in general, arbitrary errors) requires some form of redundancy, so that some kind of majority voting scheme can be used to decide what are the genuine messages and what are false. In a distributed system, the redundancy can be provided by allowing each party to send a copy of his message to each of the others. However, in the presence of faults, it is not certain that all parties actually receive the same information. The problem is to exchange sufficient information between a sufficient number of parties for all correctly functioning systems to be able to build up the same picture of what the original messages were.

This problem is often formulated as the *Byzantine Generals* (or *interactive consistency*) problem, first presented by Lamport, Shostak and Pease [80], and which we shall formulate as follows:

A commander must send a value to his $n-1$ lieutenants such that: **IC1.** All loyal lieutenants agree on the same value. **IC2.** If the commander is loyal, then every loyal lieutenant agrees on the value which he sends.

A typical group of Byzantine generals, at least one of which looks very suspicious, is shown in Figure 5.10. The conditions IC1 and IC2 are known as the *interactive consistency conditions*. In a computer system, 'loyal' systems are ones that work reliably, and 'disloyal' ones are those that may introduce errors into the messages passed.

Fig. 5.10 Four Byzantine generals

Essentially, the lieutenants receive a vector of values, $\mathbf{v} = (v_1, \ldots, v_{n-1})$, and the loyal ones must all produce the same value, say v, as result. If the values are Boolean (for example of the form 'attack'/'retreat'), a reasonable choice would be to take the majority value of the elements of the vector. If the values are in an ordered domain, the median value would be appropriate. For generality[1], we define the value of the function $majority(\mathbf{v})$ as being the value selected by a lieutenant receiving the values in $\mathbf{v}$. If no value is received from a particular participant, the algorithm should supply some default, v_{def}.

5.4.1 Using unsigned messages

Solutions to this problem depend quite critically on the assumptions made about the system. Initially, we shall assume the following:

Degree of fault-tolerance: Out of the n participants, at most t are unreliable. This defines the degree of fault tolerance required of the system. We cannot expect the protocol to work correctly if this limit is overstepped.

Network properties: Every message that is sent is delivered correctly, and the receiver of a message knows who sent it. These assumptions mean that an unreliable participant cannot interfere with the message traffic between the other participants. It would be reasonable to suppose that this could be satisfied, for example, by having a fully-connected network topology.

Timing: The absence of a message can be detected. This means that an unreliable participant cannot prevent a decision simply by doing nothing. This implies that the system operates in an essentially synchronous manner, where timeout mechanisms can be used to detect missing messages.

Note that the assumptions about the network do not prevent the participants from sending incorrect messages to one another – the generals can lie. Restricting ourselves to these assumptions is therefore often said to correspond to the use of *oral* or *unsigned* messages. We shall return later to the consequences of making other assumptions about the system.

The algorithm, of course, defines the behaviour of reliable participants; unreliable ones can do what they like! In the form of a CSP process description, the algorithm (which is recursively defined) becomes rather difficult to understand, so we present it here in a form more closely following the original (from [80]) as **Protocol 17**. We shall refer to the n participants as $P_0, \ldots, P_{n-1}$, where P_0 is the initial commander.

To see how this works, consider the case where $t = 1$ and $n = 4$. In the first step, the algorithm is performed with $t = 1$, and the initial commander sends his value v to all $n - 1$ other participants. In the second step, the algorithm is performed with $t = 0$, and each of the recipients in the previous step acts as commander for a new

---

[1] Please note: this is *not* meant to be a poor joke.

Protocol 17

Algorithm OM(n,t), t > 0:

1. The commander, P_0, sends his value to the other $n-1$ participants, $P_1, \ldots, P_{n-1}$.
2. For each i, let v_i be the value P_i receives from the commander, or else v_{def} if he receives no value. P_i then acts as commander in Algorithm $OM(n-1, t-1)$, to send the value v_i to the $(n-2)$ 'other' participants, $P_1, \ldots, P_{i-1}, P_{i+1}, \ldots, P_{n-1}$.
3. For each i, and each $j \neq i$, let v_j be the value which P_i received from P_j in step (2), during execution of algorithm $OM(n-1, t-1)$, or else v_{def} if he received no such value. P_i then uses the value $majority(v_1, \ldots, v_{n-1})$.

Algorithm OM(n,0):

1. P_0 sends his value to the other $n-1$ participants.
2. Each of $P_1, \ldots, P_{n-1}$ uses the value he receives from P_0, or uses v_{def} if he receives no value.

Fig. 5.11 Byzantine Generals protocol for at most t disloyal participants out of n, assuming unsigned messages.

round of messages, in which each of them sends to the 'other' $n-2$, from which it has not received a message. The algorithm then terminates, and the participants evaluate their final value, as *majority* of all the messages that they have received.

If all the participants are in fact reliable, then it is easy to see that all the lieutenants get 3 copies of the same message, one from each of the other participants. Suppose, however, that Lieutenant 3 is unreliable. In the first round, Lieutenants 1, 2 and 3 all receive, say v from the initial commander. In the second round, Lieutenant 2 receives v again from 1 (who is loyal), but some arbitrary value, say x from 3. Lieutenant 2 thus evaluates the final value v as $majority(v, v, x)$, which is v, as required. Likewise in the second round, Lieutenant 1 receives v from 2, and some other arbitrary value, say y, from 3. So Lieutenant 1 evaluates $majority(v, v, y)$, which is also v. In this case, both conditions IC1 and IC2 are plainly satisfied. The final case, where the original commander is unreliable, is left as an exercise.

It is a fundamental result that for unsigned messages, i.e. messages which the participants can alter arbitrarily as they pass them on, the Byzantine generals problem cannot be solved for $n \leq 3t$. Several proofs of this impossibility result can be found in the literature [45, 105]. The correctness of the algorithm for $n > 3t$ can be demonstrated by a simple inductive argument over t [80].

Generally speaking, if we have an army where we have to allow for up to t unreliable generals, the algorithm proceeds in $t+1$ rounds. In the first, we execute algorithm $OM(n,t)$, and the initial commander sends $n-1$ messages, so that each of the lieutenants receives one. Each of them then acts as commander for an execution of $OM(n-1, t-1)$, in which it sends $n-2$ messages. In this round, each lieutenant therefore receives $n-2$ messages, one from each of the other (in the context of the algorithm) commanders. For each of these $n-2$ messages, the lieutenant will act as commander for an execution of $OM(n-2, t-2)$, in which it sends $n-3$ messages to each of the 'other' lieutenants. In the context of this execution of

$OM(n-2,t-2)$, this means the set of lieutenants other than the one from which it received a message in the previous phase. Each of the $n-1$ lieutenants in total performs $OM(n-2,t-2)$ $n-2$ times, sending $n-3$ messages each time. Overall, algorithm $OM(n,t)$ is performed exactly once, while algorithm $OM(n-p,t-p)$ (for $p \in \{1,\ldots,t\}$) is performed $(n-1)\cdots(n-p)$ times, and the total number of messages sent is:

$$m = (n-1) + (n-1)(n-2) + \ldots + (n-1)(n-2)\cdots(n-t-1)$$

Thus m is $O(n^t)$, i.e. it is exponential in t. Moreover, as remarked previously, the algorithm requires $t+1$ rounds, and therefore a time proportional to $t+1$. Finally, as shown by Lamport, Shostak and Pease [80] it requires a network whose connectivity is at least $3t$-regular – i.e. such that there are at least $3t$ disjoint paths between any participant (network node) and any other. Evidently, this is an expensive algorithm in terms of resources, but it provides protection against up to t totally unreliable systems (or generals) out of n, where $n > 3t$, without putting any special requirements on the form of the messages.

Further work on the use of unsigned messages by Dolev, Fischer and others has demonstrated that some of these requirements can be slackened. For example, an algorithm resistant to t faulty systems out of n, where $n > 3t$, which uses $4t+4$ rounds and $O(n^5)$ messages is given by Dolev and Strong in [35], and one which uses $2t+3$ rounds and $O(nt+t^3 \ln t)$ messages by Fischer et al. No absolute lower bound has yet been demonstrated for the number of messages. However, it is certain that at least $t+1$ rounds are required to achieve agreement in the presence of t faulty systems.

5.4.2 Using signed messages

Whereas there is no solution to the problem using unsigned messages for t unreliable generals unless $n > 3t$, if we assume that messages can be made *unforgeable* by the addition of a *signature* which identifies the sender, then the problem is solvable for any non-trivial combination of reliable and unreliable participants, i.e. for $n > (t+1)$.

A simple algorithm using signed messages was given by Lamport, Shostak and Pease [80]. This operates under the same assumptions about the message system and timing as their algorithm using unsigned messages, and assuming the following properties of signatures:

Signatures: A signature unambiguously and correctly identifies the signer to any other participant, and cannot be forged. This implies that a signature prevents a participant who passes on a message from changing a message in an arbitrary manner: The participant may fail to pass the message on, but if it makes actual changes they will be detected.

We shall see in chapter 6 how these properties can be attained in practice.

Protocol 18

$SM[n,t:\mathbb{N}_0] \overset{\text{def}}{=} Commander[n,t] \|_{i \in NS} (P[i,t,\{\},NS] \| Timer[i]) \setminus up[i]$

$Commander[n,t:\mathbb{N}_0]$
$\qquad \overset{\text{def}}{=} (SAPA?v:\mathcal{M} \rightarrow \coprod_{j \in NS} right[j]!(v,\{0\}) \rightarrow Commander[n,t])$

$P[i:NS,t:\mathbb{N}_0,V:\mathcal{M}\text{-set},ps:NS_0\text{-set}]$
$\qquad \overset{\text{def}}{=} (left[i]?(v:\mathcal{M},ss:NS_0\text{-set}) \rightarrow$
$\qquad\qquad\qquad (\textbf{if }(\text{card }ss < t+1) \wedge (v \notin V)$
$\qquad\qquad\qquad \textbf{then }\coprod_{j \in ps-ss} right[j]!(v,ss \cup \{i\}) \rightarrow$
$\qquad\qquad\qquad\qquad\qquad (\textbf{if } V = \{\}$
$\qquad\qquad\qquad\qquad\qquad \textbf{then } up[i]!\text{SET} \rightarrow P[i,t,\{v\},ps]$
$\qquad\qquad\qquad\qquad\qquad \textbf{else } P[i,t,V \cup \{v\},ps])$
$\qquad\qquad\qquad \textbf{else } P[i,t,V,ps])$
$\qquad\qquad [\!] up[i]?t:\{\text{TIMEOUT}\} \rightarrow SAPA[i]!choice(V) \rightarrow P[i,t,\{\},ps])$

$Timer[i:NS] \overset{\text{def}}{=} (up[i]?s:\{\text{SET}\} \rightarrow (up[i]?r:\{\text{RESET}\} \rightarrow Timer[i]$
$\qquad\qquad\qquad\qquad\qquad [\!] up[i]!\text{TIMEOUT} \rightarrow Timer[i]))$

Fig. 5.12 Byzantine Generals protocol for at most t disloyal participants out of n, assuming signed messages.

Lamport, Shostak and Pease's algorithm is given as **Protocol 18** in Figure 5.12. In this figure, we again use notations of the type $\coprod_{j \in s} right[j]!y \rightarrow P$ to denote the process which offers output via the channels $right[j]$ for all $j \in s$ and then proceeds as process P, and we assume that data output via $right[j]$ will be received as input on channel $left[j]$. The notation $\|_{i \in s} R[i,\dots]$ indicates parallel composition of instances of $R[i,\dots]$ for all values of i in the set s. Each participant is identified by a number i which also functions as its signature, with the commander as number 0. The set of all subsidiary participants $\{1..n-1\}$ is denoted NS, and the set of all participants including the commander, $\{0..n-1\}$, is denoted NS_0.

Once again the protocol proceeds in up to $t+1$ rounds. In the first round, the commander creates a message by signing the data v and sends it to all the other participants. In round k, each participant accepts messages (v,ss) which have k signatures in the signature set ss, and which contain 'new' data, i.e. data v which are not already in the set of received data, V. All other messages are ignored. For each accepted message, the recipient adds the data v to set V, signs the message by adding his signature to ss so that it has $k+1$ signatures, and sends the message to all the participants who have not yet signed it. At some stage (indicated in **Protocol 18** by the receipt of TIMEOUT), the participants determine that they will receive no more valid messages, and they choose a value calculated from the contents of the set V. In the figure, it is assumed that the function $choice(V)$ evaluates this result.

Proof of correctness follows from the following analysis: If the commander is reliable, then the protocol actually terminates after two rounds. In the first round, the commander sends the message, say $(v,\{0\})$, to all the others. Each reliable participant i then includes v in its set V (which initially is empty) and sends $(v,\{0,i\})$ to all the others except 0 and i. Since they have already all received a message containing

v, no further messages are sent. In this case V only contains one value, namely v, which is the value sent by the commander. Unreliable participants may of course send invalid messages (which will be ignored) or fail to send messages. But neither of these possibilities will affect the content of V. Thus in all cases with a reliable commander condition IC2 is fulfilled, and from this IC1 follows.

Now consider IC1 if the commander is unreliable. He may then send different messages to all the others in the first round, and the procedure will then continue until in round $t + 1$ messages with $t + 1$ signatures are circulated. The problem is then to show that all the reliable participants manage to decide on the same result. This will be the case if they all construct the same set V. Thus we must show that, for arbitrary i, j, if i puts a value v into V then so does j. Now i puts v into V when it receives a message (v, ss) and $v \notin V$. If $j \in ss$, then evidently j has already put v into its own copy of V, so both i and j have v in V. If $j \notin ss$ and $(\operatorname{card} ss < t + 1)$ then i will send v on to j. On the other hand, if $j \notin ss$ and $(\operatorname{card} ss = t + 1)$ then there are no more rounds available. However, since we here suppose that the commander is unreliable, then at least one of the $t + 1$ signatories to the message must be reliable. This one must have sent the value v on to j when it first received it. Thus in all cases where i receives v and puts it into V then j also does so. Thus IC1 is also fulfilled when the commander is unreliable.

As it stands, **Protocol 18** has the same worst-case message complexity as **Protocol 17**, and still uses up to $t + 1$ rounds. However, it does use fewer messages than **Protocol 17** in cases where the commander is reliable, and it enables interactive consistency to be achieved for the minimal non-trivial case $n > (t + 1)$ rather than $n > 3t$. Dolev and Strong [36] pointed out that a simple modification reduces the worst-case number of messages to $O(nt)$. As noted above, the worst case only occurs when the commander is unreliable, and this is the only case in which participants can receive messages with different values v. In Dolev and Strong's algorithm, each participant will only pass on the *first two* different values received. This is sufficient to tell reliable participants that the commander is unreliable, and they can then choose a default value, v_{def}, which is the same for all participants.

5.4.3 Other forms of Byzantine agreement

A more precise term for the form of Byzantine agreement discussed in detail above is *strong, synchronous* Byzantine agreement. In *weak* Byzantine agreement, the consistency rule IC2 is weakened to:

IC2':   If all participants are loyal, then they all obtain the same value.

This type of consistency is what is required for *commitment* in a system with Byzantine errors, since the participants are now allowed to choose a result differing from the commander's proposal, as long as they all agree. However, weakening IC2 to 5.4.3 does not affect the complexity of the solutions significantly [77]. For example, there is still no solution with less than $t + 1$ rounds, nor is the number of messages needed to reach agreement reduced.

In *asynchronous* Byzantine agreement, the assumption that we can put a limit on the length of time which a step takes is abandoned. This means that we can no longer use timeout mechanisms to determine that a message is missing. In such systems, we need to introduce a rule that processes will always send *some* kind of response when they receive a message, even if this response merely indicates that they intend to ignore the received message. However, even if this is done, asynchronous Byzantine systems have the very unfortunate property, demonstrated by Fischer, Lynch and Paterson [46], that no consensus can be reached at all if any of the participants fails by stopping.

Finally, specific versions of Byzantine agreement for use in particular situations have been developed. An example is the Byzantine agreement algorithm for commitment described by Mohan, Strong and Finkelstein [97], and the algorithms for clock synchronisation which we discuss in the next section.

5.5 Clock Synchronisation

Some more specialised examples of protocols for reaching a consensus are the techniques for agreeing on what the time is in a distributed system. It is obvious that this is not a trivial problem, since messages always take a non-zero time to travel from any process to any other. A message arriving at process P_i can effectively only provide information about what the time was in the sending process when it was *sent off*, not what the time is when it arrives. Worse still, clocks in real systems do not necessarily run correctly or even at the same speed, so the information being passed round may not be reliable.

Clock synchronisation algorithms aim to get all (correctly functioning) clocks within a set of processes to have the same view of what the time is. A basic requirement of a correctly functioning clock is that it respects the *happened before* relation for a set of events in the set of processes. This relation, often denoted $\rightarrow$, is the smallest relation for which the following rules apply:

Local events: If a, b are events in the same process, and a occurs before b, then $a \rightarrow b$.

Message transmission: If a is the sending of a message by some process, and b is the receipt of the same message, then $a \rightarrow b$.

Transitivity: $(a \rightarrow b) \wedge (b \rightarrow c) \Rightarrow (a \rightarrow c)$

Non-reflexivity: $\neg(a \rightarrow a)$

Thus the relation $\rightarrow$ is an irreflexive partial ordering of the set of all events in the system. Interestingly, it also expresses the concept of *causal ordering*, since if $a \rightarrow b$, then a could potentially have caused b.

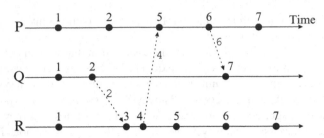

Fig. 5.13 Operation of a Lamport clock. The *numbered filled circles* indicate events in the individual processes with the corresponding values of the local clocks. *Dashed lines* show the transfer of timestamped messages.

5.5.1 Logical Clocks

A logical clock associates a value in an ordered domain with each event in a system, and the *happened before* relation is identified with the ordering relation. We define a *local logical clock* C_i in process P_i as a function which associates a value $C_i(a)$ in an ordered set, $\mathcal{V}$, with each event a in P_i. To be in accordance with the definition of $\rightarrow$, we require:

C1:   If a, b are events in the same process, P_i, and a occurs before b, then $C_i(a) < C_i(b)$.

C2:   If a is the sending of a message by P_i and b is the receipt of the same message by P_j, then $C_i(a) < C_j(b)$.

Any ordered domain will do. If we choose the natural numbers, $\mathbb{N}$, with the usual ordering, then rules C1 and C2 can be implemented in the following simple way, using a state variable T_i in process P_i to contain the value of the local (logical) time:

IR1:   Before each event in P_i, increment T_i by d, where $d > 0$.

IR2:   Timestamp each message sent by P_i with the current value of T_i. On receipt of a message with timestamp T_M by P_j, set T_j to $(\max{(T_j, T_M)} + d)$.

Clocks which follow these rules are usually known as *Lamport clocks* after their inventor [75]. The functioning of a Lamport clock with clock increment $d = 1$ in a system containing three processes is illustrated in Figure 5.13. Note that a Lamport clock merely provides a measure of the time which is good enough to be consistent with the *happened before* relation, so that it is possible to tell which order causally related events take place in. An observer who observes the system as a whole can perhaps see that the clocks in two different processes show quite different times at some instant; in Figure 5.13, for example, R gets to time 5 while Q still has time 2, while Q gets to time 7 at about the same instant that R gets to time 6. It is also easy to convince yourself that the clocks T_i in general run at the speed of whichever one of them is fastest. But as long as none of this conflicts with our view of which event happened before which, then there is no problem. Lamport demonstrates in [75] that this type of logical clock is quite sufficient for many purposes, such as determining

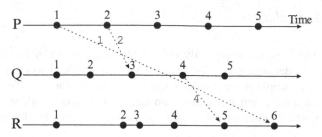

Fig. 5.14 An event sequence which does not respect causal ordering. In process R, $5 < 6$, but the first of these events cannot have caused the second.

the order in which processes attempt to access a critical region subject to mutual exclusion.

A significant problem with Lamport clocks is that $a{\rightarrow}b \Rightarrow C(a) < C(b)$, but the reverse implication is not true. This means that it is not possible just by looking at the clock values to see whether one event could logically have caused another. An example can be seen in Figure 5.14, where the event at time 5 in R is not related by the $\rightarrow$ relation to the event at time 6 in R[2]. This problem arises because only a single number is used to represent the time. More information is needed in order to tell the receiving process what the sending process knew about the other clocks in the system when it sent the message. It would then become clear that the message arriving at time 6 in R was sent before the message arriving at time 5. Mattern [86], Fidge [42] and others have proposed the use of *vector clocks* to solve this problem: A logical clock C is represented in process P_i by a vector of values, $\vec{T}_i$, whose k'th element is the latest clock value received from process P_k, and rules IR1 and IR2 above are replaced by:

IR1: Before each event in P_i, increment $\vec{T}_i[i]$ by d, where $d > 0$.

IR2: Timestamp each message sent by P_i with the current value of the vector $\vec{T}_i$. On receipt of a message with timestamp $\vec{T}_M$ by P_j, set $\vec{T}_j[k]$ to $(\max{(\vec{T}_j[k], \vec{T}_M[k])} + d)$, for all k.

For vector clocks using these rules, it follows that $a{\rightarrow}b \Leftrightarrow \vec{C}(a) < \vec{C}(b)$, where the ordering relation on vectors is defined by:

$$\vec{x} < \vec{y} \Leftrightarrow (\; \forall i \cdot (\vec{x}[i] \leq \vec{y}[i]) \land \exists i (\vec{x}[i] < \vec{y}[i]))$$

This type of logical clock, which gives a true indication of causal ordering, has been used for implementing distributed algorithms for causal broadcast [13], causal distributed shared memory [2], distributed debugging and global breakpoints and checkpoints.

---

[2] In fact, the message arriving at time 6 in R breaks the usual rules of causal ordering, since it appears both to be able to cause and be caused by the event at time 5

5.5.2 Real time clocks

A clock which in some sense correctly reflects the time as seen by an external observer is generally denoted a *real time clock*. This is in practice based on a physical clock, which in principle is incremented smoothly and continuously. We shall denote by $C_i(t)$ the time shown at real time t on the physical clock available to process P_i. The aim of clock synchronisation is to achieve the result that for all reliable clocks:

$$\forall i, j \cdot (|C_i(t) - C_j(t)| < \delta), \quad \text{for some } \delta \ll 1$$

A system of clocks for which this holds is often said to be δ-*synchronised*.

Even the best physically realisable clocks will in reality suffer from errors:

Clock drift: The clock frequency is not exactly the correct one, so as time passes the value shown on the clock will drift further and further from the correct time.

Clock variation: The clock frequencies in different clocks are different, so as time passes the values shown on the clocks in the system drift apart from one another.

We shall assume that the magnitude of such errors is limited, in the sense that all clocks fulfil the *accuracy condition*:

$$\forall i \cdot (|dC_i(t)/dt - 1| < \rho), \quad \text{for some } \rho \ll 1$$

When this is true, the drift of the clocks is sometimes said to be ρ-*bounded*[3].

Now let us consider a system where process P_i attempts to adjust its clock in accordance with messages received from P_j, which we here assume to be a reliable *clock server* containing a perfect clock. All messages sent by the server are timestamped with the current value of the server's clock. Suppose the time to send a message between the two processes is μ, which is bounded below and above:

$$\mu_{min} \leq \mu \leq \mu_{max}$$

Then it can be shown that the best result which can be achieved by a deterministic protocol will ensure that P_i's clock is synchronised to within $(\mu_{max} - \mu_{min})/2$ of the server's clock. This optimum is achieved by using the simple rule:

Deterministic synchronisation: On receiving a message with timestamp T_s from the server, a process P_i will set its own clock to $T_s + (\mu_{max} + \mu_{min})/2$.

Cristian [26] has shown that a better result can be achieved by a *probabilistic algorithm*, on the assumption that message delay is a stochastic variable distributed

---

[3] ρ-boundedness is by some authors defined by:

$$(1+\rho)^{-1} \leq (C_i(t_2) - C_i(t_1))/(t_2 - t_1) \leq (1+\rho)$$

The two formulations are equivalent in the limit $(t_2 - t_1) \to 0$

Probability density
$dF(\mu)/d\mu$

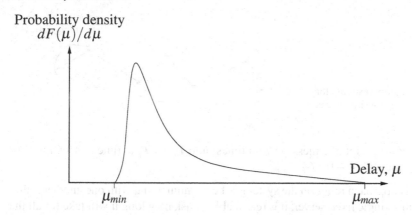

Delay, μ

μ_{min} μ_{max}

Fig. 5.15 Probability density for message delay between two given systems in a distributed system (after [26])

according to a function $F : [\mu_{min}; \mu_{max}] \rightarrow [0; 1]$, where $F(\mu)$ gives the probability that a given message will arrive within a time μ, corresponding to the probability density function shown in Figure 5.15. The protocol consists in carrying out one or more trials, each of which follows the rule:

Probabilistic synchronisation: The client, P_i, sends a message to the server and awaits a reply.
If the reply arrives timestamped T_s by the server after an interval I, the client sets its own clock to $T_s + I/2$.

It is easy to show that the client's clock is then correct to within $(I - 2\mu_{min})/2$. If better accuracy is required, the procedure is repeated until a sufficiently small value of I is obtained. The expected number of trials to achieve synchronisation to within δ is $1/F^2(\mu_{min} + \delta)$. Interestingly, this protocol only requires knowledge of a *lower* bound for the message delay, μ_{min}. Note also that it is not necessary to know the detailed form of F unless an estimate of the number of trials is required. Cristian's algorithm is one of the central elements in the Internet NTP clock synchronisation protocol [92,93], where it forms the basis of the *minimum filter* used to find the best estimate of delay and offset from a set of measurements made between a client and a clock server.

Both the deterministic and the probabilistic algorithm assume that somewhere in the network there are one or more (relatively) reliable and accurate time servers. An approach for synchronising physical real time clocks *without* using a server has been proposed by Lamport [75], who showed that δ-synchronisation can be attained if the clocks follow the implementation rules:

IRP1:   If process P_i does not receive a message at physical time t, then C_i is differentiable at t and $dC_i(t)/dt > 0$.
IRP2:   Timestamp each message sent by P_i with the current value of $C_i(t)$.

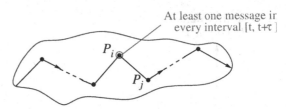

Fig. 5.16 Lamport's setup for synchronising physical clocks

> On receipt of a message with timestamp T_M by P_j at time t', set C_j to $\max(C_j(t' - 0), T_M + \mu_{min})$.

Since this approach relies on the systems all communicating with one another rather than with a single fixed server, it is reasonable to ask how long it will take for all the clocks to be synchronised. Lamport shows that under the assumptions:

1. at least one message passes between two neighbouring systems in every period τ (for $\tau \gg \mu_{max}$), as illustrated in Figure 5.16.
2. the *diameter* of the network (i.e. the number of edges in the graph between the two most distant systems) is d.

Then δ-synchronisation will be achieved for $\delta \approx d \cdot (2\rho\tau + (\mu_{max} - \mu_{min}))$ after a time no larger than $\tau \cdot d$.

5.5.3 Byzantine Clock Synchronisation

If any of the clocks are subject to arbitrary faults, Byzantine techniques are needed to ensure synchronisation. There are two approaches in common use:

Interactive convergence, where correctly working clocks exchange messages which cause their settings to converge.

Interactive consistency, where correctly working processes obtain a mutually consistent view of the time shown on the other processes' clocks, as in the Byzantine Generals algorithms discussed in Section 5.4.

A typical example of the *interactive convergence* approach is the algorithm **CNV** given by Lamport and Melliar-Smith [78, 79]. This assumes that all correctly working clocks are δ-synchronised initially, and that all processes read the clocks of all other processes. The principle is that each process P_i sets its own clock C_i to a *fault-tolerant average* of the values read, formed by taking the average after replacing all deviant values – those which deviate more than δ from $C_i(t)$ – by $C_i(t)$. The closeness with which the clocks can be synchronised (i.e. the minimum achievable value of δ) depends on how far apart they are allowed to drift before (re-)synchronisation.

In practice, it is not feasible directly to use the average *times* reported by the other processes, since the other clocks cannot all be read at exactly the same instant, and the messages reporting the times on the other clocks take a finite time to arrive. Instead, $C_i(t)$ is updated by the average *difference* between the time reported by each

Protocol 19

$P[i : NS, T : \mathbb{Z}] \overset{\text{def}}{=} (P1[i,T] \parallel Timer[i]) \setminus up[i]$

$P1[i : NS, T : \mathbb{Z}] \overset{\text{def}}{=} (SAPA?s : \{\text{SIGNAL}\} \rightarrow up!\text{SET} \rightarrow \coprod_{j \in NS-\{i\}} right[j]!s \rightarrow$
$$P2[i, [0,0,\ldots,0], T]$$
$\quad \llbracket left[k \in NS]?s : \{\text{SIGNAL}\} \rightarrow right[k]!(i,T) \rightarrow P1[i,T] \,)$

$P2[i : NS, ts : \mathbb{Z}^*, T : \mathbb{Z}]$
$\qquad \overset{\text{def}}{=} (left[k \in NS]?(j : NS, t : \mathbb{Z}) \rightarrow$
$\qquad\qquad (\text{if } |t - T| > \delta + \varepsilon$
$\qquad\qquad \text{then } P2[i, ts \dagger [j \mapsto 0], T]$
$\qquad\qquad \text{else } P2[i, ts \dagger [j \mapsto t - T], T])$
$\qquad \llbracket left[k \in NS]?s : \{\text{SIGNAL}\} \rightarrow right[k]!(i,T) \rightarrow P2[i,ts,T]$
$\qquad \llbracket tick \rightarrow P2[i,ts,T+d]$
$\qquad \llbracket up[i]?t : \{\text{TIMEOUT}\} \rightarrow P1[i, T + average(ts)] \,)$

$Timer[i : NS] \quad \overset{\text{def}}{=} (up[i]?s : \{\text{SET}\} \rightarrow (up[i]?r : \{\text{RESET}\} \rightarrow Timer[i]$
$\qquad\qquad\qquad\qquad \llbracket up[i]!\text{TIMEOUT} \rightarrow Timer[i]) \,)$

Fig. 5.17 Interactive Convergence protocol for clock synchronisation.

of the other clocks and the value of C_i at the time when this report arrives; in the average, the difference for clock, say C_k, is considered deviant (and is replaced by 0) if it exceeds $\delta + \varepsilon$, where ε is the accuracy with which a process can measure the difference between its own clock value and that of another process.

The detailed protocol – and the value of ε – depends on the mechanism used to read the clocks in the other processes. An example is shown in Figure 5.17: here synchronisation of the clocks is initiated by a user sending a SIGNAL via channel *SAPA*. This causes all the processes to be asked to send the settings on their clocks. The replies are converted to time differences, filtered to remove deviant values, and collected up in the sequence *ts* until a timer runs out, at which time their average is used to update the local timer. The event *tick* indicates some internal event which advances the local timer. A SIGNAL message arriving from another process likewise causes the local process to reply with the current value of its timer.

Like the Byzantine Generals algorithms with oral messages, this protocol requires there to be $n > 3m$ processes in total, if it is to work correctly when up to m of them are faulty. If this condition is fulfilled, and the clocks are initially δ-synchronised, then Lamport and Melliar-Smith demonstrate that the clocks will continue to be δ-synchronised after adjustment, provided δ is at least:

$$(6m+2)\varepsilon + (3m+1)\rho R$$

where R is the interval between successive (re-)synchronisations.

In contrast to interactive convergence protocols, the aim of *interactive consistency* protocols is to cause correctly working processes to get a mutually consistent view of the time shown on the other processes' clocks. This is analogous to the aim of the Byzantine Generals algorithms discussed in Section 5.4. For clocks, we require the following two conditions to be fulfilled:

IC1:   All non-faulty processes P_i, P_j agree on the same value for the clock in a third process, P_k (even if this process or its clock is faulty).

IC2:   If process P_i is non-faulty, then all other non-faulty processes obtain the clock value that it sends.

Typical examples of this approach are Lamport and Melliar-Smith's algorithms **COM** and **CSM**, which are completely analogous to the Byzantine Generals protocols **Protocol 17**, using oral messages, and **Protocol 18**, using signed messages, respectively. These protocols can maintain δ-synchronisation provided δ is respectively at least $(6m+4)\varepsilon + \rho R$ and at least $(m+6)\varepsilon + \rho R$.

5.6 Finding the Global State

As our final example of protocols for reaching consensus, we shall consider how to find the global state of a distributed system in which data items can move from one part of the system to another. There are innumerable uses for this. For example:

- Finding the total *number of files* in a distributed file system, where files may be moved from one file server to another;
- Finding the total *space occupied by files* in such a distributed file system;
- Finding the number of *control tokens* whose possession gives the right to perform certain actions in the system (see Section 4.4.3).

and so on. Obviously this can be done in a trivial way if we are allowed to have a pause in the operation of the system. We just stop the system (say, at some agreed instant of time), wait until any messages which are in transit have arrived, take a "snapshot" of the state of each of the processes, and then set the system going again. However, this is not usually a very convenient way to run a distributed system, and we would prefer a method which allows the system to continue operating at the same time as we find its global state.

A way to solve this problem has been described by Chandy and Lamport [22], and is usually known as the *distributed snapshot* algorithm. To understand the algorithm, you need to realise that the state of the system is composed of the states of the participating processes together with the states of the channels through which data (i.e. the files, tokens or whatever) pass when being transferred between these processes. The algorithm relies on two assumptions:

1. The communication channels are error-free and sequence preserving.
2. A channel delivers a transmitted message after an unknown but finite delay.

The only events in the system which can give rise to changes in the state are communication events. Each *event* is described by 5 components:

$$e \sim <P,s,s',M,c>$$

Process P goes from state s to	Message M is sent or re-
state s'	ceived on channel c.

An event $e = <P,s,s',M,c>$ is only *possible* in global state S if:

1. P's state in S is just exactly s.
2. If c is directed towards P, then c's state in S must be a sequence of messages with M at its head.

Note that this implies that simultaneous events are assumed not to occur, i.e. there is a total ordering of events. If e takes place in global state S, then the following global state is next(S,e), where:

1. P's state in next(S,e) is s'.
2. If c is directed towards P, then c's state in next(S,e) is c's state in S, with M *removed from the head* of the message seqeuence.
3. If c is directed away from P, then c's state in next(S,e) is c's state in S, with M *added to the tail* of the message sequence.

A *possible computation* of the system is a sequence of *possible events*, starting from the *initial global state* of the system. An simple example of the progress of a possible computation is shown in Figure 5.18. In the figure, and subsequently in this section, c_{ij} denotes the channel which can carry messages from process P_i to process P_j.

System configuration:

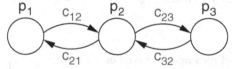

	Event						Global state S after event						
$<P$	s	s'	M	$c>$	$\Rightarrow$	$<P_1$	P_2	P_3	c_{12}	c_{21}	c_{23}	$c_{32}>$	
						<100	125	10	$<>$	$<>$	$<>$	$<>>$	
e_1	$<P_1$	100	25	75	$c_{12}>$	$\Rightarrow$	<25	125	10	$\langle 75 \rangle$	$<>$	$<>$	$<>>$
e_2	$<P_2$	125	100	25	$c_{23}>$	$\Rightarrow$	<25	100	10	$\langle 75 \rangle$	$<>$	$\langle 25 \rangle$	$<>>$
e_3	$<P_2$	100	175	75	$c_{12}>$	$\Rightarrow$	<25	175	10	$<>$	$<>$	$\langle 25 \rangle$	$<>>$
e_4	$<P_2$	175	125	50	$c_{21}>$	$\Rightarrow$	<25	125	10	$<>$	$\langle 50 \rangle$	$\langle 25 \rangle$	$<>>$
e_5	$<P_3$	10	35	25	$c_{23}>$	$\Rightarrow$	<25	125	35	$<>$	$\langle 50 \rangle$	$<>$	$<>>$
e_6	$<P_1$	25	75	50	$c_{21}>$	$\Rightarrow$	<75	125	35	$<>$	$<>$	$<>$	$<>>$

Fig. 5.18 A possible computation

Can we now find rules for when to take snapshots of the individual processes and channels so as to build up a consistent picture of the global state? To answer this question it is necessary to return to the *happened before* relation, $\rightarrow$, defined in Section 5.5. If for two events e_1, e_2, it is the case that $e_1 \rightarrow e_2$, then e_1 happened before

e_2 and could have caused it. A consistent picture of the global state is obtained if we include in our computation a set of possible events, $\mathcal{H}$, such that:

$$e_i \in \mathcal{H} \wedge e_j \to e_i \ \Rightarrow \ e_j \in \mathcal{H}$$

If e_i were in $\mathcal{H}$, but e_j were not, then the set of events would include the effect of an event (for example, the receipt of a file), but not the event causing it (the sending of the file), and an inconsistent picture would arise. The *consistent global state* found in this way is:

> $\text{GS}(\mathcal{H})$ = The state of each process P_i after P_i's last event in $\mathcal{H}$
> + for each channel, the sequence of messages sent in $\mathcal{H}$ but not re-
>   ceived in $\mathcal{H}$.

Some examples of consistent sets of events in the case of the computation of Figure 5.18 are shown in Figure 5.19(b) and (c), while an inconsistent set of events is shown in Figure 5.19(d).

Chandy and Lamport's protocol for finding a consistent set of events $\mathcal{H}$ makes use of *markers*, which are inserted in the stream of ordinary messages associated with the application. Process P_i follows the two rules:

Send markers:
> Note P_i's state.
> Before sending any more messages from P_i, send a marker on each channel c_{ij} directed away from P_i.

Receive marker: On arrival of a marker via channel c_{ji}:
> **If** P_i has not noted its state
> **Then** Send markers.
> > Note c_{ji}'s state as empty.
> **Else** Note c_{ji}'s state as the sequence of messages received on c_{ji} since
> > P_i last noted its state.

The algorithm can be initiated by any process. To start the algorithm, it is only necessary to follow the **Send markers** rule. If, for example, the progress of the basic computation is as in Figure 5.19, and P_2 initiates the algorithm at m_1 sometime between event e_2 and e_3, then the algorithm could proceed as shown in Figure 5.20. You should notice the wording here: the markers might move faster or slower along particular channels, and so arrive at their destinations earlier or later than shown in the figure. The only thing we know for certain about the progress of the markers is that they cannot overtake messages (or other markers) sent previously on the same channel, since we assume that the channels are sequence-preserving.

The various components of the state are noted down in accordance with the algorithm as follows:

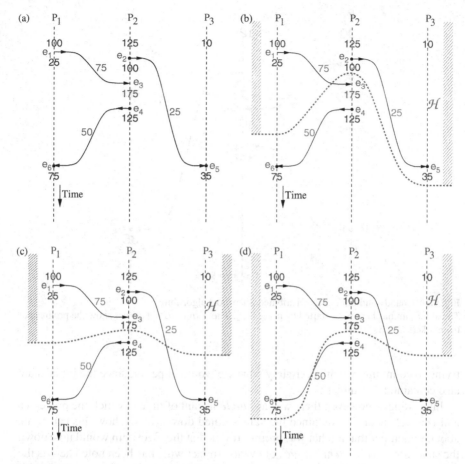

Fig. 5.19 Consistent and inconsistent sets of events. The *heavy dotted curve* demarcates set $\mathcal{H}$.
(a) Basic computation.
(b) A consistent set. $\mathcal{H}$ contains $\{e_1, e_2, e_5\}$.
(c) A consistent set. $\mathcal{H}$ contains $\{e_1, e_2, e_3\}$.
(d) An inconsistent set. $\mathcal{H}$ contains $\{e_1, e_2, e_3, e_6\}$, but not e_4, where $e_4 \rightarrow e_6$.

Marker event	Processes	Channels
m_1	$P_2 = 100$	
m_2	$P_1 = 25$	$c_{21} = \langle \rangle$
m_3		$c_{12} = \langle 75 \rangle$
m_4	$P_3 = 35$	$c_{23} = \langle \rangle$
m_5		$c_{32} = \langle \rangle$

In a practical implementation, it would of course not be quite enough just to note these component values down locally in whichever of the processes they were observed in – they would also have to be sent to the process which started the algorithm. The overall result here is a total state of 235 units of whatever it is we are

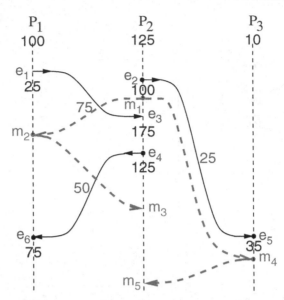

Fig. 5.20 Chandy and Lamport's Distributed Snapshots algorithm.
The algorithm has here been started by process P_2. The *heavy dashed curves* show the progress of the markers.

trying to count up, which is certainly what we would hope for, since the initial state also contained 235 units!

Interestingly, however, there was no *single* instant of time at which the processes and channels actually contained the values noted down. To see how this can come about, remember that all that was promised was that the algorithm would note down the state after a *consistent set*, $\mathcal{H}$, of events. In fact what has been noted here is the values corresponding to the set $\mathcal{H}$ in Figure 5.19(b). If the algorithm was initiated by another process, or if the markers moved faster or slower, we would effectively delineate another (consistent) set $\mathcal{H}'$ and in all probability note down another set of state components.

The key to understanding why this works is to notice that our consistent picture is based on a *partial ordering* $\rightarrow$ of events in the system. So for example in the computation of Figure 5.19(a), we know that $e_2 \rightarrow e_5$ and $e_2 \rightarrow e_3$. But we have no knowledge about the timing relationships of e_3 and e_5. With respect to the ordering relation $\rightarrow$, these two events are *incomparable*. Without fixing a total ordering (say by using a physical clock), we cannot determine what the true sequence of these events is. Passing markers round enables us to delineate a consistent set of events $\mathcal{H}$ in the sense of the partial ordering. But when we note down a process' state, we are unable to know whether the events which we have already seen in this process lay before or after incomparable events in other processes. We can in fact accept any total ordering which does not conflict with the partial ordering. We can divide events in the system into two classes:

Pre-recording events: Events in a computation which take place before the process in which they occur notes its own state.
Post-recording events: All other events.

Chandy and Lamport's algorithm finds a global state which corresponds to a *permutation* of the actual order of the events, such that all pre-recording events come before all post-recording events. The global state which is noted down is the one which would be found after all the pre-recording events and before all the post-recording events. So for example, for the computation of Figure 5.19(a), the true sequence of events is:

$$seq = \langle e_1, e_2, e_3, e_4, e_5, e_6 \rangle$$

When the markers are passed round as shown in Figure 5.20, then e_1, e_2 and e_5 are pre-recording events, and the state which is noted down, S^*, is the state after these events in the permutated sequence:

$$seq' = \langle e_1, e_2, e_5, e_3, e_4, e_6 \rangle$$

Although S^* does not necessarily correspond to any state which actually occurred at a particular instant of time, it is a state which *could possibly* have occurred, in the sense that:

- It is possible to reach S^* via a sequence of *possible events* starting from the initial state of the system, S_ι (in the example above, the sequence $\langle e_1, e_2, e_5 \rangle$).
- It is possible to reach the final state of the system, S_ϕ, via a sequence of possible events starting from S^* (in the example, the sequence $\langle e_3, e_4, e_6 \rangle$).

You should check for yourself that these sequences of events really are *possible*, starting from the given states.

Further reading

In addition to the large number of papers on specific topics referenced in the text, a number of useful review articles are available and make a good place to start further reading. Fischer [44] gives a good survey of results on Byzantine consensus. Lynch [84] presents "A Hundred Impossibility Proofs for Distributed Computing", of which a substantial number are within the area treated in this chapter. Finally, for those interested in not just the properties of these protocols but how to prove them, the article by Fischer, Lynch and Merritt [45] gives a fascinating insight into the type of mathematical methods required.

A very large number of situations can be dealt with in terms of finding the global state of a system. Chandy and Lamport's distributed snapshot algorithm is an example of a very general algorithm for this purpose. Several more specialised protocols have been developed for use for more specific purposes, such as detecting when a distributed computation terminates [33, 48] and detecting distributed dead-lock [23, 52, 88].

Exercises

5.1. Explain how **Protocol 14** would have to be modified if the size of the send window for the broadcast were to be larger than 1, i.e. if it were possible to start a broadcast with sequence number $(n+1)$ before the broadcast with number n were complete.

5.2. Give a CSP process description of Skeen's centralised, non-blocking (3-phase) commit algorithm, as sketched in the text (and described more fully in [117]).

5.3. Explain carefully what the flow of messages is in the system, if the Byzantine Generals algorithm given as **Protocol 17** is executed for $n = 4, t = 1$, when the initial commander is disloyal. Then try the case $n = 7, t = 2$, with lieutenants 2 and 3 disloyal. How many messages are sent in total in each of these two cases? Check your result against the formula in the text.

5.4. Give a CSP description of Dolev and Strong's modification of **Protocol 18** for Byzantine agreement using signed messages, as sketched in the text and described more fully in [36].

5.5. Suppose Chandy and Lamport's distributed snapshot algorithm is initiated by process P_1 just after event e_1 in the computation of Figure 5.19(a). Sketch how markers would be exchanged during the execution of the algorithm in this case. Which events are included in the set $\mathcal{H}$ during this execution of the algorithm? Which state components are noted down in the various processes, as execution of the algorithm proceeds? Which global state S^* is discovered by the algorithm in this case?

Chapter 6
Security

"And when the loss has been disclosed, the Secret Service say:
'It must have been Macavity!' – but he's a mile away.
You'll be sure to find him resting, or a-licking of his thumbs,
Or engaged in doing complicated long division sums".
"Macavity: The Mystery Cat"
T. S. Eliot.

In distributed systems, security is well-known to be an important issue, as the continual stream of computer scandals, in which 'hackers' break into supposedly secure computer installations, testifies. The first step on the way to obtaining a really secure system is to recognise that there are two basic problems in a distributed system:

1. It is difficult, perhaps even impossible, to protect the physical connections in the distributed system completely against tapping. This means that you should assume that all messages can in principle be overheard, recorded for replaying on a later occasion, or altered.

2. It is difficult to be certain that the party with whom you are exchanging messages really is the party that you believe him to be, since you cannot really 'see' who it is, but have to rely on more indirect methods of identification, which might be faked.

Naive protocols for ensuring security blatantly ignore one or both of these problems. Unfortunately, methods which appear to deal with the problems are often equally faulty. As we shall see, a formalised mechanism for reasoning about such methods is required in order to achieve the aim of a secure system.

6.1 Cryptographic Methods

Mechanisms for supporting a secure service are in general based on the use of *cryptographic* methods. These are methods for transforming data in order to hide their information content, prevent their undetected modification or prevent their unauthorised use. Generally speaking, the process of transforming data to a form where their information content is hidden – often known as *ciphertext* – is known as *encryption*, the reverse process – transforming to *plaintext* – is known as *decryption*, and a given mutual pair of encryption and decryption methods are said to form a *cryptosystem*.

Cryptographic methods are generally assumed to be able to offer at least *confidentiality* of data to their users. However, this will in fact only genuinely be the case if:

1. Encryption is perfect, in the sense that encrypted data can only be decrypted if you possess details of the authorised decryption method. This implies that the decryption method is unique, and that no combination of encrypted messages, with or without knowledge of the corresponding plaintext messages, will 'leak' sufficient information to enable the decryption method to be deduced.
2. Decryption is sensible, in the sense that if you decrypt an encrypted message using the wrong decryption method, then you get something which is plainly recognisable as nonsense. This implies that the users have some idea of what sort of messages they expect.

In general, neither of these assumptions is satisfied. However, they are often satisfied 'for all practical purposes'. For instance, a potential enemy will always need a certain amount of time to discover the required decryption method. If the encryption method is changed frequently enough, the enemy will (unless an accident which reveals the method occurs, or there is a spy who deliberately reveals it) in practice never be able to find the right method in time.

6.1.1 Encipherment

The most basic form of encryption is *encipherment*, in which an *encipherment function*,

$$E : \mathcal{M}^* \times \mathcal{K} \rightarrow \mathcal{M}^*$$

is used to transform plaintext (say, $m \in \mathcal{M}^*$) to ciphertext using a *key* (say, $k \in \mathcal{K}$), known as the *encipherment key*. A complementary *decipherment function*, D, transforms the ciphertext back to plaintext using the same or a different key, the *decipherment key*. Cryptosystems using encipherment fall into two classes:

Symmetric   systems, in which knowledge of the encipherment key implies knowledge of the decipherment key and vice-versa. An example is when the two keys are identical. Obviously this is only secure if the keys themselves are kept secret. Symmetric systems are therefore often known as *secret key* cryptosystems.

Asymmetric   systems, in which knowledge of the encipherment key does not imply knowledge of the decipherment key or vice-versa. These are often known as *public key* cryptosystems *(PKCS)*. A common arrangement is for one of the keys in fact to be made public, whereas the other one (the *private key*) is kept secret by the user.

6.1.2 Secret Key Cryptosystems

Secret key cryptosystems include most of the classic tools of the cryptographer's trade, such as substitution ciphers and transposition ciphers. In a *substitution cipher*, each symbol (letter, digit etc.) of the plaintext is encrypted by replacing it with another symbol from the same (or different) symbol set. Trivial examples are to use as a key a cyclic permutation of the letters of the alphabet, say $RSTU\ldots Q$, so that the encryption function becomes:

$$\{A \mapsto R, B \mapsto S, C \mapsto T, D \mapsto U, \ldots Z \mapsto Q\}$$

or to use an arbitrary permutation of the letters of the alphabet, say $REVB\ldots Y$, so that the encryption function becomes:

$$\{A \mapsto R, B \mapsto E, C \mapsto V, D \mapsto B, \ldots Z \mapsto Y\}$$

More complex examples include the use of *one-time pads* and the like. These are essentially random number generators, so that the substitution varies continuously and unpredictably throughout the text (or texts) to be sent, corresponding to a substitution with an infinitely long, non-repeating key. In a *transposition cipher*, the symbols of the message are left unchanged, but their positions in the message are altered.

Of these simple ciphers, only substitutions using one-time pads offer substantial protection against analysis. This is because the high redundancy of natural language permits various forms of statistical analysis of the text, such as determining the frequency of individual letters, or of sequences of two or more letters. If particular combinations of plaintext and the corresponding ciphertext are known[1], or if there is enough ciphertext without corresponding plaintext available, this type of analysis can be used to reveal the nature of the cipher.

As long ago as 1949, Shannon [114] pointed out that there are two basic techniques for counteracting this form of analysis:

Diffusion, which is the dissipation of redundancy in the plaintext by spreading it out over the ciphertext. Transposition ciphers achieve this aim in a simple way, since they typically break up sequences of letters. Encryption functions which generate symbol i of the ciphertext from several symbols (say $i-n, i-n+1, \ldots, i$) of the plaintext also enjoy this property.

Confusion, which is introduction of as much complexity into the encryption function as possible, so that it becomes difficult to deduce the key by analysis of ciphertext. This is the idea behind the more complex substitution ciphers.

Generally speaking, neither diffusion nor confusion gives much protection on its own, but a combination of the two techniques can give a relatively high degree of security.

---

[1] This does not necessarily mean that the cipher has been 'broken'. It may be possible simply to get the system to tell you the encryption of a piece of plaintext which you yourself have provided.

The best known modern secret key cryptosystem is the *Data Encryption Standard (DES)*, introduced in 1977 by the USA National Bureau of Standards [256]. This uses a 56 bit key to encrypt blocks of 64 bits of data. The 56 bit key is used to create 16 48-bit partial keys, which are used to perform 16 rounds of transformation on each block of plaintext. Each round incorporates both confusion and diffusion, by operating on the two halves of the 64 bit block in a manner described by a *Feistel network*.

Suppose in round i the two halves are L_i and R_i respectively. Then in a Feistel network the output of the round is L_{i+1} and R_{i+1}, evaluated as follows:

$$L_{i+1} = R_i$$
$$R_{i+1} = L_i \oplus SP(k_i, R_i)$$

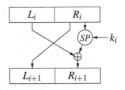

where k_i is the i'th partial key, $\oplus$ is the Exclusive OR function, and SP is some combination of bit substitutions and permutations, parameterised by the partial key. Feistel networks are used in many secret key cryptosystems, and have the useful property that they are reversible, so that the same algorithm can be used

Fig. 6.1 A round in a Feistel network

for encryption and decryption, where for decryption the steps are performed in the reverse order. The detailed properties of the cryptosystem depend on the number of rounds and on the particular SP-function chosen for use. A more detailed description of DES's SP-function can be found in [113]. In DES, the 16 rounds of transformation are preceded by a key-independent *initial transposition* of the 64 bit plaintext block, and are followed by an exchange of the two halves of the (transformed) block and then by the inverse of the initial transposition, making 19 stages of transformation in total.

This may all sound very complicated, but essentially the DES cryptosystem is a monoalphabetic substitution cipher, where each symbol in the alphabet is of 64 bits. On the other hand, it has a simple hardware implementation, which in current VLSI technology permits encryption and decryption speeds of up to at least 1 Gbit/s from commercially available chips and even higher speeds from laboratory prototypes. Its disadvantage, in common with other secret key cryptosystems, is that each *pair of users* must share a different key. So in systems with N users it becomes necessary to distribute $O(N^2)$ keys. Moreover, the key size for DES is by now much too small for high security applications. A determined enemy could find the key within a few hours by exhaustive search using a cluster of powerful computers. Multiple encryption, using several independent keys, is therefore recommended for more sensitive applications [90].

Double encryption, for example according to the scheme:

$$e = DES(k2, DES(k1, d))$$
$$d = DES^{-1}(k1, DES^{-1}(k2, e))$$

is the simplest and most obvious choice. Unfortunately, it is susceptible to *meet-in-the-middle attacks*, based on knowledge of the ciphertext which corresponds to two

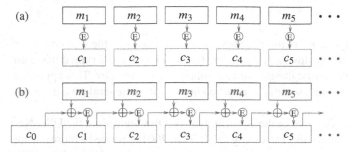

Fig. 6.2 DES modes of operation: (a) ECB mode and (b) CBC mode. Here, E is the encryption function, and $\oplus$ the exclusive or function.

or more known blocks of plaintext: Given a (plaintext,ciphertext) pair (d_1, e_1), the attacker computes a table of $DES(k, d_1)$ for all possible $k \in \mathcal{K}$ and then computes values of $x = DES^{-1}(k', e_1)$ for successive values of $k' \in \mathcal{K}$. If x equals one of the values in the table, say for $k = p$ and $k' = q$, then p and q are good candidates for the two keys $k1$ and $k2$ of the double encryption. This is checked by seeing whether $DES(p, d_i) = DES^{-1}(q, e_i)$ for one or more further (plaintext,ciphertext) pairs (d_i, e_i). If not, then the search continues with further values of k'.

Triple encryption, on the other hand, is relatively resistent to attack. A popular choice is the so-called *Triple DES* (or *3DES*) scheme, which uses three keys $(k1, k2, k3)$, so that:

$$e = DES(k3, DES^{-1}(k2, DES(k1, d)))$$
$$d = DES^{-1}(k1, DES(k2, DES^{-1}(k3, e)))$$

If the three keys are all different and of size n bits, this scheme has roughly the same resistance to attack as (single) DES with a key of $2n$ bits. Simplified schemes in which $k1 = k3$ have also been proposed, but are in fact also susceptible to meet-in-the-middle attacks [90].

Finally, DES has another problem which it shares with all other cryptosystems which operate on fixed-length blocks of data (including 3DES and the more modern AES to be described below). This is that the most obvious way of encrypting the plaintext, where each block of plaintext is directly encrypted using the same secret key, will always produce the same block of ciphertext from a given block of plaintext. This may help an attacker to deduce the secret key. This simple approach is known as the *Electronic Codebook (ECB) Mode* of operation for a block cipher, and is illustrated in Figure 6.2(a). Generally speaking, ECB mode encryption is only useful when single blocks of non-repetitive text, such as encryption keys, have to be transmitted. For longer or more repetitive transmissions, it is considered unsafe. Several other modes of operation have, however, been designed to provide more security in such cases, and are described in [257]. For general-purpose block transmission of data, the *Cipher Block Chaining (CBC)* mode illustrated in Figure 6.2(b) is usually recommended. In CBC mode, the ciphertext for block i is computed as:

$$c_i = DES(m_i \oplus c_{i-1}, k)$$

where k is the secret key, m_i is the plaintext for block i, c_{i-1} is the ciphertext for block $i-1$, and $\oplus$ is the exclusive or function. The first block is encrypted using an initial block c_0, which may be thought of as a supplement to the key. This approach ensures that a series of blocks with identical plaintext will in general give different ciphertexts.

Recognising the weaknesses of the commonly used DES algorithm, the USA National Institute of Standards and Technology (NIST) in 2001 approved a more secure symmetric cryptosystem, known as the *Advanced Encryption Standard (AES)* [259]. This is based on the *Rijndael* algorithm [27], which was the winner of a competition organised by NIST for an improved encryption algorithm for protecting non-classified data. Rijndael is an iterated block cipher with a variable block size and key size, either or both of which can be chosen to be 128, 192 or 256 bits. AES is slightly more restrictive, as the block size can only be 128 bits.

As in DES, encryption in AES proceeds in several rounds, where each round makes use of a specific *round key* derived from the main encryption key. Unlike DES, however, each round of transformation is not based on a Feistel network, but uses three distinct invertible uniform transformations, known as *layers*:

1. The *linear mixing* layer, which guarantees high diffusion over multiple rounds.
2. The *non-linear* layer, which uses parallel application of non-linear byte substitutions to each of the bytes of the block independently.
3. The *key addition* layer, which performs an Exclusive-OR of the current round key with the block produced by the previous transformations.

The number of rounds in AES depends on the key size, being 10 for key size 128 bits, 12 for key size 192 bits and 14 for key size 256 bits. The Rijndael algorithm was exposed to extensive cryptanalysis during the competition for selection as the AES, and is widely accepted to be an efficiently implementable algorithm which is resistant to all currently known types of attack. Encryption and decryption speeds in excess of 2 Gbit/s, using carefully designed hardware, have been reported. Of course, AES still suffers from the general weakness of all block ciphers which we discussed above, but use of more advanced modes of operation such as CBC alleviate this problem as in the case of DES.

6.1.3 Public Key Cryptosystems

In recent years, most attention has been paid to public key systems. Their working is illustrated in Figure 6.3. User A, traditionally known as Alice, has public key PK_A and private key SK_A, while user B, traditrionally known as Bob, uses public key PK_B and private key SK_B. By definition, Alice knows PK_B (but not SK_B) and Bob knows PK_A (but not SK_A). When Alice wishes to send secret data d to Bob, she enciphers them using Bob's public key, and therefore sends enciphered data

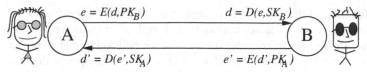

Fig. 6.3 Operation of a public key cryptosystem.

$$e = E(d, PK_B)$$

Bob can now decipher these data using his private key, to obtain

$$D(e, SK_B) = D(E(d, PK_B), SK_B) = d$$

Similarly, Alice can decipher secret data which Bob has enciphered using PK_A.

For this to offer true security, it must not be possible from publicly available information to evaluate the inverse function to E. Thus E must be a so-called *trapdoor one-way function*, where the 'trapdoor' refers to the existence of the decryption function D, for those who know the appropriate private key.

A well-known public key system is the so-called *RSA* system, after its inventors Rivest, Shamir and Adelman [110]. The basic security in RSA relies on the computational difficulty of factorising a large integer into prime factors. Given a publicly known integer, n, known as the *arithmetic modulus*, each user employs two other integers, p, the Public Exponent (which can be made public), and s, the Secret Exponent (which is kept secret), to encipher and decipher data. Data to be sent are divided into blocks, where each block is treated as the binary representation of a natural number, whose value must not exceed n. Typically, the blocks are chosen to be of l bits, where l is the largest integer for which $2^l \leq n$. To achieve confidentiality, encipherment and decipherment use the functions:

$$e = d^p \pmod{n}$$
$$d = e^s \pmod{n}$$

respectively. Such functions, of the form $x^y \pmod{n}$, are known as *modular exponentiation* functions. Efficient algorithms are known for evaluating these; for example the recursive function:

$$modexp : \mathbb{N}_0 \times \mathbb{N}_0 \times \mathbb{N}_0 \to \mathbb{N}_0$$

$modexp(x, y, n) \stackrel{\text{def}}{=}$
    if $y = 0$
    then 1
    elseif $even(y)$
    then $(modexp(x, y/2, n))^2 \bmod n$
    else $(x \cdot modexp(x, y-1, n)) \bmod n$

For an l-bit exponent y, this requires between l and $2l$ multiplications modulo n.

The inverse function to the modular exponentiation $d^p \bmod n$ is *evaluation of the integer p'th root modulo n*. Rather curiously, although algorithms for this are known, there is no known way of constructing them if we only know p and n – we also have to know the prime factors of n. If we do not know these prime factors, then we have to know s, the secret exponent, in order to decrypt the message. Thus the encryption function does indeed appear to be a *trapdoor one-way* function as required.

For the RSA algorithm, n is therefore chosen to be the product of two large primes, say $q \cdot r$, and p is chosen randomly such that:

$$\gcd(p, (q-1) \cdot (r-1)) = 1$$

i.e. such that p is relatively prime to $(q-1) \cdot (r-1)$. Then s is evaluated by Euclid's extended algorithm so that it satisfies:

$$p \cdot s = 1 \quad (\bmod\ (q-1) \cdot (r-1))$$

To understand why this is necessary, you need to know some simple results from number theory: The set of the whole numbers modulo n, $\{i \in \mathbb{N} | 0 \le i < n\}$, often known as the *set of residues* mod n and denoted $\mathbb{Z}_n$, form a commutative ring with operations addition and multiplication modulo n. A residue $a \in \mathbb{Z}_n$ is said to be *invertible* if there is an element, usually denoted $a^{-1} \in \mathbb{Z}_n$ and known as the *multiplicative inverse of a*, such that:

$$a \cdot a^{-1} \equiv a^{-1} \cdot a \equiv 1 \quad (\bmod\ n)$$

For example, in $\mathbb{Z}_5$, $2^{-1} = 3$, since $2 \cdot 3 \bmod 5 = 1$. A residue $a \in \mathbb{Z}_n$ is in fact invertible if and only if a and n are relatively prime, i.e. iff $\gcd(a,n) = 1$. The set of invertible residues in $\mathbb{Z}_n$ is often denoted $\mathbb{Z}_n^*$. For example, $\mathbb{Z}_5^* = \{1,2,3,4\}$, and $\mathbb{Z}_6^* = \{1,5\}$.

If n itself is prime, then of course all non-zero elements of $\mathbb{Z}_n$ are invertible; in such a case, $\mathbb{Z}_n$ is the finite field $\mathcal{GF}(n)$. The number of invertible residues mod n for $n > 0$ is given by *Euler's totient function*, $\phi(n)$, where by definition $\phi(1) = 1$. If n is prime, then $\phi(n) = n - 1$, as we see in the case of $\mathbb{Z}_5^*$ above; if $n = q \cdot r$, where q and r are both prime, then $\phi(n) = (q-1) \cdot (r-1)$, as we see in the case of $\mathbb{Z}_6^*$. Finally, *Euler's theorem* tells us that:

$$\gcd(a,n) = 1 \Rightarrow a^{\phi(n)} \equiv 1 \quad (\bmod\ n)$$

while a (more general) corollary to Euler's theorem gives, for primes q and r:

$$(n = q \cdot r) \wedge (0 < a < n) \Rightarrow a^{k \cdot \phi(n)} \equiv 1 \quad (\bmod\ n)$$

From these results it is easy to show that the original message is retrieved by decrypting the encrypted message, since

$$
\begin{aligned}
e^s \pmod n = (d^p \pmod n))^s \quad & \pmod n \\
= d^{p \cdot s} \quad & \pmod n \\
= d^{k \cdot (q-1) \cdot (r-1)+1} \quad & \pmod n, \text{ for some } k \\
= d \cdot d^{k \cdot (q-1) \cdot (r-1)} \quad & \pmod n \\
= d \cdot 1 \quad & \pmod n, \text{ by corollary to Euler's theorem} \\
= d
\end{aligned}
$$

Since the modulus n is publicly known, the encipherment would be compromised if it were possible to resolve n into its factors q and r, since then $(q-1) \cdot (r-1)$ would be known, and *anyone* knowing p could determine s by using Euclid's extended algorithm. However, it is generally agreed to be exceedingly difficult to resolve large integers, which are products of a few large prime factors, into their prime factors[2]. In 1977, for example, Rivest, Shamir and Adelman challenged the world to find the two factors of a number consisting of 129 decimal digits. This problem was solved in 1994 by a large team of volunteers after about 5000 MIPS-years of calculations, using the idle time on 1600 workstations over a period of about 8 months. For the best modern factorisation algorithm (the Number Field Sieve), which has an asymptotic run time of $e^{(1.923+O(1))(\ln n)^{1/3}(\ln \ln n)^{2/3}}$, it is estimated that factorisation of a 1024 bit number requires about $3 \cdot 10^7$ MIPS-years of effort. So the method is regarded as safe, provided the size of n's representation, l, exceeds 1024 bits or so. The question of how to choose good values for n is discussed in [53].

Note the careful choice of wording here: it has never been *formally proved* that modular exponentiation is a trapdoor one-way function, or even that trapdoor one-way functions exist at all. On the other hand, nobody has ever been able to show that it is not! So the security properties of the RSA cryptosystem are not mathematically clear. An advantage of the method, as with all public key systems, is that each user only needs a single key set (for RSA in fact three values: n, p and s) for all purposes. The disadvantage is that it is computationally much more demanding to evaluate the encryption and decryption functions than, say, DES or AES. The speed factor is somewhere between 100 and 1000. Speeds of the order of 1 Mbit/s for a 512 bit modulus are the best that have been achieved using specialised chips so far. For this reason, RSA is rarely used for encrypting large quantities of data. One common use for it is to encrypt SKCS secret keys for distribution to their owners. And we shall see later that RSA (and PKCSs in general) have properties which can be exploited in order to produce digital signatures and similar proofs of identity.

It is important to be aware that the basic security of the RSA algorithm can be compromised by unsuitable choice of keys or by unsuitable distribution of keys with the same modulus. For example, anyone who knows a set of keys, say for a particular modulus n, can factorise n and thus break the cryptosystem for any other user who is using that modulus. This is particularly easy if the public keys used with this modulus are relatively prime (which they usually are). Suppose in this case that two users have public keys p_1 and p_2 and both encrypt the same data, d. The attacker can then pick up the two ciphertexts:

---

[2] This must be why Macavity spends a lot of time doing complicated long division sums...

$$e_1 = d^{p_1} \bmod n$$
$$e_2 = d^{p_2} \bmod n$$

If $\gcd(p_1, p_2) = 1$, then Euclid's extended algorithm can be used to find integers u and v such that $u \cdot e_1 + v \cdot e_2 = 1$. Now one of u and v must be negative; let it be u. Euclid's extended algorithm can then be used once more to evaluate e_1^{-1}, and from this the attacker can work out:

$$(e_1^{-1})^{-u} \cdot e_2^v = d \bmod n$$

thus discovering the plaintext without the trouble of factorising n.

6.2 Integrity

Making data unreadable by the use of encryption does not necessarily preserve their integrity. The principal reason for this is that an intruder may be able to remove blocks of encrypted data, change their order, or replace them with blocks from a previous conversation (a so-called *replay attack*). Merely encrypting the data does not prevent this. We also need mechanisms which can ensure that only up-to-date data are accepted, and that their order is not interfered with.

Fig. 6.4 An intruder records an exchange of data in preparation for a replay attack

A large part of the problem here is one which we have already dealt with in Section 4.3.3. Mechanisms for ensuring temporal integrity include the use of references which uniquely identify the conversation and a numbering scheme which uniquely identifies the blocks of data. The references may, as we have seen, also merely be numbers. Or, if the distributed system can offer a universal clock, timestamps can be used.

However, in the presence of intruders who may deliberately remove or modify messages, it is not sufficient just to send the 'real' data and the reference, since an intruder could then easily fake a message by just replacing the original data with his own. To prevent this type of tampering, the message must also include some kind of *fingerprint*, which is calculated from the genuine data. If the data are changed or corrupted, the fingerprint no longer matches, and the receiver will be able to detect the fake.

The standard technique for creating such a fingerprint is to use a *one-way hash function*, also known as a *message digest*, *cryptographic checksum* or *compression function*. Like the more usual hash functions used in symbol tables and the like, a one-way hash function:

$$H : \mathcal{M} \rightarrow \mathcal{V}$$

transforms a message $m \in \mathcal{M}$ of arbitrary length to a fixed-length *hash value* $v \in \mathcal{V}$. However, a *one-way* hash function is also expected to have the properties that:

1. It is *(strongly) collision resistant*: It is computationally infeasible to find two different messages $m_1, m_2 \in \mathcal{M}$, such that $H(m_1) = H(m_2)$.
2. It is *non-invertible* (or *pre-image resistant*): Given $v \in \mathcal{V}$, it is computationally infeasible to find a message $m \in \mathcal{M}$ such that $H(m) = v$.

Both these aims are easier to achieve if the cardinality of $\mathcal{V}$ is large, so security is improved if the algorithm produces large hash values. In particular, the effort required to exploit collisions in order to compromise a hash function which produces an n-bit hash value is $O(2^{n/2})$.

Most modern one-way hash functions use more or less the same principles: The message to be hashed is divided into blocks. Each block is processed in a number of *rounds*, each of which consists of the successive application of a number of *operations*, each of which involves the application of a non-linear function and possibly also a cyclic shift, to sub-blocks of the message. The output from each block is used to determine a set of constants for use in processing the next block, until all blocks in the message have been dealt with. Three of the most widely used hash functions at present are:

MD5: This uses four rounds of 16 operations and produces a 128-bit hash value [220]. Because of the relatively small hash value space, MD5 is no longer considered secure.

Secure Hash Algorithm (SHA): This appears in four variants: SHA-1, using four rounds of 20 operations and producing a 160-bit hash value, and SHA-256, SHA-384 and SHA-512, giving 256, 384 and 512-bit values respectively [201, 260].

RIPEMD-160: This is an improved version of MD5 which uses two parallel sets of five rounds of 16 operations and produces a 160-bit hash value [201]; 128- and 256-bit variants are also defined.

On its own, a one-way hash function is not enough to ensure integrity. An intruder could simply substitute his own message, together with an appropriate reference and hash value, for the genuine one. To prevent this, it is necessary to *encrypt* the reference and hash value, for example so that the entire message then consists of the 'real' data, say d, the reference, say r, and the encrypted reference and hash value:

$$d \frown r \frown E(r \frown H(d \frown r), K)$$

where $H(x)$ is the hash value for x. It is not then possible to replace a block with a given reference with a block with another reference without knowing the encryption and decryption method and the key, here denoted K. If the references used in consecutive blocks are related to one another in some systematic manner, it is not possible to remove data blocks from the stream of data without being detected either.

To ensure integrity in a transmission from A to B, the key K needs to be A's secret key, either shared with B if an SKCS is in use, or A's private key if a PKCS is in use. In the PKCS case, an intruder can of course decrypt the encrypted part of the message (using A's public key), but this does not provide any information which she could not have worked out for herself by using the unencrypted part of the message and the (well-known) hash function. If confidentiality of the message is required, double encryption would be needed, for example using:

$$E(d\hat{\ }r\hat{\ }E(r\hat{\ }H(d\hat{\ }r),SK_A),PK_B)$$

in order for B to be sure that the message could only have been sent by A and read by B.

An alternative technique which avoids the inner encryption is to use a *Message Authentication Code (MAC)*. This is a one-way hash function, say C, with a secret key as additional parameter:

$$C : \mathcal{M} \times \mathcal{K} \to \mathcal{V}$$

so that for message $m \in \mathcal{M}$ and key $k \in \mathcal{K}$, the hash value is $C(m,k)$. Like H, C is required to be collision resistant and non-invertible. When a MAC is used, it is necessary to have the secret MAC key in order to check whether the hash value matches the message, and so an intruder cannot construct a correct hash value for a fake message. As before, message confidentiality can be ensured by an outer encryption, so that the transmitted message for MAC key MK_{AB} is:

$$E(d\hat{\ }r\hat{\ }C(d\hat{\ }r,MK_{AB}),PK_B)$$

A well-known example of a MAC is the so-called *MDx-MAC*, defined in ISO standard 9797-2 [186]. This is in fact a family of MACs, whose members are based on different basic standard hash algorithms, such as RIPEMD-160, RIPEMD-128 and SHA-1. Given a MAC key k of length L_k bits, and a standard hash function H which takes input blocks of length L_1 bits, the key k is extended to k' of length 128 bits by concatenating it with itself a sufficient number of times. k' is then used to generate three subkeys, k_0, k_1 and k_2. Subkey k_0 is then used to modify the initialisation vector of the chosen hash algorithm, while k_1 is used to modify the constants in the non-linear functions used in each round of the algorithm. The message is first hashed using the modified algorithm, H', and then a final round of the modified algorithm is applied to the result, as follows:

$$h_1 = H'(m)$$
$$h_2 = \phi'(k_2\hat{\ }(k_2 \oplus A)\hat{\ }(k_2 \oplus B)\hat{\ }(k_2 \oplus C),\ h_1)$$

where ϕ' is the modified round function, $\oplus$ is the exclusive-or function, and A, B and C are constants of the MAC algorithm which depend on the hash function chosen. For a hash value of length L_h bits, the first L_h bits of h_2 are used.

A related idea, which is particularly used with the DES cryptosystem, but which can also be used in any other system in which the plaintext is divided into blocks for encryption (including RSA, AES and many others), is to use the *Cipher Block Chaining (CBC)* mode of operation to produce a single block of ciphertext which incorporates information from the encryption of all the blocks of plaintext. Starting with an initial block c_0 (which may be thought of as a supplement to the key), consecutive blocks of plaintext are encrypted, using the appropriate encryption function E with key k, so that the ciphertext for the i'th block is:

$$c_i = E(m_i \oplus c_{i-1}, k)$$

where m_i is the plaintext for block i, c_{i-1} is the ciphertext for block $i-1$, and $\oplus$ is the exclusive or function. If the message consists of N blocks of plaintext, the N'th block of ciphertext, c_N, can simply be used as the MAC[3]; unless needed for other reasons, the remaining blocks of ciphertext can be discarded. Block chaining is the basis of the ISO standard ISO10118-2 [200] for data integrity and ISO9797-1 [185] for message authentication.

Finally, one-way hash functions can themselves be used as MACs in conjunction with a SKCS. For example, using a hash function H and a shared secret key SK_{AB}, the MAC for message $m \in \mathcal{M}$ can be evaluated as $H(SK_{AB}\widehat{\ }m)$. On its own, this is not very secure, since an attacker could add extra blocks to the message and get a new valid MAC, but more complex functions, such as $H(k1\widehat{\ }H(k2\widehat{\ }m))$, where $k1$ and $k2$ are two (possibly identical) keys, are generally regarded as secure. This is essentially the procedure followed in the HMAC algorithm described in ISO9797-2 [186].

6.3 Digital Signatures

In general, encryption ensures that data are unreadable by persons not knowing the relevant decryption method. It is thus the primary mechanism for providing *confidentiality* in a service. With the widespread use of electronic documents, there is also a need for mechanisms which make it possible to check whether a particular party is the originator (or, in some cases, the receiver) of a document. The obvious idea is to attach a *digital signature* to the document. By analogy with the traditional rules for good old-fashioned paper documents, we require that:

---

[3] ISO9797-1 also defines some more complex possibilities, involving a further encryption, decryption or truncation of c_N

Protocol 20

Message 1 $A \to T: \{d\}_{SK_{AT}}$
Message 2 $T \to B: \{(d,A)\}_{SK_{BT}}$

Fig. 6.5 Secret key signature verification protocol.
Here, SK_{pq} is a secret key for communication between p and q, and $\{m\}_k$ denotes the message m encrypted with key k.

- A signature cannot be forged, i.e. created by anyone but its rightful owner.
- A signature cannot be detached from one document and moved to another document.
- A document, once signed, cannot be modified.
- The signer of a document cannot later deny having signed it.

These requirements mean that the service which transfers the documents must offer *integrity* and *non-repudiation*. Confidentiality is not essential to the concept of a digital signature, but may obviously also be necessary if the document's contents have to be kept secret. The 'documents' themselves do not, of course, need to be ordinary text documents, such as letters or contracts; we have already seen that digital signatures can be used in the implementation of Byzantine agreement algorithms, as discussed in Section 5.4.

The basic technique for producing a non-repudiable digital signature is to encipher some data with a key which is private to the 'signer'. To show that any particular person is in fact the signer, it is then sufficient to demonstrate that only the person possessing the signer's key could have produced the signature. Such a demonstration is known as *verification* or *certification* of the source of the message.

There are two styles of signature certification:

SKCS: Here a trusted party, T, known as an *arbitrator*, is used to certify the source of a document sent from A to B. The protocol is shown in Figure 6.5. A encrypts the document, d, with a secret key SK_{AT} which A and T have in common and sends it to T. T decrypts the message to retrieve d, appends a statement that it came from A, re-encrypts it with a secret key SK_{BT} which B and T have in common, and passes the result on to B. For this method to fulfil the requirements for a signature, it is obviously essential that T can be fully trusted and that neither of the keys has been compromised.

PKCS: Digital signatures based on PKCSs use encryption with the sender's private key, SK_A, to generate the signature and decryption with the sender's public key, PK_A, to check the signature. Since everyone knows the sender's public key, no special arbitrator is needed to perform the check. For this method to fulfil the requirements for a signature, it is essential that only PK_A 'matches' SK_A and that none of the private keys SK_i has been compromised. Note that encryption with the sender's public key does not ensure *confidentiality* of the message! The purpose of the encryption here is solely to demonstrate that the sender possesses a particular secret which only she knows about.

The technique is particularly simple to use if the cryptosystem is *reversible*, i.e. if it is also true (using the notation of the previous section) that:

$$D(E(d, SK_A), PK_A) = d$$

since then the ordinary encryption and decryption functions can be used to generate and verify signatures respectively. RSA is a reversible cryptosystem in this sense. Obviously, a reversible cryptosystem also permits *message recovery*, so that the content of the original message is revealed to the verifier.

In practice, what actually gets encrypted in order to form the signature is not necessarily the message itself, since the signature would then normally be as long as the message, which may be wasteful (both of time and space, since RSA encryption is time-consuming). Instead, it is common to encrypt a *message digest* derived from the message by use of a standard one-way hash function, and to send this encrypted digest as the signature together with the plaintext message. This style of signature is known as a *digital signature with appendix*. To verify the signature, the receiver itself evaluates the digest from the plaintext message, and compares it with the decrypted signature. This is the approach used in the so-called *PKCS #1* scheme [248] and in the NIST Digital Signature Standard [258] described below.

There are two competing standard schemes for PKCS digital signatures in widespread use. The first directly uses the idea of a reversible cryptosystem as defined above and forms the basis of the ISO standard ISO9796 [183, 184]. ISO9796 does not specify a particular PKCS, but requires one which permits *message recovery*, such as RSA. The competing standard is the *Digital Signature Standard (DSS)* [258] adopted by the National Institute of Standards and Technology (NIST) in USA for use in US Federal systems. This uses a variant of the rather more complicated *El Gamal cryptosystem*, together with the SHA one-way hash function, to produce a digital signature *with appendix*. In slightly more detail, the signature algorithm (which is actually called *DSA*) makes use of the following data:

p The modulus, a prime number of size between 512 and 1024 bits
q A prime factor of $(p-1)$, of size 160 bits
h A random integer such that $1 < h < (p-1)$ and $h^{(p-1)/q} \bmod p > 1$
$g = h^{(p-1)/q} \bmod p$
$x \in \mathbb{Z}_q$
$y = g^x \bmod p$

Here (p, q, g, y) form the public key (where p, q and g can in fact be shared between a large number of users) and x is the private key. To sign a message m, a random key $k < q$ is chosen, and the signer evaluates the pair of integers (r, s) which make up the signature:

$$r = (g^k \bmod p) \bmod q$$
$$s = (k^{-1} \cdot (H(m) + x \cdot r)) \bmod q$$

It follows that both of these values are of size 160 bits. They are sent to the verifier together with the hash value of the message, $H(m)$. To verify the signature, the verifier evaluates v as follows:

$$w = s^{-1} \bmod q$$
$$u_1 = (H(m) \cdot w) \bmod q$$
$$u_2 = (r \cdot w) \bmod q$$
$$v = ((g^{u_1} \cdot y^{u_2}) \bmod p) \bmod q$$

For a correct signature, $v = r$, and the received hash value must also match the plaintext of the message, m.

6.4 Entity Authentication

Although digital signatures permit the unambiguous attribution of a single message to a particular originator, this is not in general enough to set up an authenticated two-way conversation between two entities, say A and B, so each of them is convinced that it really is talking to the other. If B receives a message signed by A, this only shows that A orginally constructed the message, not that A is currently active and just sent the message to B. So B, instead of talking to his friend A, may be fooled into talking to a malicious intruder, as illustrated in Figure 6.6.

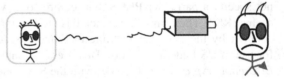

Fig. 6.6 Poor authentication: The malicious intruder has disguised himself as an innocent friend.

The general requirements for entity authentication between A and B are:

Evidence: A must produce evidence of its identity, typically by producing (or at least demonstrating knowledge of) a specific secret which unambiguously identifies A and which B can verify.

Non-transferability: B cannot use the information obtained from A to impersonate A to a third party, say C.

No third-party impersonation: No third party, say M, can succeed in impersonating A by executing the protocol with B.

No leakage: These properties must hold, regardless of how many times A and B execute the authentication protocol.

Whether these requirements can be satisfied in practice depends to a considerable extent on the type of evidence used and the style of protocol. It is customary to identify three styles of evidence:

1. **Weak authentication**, where a *password* or other simple identification code, such as a PIN code, is used as the secret.

Protocol 21

(a) Message 1 $A \to B$: N_A
Message 2 $B \to A$: $\{(N_A, A)\}_{SK_{AB}}$

(b) Message 1 $A \to B$: N_A
Message 2 $B \to A$: $\{(N_B, N_A, A)\}_{SK_{AB}}$
Message 3 $A \to B$: $\{(N_A, N_B)\}_{SK_{AB}}$

Fig. 6.7 Basic secret key entity authentication protocols for **(a)** unilateral and **(b)** mutual authentication. Here, SK_{pq} is a secret key for communication between p and q, N_p is a 'nonce' (see main text) constructed by p, and $\{m\}_k$ denotes the message m encrypted with key k.

2. **Strong authentication**, where a cryptographically secure form of *challenge and response* is used. The basic idea is that a correct response to the challenge can only be produced by a party who knows the relevant secret.
3. **Zero-knowledge authentication**, where knowledge of the secret can be demonstrated without any information about the secret being revealed at all.

We shall here focus on *strong authentication*, which is relatively secure and widely used.

6.4.1 Authentication with Secret Key Cryptosystems

In a secret key cryptosystem, each pair of parties has a mutual, secret key, and possession of this key is taken as evidence that a given entity is what it claims to be. If we assume that both A and B already know this secret, SK_{AB}, then B can authenticate itself to A by a two-way exchange of a challenge and a response, as shown in Figure 6.7(a). The quantity N_A used in the challenge is a piece of data explicitly constructed by A to identify this conversation. Such a piece of data, explicitly constructed to be fresh, is usually termed a *nonce*. This is a generalisation of the unique references used in several of the protocols of Chapter 4. For authentication purposes, a random number generated by a cryptographically secure random number generator[4] is the commonest choice, but a timestamp or other reference whose freshness can be guaranteed can also be used. In the response, B returns the nonce encrypted with the shared secret key, SK_{AB}, to A. If A can decrypt the response and find the nonce which it sent to B, it is willing to accept that it is in contact with an active entity which it can identify as B. The corresponding challenge-response protocol for *mutual authentication* of A and B involves a three-way exchange as in Figure 6.7(b). These mechanisms are two of the basic mechanisms used in Part 2 of ISO Standard 9798 for authentication using symmetric encipherment algorithms [187].

---

[4] This is a generator which produces a sequence of numbers, such that it is computationally infeasible for a third party, even after observing a long sequence, to deduce the next number which will be generated.

Fig. 6.8 Authentication via
an Authentication Server.
By suitable exchanges with
the trusted Authentication
Server, S, systems A and
B agree on a shared secret
which authenticates them to
one another.

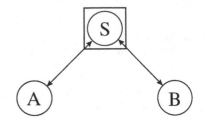

Protocol 22

Message 1 $A \rightarrow B : A$
Message 2 $B \rightarrow A : \{(A, N_B)\}_{SK_{BS}}$
Message 3 $A \rightarrow S : (A, B, N_A, \{(A, N_B)\}_{SK_{BS}})$
Message 4 $S \rightarrow A : \{(B, N_A, SK_{AB}, \{(A, N_B, SK_{AB})\}_{SK_{BS}})\}_{SK_{AS}}$
Message 5 $A \rightarrow B : \{(A, N_B, SK_{AB})\}_{SK_{BS}}$
Message 6 $B \rightarrow A : \{N'_B\}_{SK_{AB}}$
Message 7 $A \rightarrow B : \{N'_B - 1\}_{SK_{AB}}$

Fig. 6.9 Needham and Schroeder's secret key authentication protocol.
Here, SK_{pq} is a secret key for communication between p and q, N_p is a 'nonce' (see main text)
constructed by p, and $\{m\}_k$ denotes the message m encrypted with key k.

If, on the other hand, the two parties have never communicated with one another
before, and have no built-in pre-knowledge, they need a protocol to agree on the
shared secret. The usual scheme in this case is for them both to exchange messages
with a trusted *authentication server*, which in what follows we shall denote S. This
is illustrated in Figure 6.8. Several protocols, in the literature often known as *key exchange protocols* or *authentication protocols*, have been published for this purpose.
Figure 6.9 shows Needham and Schroeder's protocol [99] as modified in [100].

Protocol 22 starts (Message 1) with the initiator telling B who he is. B replies
with a so-called *authenticator* (Message 2), consisting of A's identification and a
nonce, N_B, chosen by B and encrypted with the key which B uses to communicate
with the authentication server, SK_{BS}.

A cannot decrypt the authenticator, but passes it on to the server in Message
3, which also contains the identities of both A and B and a nonce constructed by
A. Note that, at this stage, nothing has been revealed to either A or B or possible
intruders which they did not know already. Although A (and the intruders) have
seen the authenticator, it can only be read and checked by the real B or by the server.

The server, which knows all about everybody's secret keys, can now decrypt
the authenticator, and construct a new one, still encrypted with SK_{BS}, but now also
containing the new secret key SK_{AB} which is to be used for communication between
A and B:

$$\{(A, N_B, SK_{AB})\}_{SK_{BS}}$$

This is sent to A together with B's identity, A's nonce and the new key in Message 4, which is encrypted with the key which A and S use for mutual communication. This protects the vital new secret against observation by parties other than the real A.

A is now in a position to check that the reply from the server (Message 4) contained the nonce which A supplied for this conversation, and that no intruders have managed to change the intended identity of the opposite party, B. This could occur if an intruder modified Message 3 or replaced it by replaying a 'Message 3' from a previous run of the authentication protocol. If everything appears OK, A accepts the key SK_{AB} as the genuine one for use in communication with B. A then sends B, as Message 5, the modified authenticator which A has just received from the server:

$$\{(A, N_B, SK_{AB})\}_{SK_{BS}}$$

B can decrypt this message and also get the new secret key. At the same time, B can see that Message 5 is not a replay by checking its own nonce, N_B. Thus B must also believe that the identity A is the correct identity for the other party, as authenticated by the server.

The final two messages are needed in order for each party to be certain that the other exists and actually possesses the key. There is a clear analogy here to the 3-Way Handshake protocol described in Section 4.3.3, and the challenge-response schemes used in **Protocol 21**. In Message 6, B uses the new secret key to send a new nonce to A, who modifies the new nonce in some agreed manner (indicated in Figure 6.9 by subtraction of 1 from its value) to protect against simple replaying by an intruder, and returns the modified value to B, encrypted with the new secret key. In principle these exchanges could be piggy-backed on the first real messages of the conversation, but the idea of the protocol is to complete the authentication *before* exchanging any real information which might be of value.

6.4.2 Authentication with Public Key Cryptosystems

With public key cryptosystems, an entity A can prove its identity to B in one of two ways:

1. By digitally signing a challenge and sending it to B.
2. By decrypting a challenge which has been encrypted with A's public key, and which B has sent to it.

Both of these possibilities demonstrate that A has knowledge of A's private key. The basic principle is once again to use unique references (nonces) in order to establish the integrity and timeliness of the exchange. The basic protocols using the digitally signed challenges are shown in Figure 6.10, which corresponds to Figure 6.7 for SKCSs. $\{q, PK_q\}_{SK_S}$, containing the party q's identity and public key, encrypted by the secret key of S, is usually known as q's *certificate*. S is here assumed to be a trusted *authority* which can certify that q is associated with the public key PK_q. We shall consider certificates in more detail in Section 6.4.4 below. The mechanisms

Protocol 23

(a) Message 1 $A \rightarrow B$: N_A
   Message 2 $B \rightarrow A$: $(\{(B, PK_B)\}_{SK_S}, N_B, N_A, A, \{(N_B, N_A, A)\}_{SK_B})$

(b) Message 1 $A \rightarrow B$: N_A
   Message 2 $B \rightarrow A$: $(\{(B, PK_B)\}_{SK_S}, N_B, N_A, A, \{(N_B, N_A, A)\}_{SK_B})$
   Message 3 $A \rightarrow B$: $(\{(A, PK_A)\}_{SK_S}, B, \{(N_A, N_B, B)\}_{SK_A})$

Fig. 6.10 Basic public key entity authentication protocols using digital signatures for **(a)** unilateral and **(b)** mutual authentication.
Here, PK_q is q's public key, SK_q is q's private key, N_p is a nonce constructed by p, and $\{m\}_k$ denotes message m encrypted with key k..

Protocol 24

Message 1 $A \rightarrow S$: (A, B)
Message 2 $S \rightarrow A$: $\{(B, PK_B)\}_{SK_S}$
Message 3 $A \rightarrow B$: $\{(A, N_A)\}_{PK_B}$
Message 4 $B \rightarrow S$: (B, A)
Message 5 $S \rightarrow B$: $\{(A, PK_A)\}_{SK_S}$
Message 6 $B \rightarrow A$: $\{(N_A, N_B)\}_{PK_A}$
Message 7 $A \rightarrow B$: $\{N_B\}_{PK_B}$

Fig. 6.11 Needham and Schroeder's public key authentication protocol.
Here, PK_q is q's public key, SK_q is q's private key, N_p is a nonce constructed by p, and $\{m\}_k$ denotes message m encrypted with key k.

shown here are used in Part 3 of ISO Standard 9798, which describes authentication mechanisms using digital signatures [188].

The alternative technique of response by decryption of a challenge is illustrated by **Protocol 24**, which shows Needham and Schroeder's protocol for this purpose. Firstly (Messages 1 and 2), A has an exchange with the server to obtain B's public key, PK_B. This step, together with Messages 4 and 5 in which B obtains A's public key, could be omitted if it is assumed that all parties are aware of everyone's public keys. Note that the replies in both cases are encrypted with the server's private key, SK_S. This ensures *integrity* rather than secrecy, since of course anyone can decrypt such a message using the server's public key (which everybody knows!). Integrity is important, however, to protect against intruders changing the message and inserting their own identities and private keys. The reply from the server, containing B's identity and public key, encrypted with the trusted server's secret key, is B's *certificate*.

Message 3, which can only be understood by B, then tells B that someone claiming to be A wishes to communicate with him, and sends a nonce as a reference for the conversation. Of course Message 3 might have been sent by an intruder, say C, since it is encrypted with a public key. However, since B will obviously send the reply to A and encrypt it with A's public key (obtained from the trusted server), C

will not get much benefit from his efforts – although A might of course be surprised to get such an unexpected 'reply'.

After, if necessary, getting a certificate containing A's public key from the server (Messages 4 and 5), B then replies to A (Message 6), sending A's nonce and a nonce which B has just created, N_B. These are encrypted with A's public key, so that only A can understand them. Again, this message might be sent by an intruder, but now the nonces can be used to check the integrity of the exchange, just as in the Three-way Handshake protocols presented in Section 4.3.3. In fact the only real difference is the use of encryption in the current protocol. Thus the final message (Message 7) works exactly like the 'third hand' in the handshake, confirming to B that it really is A which is the other party to the conversation. The purpose of the encryption here is to ensure that only the intended recipient can understand the message.

This style of entity authentication, known as *three-way strong authentication* is used in the ISO/ITU-T Directory [180]. This is intended to support a worldwide lookup service for information on telecommunications users, electronic mail users and so on. Thus it is obviously important that unauthorised persons should not be able to change the information in the database or to read information which they are not supposed to have access to.

6.4.3 Proofs of Authentication Protocols

Informal arguments about authentication protocols are, if anything, even more prone to unsuspected errors than arguments about simple data transfer or even Byzantine protocols. The reason for this is that entity authentication is not based on the idea that the two parties merely get the same data, but on the idea that each of them *believes* that the other gets the same data – the shared secret – and that nobody else gets to see these data. Thus the proof must demonstrate that, from certain initial assumptions about what can be believed about the system, it is possible to deduce the beliefs which imply authentication.

A formal proof system for dealing with this style of proof is given by Burrows, Abadi and Needham [21]. This is based on a modal logic for beliefs, often known as *BAN logic* after its originators. A special notation is used for describing beliefs and other relevant assertions about the system. In the following description, which we have modified very slightly, P and Q are parties who communicate with one another or with third parties, K is a key, and X is a logical proposition. Messages are identified with propositions.

$P \mid\equiv X$ P believes X to be true.

$P \mid\sim X$ P once said X. This does not imply anything about how long ago this happened, but it does imply that P believed X at the time.

$P \longmapsto X$ P has jurisdiction over X. This means that P should be trusted on matters concerning X.

$P \xleftrightarrow{K} Q$ P and Q may properly communicate using the good key K. That the key is good means that it will never be discovered by anyone except P and Q or a party trusted by both of them.

$\{X\}_K$ X is encrypted using the key K.

$P \triangleright X$ P sees X. P has received a message containing X and can read it (possibly after decryption). This implies that P can also send X in subsequent messages.

$\sharp X$ X is fresh. This means that X has not been sent before the current execution of the protocol. By definition, nonces are always fresh.

$P \rightarrow Q : X$ P has sent X to Q.

In terms of this notation, the goal of authentication between two parties A and B is to establish the following beliefs for a certain key K:

$$A \models A \xleftrightarrow{K} B \tag{1}$$

$$B \models A \xleftrightarrow{K} B \tag{2}$$

$$A \models B \models A \xleftrightarrow{K} B \tag{3}$$

$$B \models A \models A \xleftrightarrow{K} B \tag{4}$$

Beliefs 1 and 2 state that both parties believe that a certain key is suitable for secure communication between them, in the sense that it is new and unknown to others (except trusted parties, such as the server). Beliefs 3 and 4 state that each party is convinced that the other party believes that the key is suitable. This may seem unnecessary, but it avoids situations such as the one in which A asks a server to generate a secret key and pass it both to A and B. In such a situation, B has no way of knowing whether A actually exists any more. Effectively, 3 and 4 state that each party believes that the other party currently exists.

    The inference system for this modal logic uses the following inference rules, which are here expanded somewhat in relation to Burrows et al. [21]. As usual, conjunction of propositions is indicated by the use of commas.

1. Message meaning

$$\frac{\Gamma \vdash P \models Q \xleftrightarrow{K} P, \; P \triangleright \{X\}_K}{\Gamma \vdash P \models Q \mid\sim X}$$

In other words, if P receives a message X encrypted with K, and knows that K is Q's key for communicating with P, then it can believe[5] that Q once said X.

2. Nonce verification

$$\frac{\Gamma \vdash P \models \sharp X, \; P \models Q \mid\sim X}{\Gamma \vdash P \models Q \models X}$$

If P believes that X is a fresh message, and that Q once said X, then it can believe that Q still believes X. Note that this is the only rule which can 'promote' a state-

---

[5] Note that "A can believe X" here and elsewhere in this section means "A can reasonably believe X". In other words, it is a valid logical deduction that A believes X.

ment involving $\sim$ to one involving $\equiv$. Effectively, it says that fresh and only fresh messages are to be taken seriously, reflecting the similar concerns which we have discussed in Chapter 4.

3. Jurisdiction
$$\frac{\Gamma \vdash P \mid\equiv Q \longmapsto X, \ P \mid\equiv Q \mid\equiv X}{\Gamma \vdash P \mid\equiv X}$$

If P believes that Q has jurisdiction over X, then it can have the same beliefs about X that Q has.

The next four rules state that P believes a set of statements if and only if P believes each of them individually:

4. And-Intro.
$$\frac{\Gamma \vdash P \mid\equiv X, \ P \mid\equiv Y}{\Gamma \vdash P \mid\equiv (X,Y)}$$

5. And-Elim.
$$\frac{\Gamma \vdash P \mid\equiv (X,Y)}{\Gamma \vdash P \mid\equiv X}$$

6. Believe And-Elim.
$$\frac{\Gamma \vdash P \mid\equiv Q \mid\equiv (X,Y)}{\Gamma \vdash P \mid\equiv Q \mid\equiv X}$$

7. Said And-Elim.
$$\frac{\Gamma \vdash P \mid\equiv Q \mid\sim (X,Y)}{\Gamma \vdash P \mid\equiv Q \mid\sim X}$$

The next two rules reflect the idea that in a secret key system, the same key is used in both directions for communications between two parties:

8. Key symmetry
$$\frac{\Gamma \vdash P \mid\equiv R \xleftrightarrow{K} S}{\Gamma \vdash P \mid\equiv S \xleftrightarrow{K} R}$$

9. Believe key symmetry
$$\frac{\Gamma \vdash P \mid\equiv Q \mid\equiv R \xleftrightarrow{K} S}{\Gamma \vdash P \mid\equiv Q \mid\equiv S \xleftrightarrow{K} R}$$

If P sees a composite statement then it also sees this statement's components, and likewise, things which P can see can be assembled into a composite statement:

10. See components
$$\frac{\Gamma \vdash P \rhd (X,Y)}{\Gamma \vdash P \rhd X}$$

11. Message composition
$$\frac{\Gamma \vdash P \rhd X, P \rhd Y}{\Gamma \vdash P \rhd (X,Y)}$$

P can see the plaintext of an encrypted statement if it has the necessary key, and can use a key which it possesses to encrypt a statement which it can see:

12. Decryption
$$\frac{\Gamma \vdash P \equiv Q \xleftrightarrow{K} P,\, P \triangleright \{X\}_K}{\Gamma \vdash P \triangleright X}$$

13. Encryption
$$\frac{\Gamma \vdash P \equiv Q \xleftrightarrow{K} P,\, P \triangleright X}{\Gamma \vdash P \triangleright \{X\}_K}$$

If P believes that part of a message is fresh, then P can reasonably believe that the entire message is fresh:

14. Freshness extension
$$\frac{\Gamma \vdash P \equiv \sharp X}{\Gamma \vdash P \equiv \sharp(X,Y)}$$

This is a consequence of the assumption that the cryptosystem offers perfect encryption, and thus also perfect integrity.

If P can see a message, and P sends the message to Q, then Q can see the message:

15. Message transfer
$$\frac{\Gamma \vdash P \triangleright X,\, P \rightarrow Q : X}{\Gamma \vdash Q \triangleright X}$$

Finally, if P has a (correct) belief about something, then P can also formulate this belief so that it can see a message expressing it:

16. Believing is seeing
$$\frac{\Gamma \vdash P \equiv X}{\Gamma \vdash P \triangleright X}$$

A correct belief is one that is derivable from the assumptions by the use of one or more of the above inference rules.

To demonstrate the use of this proof system, let us consider the Needham and Schroeder secret key protocol given previously as **Protocol 22**. The assumptions for this protocol are:

1. $A \models A \xleftrightarrow{SK_{AS}} S$
2. $S \models A \xleftrightarrow{SK_{AS}} S$
3. $B \models B \xleftrightarrow{SK_{BS}} S$
4. $S \models B \xleftrightarrow{SK_{BS}} S$
5. $S \models A \xleftrightarrow{SK_{AB}} B$

6. $A \models S \longmapsto A \xleftrightarrow{K} B$
7. $B \models S \longmapsto A \xleftrightarrow{K} B$
8. $A \models S \longmapsto \sharp(A \xleftrightarrow{K} B)$

9. $A \models \sharp N_A$
10. $B \models \sharp N_B$
11. $S \models \sharp(A \xleftrightarrow{SK_{AB}} B)$

12. $A \rhd N_A$
13. $B \rhd N_B$
14. $B \rhd N'_B$

Assumptions 1–5 and 9–11 are routine. Assumptions 6 and 7 state that the clients, (A, B), trust the server, S, to make new keys for A and B. Assumption 8 states that A furthermore trusts S to generate a new key which can also be used as a nonce. Finally, assumptions 12–14 state that A and B can see nonces which they have invented for themselves.

The protocol can be described in terms of abstract messages, rather than the concrete ones given before, as:

Message 1 $A \rightarrow B$:
Message 2 $B \rightarrow A$: $\{N_B\}_{SK_{BS}}$
Message 3 $A \rightarrow S$: $(N_A, \{N_B\}_{SK_{BS}})$
Message 4 $S \rightarrow A$: $\{(N_A, A \xleftrightarrow{SK_{AB}} B, \sharp(A \xleftrightarrow{SK_{AB}} B), \{(N_B, A \xleftrightarrow{SK_{AB}} B)\}_{SK_{BS}})\}_{SK_{AS}}$
Message 5 $A \rightarrow B$: $\{(N_B, A \xleftrightarrow{SK_{AB}} B)\}_{SK_{BS}}$
Message 6 $B \rightarrow A$: $\{(N'_B, A \xleftrightarrow{SK_{AB}} B)\}_{SK_{AB}}$
Message 7 $A \rightarrow B$: $\{(N'_B, A \xleftrightarrow{SK_{AB}} B)\}_{SK_{AB}}$

The initial part of the proof demonstrates that Messages 1–3, together with the assumptions, enable S to see the things which are necessary in order to send Message 4, and that these can be encrypted with the key SK_{AS}:

$$S \triangleright \{(N_A, A \xleftrightarrow{SK_{AB}} B, \sharp(A \xleftrightarrow{SK_{AB}} B), \{(N_B, A \xleftrightarrow{SK_{AB}} B)\}_{SK_{BS}})\}_{SK_{AS}}$$

We leave this part of the proof as an exercise. The proof continues as follows:

1. $\Rightarrow \{..., \text{Message 4 transfer}\}$

$$A \triangleright \{(N_A, A \xleftrightarrow{SK_{AB}} B, \sharp(A \xleftrightarrow{SK_{AB}} B), \{(N_B, A \xleftrightarrow{SK_{AB}} B)\}_{SK_{BS}})\}_{SK_{AS}}$$

2. $\Rightarrow \{1, \text{Assumption 1, Message meaning}\}$

$$A \mid\equiv S \mid\sim (N_A, A \xleftrightarrow{SK_{AB}} B, \sharp(A \xleftrightarrow{SK_{AB}} B), \{(N_B, A \xleftrightarrow{SK_{AB}} B)\}_{SK_{BS}})$$

3. $\Rightarrow \{\text{Assumption 9, Freshness extension}\}$

$$A \mid\equiv \sharp(N_A, A \xleftrightarrow{SK_{AB}} B, \sharp(A \xleftrightarrow{SK_{AB}} B), \{(N_B, A \xleftrightarrow{SK_{AB}} B)\}_{SK_{BS}})$$

4. $\Rightarrow \{2, 3, \text{Nonce verification}\}$

$$A \mid\equiv S \mid\equiv (N_A, A \xleftrightarrow{SK_{AB}} B, \sharp(A \xleftrightarrow{SK_{AB}} B), \{(N_B, A \xleftrightarrow{SK_{AB}} B)\}_{SK_{BS}})$$

5. $\Rightarrow \{4, \text{And-elim}\}$

$$A \mid\equiv S \mid\equiv A \xleftrightarrow{SK_{AB}} B$$

6. $\Rightarrow \{5, \text{Assumption 6, Jurisdiction}\}$

$$\boxed{A \mid\equiv A \xleftrightarrow{SK_{AB}} B}$$

7. $\Rightarrow \{4, \text{And-elim}\}$

$$A \mid\equiv S \mid\equiv \sharp(A \xleftrightarrow{SK_{AB}} B)$$

8. $\Rightarrow \{7, \text{Assumption 8, Jurisdiction}\}$

$$A \mid\equiv \sharp(A \xleftrightarrow{SK_{AB}} B)$$

9. $\Rightarrow \{1, \text{Assumption 1, Decryption}\}$

$$A \triangleright (N_A, A \xleftrightarrow{SK_{AB}} B, \sharp(A \xleftrightarrow{SK_{AB}} B), \{(N_B, A \xleftrightarrow{SK_{AB}} B)\}_{SK_{BS}})$$

10. $\Rightarrow \{9, \text{See components}\}$

$$A \triangleright \{(N_B, A \xleftrightarrow{SK_{AB}} B)\}_{SK_{BS}}$$

11. $\Rightarrow \{10, \text{Message 5 transfer}\}$

$$B \triangleright \{(N_B, A \xleftrightarrow{SK_{AB}} B)\}_{SK_{BS}}$$

12. $\Rightarrow \{11, \text{Assumption 3, Message meaning}\}$

$$B \mid\equiv S \mid\sim (N_B, A \xleftrightarrow{SK_{AB}} B)$$

13. $\Rightarrow \{\text{Assumption 10, Freshness extension}\}$

$$B \mid\equiv \sharp(N_B, A \xleftrightarrow{SK_{AB}} B)$$

14. $\Rightarrow \{12, 13, \text{Nonce verification}\}$

$$B \mid\equiv S \mid\equiv (N_B, A \xleftrightarrow{SK_{AB}} B)$$

15. $\Rightarrow \{14, \text{Believe And-elim.}\}$

$$B \mid\equiv S \mid\equiv A \xleftrightarrow{SK_{AB}} B$$

16. $\Rightarrow \{15, \text{Assumption 7, Jurisdiction}\}$

$$\boxed{B \mid\equiv A \xleftrightarrow{SK_{AB}} B}$$

17. $\Rightarrow \{11, \text{Assumption 3, Decryption}\}$

$$B \triangleright (N_B, A \xleftrightarrow{SK_{AB}} B)$$

18. $\Rightarrow$ {17, See components}

  $B \rhd A \overset{SK_{AB}}{\longleftrightarrow} B$

19. $\Rightarrow$ {18, Assumption 13, Message composition, Encryption}

  $B \rhd \{(N'_B, A \overset{SK_{AB}}{\longleftrightarrow} B)\}_{SK_{AB}}$

20. $\Rightarrow$ {19, Message 6 transfer}

  $A \rhd \{(N'_B, A \overset{SK_{AB}}{\longleftrightarrow} B)\}_{SK_{AB}}$

21. $\Rightarrow$ {6, 20, Message meaning}

  $A \models B \mid\sim (N'_B, A \overset{SK_{AB}}{\longleftrightarrow} B)$

22. $\Rightarrow$ {8, 21, Nonce verification}

  $A \models B \models (N'_B, A \overset{SK_{AB}}{\longleftrightarrow} B)$

23. $\Rightarrow$ {22, Believe And-elim.}

  $\boxed{A \models B \models A \overset{SK_{AB}}{\longleftrightarrow} B}$

24. $\Rightarrow$ {20, Message 6 transfer}

  $B \rhd \{(N'_B, A \overset{SK_{AB}}{\longleftrightarrow} B)\}_{SK_{AB}}$

25. $\Rightarrow$ {24, 16, Message meaning}

  $B \models A \mid\sim (N'_B, A \overset{SK_{AB}}{\longleftrightarrow} B)$

26. $\Rightarrow$ {Assumption 10, Freshness extension}

  $B \models \sharp(N'_B, A \overset{SK_{AB}}{\longleftrightarrow} B)$

27. $\Rightarrow$ {25, 26, Nonce verification}

  $B \models A \models (N'_B, A \overset{SK_{AB}}{\longleftrightarrow} B)$

28. $\Rightarrow$ {27, Believe And-elim.}

  $\boxed{B \models A \models A \overset{SK_{AB}}{\longleftrightarrow} B}$

The four framed beliefs, which follow from steps 6, 16, 23 and 28, are the beliefs required for demonstrating authentication.

6.4.4 Certification Authorities

A *certificate* is a structure which can be exchanged with other parties to provide proof of identity. Certificates are particularly important in systems which use PKCSs, so that users can be certain who owns the public keys which are in use. For electronic commerce, the use of certificates is usually considered essential, so that customers, traders and financial institutions can all identify themselves to one another in a trustworthy manner. We have in previous examples used simplified forms of certificate which just contained the owner's identity and public key. In reality, most certificates nowadays are so-called *X.509v3 certificates*, i.e. they follow version 3 of the ITU-T standard X.509, originally designed for use with the ITU-T Directory [180]. A basic X.509v3 certificate contains:

- The version of the X.509 standard which applies to the certificate (for example, version 3).
- An identification of the owner, A.
- The owner's public key, PK_A.
- A description of the encryption algorithm for which the key is intended (for example, RSA).
- The period of validity of the certificate.
- An identification of the particular certificate, such as a serial number.
- A description of the algorithm used for generating the issuer's signature (for example SHA-1 hash with RSA encryption).
- An identification of the issuer of the certificate, S.
- The issuer's digital signature, DS_S, for the content of the certificate.

Additional information may appear in the form of *extensions*, which can describe the applications for which the key has been issued, the security policy associated with the certificate, the Web site at which information about revoked (cancelled) certificates can be found, and so on. Since X.509 certificates were originally designed for use with the ITU-T Directory, the identities of the owner and the issuer are specified as *X.500 names* in terms of a set of *attributes*; we shall describe these in more detail in Section 7.1.1. The issuer is expected to be a trusted party, in the sense described in the previous sections, and is known as a *Certification Authority (CA)*. Since the certificate associates its owner, A, with a public key, PK_A, it is often said to be a certificate *for the owner's public key*.

In the real world, there are not one but many Certification Authorities, and the problem arises of how users whose certificates are issued by *different* authorities can identify themselves to one another in a trustworthy manner. A model which defines which relationships of trust exist between multiple CAs is denoted a *trust model*. In many practical systems, the trust model is *hierarchical*, so that for one CA, say CA_i, to trust a certificate issued by another, say CA_j, it must be able to refer to a common ancestor in the hierarchy, say CA_a, who can confirm that CA_j's certificate is genuine. This idea is illustrated in Figure 6.12. An arrow from X to Y in the figure indicates the relationship Y can trust X, implying that X can issue a certificate for Y's public key. To validate a certificate issued by a given CA_j, it is necessary to be able to follow an unbroken directed path from a CA which the verifier trusts *a priori* to CA_j. Such a path is known as a *certification path*.

Hierarchical trust models come in several variants, depending on whether it is possible for a CA lower in the hierarchy to certify the public keys of its immediate superior or not. Figure 6.12(a) depicts a *strict hierarchical* (or *rooted chain*) model, in which certificates can only be issued for inferiors. It is then necessary for CA_i to know (and trust) the public key of the *root* of the hierarchy and to apply to the root in order to be able to trace a certification path down to the authority, CA_j, which issued the certificate in question. For example, to verify a certificate issued by CA_3, CA_2 would follow the procedure:

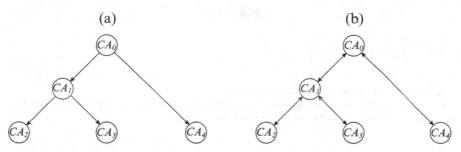

Fig. 6.12 Hierarchical trust models.
(a) In a strict hierarchical model, a CA can only issue a certificate for CAs which are its immediate inferiors. (b) In a hierarchy with reverse certificates, a CA can also certify the public key of its immediate superior, so trusted information can propagate both up and down in the hierarchy.

1. Apply to the root CA_0 to get a certificate $\{(CA_1, PK_1)\}_{SK_0}$, signed by CA_0, associating CA_1 with the public key PK_1. By using the trusted public root key, PK_0, this certificate can be opened to obtain a trusted copy of PK_1.
2. Apply to CA_1 to get a certificate $\{(CA_3, PK_3)\}_{SK_1}$, signed by CA_1, associating CA_3 with the public key PK_3. By using the key PK_1 just obtained from CA_0, this certificate can be opened to obtain a trusted copy of PK_3.
3. Use PK_3 to verify the certificate $\{(U, PK_U)\}_{SK_3}$, signed by CA_3, which is of interest.

Figure 6.12(b) depicts a hierarchy with *reverse certificates*, where a CA can also certify the validity of its superior's key. In this case, CA_i can check the validity of a certificate issued by CA_j by tracing a path up the hierarchy to the nearest common ancestor and down to CA_j, and the procedure for CA_2 to verify a certificate issued by CA_3 becomes:

1. Look up locally to find a reverse certificate $\{(CA_1, PK_1)\}_{SK_2}$, signed by CA_2, associating CA_1 with the public key PK_1. This gives CA_2 direct access to a trusted copy of PK_1.
2. Apply to CA_1 to get a certificate $\{(CA_3, PK_3)\}_{SK_1}$, signed by CA_1, associating CA_3 with the public key PK_3. By using the trusted key PK_1, this certificate can be opened to obtain a trusted copy of PK_3.
3. Use PK_3 to verify the certificate $\{(U, PK_U)\}_{SK_3}$, signed by CA_3, which is of interest.

Some systems, including those based on the ITU-T X.509 standard [180], allow more general trust models, such as general digraphs, in which any CA may certify the validity of any other CA's public key. This tends to reduce the lengths of the necessary certification paths, making the protocol more efficient.

Protocol 25

Message 1 $A \rightarrow B$: $\alpha^{x_A} \bmod q$
Message 2 $B \rightarrow A$: $\alpha^{x_B} \bmod q$

Fig. 6.13 Diffie-Hellman key agreement protocol.
Here, α is a publicly known integer which is a primitive root of a publicly known prime q, and x_A and x_B are secret integers known only to A and B respectively.

6.5 Key Exchange

Key exchange (or *key establishment*) is the general term for the activity of making a shared secret available to two or more parties. In many cases, as we have seen, key exchange may be an integral part of the entity authentication process, but there are several situations in which this may not be appropriate. In particular, two parties may wish to change their encryption keys from time to time during an exchange, in order to protect themselves against possible key compromise due to their inadvertently exposing their keys or due to a successful attack by an adversary. When they change their keys, they do not necessarily wish to go through the complexity of the general authentication protocols presented in the previous section.

Key exchange can be based on two fundamental techniques:

Key transport,   (or *key distribution*, in which one party creates or derives the new secret key and (securely) transfers it to the other party or parties.

Key agreement,   in which each of the parties contributes a *share* of the information needed to derive the new secret key. A party can only evaluate the new secret when it has accumulated all the shares.

The key exchange methods which we have considered in connection with entity authentication have all been based on *key transport*. The essential feature of all these is that the creator of the key sends an encrypted message, containing the new key, some kind of nonce (a timestamp or sequence number) to guarantee freshness, and possibly a digital signature, to the party who is to receive the key. These requirements ensure confidentiality of the new key, integrity and sender authentication. In some contexts, information about the *lifetime* of the key may also be desired. Keys expire at the end of their lifetime and must be replaced by this time at the very latest.

An important example of a *key agreement* protocol is the *Diffie-Hellman protocol*, historically the first practical solution to the problem of key distribution over an insecure communication channel [30]. The protocol is given as **Protocol 25** in Figure 6.13. The shared secret which can be evaluated by both A and B after this exchange is:

$$K = \alpha^{x_A \cdot x_B} \bmod q$$

which is used as the new secret key. Note that A's personal secret x_A is not revealed directly to B (or to any adversaries who may be listening), and it is computationally

a)

$$K_A \quad A \qquad\qquad\qquad\qquad\qquad\qquad\qquad\qquad B \quad K_B$$

$$\alpha^{x_A}$$

$$\alpha^{x_A x_B} \qquad\qquad\qquad\qquad\qquad \alpha^{x_B} \qquad \alpha^{x_A x_B}$$

b)

$$K_A \quad A \qquad\qquad\qquad M \qquad\qquad B \quad K_B$$

$$\alpha^{x_A}$$

$$\alpha^{x'_A}$$

$$\alpha^{x_B} \qquad \alpha^{x'_A x_B}$$

$$\alpha^{x_A x'_B} \qquad\qquad \alpha^{x'_B}$$

Fig. 6.14 An attack on the Diffie-Hellman protocol.
(a) Normal operation; (b) During man-in-the-middle attack

Protocol 26

Message 1 $A \rightarrow B$: $\alpha^{x_A} \bmod q$
Message 2 $B \rightarrow A$: $(\alpha^{x_B} \bmod q, \{S_B(\alpha^{x_B}, \alpha^{x_A})\}_K)$
Message 3 $A \rightarrow B$: $\{S_A(\alpha^{x_B}, \alpha^{x_A})\}_K$

Fig. 6.15 Station-to-Station key agreement protocol.
Here, α is a publicly known integer which is a primitive root of a publicly known prime q, and x_A and x_B are secret integers known only to A and B respectively. K is the secret key evaluated as $\alpha^{x_A x_B} \bmod q$ by both A and B, $S_i(m)$ denotes message m digitally signed by party i, and $\{m\}_k$ denotes message m encrypted with key k.

infeasible for B to evaluate x_A from ($\alpha^{x_A} \bmod q$). Likewise, B's personal secret x_B is not revealed directly to A. Nevertheless, they each receive enough information to evaluate the new shared secret, K.

Whereas the basic Diffie-Hellman protocol is secure against passive attackers, who just listen to the exchange of messages, it is *not* secure against active attackers who can replace messages by new ones. The classic attack is a so-called *man-in-the-middle attack*, in which an attacker M intercepts and changes the messages going from A to B and vice-versa. This is illustrated in Figure 6.14(b). The attacker M replaces A's message α^{x_A} by $\alpha^{x'_A}$ and B's reply α^{x_B} by $\alpha^{x'_B}$, where both x'_A and x'_B have been invented by M. This means that A computes the new key $K_A = \alpha^{x_A x'_B}$ and B the new key $K_B = \alpha^{x'_A x_B}$. However, M also possesses all the information needed to compute both these keys, and is therefore in a position to decrypt all messages sent from A to B and *vice versa*, and to re-encrypt them using the intended receiver's key. Thus neither A nor B is aware that their exchange of messages is compromised.

The obvious problem is that the messages in **Protocol 25** contain no information which securely identifies their sender or which ensures integrity. A large number of proposals for ways to improve this situation have been made. As an example, let us consider Diffie, van Oorschot and Wiener's *Station-to-Station (STS) protocol* [31], as given in **Protocol 26**. The STS protocol is the basis of the Oakley Key Determination Protocol [242] used within the IPsec suite of Network layer security protocols [233]. This protocol sends an encrypted, signed copy of the exponentials used to evaluate the shared secret key together with the exponentials themselves. This enables the recipients to check the integrity and source of the received information. As in the three-way handshake and similar protocols, the third message confirms to B that the new key K is actually shared with A. These additional features protect the protocol against the simple man-in-the-middle attack shown in Figure 6.14. However, users of the protocol should still take care, as you will see if you try to solve Exercise 6.9. You should never underestimate the difficulty of designing a correct and secure key exchange protocol!

6.6 Non-cryptographic Methods

Not all forms of security can be provided solely by the use of cryptographic methods. Some other – rather obvious – techniques are:

Traffic padding   used to produce a constant flow of traffic between users of a service so that information about traffic flow cannot be used to deduce the level of activity of the users.

Routing control   to ensure that data are not routed via 'sensitive' sub-networks, where they perhaps could more easily be tapped. The general subject of routing is discussed in the next chapter.

Passwords   which are typically used for access control.

Smart cards   which may be used to contain secret information for access control, keys or other personal information or which can be used to compute cryptographic functions using a combination of information stored on the card and information supplied by the user.

Protected channels   which because of their technical properties, routing or other features are resistant to external threats.

Firewalls   which are network components which prevent undesired or malicious traffic from passing into parts of the network where a high level of security is required.

We shall not go into further details of these methods here.

Further reading

For the basic concepts of security in distributed systems, Part 2 of the OSI Reference Model [134] is a good source of definitions, and contains some useful tutorial matter on where in the system it is most appropriate to deal with various kinds of threat. A large number of general texts on security in computer systems are available, such as Stallings' "Cryptography and Network Security" [122] and Pfleeger & Pfleeger's "Security in Computing" [106]. These also cover aspects of security which we have not had space to consider here, such as malicious software (vira, worms and other "malware"), operating system security and organisational and legal aspects of security. Bishop's book "Computer Security" [15] gives a more abstract technical review of the area, with emphasis on the basic principles. General reviews can also be found in many books on the architecture and design of distributed systems, such as reference [98].

Brassard's monograph "Modern Cryptology" [18] is a good modern review of cryptographic methods, which discusses not only the well-known DES and RSA methods, but also methods based on newer research, such as keyless cryptography and quantum cryptography. Schneier's book "Applied Cryptography" [113] gives a comprehensive review of cryptographic methods and a detailed presentation of concrete algorithms. More mathematical aspects of cryptography are dealt with in the "Handbook of Applied Cryptography", edited by Menezes, van Oorschot and Vanstone [89]. The proceedings of the annual conference on Advances in Cryptology report on the most recent developments.

Exercises

6.1. In a distributed system which uses a public key cryptosystem, there are two distinct forms of double encryption which assure the receiver, say B, that only the sender, say A, could have sent a message m and only the receiver can read it:

1. $E(E(m, PK_B), SK_A)$
2. $E(E(m, SK_A), PK_B)$

Can B conclude the same about these two messages? If not, in what essential manner do they differ?

6.2. Suppose A forms a digital signature for message m by encrypting a message digest (hash value) for m with A's private key, SK_A, as suggested in the text. It is then possible for A to deny having sent the message, by claiming that an intruder had stolen the secret key and sent the message without A's knowledge. Suggest ways of avoiding this problem.

6.3. Unique identification of a sender, A, by a digital signature based on a reversible public key crytosystem relies on the assumption that a message enciphered by A using his secret key SK_A can only be deciphered using a unique key, K, which is A's public key, PK_A. Is it in fact certain that such a unique key exists?

Note: In the general case, this is a very challenging problem, so you may restrict your answer to the RSA cryptosystem. (Even so, you may need to investigate quite a lot of literature to find the answer.)

6.4. In the text, the initial part of the proof of correctness of Needham and Schroeder's authentication protocol is missing. Use the proof system given in the text to prove that in fact Messages 1–3 of the protocol, together with the assumptions given on page 179, enable us to infer that S can see the things necessary to send Message 4 and that they can be encrypted with key SK_{AS}, i.e. that:

$$S \triangleright \{(N_A, A \xleftrightarrow{SK_{AB}} B, \sharp(A \xleftrightarrow{SK_{AB}} B), \{(N_B, A \xleftrightarrow{SK_{AB}} B)\}_{SK_{BS}})\}_{SK_{AS}}$$

6.5. The protocol for secret key authentication originally given by Needham and Schroeder in [99] differs from the final version given here as **Protocol 22**, essentially by omitting messages 1 and 2. The protocol was:

> Message 1 $A \rightarrow S$: (A, B, N_A)
> Message 2 $S \rightarrow A$: $\{(B, N_A, SK_{AB}, \{(A, SK_{AB})\}_{SK_{BS}})\}_{SK_{AS}}$
> Message 3 $A \rightarrow B$: $\{(A, SK_{AB})\}_{SK_{BS}}$
> Message 4 $B \rightarrow A$: $\{N_B'\}_{SK_{AB}}$
> Message 5 $A \rightarrow B$: $\{N_B' - 1\}_{SK_{AB}}$

This protocol turned out to be inadequate to ensure authentication, and had to be modified as shown in **Protocol 22**. Explain what the weakness of this protocol was, and why the modifications are a cure for the weakness.

6.6. In a secure distributed system which uses a public key cryptosystem, a mechanism is needed for the distribution of public keys. It is obviously important that this distribution cannot be 'faked', so that, say, a message claiming to give the public key for the police has actually been sent out by a group of drug barons. Suggest a protocol for solving this problem. Make sure to describe carefully which of the messages sent in the protocol are encrypted, by whom they are encrypted and decrypted, and which keys are used in each instance.

Is your protocol also suitable for the distribution of secret keys in secret key cryptosystems?

6.7. In many computer systems, the user has to type in a password in order to obtain access to any particular system. Discuss the various ways in which this password might be revealed to persons who are not supposed to know it. You should bear in mind that the system on which the user actually types in the password may be connected to the system to which access is desired by some kind of communication network. Then suggest how the methods discussed in this chapter could be used to prevent unauthorised persons from obtaining the password.

6.8. When certificates are used to provide authentication, it is important that a certificate can be *revoked* if it is no longer valid – for example, if the key which it contains is known to be compromised, or if the owner of the certificate ceases to exist. Suggest a suitable protocol for dealing with revocation in the case of a system with multiple certification authorities, based on an hierarchical trust model.

6.9. The Station-to-Station protocol given as **Protocol 26** is sensitive to a type of man-in-the-middle attack in which the attacker changes the first message from A to B, so that it looks as though it came from a third party, C. (Technically, this can be done by changing the sender address in the PDU.) B then replies to the intruder, who sends the reply on to A. When A sends its third message, it belives that it is talking to B, whereas B believes it is talking to C. Suggest ways of avoiding this type of attack.

For a bigger challenge, try to use BAN logic to prove that your improved protocol offers correct assurances to the parties involved.

Chapter 7
Naming, Addressing and Routing

> "... The name of the song is called 'Haddock's Eyes'."
>
> "Oh, that's the name of the song, is it?" Alice said, trying to feel interested.
>
> "No, you don't understand," the Knight said, looking a little vexed. "That's what the name is called. The name really is 'The Aged Aged Man'."
>
> "Then I ought to have said, 'that's what the song is called'?" Alice corrected herself.
>
> "No, you oughtn't: that's another thing. The song is called 'Ways and Means': but that's only what it's called, you know!"
>
> "Well, what is the song, then?" said Alice, who was by this time completely bewildered.
>
> "I was coming to that," the Knight said. "The song really is 'A-sitting on a Gate': and the tune's my own invention".
>
> "Alice through the Looking-Glass"
> Lewis Carroll

In the previous chapters of this book, we have implicitly assumed that the sender of a message knows the identification of its intended receiver, and that the service which the sender uses to pass the message knows not only the location of the destination within the distributed system, but also how to get there. The senders and receivers have, of course, been active objects (described by processes) within the system. More generally, we may need to have a similar sort of knowledge about passive objects, such as data which we wish to get hold of. The question now arises as to where all this knowledge comes from, and how it is passed round in the system. In this chapter we shall try to answer this question.

7.1 General Principles of Naming and Addressing

Following the terminology of Shoch [115], which has been taken over in a somewhat modified form by ISO, we distinguish between the following types of identifier for an object in a distributed system:

- A **name**, which is an identifier permanently associated with an object, regardless of the object's location within the distributed system.
- An **address**, which is an identifier associated with the current location of the object.
- A **route**, which is an identifier associated with the path to be followed in order to reach the object.

The general requirement for a scheme of identifiers in a distributed system is that it must make it possible to deal with situations where:

1. Objects can move from one system to another.
2. References may be made to objects within a general class, with automatic selection of an appropriate object from the class, according to some convenient selection criterion such as efficiency of access. Identifiers which can be used in this way are often denoted *Generic Identifiers* or *Anycast Identifiers*.
3. The same identifier can be used to refer to a whole class of objects, so that many objects have the same identifier. Identifiers of this type are often denoted *Group Identifiers* or *Multicast Identifiers*.
4. The same object may be referred to by different identifiers, for example from different entities or different systems. If this is possible, we say that the identification system permits *Alias Identifiers* or *Equivalence Identifiers*.

The distinction between names and addresses makes it possible to deal with the first situation, involving the construction of a (possibly distributed) *directory*, which can be abstractly described as a mapping from names to addresses.

Generic identifiers can in principle also be dealt with by means of a directory, which in this case must be a mapping from names to sets of addresses. However, as we shall see later, this is not always a very sensible approach, as it may not be convenient (perhaps not even possible) permanently to maintain instances of all possible generically identified objects on all systems where they might be required. It may therefore be necessary to create a new instance of an object when it is referred to, and this is not compatible with the classical idea of a passive directory used only for lookup purposes.

How alias identifiers are dealt with depends on the purpose for which they have been introduced. There are a number of important possibilities:

- To allow the 'external' name of an object seen from other parts of the distributed system to be different from the name used locally by, say, the local operating system (*OS*). This makes it possible to set up a uniform global identifier scheme which hides the fact that objects are in fact distributed over many systems.
- To allow several global identifiers for the same object ('global aliases').
- To allow human users to use different identifiers from the internal identifiers used within the computers.

In this connection it is convenient to introduce the concept of a *local implementation identifier*, which is an identifier acceptable to the local OS of the system in which the object is located. The same object may be identified within its local system by another identifier, which we shall call a *unique local identifier*, which has a form which follows some global convention within the distributed system, and which is therefore globally acceptable, though only *unique* within the scope of, say, a single system or entity. Finally, the object may be identified throughout the distributed system by one or more *global identifiers*, which uniquely identify the object everywhere.

To deal with all these identifiers, a set of mappings is in general required, defining the correspondences between local unique identifiers and local implementation identifiers, and between global identifiers and local implementation identifiers. These mappings are sometimes known as the *local contexts* and the *global context* respectively. Some of the mappings may, of course, be identity mappings, and will in general be so in *homogeneous* distributed systems (i.e. ones whose component systems are identical – at least with respect to naming conventions).

We can formalise these ideas a little more, as follows:

$$
\begin{aligned}
\textit{Directory:} && NAME &\mapsto ADR \\
\textit{or:} && NAME &\mapsto ADR\text{-set} \\
\textit{Routing\_context:} && ROUTE &\mapsto ADR^* \\
\textit{Local\_context:} && ULID &\mapsto LIID \\
\textit{Global\_context:} && GLID &\mapsto LIID
\end{aligned}
$$

where

$$
\begin{aligned}
\text{Name,} && NAME &\subseteq ID \\
\text{Address,} && ADR &\subseteq ID \\
\text{Route,} && ROUTE &\subseteq ID \\
\text{Global identifier,} && GID &\subseteq ID \\
\text{Unique local identifier} && ULID &\subseteq ID \\
\text{Local implementation identifier} && LIID &\subseteq ID
\end{aligned}
$$

where *ID* is the domain of identifiers.

The strategic questions to be answered in connection with naming and addressing within a particular distributed system are then:

1. What types of identifiers (names, addresses, routes) are to be used in each protocol layer for referring to active and passive objects respectively?
2. If names are to be used, how are the *Directory* and *Routing_context* mappings to be implemented?
3. Are generic identifiers required?
4. What scheme of global and/or local identifiers is to be used, and how are the mappings from these to local implementation identifiers to be implemented?
5. Are alias names other than those implied by the local and global context mappings required, and at what level (several GIDs, several ULIDs within each system, several LIIDs)?

There are no absolute answers to these questions. However, the way in which they are answered in a particular system may have considerable influence, both with respect to 'what can be done' within that system, and with respect to the efficiency of the transfer of information within the system. What follows is therefore a series of general ideas on this subject, rather than a set of hard and fast rules for what to do.

7.1.1 Naming Strategies in the Upper Layers of the System

The upper layers of a distributed system offer a service to a conceptual 'application user'. In general, this gives the user one of two possible views of the system:

1. The **transparent view**, where the user cannot see that the system on which she runs her application is distributed. This implies either that the individual systems at the various locations are completely homogeneous (they are then often said to be *monotype*), or that all objects are identified by global identifiers whose structure does not reveal the location of the object within the network. If the latter is true, then the identifiers are global *names* rather than addresses or routes.
2. The **system-specific view**, where the user specifically refers to the location of the desired object when referring to it. This implies that the user provides some kind of address in order to identify the object.

Generally speaking, the system-specific view is preferred in distributed systems which have the character of pure networking systems, where the network merely provides remote access to any of the host computers which are attached to it, but where there is little or no cooperation between these computers during the execution of applications. When extensive cooperation between the individual systems during the execution of an application is envisaged, the transparent view is normally preferred.

Since it may also be desirable to provide the application user with access to services both by generic identifier and specific identifier, there are four principal identifier schemes available. For example, to specify that we wish to communicate with a process offering a line printer service (i.e. acting as spooler for a line printer), we might be able to choose as shown in the following table:

	View	
Identification	Transparent	Specific
Generic	'any line printer service'	'any line printer service on system XXX'
Specific	'any PostScript™ printer service'	'the PostScript™ printer service on system XXX'

A particularly general way of dealing with all these possibilities is offered by naming based on *attributes*. This is the scheme used in the ISO/ITU-T Directory [173, 174, 178, 179], and often referred to as *X.500 naming*, after the series of ITU-T recommendations (X.500 to X.521) which describe it. In such a naming scheme, each 'name' consists of a list of attributes. Some of these correspond to what we would ordinarily consider a name, others describe various properties of

Table 7.1 Attributes for X.500 naming (after [178]).

Attribute & Mnemonic	Description
Labelling attributes	
Common name, CN	The usual name for the object.
Surname	The family name of a person.
Serial number	The serial number of a device.
Geographical attributes	
Country name, C	
Locality name, L	
State or province name, S	
Street address	
Organisational attributes	
Organization name, O	The company or institution.
Organizational unit name, OU	The department, group or unit.
Title, T	The title or function of a person.
Explanatory attributes	
Description	Descriptive information: interests, keywords, etc.
Search guide	Suggested search criteria.
Business category	The occupation or similar of a person.
Postal addressing attributes	
Postal address	
Postal code	
Telecommunications addressing atributes	
Telephone number	
Telex number	
Teletex terminal identifier	
Facsimile telephone number	
X121 address	(see Section 7.2.1)
International ISDN number	
OSI Application attributes	
Presentation address	(see Section 7.2.1)
Supported Application Context	(see Section 10.2)
Relational attributes	
Member	A group of names associated with an object.
Owner	The name of an object responsible for some other object(s).
See Also	A reference to other entries in the directory which describe the same object.
Security attributes	
User password	
User certificate	(see Section 6.4.2)

the object or user concerned, such as its organisational properties ('in the R&D Department'), telephone number, occupation, location, aliasing information, authentication information and so on. A selection of the attributes proposed for use in X.500 naming [178] is given in Table 7.1. To name an object, it is necessary to supply a set of attributes which describe it sufficiently uniquely for the purpose in hand; this will obviously depend on whether generic or specific identification is required. Since some of the attributes may describe the system to which the object or person is attached, they make it possible to cater for both transparent and system-specific naming strategies.

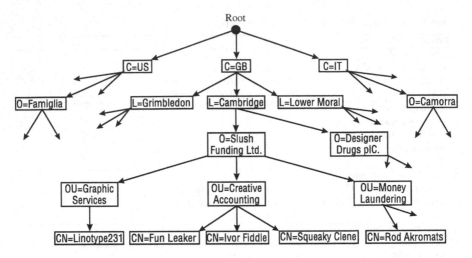

Fig. 7.1 An X.500 Directory Information Tree.

Although this is not essential, most proposals for using attributed-based naming assume that the attributes are arranged in some kind of hierarchy. This simplifies lookup, by making it possible to check off the more general attributes (such as the country where the object is located) before going on to the more specific ones. It also makes it possible to divide the directory up into hierarchically organised domains, which can be administered by different authorities. We shall look at some of the consequences of this in Section 7.1.3 below. In X.500 the hierarchy is known as the *Directory Information Tree (DIT)*.

An example of an X.500 DIT is shown in Figure 7.1. Note that, although it is a tree, it is not a strict layered hierarchy, as the Locality attribute is sometimes above the Organisational Unit attribute, and sometimes below it, depending on how the administrators of the different domains determine that things should be organised. Given this particular DIT, the name:

{C=GB, L=Cambridge, O=Slush Funding Ltd., CN=Ivor Fiddle}

would uniquely identify the person known as Ivor Fiddle, and so in fact would the name:

{C=GB, O=Slush Funding Ltd., CN=Ivor Fiddle}

Of course, this only works if Slush Funding Ltd. have no Ivor Fiddles working for them at other localities than Cambridge or in other organisational units than the Creative Accounting department.

A particular example of the use of X.500 names is in systems for handling electronic mail according to the ISO MOTIS and ITU-T MHS standards [191], where they are usually referred to as *O/R names*. O/R stands for Originator/Recipient, reflecting the fact that they identify the sender or receiver of the electronic mail.

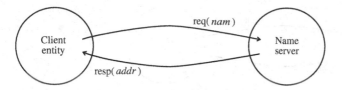

Fig. 7.2 Obtaining an address from a name server.
The name *nam* is passed to the server, and the corresponding address *addr* is returned to the client.

7.1.2 *Directories and Servers*

If the transparent view is to be offered to users, there must be a global naming scheme with globally available directories. A convenient way to implement these in many distributed systems is by means of a so-called *name server*.

A *server* is a specialised active object (most often a software process) which mediates, and in many cases controls, access to objects of a particular type. In the case of a name server, these objects are directory entries – mappings from names to addresses. Access to the server typically follows the RPC convention described in Section 4.3.2. For a name server, the calling parameter is usually just the name for which the corresponding address is required, and the return parameter is the address. This is illustrated in Figure 7.2.

A name server can be implemented for names valid within any convenient scope (in OSI Reference Model notation: any *domain*), such as a single layer, a single sub-network or a single system. In the last case, the names may either be global names referring to objects in the relevant system, or they may be local unique names. If local names are used, a globally valid directory can only be constructed by providing an additional server which can construct unique global names from the local names and knowledge of their locations.

A name server within a layer normally only contains the names of other active elements (entities) associated with the layer, and providing services to the users of this layer. The nature of the registered entities depends strongly on the layer and the system architecture, since different architectures make use of different degrees of specialisation among entities. As an example, consider the Application Layer, i.e. that layer which directly offers services to the application processes and their users. Two common architectures present themselves:

1. **Server-based:** In this architecture, the distributed system is partitioned into a set of specialised systems, each offering a particular application-related service to the user. Traditional examples are: clock servers, printer servers, terminal cluster servers, file servers, database servers and language translator (compiler) servers, each providing access to the objects its service type implies.
2. **General entity:** In this architecture, most commonly associated with large heterogeneous networks offering OSI services, the entities of the Application Layer

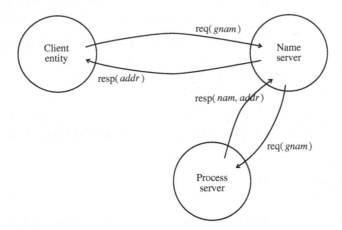

Fig. 7.3 Creating an instance of a generic object by using a process server.
The generic name *gnam* is passed to the name server, which requests the process server to create an instance of the object and then returns its address *addr* to the client.

offer general combinations of services, and give access to general facilities within their host systems.

In other layers, the distinction between these architectures is less clear, as layer entities are more likely to be identical in all systems, so that the same service is offered everywhere.

When an entity is started, it must announce its presence to the name server, sending its name and address. When it terminates, the name and address must be removed again. Objects controlled by servers, on the other hand, are catalogued by their own server and are not directly registered by the name server. It should be obvious that the name server's own address must be constant and well-known to everyone, so that it can always be consulted or reported to.

This organisation is appropriate if specific identifiers are used. If generic identifiers are used, there are two possibilities: One is for the name server to contain the addresses of all relevant instances; when asked for an address, it can reply with the 'nearest' one to the enquirer. This is only appropriate if all possible instances of the generic object are available all the time. This may be a very wasteful disposition. An alternative policy is to create a new instance as and when required, and in this case the name server will ask a *process server* to create the required instance and return its address. This is illustrated in Figure 7.3.

A final variation on the name server theme is the *trader*. This mediates contact to a suitable object on the basis of requirements specified by the client. Typically, these requirements would specify the *interfaces* (expressed in terms of function names and the corresponding argument types and result types) for the functions to be provided by the object, and the trader then tries to find an object which offers at least the required functionality. This type of server is, for example, often found in distributed

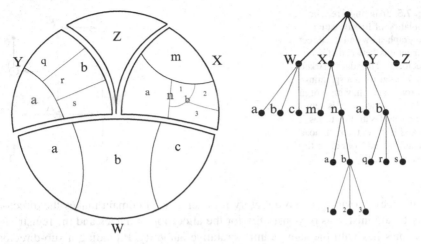

Fig. 7.4 A distributed system with domain structure (after [141]).
Left: The domain structure of the system; **Right:** The logical tree structure of the domains.

systems which are constructed from objects in accordance with the *Common Object Request Broker Architecture (CORBA)* specifications, a set of industry standards for distributed object-oriented systems [101].

7.1.3 Distributed Directories

In a small distributed system, based on a small physical network, the Application Layer name server is usually centralised, in the sense that it is implemented on a single physical system. This corresponds to there being a single *naming domain* at this level. As networks become larger, there are administrative and technical advantages in dividing them up into several logical or physical domains. Logical domains are convenient to administer, as they may be associated with different organisations or different parts of an organisation. A division into physical domains is usually motivated by technological considerations. For example, a large network may consist of several sub-networks. If it is a Wide Area Network, offering public network services, the sub-networks may correspond to different geographical regions, different countries, and so on. In Local Area Networks, the sub-networks may be based on different technologies, for example with a high-capacity backbone network which connects several lower-capacity networks, which in turn reach out to the individual user workstations or whatever.

The overall structure of the identifier space (the names if it is a logical domain structure, or the addresses if it is a physical domain structure) then becomes as shown in Figure 7.4.

Within such systems, it is convenient to distribute the directory, so that a sub-directory is implemented within each sub-domain (at least down to a certain depth

Fig. 7.5 Spanning Tree for
Emulation of Broadcasting.
The graph shows all the direct
connections between sub-
directories. The edges marked
with *arrows* form a spanning
tree for the graph, with root in
A. From A the query is sent
to the set of sub-directories
marked B, from them to those
marked C, and from them to
those marked D.

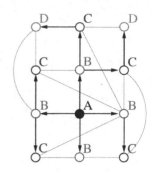

in the tree). Providing a sub-directory for each logical domain makes the directory easy to administer, as responsibility for the allocation of names and the registration of names lies with the same administratative authority. Providing a sub-directory for each physical domain offers the potential advantage of robustness with respect to failures within sub-networks. However, distribution of the directory can also give rise to a number of difficulties, which have to be taken care of.

Using Broadcasts for Directory Lookup

Lookup in a distributed directory cannot always be dealt with by a simple exchange of messages between the user and its local name server – if the name to be looked up is not known in the local sub-directory, there must be a protocol for passing on the enquiry to other sub-directories. One obvious possibility is to broadcast the query to all sub-directories. Unfortunately, unless the network has been specially designed for this purpose, a true broadcast service is unlikely to be available, precisely because the network is partitioned into sub-networks. Broadcasting will therefore have to be emulated by a series of point-to-point communications. As we have seen in Chapter 5, this may be an expensive solution, both in terms of time and messages sent. The best that can be done is often to allow the enquiry to spread out among the sub-directories in a tree-like manner: the local sub-directory to the initial enquirer asks those sub-directories which it can contact directly (or those that are 'nearest' in some sense), and waits for their replies. Each of them either replies itself, if it knows the answer, or asks a new sub-set of sub-directories and waits for their reply, and so on.

For efficiency, it will usually be desirable to ensure that sub-directories do not get asked more than once. A simple way to ensure this is by only sending queries along the branches of a *spanning tree* (in the graph-theoretical sense) covering all sub-directories, as illustrated in Figure 7.5. Separate spanning trees must, of course, be defined for each individual sub-directory as root. Construction of the spanning trees can be based on pre-knowledge of the topology of the network, or by using a distributed algorithm.

Figure 7.5 only shows how the *query* is propagated through the tree of sub-directories. There are then two strategies for how to return the *replies*: In the *chaining* strategy, a sub-directory which can answer the query sends its reply back to the system (the original client or one of the intermediate sub-directories) from which it received the query, which then passes the reply on to the system from which *it* received the query and so on. Thus propagation of queries spreads out through the spanning tree as a wave from the root to the leaves, and collection of replies as a wave from the leaves to the root, as in the *diffusing computations* used in the broadcast protocols discussed in Chapter 5. In the alternative strategy, sometimes known as *(direct) referral*, a sub-directory which can answer the query sends its reply directly back to the *originator* of the query at the root of the spanning tree. This may increase efficiency in the system. In practical systems with distributed directories, the originator will of course – regardless of which reply strategy is used – usually *cache* recent replies, in order to avoid unnecessary lookup operations in the common case where the same information is to be used several times within a short period of time.

When the distributed system to be covered by the directory becomes very large, simple-minded broadcasting is no longer an efficient way of disseminating queries, since there may be thousands or even millions of sub-directories which have to be consulted before the response to a query can be found. A number of heuristics which shorten the lookup process have therefore been investigated. A good example of this is found in the Internet Domain Name System (DNS), which is intended to offer directory services throughout the global Internet, and which we consider in the next section.

Replicated Directories

Another possible solution to the lookup problem is to arrange for there to be several copies of all or part of the directory. The directory is then said to be (fully or partially) *replicated*. Note that with full replication each sub-directory covers the complete naming domain of the entire distributed system. In very large networks, this is impractical, but in smaller networks it can be a useful technique, especially as it gives excellent protection against failure of a single sub-directory. Lookup is then easy, but insertion of new entries in the directory requires some kind of broadcasting, and so does deletion of entries when an object catalogued in the directory becomes unavailable.

If the broadcast is not 'instantaneous', or if it can fail to reach some destinations, there is the potential problem that different sub-directories at certain times may contain different information, and thus be inconsistent. To some extent, this situation can be avoided by the use of protocols which are more complex than simple broadcasts, such as the two-phase commit protocol presented in Chapter 5. However, it is only *to some extent*. The problem is that commit protocols are designed only to carry out the requested changes if all parties agree to them. A little thought will (hopefully) convince you that this can often be acceptable when directory entries have to be *inserted*, i.e. when a new object becomes available, since the worst thing that can happen is more or less that a long time may pass before the rest of the system gets to know that this object is available. When an object has to be *deleted*, the commitment protocol is counter-productive, since it prevents anyone being told about the demise of the object until everyone has been told about it! This is not much help if the object already is dead and unable to take part in any further activity.

On the whole, a better strategy is usually to use a simple protocol for spreading information about directory changes, and to construct the protocols used to access objects in such a way that they are resilient to finding 'nobody at home'. In other words, a user first tries to communicate with an object at whatever address the nearest sub-directory tells her (or even at the last known address which she herself can remember without consulting the directory). If this fails, she asks the sub-directory again after a suitable delay. This procedure continues until success is obtained, or until the user decides to give up. The same strategy is equally useful with centralised directories, to guard against the possibility that the object has moved (or been *re*moved) since the directory was consulted.

Constructing Unique Global Names

A second problem with distributed directories is how to ensure uniqueness of global names. As with many other problems in distributed systems, the possible solutions fall into three classes:

1. **Centralised.** A central facility allocates (and deallocates) unique global identifiers on demand. The facility could, for example, be incorporated in a process server. Potentially this gives a problem of reliability, just as with a centralised name server, but in practice this problem does not seem to be important.
2. **Isolated.** Each system allocates its own identifiers without explicit reference to other systems. This is more robust than the centralised strategy, but requires a system-wide convention for how global identifiers are to be chosen, to avoid name conflicts. Essentially, this obliges global names in fact to be global addresses, in the sense that the identifier space is partitioned, and each partition is associated with a particular system. (How else would you define an address?) This suits the system-specific view of objects discussed in the previous section, but not the transparent view. This is the strategy proposed in ISO Standard 11578 [208], according to which a *Universal Unique Identifier (UUID)* is constructed by concatenating the time of day, the address of the system and a random number.
3. **Truly distributed.** Each system allocates global identifiers after reference to the others. This can be more robust than the centralised strategy, although robust algorithms (as discussed above) can give poor response if some systems are unable to answer queries due to failure. Generally speaking, it will also be necessary to use broadcasting, which again may be expensive.

Compromise strategies, such as having a centralised allocator for each sub-domain, corresponding to (say) a sub-network, are evidently also possible. So the system designer has a whole spectrum of combinations at his or her disposal, depending on the system requirements for robustness, cost (in some general sense), system transparency and response time. General rules for what to choose can not be given here.

7.1.4 Internet Naming and the Internet DNS

A well-known example of a domain-oriented naming strategy is the one used in the Internet for identifying systems at the Network Layer and above. The names are generally known as *host names*, although strictly speaking they identify network interfaces. Since a host may have several network interfaces (for example, if it lies on the boundary between two sub-networks) and since alias names are also permitted, a host may have several names. A name is conventionally written as a series of elements separated by dots. For example:

```
www.rfc-editor.org
hobbits.middle-earth.net
student31.imm.dtu.dk
itsy.bitsy.polkadot.bikini.fr
stop.it
```

An Internet host name has no fixed length and its structure reflects the *administrative domains* which are responsible for allocating the name. The elements of the name are given from left to right in order of increasing significance. For example, `www.rfc-editor.org` refers to the the system `www` within the sub-domain `rfc-editor` within the top level domain `org`.

The top level domain is usually a two-letter code referring to a particular country (`dk`, `it`, `uk`, `ru`,...) or to a general class of names (`org`, `net`, `mil`, `com`,...), each of which has its own *naming authority* responsible for allocating names. For example, names in the top level domain `dk` are administered by the Danish naming authority, those in `ru` by the Russian authority, and so on, while names in `org` (which belong to non-profit organisations) are administered by the Public Interest Registry in Virginia, USA, those in `net` and `com` by Verisign Global Registry Services and so on[1]. A full list of the rules can be found in reference [221], and a list of the current "generic domains", published by the *Internet Assigned Numbers Authority (IANA)*, which administers names and addresses in the Internet, can be found on the Web at:

`http://www.iana.org/domain-names.htm`

Note that Internet host names really are *names* and so do not necessarily tell you anything about where in the world the system is located or what services it offers,

---

[1] In practice, the domain administrator often passes on the task of actually registering the names to one or more companies which act as registrars.

just as your personal name does not tell anything about where *you* are located or what you do. The Internet name just tells you about where the name has been registered. And although it is conventional to give hosts which offer particular services names which reflect these services (so the name of the Web server in domain xxx often has the name www.xxx, and the mail server the name mail.xxx), there is no guarantee that this is the case.

In many cases, for practical reasons, the top-level registration authority delegates the ability to register names to the sub-domains under its control. So for example, with a name such as student31.imm.dtu.dk, the sub-domain name dtu would be registered directly with the dk authority, the sub-sub-domain name imm would be registered with an authority for dtu.dk, and the actual host name student31 would be registered with an authority for imm.dtu.dk.

The mapping between names and the corresponding addresses is maintained via the *Domain Name System (DNS)* [217, 218], a distributed directory into which information can be inserted and from which information can be retrieved by using the DNS Application layer protocol. The DNS contains mappings for both the forward (name-to-address) and inverse (address-to-name) directions of lookup. Since a separate server containing a sub-directory is typically used for each top-level domain and sub-domain in the Internet, the DNS protocol uses heuristics in order to make searching in the large number of sub-directories more efficient than the naive broadcasting strategy described in Section 7.1.3.

The DNS pre-supposes that each host contains a certain amount of information about commonly-used name-address mappings, accessible locally by a system component known as a *resolver*. This locally stored information is composed of initial information loaded when the system is initialised, together with *cached* results from recent queries. If the resolver cannot find the required mapping locally, it will send a query to a DNS server which it knows about. Two modes of lookup are defined:

1. **Iterative lookup:** If a DNS server does not know the answer to an incoming query, it will refer the originator of the query to one or more further servers on which the requested information may possibly be available. It is up to the originator to decide how to exploit this *referral* information. If a DNS server knows the answer to the query, it will reply directly to the originator. This mode of lookup must be supported by all servers.
2. **Recursive lookup:** If a DNS server does not know the answer to the query, it will automatically pass it on to one or more other DNS servers which it believes will know the answer. If they do not know the answer, they pass it on to further servers, and so on in a recursive manner. Responses to queries are returned to the originator of the query by the directory chaining strategy described above. Servers have the option of whether or not to support this mode of lookup.

These query modes are illustrated in Figure 7.6 on the next page.

Parameters in the query are used to specify which direction of lookup (forward or inverse) is required, and which mode of lookup is preferably to be used. Remember, however, that servers do not need to support recursive lookup; if a recursive lookup query arrives at a server which does not support this feature, the server is allowed

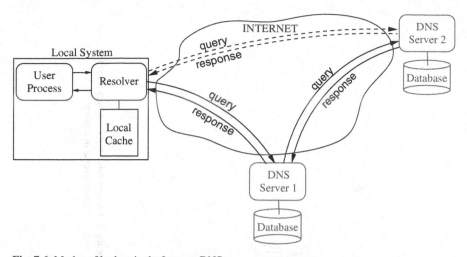

Fig. 7.6 Modes of lookup in the Internet DNS.
The *full arrows* indicate the progress of a query which propagates recursively to DNS Server 1 and DNS Server 2, and the corresponding response from DNS Server 2 back to the resolver. The *dashed arrows* indicate the final step of an iterative lookup, where DNS Server 1 has referred the resolver to DNS Server 2.

to reply with a referral as in iterative lookup. A further characteristic of the Internet DNS is that, in addition to caching recently used name-address mappings, the servers can explicitly fetch mappings for complete domains from other servers, in order to have the information available locally. This feature, known as *zone transfer*, makes it possible to introduce a controlled amount of replication in the directory.

In principle, DNS servers can point to more knowledgeable servers anywhere in the Internet. In practice, the sequence in which servers will be asked generally follows a standard heuristic which reflects the hierarchical domain naming structure: Just as names are generally registered via a hierarchy of registration authorities, so name-address mappings are registered in a hierarchy of name servers, as illustrated in Figure 7.7. So after a query from a resolver has initially been sent to the DNS server in the local (sub-)domain, it will then if necessary be sent to a so-called *root server* for the top-level domain referred to in the query, and then successively to servers for lower and lower sub-domains of this top-level domain, until the answer is found or the search terminates wihout an answer. For example, if the resolver and the local domain server do not know the answer, a query referring to student31.imm .dtu.dk will first be directed to an *authoritative server* for dk, and then (if necessary) successively to authoritative servers for dtu.dk and imm.dtu.dk. As in the case of naming authorities, the authoritative server for a particular domain will usually, for practical reasons, initially just contain information about the sub-domains immediately below it in the name hierarchy. But as time goes by, it may accumulate information about further sub-domains by means of caching or zone transfers.

In addition to the well-known generic domains and country domains, the Internet DNS contains a special naming domain, in-addr.arpa, which is used to simplify

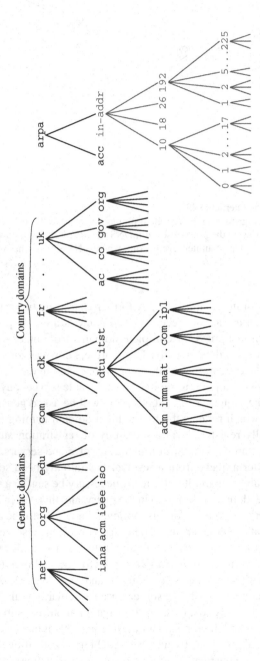

Fig. 7.7 Domain and name server hierarchies in the Internet DNS

Only some of the Internet domains are shown. Typically, an authoritative name server for each naming domain contains name-address mappings for at least the domains at the level immediately below it in the tree. The special domain arpa. in-addr contains inverse mappings.

Table 7.2 Important types of Resource Record in the Internet DNS

RR Type	Content of Rdata
A	The address corresponding to the Owner Name
CNAME	The canonical name corresponding to the Owner Name, when the latter is an alias.
MX	The name of a host which is willing to act as a mail exchange for the Owner, and a priority used to choose a suitable mail exchange if there are several candidates.
NS	The name of the authoritative name server for the Owner's domain.
PTR	The name of a location in the name space. (Typically used to give the name corresponding to an address in the `in-addr.arpa` domain.)

the task of inverse lookup). The name servers for sub-domains immediately below `in-addr.arpa` contain address-to-name mappings for *physical networks* and *gateways*, while those further down in the hierarchy contain the mappings for individual systems. So, for example, to look up the Internet name corresponding to the Internet address `10.2.23.27` (see Section 7.2.2), a query which cannot be answered locally will be sent to an authoritative name server for domain `10.in-addr.arpa`, and then if necessary to a name server for `2.10.in-addr.arpa`, and finally to one for `23.2.10.in-addr.arpa`.

The actual directory databases used in the Internet DNS need amongst other things to store information about forward and inverse mappings, alias names, and pointers to other servers. This information is stored in *Resource Records (RRs)* of different types. Each RR contains fields specifying:

- **Owner Name:** The name of the node in the naming tree which the RR describes;
- **Time-to-Live (TTL):** The time left before the RR will be discarded. This is used to limit the lifetime of cached RRs;
- **Type:** The type of the RR;
- **Rdata:** Information specific for the given type of RR.

The content of the RData in the most important types of RR is summarised in Table 7.2.

7.2 Addressing Structures

The directory concept neatly solves the problem of how to allow objects to move round in a distributed system, by permitting a clear distinction to be kept between names and addresses. Thus names and addresses can have quite different structures, and, in particular, the structure of addresses can be chosen to permit efficient solution of the 'real' addressing problem:

1. How to find the way to the destination system.
2. At the destination system, how to recognise that the PDU is in fact intended for a protocol entity within that system.

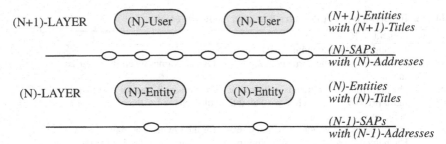

Fig. 7.8 Names and Addresses in the OSI Reference Model

For generality, we shall discuss addressing in terms of a layered architecture, using OSI notation. The basic concepts are illustrated in Figure 7.8. An *(N+1)-Entity*, which lies within the (N+1)-Layer, acts as an *(N)-User*, i.e. as a user of the *(N)-Service*. In general, it is identified by a name, known as an *(N+1)-Title*, and is attached to an *(N)-SAP*. This (N)-SAP is identified by an *(N)-Address*, to which other (N)-Users may direct (N)-SDUs which are intended for this (N)-User.

In terms of this notation, there are three basic addressing structures which may be used for constructing the (N)-Address [40]:

1. **Hierarchic**, in which case it is constructed from the (N-1)-Address associated with the (N)-Entity which takes part in the provision of the (N)-Service offered at the (N)-SAP concerned. The (N)-Address is constructed from the (N-1)-Address by concatenation with a *selector*, which for (N)-Addresses is usually denoted an *(N)-Selector*:

$$(N)\text{-}address = (N-1)\text{-}address \,\widehat{}\, (N)\text{-}selector$$

This permits conversations associated with several (N)-SAPs to go via the same (N-1)-SAP, a technique often known as *address multiplexing*.

2. **Partitioned**, in which case it is constructed by concatenation of a *Domain Identifier* with a *Sub-domain address*, where each domain is associated with a group of (N)-SAPs within the network, and the sub-domain addresses select particular (N)-SAPs within the given domain:

$$(N)\text{-}address = (N)\text{-}domain\text{-}id \,\widehat{}\, (N)\text{-}sub\text{-}domain\text{-}address$$

It is an assumption with this form of addressing that domains are completely disjoint, and that sub-domains within a domain are similarly disjoint. However, sub-domains may themselves be partitioned into sub-sub-domains, and so on in a recursive manner. With this form of addressing, (N)-Addresses are not related in any particular way to (N-1)-Addresses, so the (N)-Entities must explicitly maintain or use an address mapping function from (N)-SAPs to (N-1)-SAPs within the (N)-Layer. In return for this, this form of addressing can ease the implementation of the routing function, if the domains are associated with natural divisions in the network – such as sub-networks. We have already discussed how this can come about in connection with directory implementations.

3. **Flat,** in which case the (N)-Addresses are not directly related to the (N-1)-Addresses or to any division of the address space into domains. This addressing structure does not give the (N)-Entity any help at all, but obliges it explicitly to keep track of the relationship between (N)-SAPs and their associated (N-1)-SAPs and also of routing information.

7.2.1 OSI Addressing

The general addressing structure for use within OSI standards is described in Part 3 of the OSI Reference Model (Reference [135]). Basically, this states that within layers above the Network Layer, an *hierarchic* addressing structure is used. Directories are then only required for the Application Layer and the Network Layer. The Application Layer directory responds to enquiries concerning a named Application Process (Presentation Service User) instance by providing the enquirer with the P-address [2] of the PSAP to which the P-User is attached. The hierarchical addressing principle is then consistently applied through the upper four layers of the architecture, as follows:

$P\text{-}address = N\text{-}address\,\hat{}\,T\text{-}selector\,\hat{}\,S\text{-}selector\,\hat{}\,P\text{-}selector$

$S\text{-}address = N\text{-}address\,\hat{}\,T\text{-}selector\,\hat{}\,S\text{-}selector$

$T\text{-}address = N\text{-}address\,\hat{}\,T\text{-}selector$

In the Network Layer, the structure of the Network Address is defined in a general manner in [135], and more specifically in the Network Service standard, (Reference [141]). This decrees that OSI N-Addresses shall have the partitioned form. This is hardly surprising, as one of the functions of the Network Layer is to perform route selection. This can be made significantly easier if partitioned addresses are used. Partitioned addressing structures have in fact traditionally been used in many types of communication network. Well-known examples are the telephone network, and public international data networks, in which addressing follows ITU-T Recommendation X.121. In the telephone network, the address ('number') has the structure of a country code, followed by an area code, followed by a 'subscriber number'. In X.121 there are several possibilities, one of them essentially the same as for telephones, the other with just a Digital Network Identifier Code (DNIC) followed by a subscriber number. This type of partitioned address is illustrated in Figure 7.9.

Within the Network Layer, a further directory is envisaged, which relates physical system identifiers to Network Addresses, and (if desired) to routes. The maintenance of this routing information will be discussed in the next section. In practice,

---

[2] In OSI work, it is common practice to abbreviate layer names by their initial letters or similar: Thus, P-Address for Presentation Address, P-User for Presentation Service User, and similarly S- (Session), T- (Transport), N- (Network), D- (Data Link) and Ph- (Physical).

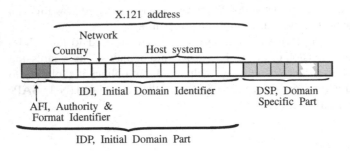

Fig. 7.9 ISO Network addressing using X.121 addresses.
The AFI in the ISO Network address identifies the type of address in use by means of a 2-digit code. For an X.121 address, the code is 36 when the DSP is in a BCD encoding, and 37 when it is in a pure binary encoding; the actual X.121 address (the IDI) consists of up to 14 digits in a BCD encoding.

the 'physical system identifier' is often an identification for the hardware adaptor card used to attach the system to the network. For example, in a local area network it will almost always technically speaking be a Media Access Control (MAC) address, such as an Ethernet or Token Ring address.

7.2.2 Internet addressing

The addressing structure used in networks which utilise the Internet protocol suite is a simplified version of the OSI structure. Within the Network Layer, which uses the DoD Internet protocol (IP), systems are identified by a partitioned address, usually known as an *IP address*. The *Domain Name System (DNS)* is used to map the human-readable system names ("host names"), which are partitioned to reflect an administrative domain structure (see Section 7.1.4) to IP addresses.

In the classic version of the IP protocol (known as IPv4 [210]), the address is represented by 32 bits. Originally, the leading bits indicated the so-called *class* of the address. This specifies whether the address is for a single host or a multicast group, and in the case of a single host determines the length of the network identifier and host identifier, reflecting some historical idea about how many hosts the network is likely to have. The number of bits which identify the network (or indicate that the address is the address of a multicast group) is often specifed by a so-called *netmask*, which is the pattern of bits which can be used to remove the *host id* or *multicast group id* part of the address. The general structure of the address is shown in Table 7.3. The traditional human-oriented representation of Internet IPv4 addresses and netmasks is as a sequence of four (decimal) integers, where each number lies in the range [0..255] and is the decimal value corresponding to 8 bits of the address. So for example 129.131.68.63 must be a Class B address (the leading bits of the first octet are 10), with network ID 000001 10000011 and

Table 7.3 IPv4 address structure and netmasks for class-based addressing

Network Class	Leading bits	Network ID (bits)	Host ID (bits)	Netmask
A	0	7	24	255.0.0.0
B	10	14	16	255.255.0.0
C	110	21	8	255.255.255.0
Multicast	1110	Group ID (28 bits)		240.0.0.0

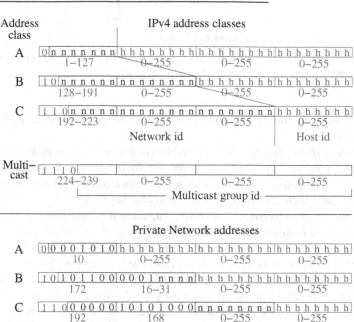

Fig. 7.10 IPv4 addresses (above) and Private Network addresses (below) for class-based addressing

host ID 01000100 00111111. Similarly, 224.0.1.1 is a multicast address for multicast group number 257 (the group used for the Network Time Protocol, NTP). Figure 7.10 illustrates the address structure in more detail.

Not all $2^{32} - 1$ addresses can be used freely. Traditionally, host IDs consisting entirely of 0-bits are not used, while a host ID consisting entirely of 1-bits is used as the *broadcast address* for the network concerned: any traffic sent to this address will be directed to *all* systems within that network. Furthermore, a subset of the IP addresses in each class is allocated for use in systems which will *not* be connected (directly) to the Internet. These are known as *Private Network (PN)* addresses, and are of course not globally unique: There can be many systems with the address, say, 192.168.25.1 in the world! PN addresses are commonly used in networks set up for testing purposes and also in *computer clusters*. Typically, the individual computers in the cluster do not need to be accessed directly from the Internet. Instead, all access goes via a front-end system (which has a public Internet address) which

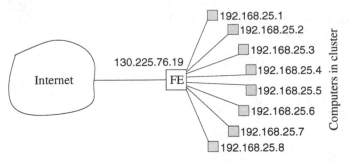

Fig. 7.11 A computer cluster with private network addresses. Only the front-end (FE) has a public Internet address and can therefore be contacted directly via the Internet.

passes on traffic to and from the cluster computers. This is illustrated in Figure 7.11.

In the more recent *IP Version 6 (IPv6)*, the addressing scheme is extended, so that the address is represented by 128 bits (conventionally denoted by 8 groups of 4 hexadecimal digits, separated by colons), and several more address classes, each identified by a particular pattern of leading bits, are available [232].

In practice, class-based addressing is inconvenient, since it is based on the idea that networks only come in three sizes: Small (Class C, up to $2^8 - 2 = 254$ hosts[3]), Medium (Class B, up to $2^{16} - 2 = 65\,534$ hosts) or Large (Class A, up to $2^{24} - 2 = 16\,777\,214$ hosts). Organisations want to be able to have networks with numbers of hosts given by any power of 2. This is made possible by the so-called *Classless Inter-Domain Routing (CIDR)* scheme of addressing [252]. When CIDR is used, the number of bits used to identify the network is included in the human-readable form of the address, and is passed to all routers which need to be able to find the network concerned. For example, an IPv4 CIDR address 130.225.69.17/23 indicates that the first 23 bits of the address identify the network and the remaining 9 bits indicate the system within the network. It is common practice to use the address where the host bits are all 0 to refer to the network itself; thus the network in the above example would be identified as 130.225.68.0/23, and its netmask would be 255.255.254.0. Correspondingly, the network broadcast address would be 130.225.69.255/23, where all the host id bits are set to 1. These ideas are illustrated in Figure 7.12 on the facing page.

In the Internet, application protocols rely directly on a connection-mode or connectionless-mode Transport service, and do not make use of separate Session and Presentation layers as in the OSI Reference Model. The overall addressing structure is therefore reduced to:

$$T\text{-}address = N\text{-}address \,\hat{}\, T\text{-}selector$$

where the *T-selector* is known as a *port*. In contrast to the OSI scheme, where T-selectors are used exclusively for multiplexing purposes and the individual selec-

---

[3] Rember that host id 00000000 is not used, and 11111111 is used as the broadcast address.

	Decimal IP addresses	Binary IP addresses
Unused	130.225.68.0	10000010 11100001 0100010 0 00000000
	┌ 130.225.68.1	10000010 11100001 0100010 0 00000001
	│ :	:
	│ 130.225.68.255	10000010 11100001 0100010 0 11111111
Hosts	│ 130.225.69.0	10000010 11100001 0100010 1 00000000
	│ 130.225.69.1	10000010 11100001 0100010 1 00000001
	│ :	:
	└ 130.225.69.254	10000010 11100001 0100010 1 11111110
Broadcast	130.225.69.255	10000010 11100001 0100010 1 11111111
Netmask	255.255.254.0	11111111 11111111 1111111 0 00000000

Fig. 7.12 Addresses and the netmask in a CIDR network with 23-bit network id

Table 7.4 Some common assigned Internet ports

Application	Port	Application	Port
FTP data	20	POP3	110
FTP control	21	NNTP	119
TELNET	23	NTP	123
SMTP	25	IMAP	143
DNS	53	LDAP	389
HTTP	80	HTTPS	443

tors have no specific meaning, a long series of the ports available in the Internet addressing scheme have conventionally been allocated for use with particular application protocols. In particular, most standard Internet applications have been assigned a port number between 1 and 1023 by the *Internet Assigned Numbers Authority (IANA)* for use by servers offering the particular application. Some examples are shown in Table 7.4. For all these examples, the port numbers are identical for the connection-mode (TCP) and connectionless-mode (UDP) transport protocols, though this is not necessarily always the case. Port numbers from 1024 up to 49151 can be *registered* with the *IANA* for use with specific applications, while those from 49152 and up can be used freely, for example when ports have to be *dynamically allocated*. A complete and up-to-date list is maintained by the IANA, and can be seen on the Web page:

        http://www.iana.org/assignments/port-numbers

In the Internet, the translation between network (IP) addresses and physical system identifiers is mediated by an *Address Resolution Protocol (ARP)*. This involves broadcasting a request to all systems in the local sub-net, specifying the IP address for the system whose physical system identifier is needed; the system with this IP address must then reply with the corresponding physical system identifier [214]. No centralised directory is involved, but the individual systems often cache translations which they use frequently.

Table 7.5 Attributes characterising O/R addresses

Attribute	Mnemonic
Country name	C
Administration domain name	ADMD, A
Private domain name	PRMD, P
Organization name	ORG, O
Organizational unit names	OU
Personal name	
Surname	S
Given name	G
Initials	I
Generation qualifier	GQ

7.2.3 MOTIS/MHS Addressing

Message handling (electronic mail) systems, in ISO known as MOTIS and in ITU-T as MHS (or more popularly as *X.400* systems after the series of ITU-T recommendations which govern their operation), use a more complex style of addressing [192], based on the use of *attributes* like the X.500 naming scheme discussed in Section 7.1.1 above. In fact, the X.400 address could well be part of an X.500 name, just as we have previously seen that an X.121 address or ISDN number can be part of it. Each X.400 address is itself made up of a number of (sub-)attributes, which together characterise the location of the service user who sends or receives an electronic mail message. This location is in MOTIS/MHS known as the user's *O/R address*, by analogy with the user's O/R name.

In the X.400 standards it is envisaged that electronic mail can be delivered in several different ways: To a user in a computer system, to an identifiable terminal in a network, or even by so-called physical delivery by ordinary post. The form of the attribute list depends on the intended form of delivery. Here we shall only consider addressing for delivery to a user in a computer system. The attributes which can be specified are listed in Table 7.5.

These attributes describe the address in an hierarchical manner, with each country divided up into two levels of domain, with one or more domains administered by public telecommunication operators as the upper level, and privately administered domains (each of which is subordinate to a particular public domain) as the lower level. Domains are in turn divided into organisations, which typically correspond to companies, universities, user groups or the like; organisations are divided into organisational units such as departments or sections (there may in fact be up to four levels); and organisational units are divided into separately identifiable users.

As long as the address is unambiguous, several of the attributes may be omitted. The Country-name and Administration-domain-name attributes are mandatory, while the remainder are included as required by the administration or private domain in which the user is located. If the Personal-name attribute is used, the Surname component is mandatory and the remaining components are optional. Thus there is no fixed format for the address; each of the attributes is encoded together

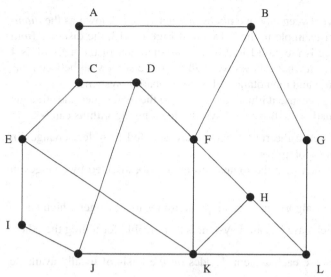

Fig. 7.13 An Example Network.

with a type code indicating which of the attributes it is, using BASN.1 encoding, which we shall describe in more detail in Chapter 8.

7.3 Routing

Routing is the function of finding a suitable path for PDUs to take from one SAP to another. In the OSI Reference Model architecture, this function is only relevant within the Network Layer, as this is the only layer in which there is a concept of a *path* between a source and destination, which may involve passing intervening systems in which there is a choice of path. In the Data Link Layer, communication takes place between service users in directly connected systems, whereas in the Transport Layer and above, all transmission is end-to-end, and the intervening systems (if any) are quite invisible.

Figure 7.13 shows an example of a network. For the purposes of discussing routing, we assume this is a physical network, with the *nodes* of the network occupied by *systems*, and the *edges* of the network implemented by *communication links* of some kind. To remind you of some useful graph-theoretical notation: Two nodes are said to be *adjacent* if there is an edge directly connecting them; the two nodes are then said to be *end-points* of the edge. A *path* consists of a sequence of adjacent nodes; the first and last nodes of the sequence are the end-points of the path. The remaining nodes (if any) are said to be *intermediate nodes* of the path. The path between two nodes which has fewest edges is known as a *geodesic* for those nodes. The number of edges which it contains is the *distance* between the nodes. The length of the longest geodesic between any two nodes in a network is known as the *diameter* of the network. For example in the network of Figure 7.13, the distance from L to C is 3 (the geodesic is the path LKEC), and the diameter of the network is 4 (a geodesic from I to B). In what follows we shall alternate somewhat between this graph-theoretical notation and the notation of communication systems.

Routing is interesting because it illustrates almost all the techniques and strategic choices which can be made in a distributed system. Routing algorithms can be:

- **Adaptive**, in which case the routes chosen are adapted to reflect changes in traffic patterns or net topology, or
- **Non-adaptive**, in which case the routes chosen are not affected by changes in traffic or topology.

Furthermore, the adaptive algorithms can adapt the routes in a manner which is:

- **Centralised**, in which case a central system is responsible for telling the others which routes to use,
- **Isolated**, in which case each system decides on the basis of locally available information which routes to use,
- **Truly Distributed**, in which case the systems explicitly exchange information with the aim of agreeing on a globally optimal set of routes.

These methods will be illustrated in the following sections.

7.3.1 Flooding

The simplest non-adaptive routing algorithm which can be imagined is to try out all conceivable routes which might lead toward the destination. In other words, in each system to send a copy of the PDU out to all adjacent systems, except the system from which the PDU arrived. This is usually known as *flooding*. Obviously, the final destination will (under normal circumstances) receive many copies of each message, via different routes, and must throw away redundant duplicates. Also, some mechanism is required to terminate the continued generation of more and more copies of the PDU, as the already generated copies pass through the network. The simplest technique is to include a *hop counter* in each PDU, and to initialise this counter to the maximum number of edges of the network along which the PDU (and all copies derived from it) is allowed to pass. Every time a PDU (in several copies!) is transmitted from a system, its counter is decreased by one. If a PDU arrives with counter value zero, it is discarded without being sent on. If the initial sender knows the graph-theoretical distance to the final destination, then it can use this value to initialise the hop counter. Otherwise the diameter of the network can be used. The protocol is shown in Figure 7.14.

For example, in the network of Figure 7.13, the routes with not more than 6 hops from F to G shown in Figure 7.15 would be discovered by flooding. Since the network has diameter 4, a strategy which discarded PDUs after 4 hops would in this case remove all the routes with loops and leave five useful alternatives.

Protocol 27

$$Node[i:\mathrm{N}_0] \stackrel{\text{def}}{=} (SAPA[i]?(dst:\mathrm{N}_0,x:\mathcal{M}) \rightarrow$$
$$\coprod_{j\in ns(i)} link[j]!(i,dst,hops(i,dst),x) \rightarrow Node[i]$$
$$[\![link[k\in ns(i)]?(src:\mathrm{N}_0,dst:\mathrm{N}_0,h:\mathrm{N}_0,x:\mathcal{M}) \rightarrow$$
$$(\textbf{if } dst = i$$
$$\textbf{then } SAPA[i]!x \rightarrow Node[i]$$
$$\textbf{elseif } (src = i) \vee (h = 0)$$
$$\textbf{then } Node[i]$$
$$\textbf{else } \coprod_{j\in ns(i)-\{k\}} link[j]!(src,dst,h-1,x) \rightarrow Node[i]))$$

Fig. 7.14 Flooding. In the protocol, $ns(i)$ is the set of indices for channels leading to the neighbours of node i, and $hops(i,j)$ is the number of hops from node i to node j.

No. of hops

2	FBG		
3	FHLG	FKLG	
4	FKHLG	FHKLG	
5	FDCABG	FDJKLG	FKHFBG* FHKFBG*
6	FKECABG	FDCEKLG	FDJKHLG FHKFHLG*
	FKHFKLG*	FKJDFBG*	FDJKFBG*

Fig. 7.15 Routes from F to G with not more than 6 hops. The routes marked with an asterisk contain loops.

Although apparently a primitive method, flooding has a number of areas of use. One area in which it is popular is in military networks, where the individual systems may disappear from one minute to the next. The robustness of flooding to loss of nodes or edges in the network is plainly an advantage here. It must also be noted that flooding is certain to find the shortest and the quickest route(s) between any two systems, since it simply tries all routes in parallel! This can be an advantage if the quickest route has to be guaranteed, and is exploited in the exploratory phase of the so-called *source routing* described in Section 7.3.7 below.

7.3.2 Static Routing

In *static routing* (or *directory routing*), each system makes use of a *routing table* with an entry for each other system in the network. In system i, the entry for system j specifies one or more nodes adjacent to i, to which i will send traffic whose ultimate destination is j.

If more than one node is specified, there is some fixed rule for choosing between them. This may be based on some classification of the PDU to be sent, such as its length (since some routes may be able to carry longer PDUs than others), security requirements, urgency or the like – the kind of properties usually referred to as the *Quality of Service* (QOS) of the network. If there is no such basis for making the choice, or if several routes offer the same quality of service, then the rule may simply be to have a pre-determined probability for choosing each particular one. The probabilities can be chosen, for example, to minimise the average time for transmission between arbitrary pairs of nodes in the network. This time is a function of the load applied to each communication link between adjacent systems (which of course is related to the probability of choosing a particular link) and to the capacity of these links.

A common approximation is to evaluate this time using a simple queueing network model, assuming M/M/1 queues for transmission on each link. For a network with m links and n systems, this leads to the formula:

$$\overline{T} = (1/\gamma) \sum_{k=1}^{m} \frac{\lambda_k}{\mu C_k - \lambda_k}$$

where

$$\lambda = \sum_{k=1}^{m} \lambda_k$$

$$\gamma = \sum_{i=1}^{n} \sum_{j=1}^{n} \gamma_{ij}$$

and where λ_k is the mean rate (PDUs per unit time) at which PDUs are generated for transmission along link k, γ_{ij} is the mean number of PDUs per unit time to be sent from system i to system j, C_k is the capacity of link k in bits/unit time, and $1/\mu$ is the mean PDU size in bits. A Poisson process for the generation of PDUs and an exponential distribution of PDU sizes is assumed here.

Evidently the capacities of the links, C_k, are pre-determined. If the traffic pattern, γ_{ij}, is reasonably constant, then $\overline{T}$ can be minimised once and for all by adjustment of λ_k, the rate at which traffic is offered to the individual links. The ratio of the values of λ_k for the various links starting in a given system can then be used to determine the probability with which these links should be chosen. Note that all these calculations are performed when the network is set up, and are not dynamically adjusted to suit the actual traffic while the network is running; the routing algorithm is completely static. The method is obviously best suited to networks whose topology and traffic do not change much with time. Its particular advantage is that, once the table has been worked out, the algorithm used in each system is extremely simple.

7.3.3 Tree Routing

If the network has a tree-like topology, there is only one route from any node to any other node. Thus it is unnecessary to consider alternative routes, and adaptive routing is not an issue. In each node, the edge to be used in order to follow a path to the final destination is fixed by the topology. If the addressing structure used in the network is flat or hierarchical, then static tables can be used, as described in the

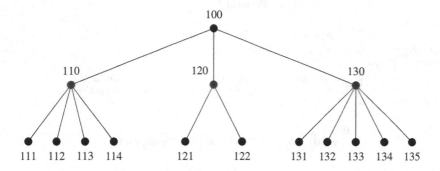

Fig. 7.16 Partitioned Addressing in a Tree Network.

previous section. However, if the addressing structure is *partitioned* to reflect the tree structure, then routing can be performed without the use of tables at all. For a tree with depth N, the address for a node will consist of an N-tuple, where the first element specifies which sub-tree at the root level the node belongs to, the second element specifies which sub-tree of this sub-tree the node belongs to, and so on. A simple example is seen in Figure 7.16.

In a network of this type, the route to be chosen at a node at depth i is determined by comparison of the *i-prefix* (the first i elements) of the address of that node with the i-prefix of the destination address. If these prefixes are different, the PDU is sent up the tree (to level $i - 1$). If they are the same, the PDU is either kept (if the whole address already matches) or sent down the tree to the node whose $(i + 1)$-prefix matches. If there is no such node, the address is in error, and the PDU can be discarded.

Although we have described this algorithm in terms of a tree of simple nodes, it can also be applied with small modifications even when the nodes of the tree are themselves networks – or, more correctly sub-networks, as illustrated in Figure 7.4. A network made up of sub-networks joined together in a tree-like structure is often known as a *hierarchical* network.

7.3.4 Centralised Adaptive Routing

In a network with a general topology, in which there are alternative routes between pairs of nodes, static routing techniques do not give optimal results if the traffic pattern begins to differ significantly from the pattern assumed when the routing tables were set up. Some links may become more or less unused, while others become overloaded. This will lead to long delays for transmission to certain destinations, or even to complete lack of the necessary buffer resources for containing the PDUs which are to be sent off. These phenomena are generally known as *congestion*, a subject which we shall look at in more detail later in this chapter.

Protocol 28

$$RCC \overset{\text{def}}{=} (C[default : (\mathbb{N}_0^*)^*] \parallel Timer[0]) \setminus \{up[0]\}$$

$$C[gtab : (\mathbb{N}_0^*)^*] \overset{\text{def}}{=} (up[0]!\text{SET} \rightarrow C1[gtab,[\,]])$$

$$C1[gtab : (\mathbb{N}_0^*)^*, new : Info^*]$$
$$\overset{\text{def}}{=} (link[k \in ns(0)]?(src : \mathbb{N}_0, inf : Info) \rightarrow C1[gtab, new\,\hat{}\,inf]$$
$$[\![up[0]?t : \{\text{TIMEOUT}\} \rightarrow C2[evaluate(gtab, new), \text{len } gtab - 1]\,)$$

$$C2[gtab : (\mathbb{N}_0^*)^*, n : \mathbb{N}_0]$$
$$\overset{\text{def}}{=} (\textbf{if } n = 0$$
$$\textbf{then } C[gtab]$$
$$\textbf{else } link[gtab(0)(n)]!(n, gtab(n)) \rightarrow C2[gtab, n - 1]\,)$$

$$P[i : \mathbb{N}_0, rtab : \mathbb{N}_0^*] \overset{\text{def}}{=} (P1[i : \mathbb{N}_0, rdef : \mathbb{N}_0^*] \parallel Timer[i]) \setminus \{up[i]\}$$

$$P1[i : \mathbb{N}_0, rtab : \mathbb{N}_0^*] \overset{\text{def}}{=} (up[i]!\text{SET} \rightarrow P2[i, rtab]\,)$$

$$P2[i : \mathbb{N}_0, rtab : \mathbb{N}_0^*] \overset{\text{def}}{=} (link[k \in ns(i)]?(dst : \mathbb{N}_0, rtab' : \mathbb{N}_0^*) \rightarrow$$
$$(\textbf{if } dst = i$$
$$\textbf{then } P2[i, rtab']$$
$$\textbf{else } link[rtab(dst)]!(dst, rtab') \rightarrow P2[i, rtab]\,)$$
$$[\![link[k \in ns(i)]?(src : \mathbb{N}_0, inf : Info) \rightarrow$$
$$link[rtab(0)]!(src, inf) \rightarrow P2[i, rtab]$$
$$[\![up[i]?t : \{\text{TIMEOUT}\} \rightarrow link[rtab(0)]!(i, getinfo()) \rightarrow P1[i, rtab]\,)$$

$$Timer[i : \mathbb{N}_0] \overset{\text{def}}{=} (up[i]?s : \{\text{SET}\} \rightarrow (up[i]?r : \{\text{RESET}\} \rightarrow Timer[i]$$
$$[\![up[i]!\text{TIMEOUT} \rightarrow Timer[i])\,)$$

Fig. 7.17 Distribution of routing tables from a control center

As long as the capacity of the network is not actually exceeded by the amount of traffic generated, delays can usually be reduced (or avoided) by using a better routing algorithm, which adapts to changing traffic patterns, and chooses routes which avoid heavily loaded parts of the net as much as possible. If the adaptation is sufficiently dynamic, both short term bursts of traffic and longer term changes in the traffic pattern can be taken care of.

One of the first forms of adaptive routing to be developed was *centralised* adaptive routing. Here, one system takes on the rôle of *Routing Control Centre* (RCC). From time to time, each other system sends the RCC information about observed delays, the lengths of its internal queues for transmission along particular links, broken links and so on. The RCC uses this information to calculate new routing tables, which are sent out to the individual systems. These routing tables contain the same type of information as with static routing – but of course they are not static.

The protocol for distributing the routing tables is given as **Protocol 28** in Figure 7.17. In the figure, the control center is described by the process *RCC* and the i'th system $(i > 0)$ by $P[i, rtab]$, where $rtab$ is the local routing table. $gtab$ is the global set of routing tables in the RCC. Its j'th element, $gtab(j)$, is a routing table for the j'th system (where system 0 is the RCC itself), and $evaluate(gtab, new)$ evaluates a new set of routing tables from the previous set together with the information *new* received from the other systems. In the i'th system, new settings from the RCC are received from time to time, and relevant local information for transmission to the RCC is extracted by the function $getinfo()$ every time the local timer ($Timer[i]$) runs out. As in **Protocol 27**, $ns(i)$ is the set of indices for the channels leading to the neighbours of system i.

The particular advantage of this method is that the RCC accumulates global knowledge and therefore in principle makes a globally optimal decision. Unfortunately, there are a number of disadvantages:

- It takes time for the information about the individual systems to reach the RCC, time to calculate the new routing tables (a distinctly non-trivial optimisation calculation), and time to distribute the new routing tables again. Thus the modified route has been evaluated on the basis of information accumulated a 'long' time ago. This will often make the method unsuitable for adaptation to rapid changes in traffic.
- When the RCC distributes new routing tables, those systems nearest the RCC get their new tables first, perhaps quite a while before the systems furthest from the RCC. This may lead to temporary inconsistencies in the routing strategies used by different systems, and thus to confusion or congestion. This is particularly a problem when drastic changes have occurred – for example if the new routing tables have been calculated in response to a change in network topology resulting from a total failure of a system or link.
- The algorithm does not work if the RCC fails. So either the RCC must be made hardware redundant, or there must be some way of selecting a back-up RCC from among the other systems, or one must accept that the network essentially uses static routing during periods when the RCC is unable to function. Similar considerations apply if one part of the network can become cut off from the RCC, for example due to link or system failures.

In practice, however, centralised adaptive routing, like static routing, is very common, presumably because the effort of evaluating routes can be concentrated in a single system, which can be specially developed for the purpose.

7.3.5 Isolated Adaptive Routing

In *isolated* algorithms, each system determines what to do on the basis of information which it itself possesses, without deliberate exchange of relevant information with other systems.

A typical simple example is the so-called *hot potato* algorithm, suggested by Baran [4]. When a PDU arrives at (or is generated in) a given system, it is sent out along the link which has the shortest queue. Sometimes this is combined with a static routing table, in the way that the choice of outgoing link is first made on the basis of the table. Then, if the queue for that link is too long (say, larger than some threshold), the hot potato rule is used to choose another link instead. This type of combination diverts some traffic from the routes given in the table when those routes are heavily loaded.

Another example, also due to Baran, is *backward learning*. This algorithm derives information from PDUs *arriving from* a particular system, in order to deduce what to do with traffic *going to* that system. Generally speaking, when this method is used, the PDUs must contain information which makes it possible to estimate how good or bad their route was. For example, the original sender can *timestamp* each PDU, or include a *hop counter* which is counted up every time a PDU is passed between adjacent systems. When a PDU from, say, system A arrives at system B via link k (whether or not B is its final destination), then B can see how long the PDU has been on its way, or how many systems it has been through on the way. It can then use this information as a measure of how good link k is as a potential route *towards A*. If k appears to be better than B's current choice for traffic toward A, then k is chosen for use until further notice.

For this method to work well, each system must continually estimate the goodness of all its outgoing links, so that it can see whether a particular one is better than its current choice. Rather oddly, in the original method, the current choice was not continually monitored once it had been chosen – its properties were assumed to remain constant. This works fine if the problem is just that we do not know what the best route is when we start the network: we start from some arbitrary assignment of routes, and improve them using backward learning. However, systems then only react to *improvements* and not to changes for the worse. So, if there is a risk that some routes may get *worse*, then from time to time we must reinitialise the routing tables and start backward learning again. On the whole, it is probably better to do the job properly, even if this means more administration in each system.

An interesting type of backward learning is used in the so-called *transparent bridging* routing favoured in ISO for routing between segments of a complex local area network [198]. This is based on the idea that it is possible to move from one segment to another at particular nodes which act as *gateways* or *bridges*. Technically, this means that they are in the MAC (Medium Access) sub-layer of the Data Link layer of the OSI architecture, but from an abstract point of view they essentially perform routing between sub-networks. As in backward learning, the bridges accumulate information about which route to use for traffic *to* a system, say A, by noting which sub-network traffic *from A* arrives on. However, their operation is somewhat more refined than simple backward learning, as they assume that the only permitted routes lie on a spanning tree which spans the network. This means that routes which do not follow the branches of the spanning tree can be excluded and do not need to be noted down. The spanning tree is determined when the network is started, and again whenever any important topological change (such as failure of a bridge) occurs. Essentially, this gives the signal for the start of a new learning process.

7.3.6 Distributed Adaptive Routing

In this class of algorithm, the systems explicitly exchange information which enables them to build up a global picture of the state of the network, and thus to select an optimal route to any other system. Once again, there are several possibilities for what we might want to use as a measure of a good route: how long time a PDU will take to reach the destination via that route, how many systems the PDU will have to be handled by on the way, and so on.

Let us assume that we use time as our measure. At regular intervals, each system will send its own estimates of the times required for PDUs to get from that system to other systems in the network. There are two basic strategies for how to do this:

1. **Distance vector routing**, in which system i sends its *neighbours* a set of estimates (a "distance vector") of how long it will take to get to each of the systems $1, 2, \ldots, N$ in the network.
2. **Link state routing**, in which system i sends to each of the systems $1, 2, \ldots, N$ in the network a set of estimates of how long it will take to get to each of i's neighbours.

Distance Vector Routing

In distance vector routing, also known as Bellman-Ford routing after its original developers, each system sends its *neighbours* a set of estimates of how long it will take to get to each of the systems in the network and will correspondingly receive estimates from each of its neighbours. In addition, it will itself try directly to measure how long it takes to reach each of these neighbours; this can be done by sending 'probes' – PDUs which are at once returned by the receiver. Given the neighbours' estimates of how long it takes to reach any system from them, and its own estimates of how long it takes to reach each of the neighbours, the system finds, for each possible destination in the network, the combination which gives the quickest route. This is illustrated in Figure 7.18, which shows an example of routing information for system F in the network of Figure 7.13.

Here, for example, we see that system F has estimated that the times required to send a PDU to B, D, H and K are respectively 8, 6, 10 and 4 time units. From the information received from these neighbours, F can see for example that system I can be reached in 41 time units from B, 26 from D, 33 from H and 27 from K. Thus the shortest time is the minimum of (41+8), (26+6), (33+10) and (27+4), i.e. 31 time units, obtained by going via K. Traffic for I is therefore routed via K until further notice. Although it is not necessarily the case that the algorithm produces a globally optimum route in the first step after a change in the network, it is possible to prove that this algorithm converges to give the best routes in any finite network after a finite number of steps. The protocol can be extended in a simple way to make it possible to deal with topology changes; for example, a time 'infinity' (represented by a value larger than any which can occur in practice) can be sent to indicate that

	Estimates from: B D H K				Estimated Route optimum via	
A	16	8	24	28	14	D
B	0	14	18	12	8	B
C	19	5	21	15	11	D
D	14	0	16	10	6	D
E	29	15	20	15	19	K
F	10	5	10	5	0	–
G	15	29	24	25	23	B
H	18	16	0	6	10	H
I	41	26	33	27	31	K
J	21	7	17	11	13	D
K	12	10	6	0	4	K
L	26	19	8	9	13	K

Fig. 7.18 Exchange of Information in Distance Vector Routing.

Local estimates of time to reach:

B	D	H	K
8	6	10	4

a route is completely unavailable. This extension is used in the Internet RIP routing protocol [243], amongst others.

Like backward learning, distance vector routing has the problem that it tends to react much more slowly to degradation in the network than it does to improvements. In unfavourable circumstances, it may even demonstrate a type of unstable behaviour known as "counting to infinity" after a topology change occurs. Suppose, for example, the link AC in the network of Figure 7.19(a) breaks at time t_0, giving the network of Figure 7.19(b). If node A detects this failure, it will at time t_1 deduce that the best route to C now costs 3 time units and goes via B, whereas node B will still believe that the best route to C goes via A and costs 2 units. They then exchange this new information, which causes each of them to think that the best route now costs one more unit. They then exchange this new information, which causes each of them to think that the best route now costs yet one more unit. And so on. The basic problem is that A and B cannot see that each of them thinks the best route goes via the other.

Link State Routing

Problems of this type do not appear in *link state routing*, which has largely replaced distance vector routing in most networks, and is the currently preferred routing algorithm in the Internet. The basic algorithm is, as mentioned previously, for each node to measure the delay to each of its neighbours, and to distribute this information to all other systems in the network. Figure 7.20 shows an example of this routing information in the network of Figure 7.13. Once a node has received a PDU containing link state information from each of the other nodes, it can construct a picture of the state of the entire network, with information about the delay involved in passing each edge (link) in the network. It can then use any of a number of *short-*

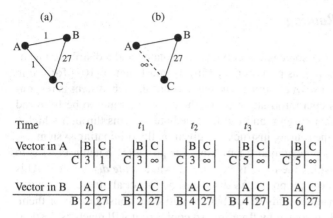

(a)   (b)

Time t_0 t_1 t_2 t_3 t_4

Vector in A

	B	C
C	3	1

	B	C
C	3	∞

	B	C
C	3	∞

	B	C
C	5	∞

	B	C
C	5	∞

Vector in B

	A	C
B	2	27

	A	C
B	2	27

	A	C
B	4	27

	A	C
B	4	27

	A	C
B	6	27

Fig. 7.19 Counting-to-infinity in Distance Vector Routing

Source Link State Information

Source					
A	B 16	C 3			
B	A 16	F 8	G 15		
C	A 3	D 5	E 10		
D	C 5	F 6	J 7		
E	C 10	I 10	K 15		
F	B 8	D 6	H 10	K 4	
G	B 15	L 16			
H	F 10	K 6	L 8		
I	E 10	J 16			
J	D 7	I 16	K 11		
K	E 15	F 4	H 6	J 11	L 9
L	G 16	H 8	K 9		

Fig. 7.20 Exchange of Information in Link State Routing

est path algorithms to find the route giving the least delay for any given destination. A popular choice is Dijkstra's shortest path algorithm [32], which is described in innumerable works on graph algorithms. The actual distribution of the link state information from each source to all other nodes is typically done by an optimised form of flooding, where link state PDUs which have already been seen once are not passed on to other nodes. Link state routing is the basis of the Internet *Open Shortest Path First (OSPF)* routing protocol [231]. This is currently the commonest *interior gateway routing protocol*, which is the class of protocol used for routing within a so-called *Autonomous System (AS)*, i.e. a portion of the Internet administered by a single organisation. Routing *between* ASs is generally done by the *Border Gateway Protocol (BGP)*, which is a distance vector protocol [251].

7.3.7 Exploratory Routing

A final variation, which lies somewhere between an isolated and a distributed technique, is *exploratory routing*, as proposed by Pitt, Sy and Donnan [107] for use in connection with so-called *source routing*. In source routing, each system is responsible for maintaining its own information about the complete route to be followed in order to reach any other system, and the intermediate systems through which a PDU passes just follow the routing instructions given by the originating system.

Exploratory routing is a technique for making this possible: When a PDU is to be sent to a system for which the route is not yet known, a *route discovery* PDU is sent out first for exploratory purposes. As discussed by Pitt et al., there are several possible strategies for handling this PDU, but we will only consider one of them. Here, the discovery-PDU is routed by flooding, so copies of it will reach its destination by (in principle) all possible routes, or at any rate all the shortest ones. When a copy of the outgoing discovery-PDU is passed from one system to another, the addresses of the systems which it passes are recorded in the PDU. Thus when the final destination receives a copy of a discovery-PDU, it can see which route this copy has followed. For example, returning again to Figure 7.13, destination G would receive copies of the discovery-PDU with recorded routes:

FBG, FHLG, FKLG, FKHLG, FHKLG

for an exploratory phase started from node F, using flooding with a distance limit of 4 hops, as shown in Figure 7.15. The destination then returns each copy to the sender. A discovery-PDU on its way back to the original sender is routed back along the route which it followed on the outgoing trip, by making use of the route recorded in the PDU.

This procedure results in the originator receiving a number of copies of the discovery-PDU back from the destination, each of them containing infomation about the route followed. By some appropriate criterion – time taken, number of intermediate systems, maximum permitted PDU size, or whatever – the originator then chooses the 'best' route, and this is used for the subsequent data-PDUs to be sent to this destination. When exploratory routing is used to support source routing, the data-PDU carries a description of the entire route as well as the address of the destination, and it is this description, rather than the destination address, which is used to guide the PDU through the network.

The protocol is given in Figure 7.21. In the figure, the discovery-PDUs are headed by the keyword DISCOVER, the replies by ROUTE and the data-PDUs by DATA. In the version of the protocol shown in the figure, the original sender (process *Syst*) sends out a discovery-PDU when it needs to send data to a destination for which it does not currently know the route. The discovery-PDU is distributed by flooding, and the replies are collected up (process *Pend*) until a timer runs out. Replies arriving after the timer runs out are ignored. The function *best*(*replies*) is used to evaluate the best of the replies according to the desired criterion, and the selected route is inserted in the sender's routing table, denoted *routes*, by the function *adjust*.

Protocol 29

$Node[i : \mathbb{N}_0, routes : (\mathbb{N}_0^*)^*]$
$\quad \overset{\text{def}}{=} (Syst[i, routes] \parallel Timer) \setminus \{up\}$
$Syst[i : \mathbb{N}_0, routes : (\mathbb{N}_0^*)^*]$
$\quad \overset{\text{def}}{=} (SAPA?(dst : \mathbb{N}_0, x : \mathcal{M}) \rightarrow$
$\qquad (\textbf{if } routes(dst) = []$
$\qquad \textbf{then } \coprod_{j \in ns(i)} link[j]!(\text{DISCOVER}, i, dst, hops(i, dst), [j]) \rightarrow$
$\qquad\qquad\qquad\qquad\qquad\qquad up!\text{SET} \rightarrow Pend[i, routes, dst, x, []]$
$\qquad \textbf{else } Send[i, routes, dst, x])$
$\quad [\![link[k \in ns(i)]?(d : \{\text{DISCOVER}\}, src : \mathbb{N}_0, dst : \mathbb{N}_0, h : \mathbb{N}_0, sl : \mathbb{N}_0^*) \rightarrow$
$\qquad (\textbf{if } dst = i$
$\qquad \textbf{then } link[k]!(\text{ROUTE}, src, dst, 1, [k]\hat{\ }sl) \rightarrow Syst[i, routes]$
$\qquad \textbf{elseif } (src = i) \vee (h = 0)$
$\qquad \textbf{then } Syst[i, routes]$
$\qquad \textbf{else } \coprod_{j \in ns(i) - \{k\}} link[j]!(\text{DISCOVER}, src, dst, h - 1, [j]\hat{\ }sl) \rightarrow Syst[i, routes])$
$\quad [\![link[k \in ns(i)]?(r : \{\text{ROUTE}\}, src : \mathbb{N}_0, dst : \mathbb{N}_0, h : \mathbb{N}_0, sl : \mathbb{N}_0^*) \rightarrow$
$\qquad (\textbf{if } src = i$
$\qquad \textbf{then } Syst[i, routes]$
$\qquad \textbf{else } link[sl(h + 1)]!(\text{ROUTE}, src, dst, h + 1, sl) \rightarrow Syst[i, routes])$
$\quad [\![link[k \in ns(i)]?(r : \{\text{DATA}\}, src : \mathbb{N}_0, dst : \mathbb{N}_0, sl : \mathbb{N}_0^*, x : \mathcal{M}) \rightarrow$
$\qquad (\textbf{if } dst = i$
$\qquad \textbf{then } SAPA!(src, x) \rightarrow Syst[i, routes]$
$\qquad \textbf{else } Send[r, src, dst, sl, x]))$

$Pend[i : \mathbb{N}_0, routes : (\mathbb{N}_0^*)^*, dst : \mathbb{N}_0, x : \mathcal{M}, replies : (\mathbb{N}_0^*)^*]$
$\quad \overset{\text{def}}{=} (link[k \in ns(i)]?(d : \{\text{DISCOVER}\}, src : \mathbb{N}_0, dst : \mathbb{N}_0, h : \mathbb{N}_0, sl : \mathbb{N}_0^*) \rightarrow$
$\qquad (\textbf{if } dst = i$
$\qquad \textbf{then } link[k]!(\text{ROUTE}, src, dst, 1, [k]\hat{\ }sl) \rightarrow Pend[i, routes, dst, x, replies]$
$\qquad \textbf{elseif } (src = i) \vee (h = 0)$
$\qquad \textbf{then } Pend[i, routes, dst, x, replies]$
$\qquad \textbf{else } \coprod_{j \in ns(i) - \{k\}} link[j]!(\text{DISCOVER}, src, dst, h - 1, [j]\hat{\ }sl) \rightarrow$
$\qquad\qquad\qquad\qquad\qquad\qquad\qquad Pend[i, routes, dst, x, replies])$
$\quad [\![link[k \in ns(i)]?(r : \{\text{ROUTE}\}, src : \mathbb{N}_0, dst : \mathbb{N}_0, h : \mathbb{N}_0, sl : \mathbb{N}_0^*) \rightarrow$
$\qquad (\textbf{if } src = i$
$\qquad \textbf{then } Pend[i, routes, dst, x, replies\hat{\ }(h, sl)]$
$\qquad \textbf{else } link[sl(h + 1)]!(\text{ROUTE}, src, dst, h + 1, sl) \rightarrow$
$\qquad\qquad\qquad\qquad\qquad\qquad Pend[i, routes, dst, x, replies])$
$\quad [\![link[k \in ns(i)]?(r : \{\text{DATA}\}, src : \mathbb{N}_0, dst : \mathbb{N}_0, sl : \mathbb{N}_0^*, x : \mathcal{M}) \rightarrow$
$\qquad (\textbf{if } dst = i$
$\qquad \textbf{then } SAPA!(src, x) \rightarrow \qquad\qquad\qquad Pend[i, routes, dst, x, replies]$
$\qquad \textbf{else } Send[src, dst, sl, x]))$
$\quad [\![up?\{\text{TIMEOUT}\} \rightarrow Send[i, adjust(routes, best(replies)), dst, x])$

$Send[i : \mathbb{N}_0, routes : (\mathbb{N}_0^*)^*, dst : \mathbb{N}_0, x : \mathcal{M}]$
$\quad \overset{\text{def}}{=} (link[\text{hd } routes(dst)]!(\text{DATA}, i, dst, \text{tl } routes(dst), x) \rightarrow Syst[i, routes])$

Fig. 7.21 Exploratory routing

As in **Protocol 28**, the routing table is modelled as a sequence of sequences, whose j'th element gives the route to destination system j.

An obvious advantage of this routing protocol is that intermediate systems can be made simpler, as they do not have to maintain routing tables. In fact it is sometimes presented as a method for table-free routing. This is, however, not strictly the case, since the burden of maintaining the tables is merely transferred to the originating systems. Another potential advantage follows from the use of flooding in the exploratory phase: all the best routes are discovered, and each originating system can then use any appropriate criteria for choosing among them. The disadvantage is that flooding is expensive, and has to be performed every time that an originator wants to send to a new destination.

In source routing as described by Pitt et al., the discovered route is used until further notice, or until the originator finds out that PDUs sent via this route are not getting through to the destination. In fact, in Pitt et al.'s proposal this method, like the transparent bridging method discussed previously, is intended for use for routing between sub-networks, such as interconnected segments of a complex local area network (LAN); in particular, the method is used for routing in networks made up from multiple token rings [199]. Here the routing problem is one of finding which gateway or bridge between two sub-networks to pass through. Failure of such a gateway or bridge can be expected to be detected fairly quickly. If this happens, a new exploratory phase is set going to find a new route.

Another area in which exploratory routing is popular is in so-called *Mobile Ad Hoc Networks (MANETs)*. In a MANET, a collection of mobile nodes communicate via a temporary (and often dynamically changing) wireless network without any centralised administration. Each wireless transmitter has a finite range, and as the transmitting nodes move round in the mobile network, nodes which previously have been able to communicate with one another become unable to do so, so a new route has to be found. This is illustrated in Figure 7.22. The dashed circles round some of the nodes in the figure indicate the ranges of the nodes' transmitters.

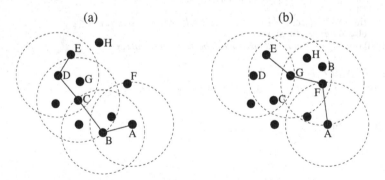

Fig. 7.22 Routing in a MANET.
(a) Initially, a route from A to E via B, C, and D is in use.
(b) After B, G and H move, a new route from A to E is needed, as B is no longer within range of A. The new route goes via F and G.

In this situation, exploratory routing offers obvious advantages over more static, table-based algorithms. Typical examples are the *Dynamic Source Routing (DSR)* [71] and *Ad Hoc On-Demand Distance Vector (AODV)* [249] routing protocols. Both of these use optimised forms of flooding for route discovery, in order to reduce overhead. For example, in DSR an intermediate node will only pass on a discovery-PDU for a given source and destination if it has not recently handled a discovery-PDU for the same source and destination, while in AODV an intermediate node which already knows a route to the final destination will not pass on the discovery-PDU, but just return the route which it knows. Once a route has been discovered, DSR attempts to check whether it continues to be valid by checking whether each message is passed on by the next system along the route (this is easy in a wireless network, as the transmission can be overheard); if this does not occur, a new exploratory phase is set going. AODV uses a more active policy in which each node sends out *Hullo* messages at suitable intervals to each destination which it knows about; a new exploratory phase is set going if no reply is received.

7.4 Congestion

A problem closely connected with routing is the avoidance of congestion in a network. In fact, as mentioned above, congestion can be notably reduced by good routing, since traffic can often be routed to avoid heavily loaded parts of the network. Unfortunately, however, routing is not a universal cure for congestion, which may also arise because more traffic is generated (in certain parts of the network in certain periods) than the network can bear.

Congestion control, like routing, requires global decisions if it is to be effective – otherwise the congested area just moves off to another part of the network. But, as with routing, it may be possible to produce a good approximation to a global solution without any system using more than its own local knowledge.

The general symptoms of congestion are poor throughput, extended delivery times and possibly complete failure to deliver PDUs. Typical behaviour with increasing network load is illustrated in Figure 7.23. Up to the *knee*, throughput approximately follows the ideal curve (dashed), asymptotically approaching the limit of the network capacity, while the delay remains more or less constant. Over a range of loads between the knee and the cliff, the throughput stagnates and delays increase markedly. Finally, if load increases beyond the *cliff*, a so-called *congestion collapse* may occur, with a dramatic drop in throughput and increase in delays.

The symptoms of congestion arise when the total demands made on network resources, such as buffers, link capacities and processor capacities, exceed the quantities of these resources actually available. Two radically different approaches to dealing with congestion are therefore:

- **Resource creation:** create more of the resources which are in short supply.
- **Demand reduction:** reduce the demand to match the currently available level of resources.

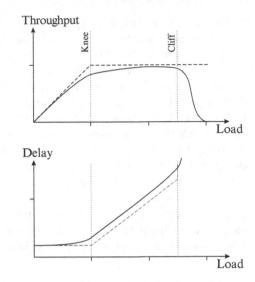

Fig. 7.23 Schematic network behaviour with increasing load.

Most interest has been focussed on demand reduction techniques. These fall into two groups:

- **Service denial**, where new connections cannot be established unless there are resources for them. This is the preferred technique in many telecommunications systems, such as the ordinary telephone system.
- **Service degradation**, where some or all systems are required to reduce the traffic load which they generate, or to re-schedule it so that the overall demands never exceed the available resource capacity in the network.

Service denial schemes are commonly associated with pre-allocation of resources in the source, destination and intermediate systems (if any) when a connection is set up. For example, a suitable amount of bandwidth needs to be reserved on all links on the chosen route, and suitable numbers of buffers need to be allocated to store the passing PDUs. In particular, it is necessary to allocate, for the lifetime of the connection, W_s buffers in the sending system and W_r buffers in the receiving system, where W_s and W_r are the send and receive window sizes agreed when the connection is set up. Since the resources need to remain allocated until the connection is broken, regardless of whether they are utilised, this approach can be very expensive in terms of buffer space. From the very nature of things, it is unsuitable for use in connectionless-mode operation.

Service degradation schemes are characterised by the techniques which they use for reducing traffic as congestion approaches. It is important to realise that this is a problem in control engineering, which requires an appropriate response (traffic reduction) to an indication of congestion. Jain [69] has pointed out that there are two slightly different ways of going about this, depending on whether the aim is to maintain the load at a level round the "knee" or just below the "cliff" of the throughput/load curve, as illustrated in Figure 7.23. These are sometimes denoted *congestion avoidance* and *congestion control* respectively. We shall here consider four commonly used techniques for dealing with congestion, which use increasingly direct forms of feedback from the network to achieve their aim:

1. Discarding of PDUs.
2. Limiting the number of PDUs in transit at any time.
3. Timeout-based congestion control.
4. Explicit feedback.

In certain systems, attempts are made to use ordinary *flow control* as a form of congestion control. A well-known example is the ARPANET. However, this is unsatisfactory, as flow control aims to prevent a receiver being overrun by traffic generated by a specific sender, and not to limit the total amount of traffic between all possible sender-receiver pairs. In a congested network, it is highly possible that the receiver never actually receives any data at all. We shall therefore not consider this method in more detail here.

7.4.1 Discarding

A simple but effective form of congestion control based on an *isolated* algorithm is simply to *discard* any PDUs for which no buffers are available. This causes the reliability of the service to drop, in the sense that PDUs are lost and will at some stage probably have to be retransmitted. However, it may enable other aspects of the overall quality of service – such as throughput – to be maintained, since congestion no longer has a disturbing effect.

Arbitrary discarding of PDUs may be counter-productive: discarding an acknowledgment, for example, may mean that we lose the opportunity to release one or more buffers containing data-PDUs which we have transmitted. So in practice some buffers are always kept available so that incoming PDUs can be inspected. Irland [67] investigated a number of policies for how to allocate the remaining buffers, which can be used for outgoing traffic. Supposing that t_i buffers are made available for the queue of PDUs waiting for link i, then PDUs to be transmitted by that link will be discarded when the length of the queue exceeds the threshold t_i. Irland used a Markov model to analyse how t_i should be related to the total number of buffers, n, available for all links. The optimum is a complex function of the traffic. However, Irland discovered that a close approximation to the optimum could often be achieved by using the same value of t_i, say $\hat{t}$, for all links, independent of the traffic pattern. This is often called a *restricted buffer sharing* policy, as the pool of buffers is shared evenly among the links. Intuitively, it gives a good result because it ensures that the busiest links do not hog all the buffers, as they would tend to do in an *unrestricted* (demand controlled) buffer sharing policy. Irland found that the best value for $\hat{t}$ was given by a simple rule, which he called the *Square Root rule*: If there are g outgoing links from the system, then a good value of $\hat{t}$ is approximately $n/\sqrt{g}$.

7.4.2 Limiting the Number of PDUs

Davies [29] proposed a more distributed method for congestion control than simple discarding. His method is explicitly to limit the number of PDUs which can be in transit at any one time. This is known as *isarithmic* control[4]. The mechanism is to use a set of *tokens* which circulate within the network. When a system wishes to generate a PDU, it must first capture a token. When the PDU arrives at its ultimate destination, the receiving system regenerates the token. This ensures that the global strategy of limiting the number of PDUs is realised. However, there may still be local congestion, which this typically distributed form for control can do little about.

This method also presents the interesting problem of how to ensure a distribution of tokens which offers systems a *fair* service. In a net with arbitrary topology there is no simple distributed algorithm for ensuring this, but a possible way out is to use a centralised token distributor, which sends tokens towards each system in turn. Alternatively, a 'logical ring' can be defined covering all the nodes in the network, such that tokens are passed round from one system to another in some pre-determined order.

An even more delicate problem is what to do if tokens can get lost. Firstly, we need a method for counting the number of existing tokens (strictly, free tokens + PDUs in transit), and secondly we need a mechanism for generating new tokens to replace the lost ones. Counting the tokens is not a trivial task if the network is actually working, as tokens are continually being passed round from one system to another. One possibility is simply to 'freeze' the network from time to time while the audit takes place, but this is not always acceptable. This is obviously a situation where Chandy and Lamport's snapshot algorithm [22] for dynamically determining the global state of a distributed system (see Section 5.6) would be appropriate. The auditing algorithm must be initiated by some supervisory system from time to time, and the same supervisory system would typically also be responsible for generating replacement tokens when needed.

7.4.3 Timeout-based control

Timeout-based techniques are based on the assumption that timeouts indicate PDU loss or excessive delays and are therefore good indicators of congestion. If a sender experiences a timeout, the send window size W_s should be reduced; after a period with no timeouts, the window can gradually be opened again. An analysis by Chiu and Jain [25] demonstrates that the choice of additive or multiplicative rules for the increase and decrease algorithms has a marked effect on the stability and fairness of the service provided by the network. To ensure a stable and fair result, the window size should be decreased by a multiplicative factor and increased by an additive term up to some suitable limit:

---

[4] From the Greek: $\iota\sigma\sigma\varsigma$: equal, $\alpha\rho\iota\theta\mu\sigma\varsigma$: number.

On congestion: $W_s^{(i)} = W_s^{(i-1)} \cdot d$

No congestion: $W_s^{(i)} = \max\left(W_s^{(i-1)} + u, W_{max}\right)$

where $W_s^{(k)}$ is the k'th estimate of the send window size, and $0 < d < 1$. This approach is used in most modern implementations of TCP, the ISO Class 4 Transport Protocol (ISO TP4) and other similar connection-mode Transport Layer protocols.

The TCP scheme is in fact slightly more complicated, since it also incorporates a mechanism to ensure that a stable state is achieved without oscillating behaviour due to a sudden influx of PDUs when a connection is first opened or is recovering from congestion. This mechanism, due to Van Jacobsen [68], is known as *slow-start*, and makes use of a *congestion window*, of size say W_c, for each transmission direction in each connection. When the connection is opened, $W_c = 1$. After each acknowledgment from the receiver, the size of the sender's congestion window is increased by 1. The size of the sender's send window is:

$$W_s = \min\left(W_c, W_r'\right)$$

where W_r' is the size of the receiver's receive window, as announced by the receiver. The effect of slow-start is to ensure that the system gradually approaches a state where it is *self-clocking*, in the sense that the sender sends a PDU only when it receives an acknowledgment for some previous PDU. This means that the inter-PDU interval exactly matches the time required to send a PDU on the slowest link in the path between sender and receiver. Sending at a faster rate would clearly lead to congestion on the link concerned. This is illustrated in Figure 7.24, which shows the behaviour of a new connection with and without slow-start. With slow-start, the throughput asymptotically approaches the available bandwidth after a delay (the 'slow start'). Without slow-start, there are many retransmissions, and the effective throughput is reduced to about a third of the available bandwidth.

To combine this mechanism with the congestion avoidance algorithm, slow-start is used after a timeout until the send window has reached half its value before the timeout. Essentially, this gives a congestion avoidance algorithm where $d = 0.5$, with a 'pre-phase' consisting of the slow-start. Once the send window has reached half its original size, subsequent acknowledgments trigger the ordinary congestion avoidance scheme, which in TCP causes W_c to be increased by $1/W_c$, and where W_s is related to W_c and W_r' as above. The choice of $1/W_c$ as the increment means that the send window in fact increases by at most one for each round-trip time from sender to receiver and back, thus ensuring that the system remains self-clocked.

Systems which use timeout-based mechanisms to counteract congestion need to rely on good values of the round trip time, R, in order to choose an appropriate time-out setting. It is not a trivial task to obtain a good estimate of R, since measurements of R are subject to statistical variation. The technique used in TCP is to evaluate the i'th estimate, $R^{(i)}$, from the $(i-1)$'th estimate and the i'th sample, $M^{(i)}$, of the round trip time (i.e. the time from a PDU is transmitted until it is acknowledged) according to the formula:

Sequence number

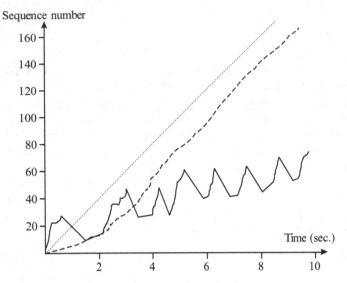

Fig. 7.24 Behaviour of a TCP connection (after [68]).
The *dotted line* corresponds to the available bandwidth through the network. The *dashed curve* shows the behaviour with slow-start, and the *full curve* the behaviour without slow-start.

$$R^{(i)} = (1 - g) \cdot R^{(i-1)} + g \cdot M^{(i)}$$

Here g is a *gain factor* $(0 < g < 1)$ which is determined from the variance in the samples, so that a large variance results in a small value of g. Since a communications network is a *linear system*, R converges to the true average exponentially with time constant $1/g$. The retransmission timer value is evaluated from the latest value of R as:

$$T_r = \min (T_{max}, \ \max (T_{min}, \beta \cdot R))$$

where T_{max}, T_{min} are upper and lower bounds for the timeout value and β is a delay variance factor in the region of 2.

Since poor estimates of the timeout setting give rise to excessive retransmissions, which in turn may cause more congestion and further delays, the retransmission timeout timer value is doubled after each unsuccessful retransmission. As in the case of the CSMA/CD protocol described by **Protocol 11**, this mechanism, known as *Binary Exponential Backoff* ensures stability in the system. After a successful retransmission, the normal way of evaluating the round trip time – and thus the timer value – is recontinued.

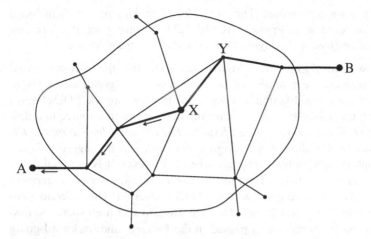

Fig. 7.25 Congestion control using choking.
System X has detected excessive utilisation of the link from X to Y. Traffic from A to B is to be
routed via this link. On receiving a PDU which is on its way from A to B, X will send a choke
packet *(arrows)* back to A to tell it to reduce the traffic from A to B.

7.4.4 Explicit feedback

The final group of techniques which we shall consider make use of explicit information from the network in order to reduce load. These techniques are essentially all
variants of the *choking* protocol proposed by Majithia et al. [85] in the 1970's. Choking is a method for congestion limiting, in which the decision to react to congestion
is taken locally, but results in control PDUs being sent round in the network carrying orders to reduce the flow. Essentially, each system monitors the utilisation of its
outgoing links. The measure of utilisation can be the number of PDUs transmitted
per unit time, the queue length or whatever is convenient. Whenever the utilisation
rises above a certain threshold, the link is noted as being in a *warning* state. If a
PDU arrives which should be sent on via a link in a warning state, a control PDU,
known as a *choke packet*, is sent back to the original sender of the PDU, informing it
of the PDU's destination, as illustrated in Figure 7.25. This sender must then reduce
the traffic for that destination by an agreed percentage for a certain period. If further
choke packets arrive after this period is over, the generated traffic is reduced even
further. If no further choke packets arrive within a further period of time, the traffic
may be increased again. As in the case of timeout-based control (which is based on
implicit information from the network), a multiplicative decrease and an additive
increase in the traffic is necessary in order to achieve a stable, fair result.

   This method is interesting because it uses a form for distributed control based on
an isolated decision algorithm. It also attacks the congestion problem at its root –
where the excess traffic is generated. The idea is such an attractive one that it is
perhaps not surprising that it has turned up in several other contexts since Majithia

et al.'s original paper was published. The basic idea of choking packets is included in the Internet Control Message Protocol (ICMP) [211] for managing IP, where they are known as *Source Quench messages*. Two more modern examples are:

Rate-based Flow Control in ATM: Modern telecommunication networks based on the ATM protocol use a number of congestion control algorithms, all essentially based on variants of Majithia's scheme. In an ATM network, PDUs known as *cells* pass through one or more *switches* on their way from a source to a destination. The basic scheme is to set an *Explicit Flow Control Indication (EFCI)* marker in data cells as they pass through a switch in which congestion is detected. In contrast to Majithia's original scheme, however, it is the final destination which sends information back to the source (in a *Resource Management (RM)* cell) if a data cell is received with the EFCI marker set. The different algorithms differ with respect to whether RM cells are also sent from source to destination, how much information is passed in the forward- and backward-going RM cells, and how the source of the data adjusts in response to the information received, in order to achieve a stable flow which is a fair share of the total flow [70].

Explicit Congestion Notification (ECN) in TCP/IP: ECN is a variant of Majithia's scheme proposed for use in networks which use the TCP/IP protocol suite [109]. This is slightly more complicated than Majithia's scheme, because two protocol layers are involved: The Transport Layer, using the TCP protocol, and the underlying Network Layer, using IP, so that TCP PDUs are embedded within IP PDUs for transmission. If ECN is not in use, and congestion is detected at an intermediate IP system (an *IP router*), the IP PDU and the TCP PDU (or PDUs) which it contains are just discarded. If ECN is in use[5], the corresponding IP PDUs are marked with an *ECN Capable Transport (ECT) marker*. If congestion is detected at an intermediate system, IP PDUs with an ECT marker are not discarded unless the congestion is very severe. Instead, they are just marked with a *Congestion Experienced (CE) marker*. The ultimate destination for the TCP PDU received in an IP PDU with a CE marker must then inform the originator of the TCP PDU that a reduction of traffic is required. It does this by marking all TCP acnowledgments with an *ECN echo (ECNE) marker*, until the originator sends a TCP PDU with its *Congestion Window Reduced (CWR) marker* set. This is illustrated in Figure 7.26.

7.4.5 Deadlock

A spectacular form of congestion in networks is *deadlock*, where two or more systems are unable to forward messages to one another at all. The most usual reason for this is that each of the systems involved is waiting for a buffer to become free in

---

[5] This may be the case for all traffic, or just for selected TCP flows between particular pairs of end systems.

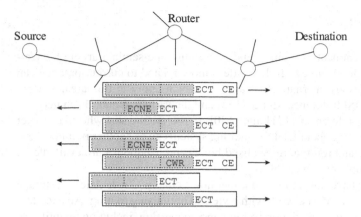

Fig. 7.26 TCP/IP congestion control with ECN.
ECN capable IP PDUs are not discarded if a router through which they pass detects congestion, but they are marked with a CE marker. The receiver of a TCP PDU *(shaded)* which arrives in a CE-marked IP PDU will mark its acknowledgments with ECN-echo until the source of the TCP PDUs sends one marked CWR to show that it has reduced its rate of transmission.

one of the others, in a cyclic manner: A waits for B, which waits for C, which waits for A, or the like. This is known as *store-and-forward deadlock*. A variant of this is the *reassembly deadlock* discussed in Section 4.6.

Any technique which reduces congestion due to buffer shortage, and thus ensures that there are always some free buffers in all systems, can prevent store-and-forward deadlock. More specific techniques for avoiding buffer deadlocks usually rely on some form of *resource ordering*: Resources are given some linear or partial ordering, $\preceq$, and a process which has acquired resources of rank r in this ordering may only request resources of rank $\succ r$. This is analogous to the well-known techniques for deadlock avoidance in resource allocation in operating systems.

There are several popular ranking schemes for deadlock avoidance. One of the simplest, which is generally attributed to Merlin and Schweitzer [91], is based on counting hops performed by the messages: A messsage is placed in a buffer of rank r (or less, if there are any such available) when it arrives at the r'th system along its route. For this to work correctly, the routing scheme must ensure that the maximum number of hops, n_{max}, used on a route between two arbitrary systems is known. It is then fairly easy to show that if all systems have buffers of ranks $1 \ldots n_{max}$, and if messages which arrive at their final destination are removed from their buffers within a finite time, then unbounded waiting for buffers cannot occur as messages are forwarded through the network. Informally, the argument is that removal of the message at the ultimate destination, say S_n, releases a buffer of rank, say, n. This enables a message which has gone $n-1$ hops to be passed on to S_n from, say, system S_{n-1}, and thus releases a buffer of rank $n-1$ in S_{n-1}, which enables a message which has gone $n-2$ hops to be passed on from some other system, and so on. A more formal proof, and a good review of this area in general, can be found in [56].

Further reading

For a theoretical treatment of naming and addressing, the seminal article by Watson [126] offers a good survey of ideas. Ideas more related to current practice can be found in the various international standards which apply in this area, starting with Part 3 of the OSI Reference Model [135] and the various standards on network addressing, such as references [141] and [130]. If you are the sort who likes to get his fingers dirty, reading about UNIX™ mailing systems gives another point of view, both on addressing and routing. Specialised books and handbooks are available on this topic, for example reference [50].

In this book we have not said much about how actually to calculate or estimate quantitative parameters of a network with a view to optimising routing. An excellent source with much useful material on routing and congestion, including quantitative aspects, is Bertsekas and Gallagher's book "Data Networks" [11].

The types of routing which we have concentrated on here are the ones most used in loosely-coupled distributed systems, where the physical separation of the component systems is 'large' and the topology of the network (for cost reasons) correspondingly sparse. In tightly-coupled multiprocessor systems, where the separation is 'small', more fully-connected networks are often used, and special routing algorithms have been developed to take advantage of this. An area of particular theoretical and practical interest is networks with an *n-dimensional binary hypercube* or *Boolean cube* topology, in which each system is connected to its neighbours in n dimensions. For a historical review see for example reference [59]. Optimal routing in hypercubes has been described by Bertsekas and his co-workers [12]. In multiprocessor systems, it is important that routing does not lead to deadlock, as the timing requirements are generally strict and deadlock detection and recovery are therefore impracticable. Much work has therefore gone into finding deadlock-free algorithms, such as Dally and Seitz' *wormhole routing* [28, 37].

Exercises

7.1. Confidential Connections Ltd. offers a large number of distributed services to industry, including a so-called *Secure Directory* service, which on demand can give addresses (in the OSI sense of the word) or other information about named users or service operators. The service is secure in the sense that:

- Information may only be supplied to subscribers to the service.
- Changes in the directory may only be made by the subscriber whose information is to be changed.

This is ensured by operating the directory service as an *authenticated service* with digital signatures based on a public key cryptosystem (PKCS).

Assume that the directory is to be distributed, but that there is only one copy of the information about any particular subscriber, and that this copy may be on any system. Propose an algorithm which can be used for *lookup* in the directory. Your proposal could conveniently take the form of a description of the sequence in which things take place, from the moment when a user asks the service for information about a subscriber until this information is supplied (or the user is told that they for some reason are inaccessible). Specify carefully which messages are sent between the various parts of the system, together with the content of these messages (in rough terms!). If messages are to be encrypted, then specify who is to encrypt them, which key is to be used and what the purpose of the encryption is.

Then describe (in a similar manner) an algorithm which can be used for *changing* the information about a subscriber in the directory.

Finally, describe (in a similar manner) an algorithm for *changing* the information about a subscriber, but now assuming that the directory is *fully replicated*.

7.2. An alternative strategy for handling source routing is to send out a discovery-PDU via a broadcast, rather than using flooding. The address of the destination whose route is to be found is incorporated in the discovery-PDU in a special field. A system which receives a broadcast discovery-PDU containing its own address in the special field *replies* to the originator of the discovery-PDU by using flooding. The result of this is that the originator, as in the strategy discussed in Section 7.3.7, receives messages from the desired system via all possible routes between the two systems.

Give a CSP description of this version of source routing, and then compare the strategy described here with the one described in Section 7.3.7, paying attention to factors such as the traffic generated in the network, the traffic generated at the nodes, and any other efficiency properties which you consider relevant.

7.3. As stated in the text, the Dynamic Source Routing (DSR) protocol often used in MANETs uses an optimised form of flooding for route discovery. An intermediate node will only pass on a discovery-PDU for a given source and destination if it has not recently handled a discovery-PDU for the same source and destination. Give a CSP description of this form of flooding. You may assume that each discovery-PDU for a given source and destination contains a sequence number, so a "recently handled" discovery-PDU for the same source and destination can be recognised by looking at this number.

7.4. The Royal Library of the Kingdom of Wom, whose population are famous (at least among computer ethnologists) for reading a lot but writing very little, has decided to introduce the latest technology in all its branches, which are distributed throughout the kingdom. As a result of a general IT initiative in Wom during the 1990's, each branch has a computerised catalogue of all the books and journals which it possesses. However, due to a lack of internal coordination in the Royal Library, these catalogues are based on a variety of different computer systems. Even worse, up to now it has been necessary for any citizen of Wom, who wanted to find a book which was not in his or her local branch, personally to get in touch with other branches where the desired work might be available. This has given rise to severe administrative difficulties for the librarians, who by now spend most of their time on the telephone answering questions from citizens in distant parts of the kingdom.

The Master of the Royal Library has therefore decreed that a distributed catalogue is to be created on the basis of the existing branch catalogues. An army of consultants has been hired to consider, together with the librarians and other royal administrators, what requirements should be placed on this catalogue. Their main conclusions are as follows:

1. The Royal Exchequer requires that the existing computerised catalogues in the individual branches are to be preserved.
2. The Royal Environment Ministry requires that the individual branches turn off their machines when the branch is closed.
3. The librarians agree that all updates to the catalogues, when a branch obtains a new work or is obliged to write off an old one, are to be performed on the local branch catalogue only.

Your task is to give a formal description of parts of this distributed catalogue system for approval by the consultants. (Don't worry – computer consultants in Wom all have a modern education in computer science and can read CSP!) You should note that the easiest way to fulfil the first requirement is to specify an interface which the various local systems all have to use. You do not need to go into details of how they match their local systems to this interface. To fulfil the second requirement, this interface should allow the branches to 'sign on' (for example, when they open in the mornings) and 'sign off' (for example, when they close in the evening) as well as to send and receive actual queries to or from other systems. You should specify the interface, which corresponds to the *service* offered by the distributed catalogue, as a set of one or more CSP processes. You should then specify the *protocol* to be used in order to provide this service, also in the form of a set of CSP processes.

7.5. Develop an implementation of a simple *trader*, as described in Section 7.1.2. This must be able to register the signatures (the function names and argument and result types) of the functions associated with a named interface, together with the addresses of servers which offer this interface. Given a request specifying one or more signatures, it must return the address of a server which offers an interface containing functions with these signatures. It will be necessary to design representations for signatures involving a suitable set of standard types, including both simple types ($\mathbb{N}$, $\mathbb{Z}$, $\mathbb{B}$, ...) and composite types, such as arrays and lists. (Remember that it is important that the representation makes it possible to distinguish arguments from results.) You will also need to design suitable data structures which can be used to store signatures, so that they can easily be matched to incoming requests.

7.6. In the Internet DNS, *zone transfers* are used to fetch complete name-address mappings from other name servers. This is often considered a security risk: A malicious intruder could set up a fake name server which could provide false mappings by responding faster to requests for zone transfers than the genuine name server. Which of the security techniques discussed in Chapter 6 would you use in order to avoid this problem?

Chapter 8
Protocol Encoding

Anteater: *"Actually, some trails contain information in coded form. If you know the system, you can read what they're saying just like a book."*
Achilles: *"Remarkable. And can you communicate back to them?"*
Anteater: *"Without any trouble at all. That's how Aunt Hillary and I have conversations for hours"*.

"Gödel, Escher, Bach"
Douglas R. Hofstadter

According to our definition in Chapter 1, the representation rules for PDUs are just as much part of the protocol as the rules of the exchange of PDUs. However, until now we have ignored this topic completely, describing the contents of PDUs in an abstract manner as records with fields of more or less standard elementary or composite data types. The representation rules are chosen so as to fulfil a number of general objectives in relation to the protocol:

1. **Efficiency:** The information in the PDU should be coded as compactly as possible.
2. **Delimiting:** It must be possible for the receiver to recognise the beginning and end of the PDU.
3. **Ease of decoding:** It should be easy for the receiver to find out exactly what information it has received.
4. **Data transparency:** The representation should be such that arbitrary sequences of bits can be sent as data within the PDU.

To a certain extent, these rules are in conflict with one another, so compromises usually have to be accepted.

In practice, there are three principal ways of representing the fields of a PDU when it is transmitted:

1. **Simple binary** – or *'ad hoc'* – encoding in which fixed groups of bits within the PDU are used to represent the values of the fields in an arbitrary manner.
2. **Type-Length-Value (TLV)** encoding, in which each field is described by a triplet of sub-fields. The first of these gives the *type* of the field, the second gives the *length* of the representation of the third sub-field, while the third sub-field gives the actual *value* of the field.

Table 8.1 Abstract PDUs for HDLC [131]

PDU type	Abstract description	
Information	$Ipdu$:	$(n_s : \mathbb{N}_0,\ ack_r : \mathbb{N}_0,\ PF : \mathbb{B},\ info : \mathscr{M})$
Receive ready	$RRpdu$:	$(ack_r : \mathbb{N}_0,\ PF : \mathbb{B})$
Receive not ready	$RNRpdu$:	$(ack_r : \mathbb{N}_0,\ PF : \mathbb{B})$
Reject	$REJpdu$:	$(ack_r : \mathbb{N}_0,\ PF : \mathbb{B})$
Selective reject	$SREJpdu$:	$(ack_r : \mathbb{N}_0,\ PF : \mathbb{B})$
Set NR mode	$SNRMpdu$:	$(PF : \mathbb{B})$
Set AR mode	$SARMpdu$:	$(PF : \mathbb{B})$
Set AB mode	$SABMpdu$:	$(PF : \mathbb{B})$
Set NR mode extended	$SNRMEpdu$:	$(PF : \mathbb{B})$
Set AR mode extended	$SARMEpdu$:	$(PF : \mathbb{B})$
Set AB mode extended	$SABMEpdu$:	$(PF : \mathbb{B})$
Disconnect	$DISCpdu$:	$(PF : \mathbb{B})$
Unnumbered acknowledge	$UApdu$:	$(PF : \mathbb{B})$
Unnumbered information	$UIpdu$:	$(PF : \mathbb{B},\ info : \mathscr{M})$
Exchange identification	$XIDpdu$:	$(PF : \mathbb{B},\ info : \mathscr{M})$
Test	$TESTpdu$:	$(PF : \mathbb{B},\ info : \mathscr{M})$
Frame reject	$FRMRpdu$:	$(PF : \mathbb{B},\ info : \mathscr{M})$

3. **Matched tag** encoding, in which each field is headed by a *start tag* which contains a keyword identifying the field, and is terminated by a *terminator*, which often has the form of a matching *end tag*.

We shall consider these in turn.

8.1 Simple Binary Encoding

Simple binary encoding offers the most compact representation of the fields of the PDU, because there is no need for type or length indicators. The price to be paid for this is generally speaking a lack of flexibility. Thus this style of coding is preferred for protocols which only use a few types of PDU with fixed contents. This is generally the case for protocols in the lower layers of the OSI Reference Model.

An example is the HDLC protocol used in the Data Link layer [131]. From an abstract point of view, this is a protocol for providing a full duplex connection-mode service, with a two-way window protocol using sequence numbers counted *modulo 8* (or, optionally, *modulo 128*) in the data transfer phase. There are 17 types of PDU, which can be described abstractly as shown in Table 8.1. Here, the *info* field carries the body of the message, n_s the sequence number of the message, and ack_r the sequence number of the message being acknowledged. The *PF* field carries the so-called *Poll/Final* information, whose meaning depends on whether the PDU is sent as a *command* to produce some kind of reaction from the other party, or whether it is a *response* to a command (see Chapter 9). Roughly speaking[1], if it is a

---

[1] The full rules are somewhat more complicated, depending on the mode of operation of the data link. The rules given here correspond to Normal Response Mode (NRM).

Table 8.2 Encoding of Control field in HDLC protocol PDUs.
This shows the standard 8-bit encodings of the control field. The Control field in I- and S-PDUs can also be encoded in a 16-bit Extended Encoding:

I: 0nnnnnnn paaaaaaa   S: 10ss0000 paaaaaaa

Format	Code	Interpretation	
I	0nnn paaa	nnn= binary representation of n_s	
		aaa= binary representation of ack_r	
		p=1 $\Rightarrow$ PF = true.	
S	10ss paaa	aaa= binary representation of ack_r	
		p=1 $\Rightarrow$ PF = true	
		ss= 00: RRpdu,	10: RNRpdu,
		01: REJpdu,	11: SREJpdu
U	11xx pyyy	p=1 $\Rightarrow$ PF = true	
		xxyyy= 00001: SNRMpdu,	11000: SARMpdu,
		11100: SABMpdu,	00010: DISCpdu,
		11011: SNRMEpdu,	11010: SARMEpdu,
		11110: SABMEpdu,	00110: UApdu,
		00000: UIpdu,	11101: XIDpdu,
		00111: TESTpdu,	10001: FRMRpdu.

command, PF = true indicates that the other party is being *polled* for data. If it is an *Ipdu* response, PF = true indicates that this is the *final* portion of data in a sequence sent in response to being polled. If it is any other type of PDU sent as a response, PF = true indicates that there are no data to send in response to being polled.

All these PDUs are coded in the basic format:

Flag	Address	Control	Information	FCS	Flag
01111110	$8n$ bits	8/16 bits	m bits	16/32 bits	01111110

Here, the *FCS* bit field is a polynomial checksum for the Address, Control and Information fields, evaluated using the CRC-CCITT generator poynomial (for 16-bit checksum) or CRC-32 (for 32-bit checksum). The *Address* bit field contains an n-octet bit sequence identifying the intended receiver of the PDU, and the *Information* bit field contains the coding of the *info* field of the PDU, if any. It may be of arbitrary length, including 0; a length of 0 indicates that the PDU carries no data.

The *Control* bit field gives the type of the PDU, together with the n_s, ack_r and PF control fields of the PDU where appropriate, according to the coding scheme given in Table 8.2. Note that three variants are used, corresponding to various classes of PDU[2]: *I-format* (Information transfer format) for I-PDUs, *S-format* (Supervisory format) for RR, RNR, REJ and SREJ PDUs, which carry acknowledgement numbers but no data, and *U-format* (Unnumbered format) for the remaining types of PDU, which carry no numbers, but may or may not carry data. As can be seen, the values of n_s and ack_r are represented in a pure binary representation for natural numbers (in $\{0..7\}$ for the standard encoding and $\{0..127\}$ for the extended

---

[2] In HDLC, a PDU is known as a *frame*

encoding), while all the other fields are represented in an arbitrary manner chosen for the compactness of the encoding.

The individual bits of an HDLC PDU are usually transmitted in a synchronous manner, but the protocol is essentially *asynchronous*, in the sense that a new PDU can follow at any time after the previous one. The gap between consecutive PDUs is filled with some kind of idling bit pattern, for example all 1-bits. To indicate to the receiver when a new PDU is about to start, the beginning of the PDU is marked with a *Flag* field containing a fixed bit pattern, 01111110.

Since HDLC, like most modern data transfer protocols, permits the lengths of PDUs to vary arbitrarily (in practice up to some maximum number of bits), the receiver has the problem of how to know what the length of the PDU is. The solution in HDLC is to mark the end of the PDU with another *Flag* field. This unfortunately conflicts with the general aim of achieving *data transparency*. Obviously, an HDLC PDU must not contain a bit sequence 01111110 between the two flags, or the receiver will imagine that this sequence is intended to mark the end of the PDU. The solution to this problem is to transform the entire body of the PDU (i.e. the sequence of bits between the two flags), using a technique known as *bit stuffing*: The sender inserts an extra 0-bit in the body after every sequence of five consecutive 1-bits, and the receiver removes any 0-bit which follows five consecutive 1-bits.

The need to mark the beginning and end of the PDU vanishes if all PDUs have the same length and the protocol is *synchronous*. In this case, consecutive PDUs follow one another at constant intervals of time, as in the classical TDM protocols discussed in Section 4.5.1. In practice, various intermediate styles of protocol are found. An interesting, but *very* complex example is the *SDH* (Synchronous Digital Hierarchy) protocol [253] used in many modern telecommunication systems. Here, the 'frames' for holding data follow a synchronous scheme, and the data units all have the same length, but the position of the data within the frames is allowed to vary. This permits the originator to supply the data slightly early or late in relation to the strictly synchronous frame timing. Typically this is necessary because the clock used to generate data within the sending system drifts slightly with time. To make it possible for the receiver to find the data, each frame contains a *pointer* (at a fixed position near the beginning of the frame), indicating where the actual data in this frame start. This is adjusted by the sender as required.

8.2 TLV Encoding

TLV encoding offers more flexibility than simple binary encoding, in the sense that it becomes possible to omit fields from a PDU, since the fields which are in fact included are unambiguously identified by their type sub-fields, and their lengths are given by explicit length sub-fields. A simple example of this form of encoding is found in the ISO Transport Layer protocols [138], where the so-called *variable part* of each PDU is encoded in this way. This part of the PDU can in principle contain a large number of optional pieces of information, of which maybe only two or three

Table 8.3 Encoding of fields in variable part of ISO Transport Protocol PDUs. All lengths are measured in octets, and are encoded in an 8-bit unsigned binary representation. x, y and z are arbitrary. Times and other integer values are encoded in unsigned binary representations.

Field	Type code	Length	Value code
Checksum	1100 0011	2	Binary representation of checksum.
Calling TSAP	1100 0001	x	Binary representation of address.
Called TSAP	1100 0010	x	Binary representation of address.
TPDU size	1100 0000	1	8-bit binary representation of $\lceil \log_2 l \rceil$, where $l = $ length of the TPDU in octets.
Version no.	1100 0100	1	0000 0001
Protection	1100 0101	y	User defined.
Extra options	1100 0110	1	0000 mnpq, where: q=1 $\Rightarrow$ use of T-expedited data required, p=1 $\Rightarrow$ don't use checksum, n=1 $\Rightarrow$ use receipt confirmation, m=1 $\Rightarrow$ use N-expedited data.
Alt. classes	1100 0111	n	Codes for n alternative protocol classes.
Ack. time	1000 0101	2	16-bit binary representation of max. time needed to produce an acknowledgement (msec).
Throughput	1000 1001	12	Max. throughput; or
		24	Max. throughput, average throughput. Each throughput is specified by 4 integers in 16-bit binary representations: target value, calling→called (oct/sec), min. acceptable, calling→called (oct/sec), target value, called→calling (oct/sec), min. acceptable, called→calling (oct/sec).
RER	1000 0110	3	8-bit binary representations of: $\lceil \log_{10} t \rceil$, where $t = $ target value, $\lceil \log_{10} t \rceil$, where $t = $ min. acceptable value, $\lceil \log_2 s \rceil$, where $s = $ TSDU size of interest.
Priority	1000 0111	2	16-bit binary representation of priority (as integer value, 0=highest priority).
Transit delay	1000 1000	8	16-bit binary representations of: target delay, calling→called (msec), max. acceptable delay, calling→called (msec), target delay, called→calling (msec), max. acceptable delay, called→calling (msec).
Reassign time	1000 1011	2	16-bit binary representation of reassignment time, TTR (sec).
Clearing code	1110 0000	z	Additional information about the reason for clearing the connection.

are actually needed in any particular case. The *fixed part* of the PDU, which contains mandatory fields, is encoded using a simple binary encoding. Although a TLV encoding of any particular piece of information will always be longer than a simple binary encoding, the encoding of the complete PDU will usually be more compact if TLV encoding is used for optional fields. The TLV coding used in Transport Layer PDUs is shown in Table 8.3.

This style of coding is also found in the ISO OSI connectionless-mode Network protocol [142] the Internet IP protocol [210] and the ISO OSI connection-mode

Session protocol [140]. The type codes are quite arbitrary, and do not convey any explicit information about the encoding of the value field.

8.3 ASN.1 Encoding

A more refined form of TLV encoding is to be found in the so-called *Basic Encoding Rules for ASN.1* [159]. ASN.1 [158] is a notation for denoting the abstract syntax of data (i.e. for describing data in a representation-independent manner), and is widely used for describing data structures for use in the Application Layer of the OSI protocol hierarchy. This is convenient, because it then becomes possible to describe algorithms and applications in a manner which is independent of the ways in which the data structures are represented on individual systems.

8.3.1 ASN.1 Types

As with most other notations for denoting abstract syntax, including the VDM-like notation used in this book, ASN.1 permits us to construct data types from a series of *simple types* which may be composed in various ways to form *structured types*. In addition, *subtypes* of types can be specified. The notations for ASN.1's simple types are listed in Table 8.4(top), and the notations for constructing structured types and subtypes in Table 8.4(middle) and (bottom) respectively. Both simple and structured types can be marked with a *tag*, so that apparently identical types can be differentiated. A tag is made up of a *class* specification, which delimits the scope of the tag, together with a *number*. For example the types:

    BOOLEAN
    [APPLICATION 3]BOOLEAN
    [APPLICATION 4]BOOLEAN

are different. The classes and their scopes are shown in Table 8.5. A tag's number must of course be unambiguous within the relevant scope – for example, for a type tagged as *APPLICATION* within the application concerned. Untagged simple or structured types are implictly *UNIVERSAL*, with numbers as shown in Table 8.6. The *CHOICE* and *ANY* types have no numbers of their own – the number of the type actually chosen is used.

Table 8.4 Simple types (top), structured types (middle) and subtypes (bottom) in ASN.1. In addition, there is a *universal type*, denoted *ANY*, and a set of 'ready-made' *useful types*, for specialised purposes such as giving the date and time.

Type notation	Denoted set of values
BOOLEAN	Truth values: true, false.
INTEGER	The whole numbers.
ENUMERATED {*NamedNumberList*}	The whole numbers given in *NamedNumberList*, which may be referred to by the associated names.
REAL	The real numbers expressible in the form $m \cdot B^e$ (where m and e are arbitrary integers and B is 2 or 10), together with $+\infty$ and $-\infty$.
BIT STRING	Sequences of 0 or more bits.
OCTET STRING	Sequences of 0 or more arbitrary octets.
xxxString	Character strings from pre-defined character set *xxx*.
NULL	The empty set.
OBJECT IDENTIFIER	Arbitrary identifiers ('tokens').

Type notation	Denoted set of values
SEQUENCE{*TypeList*}	Sequences whose elements correspond in number and order to the types in the type list, possibly with omissions (denoted in the type list by *OPTIONAL*), which may have default values (denoted by *DEFAULT*).
SEQUENCE OF Type	Sequences of 0 or more elements of the type given by *Type*.
SET{*TypeList*}	Sets with one member from each of the types in the type list, possibly with omissions (*OPTIONAL*), which may have default values (*DEFAULT*).
SET OF Type	Arbitrary subsets of *Type*.
CHOICE{*TypeList*}	Union type of the types in the type list.

Subtype notation	Denoted set of values
AlternativeList	For arbitrary parent types: the values explicitly given in *AlternativeList* (for example: $(3|5|7|11|13)$).
Lower..Upper	For (possibly tagged) *REAL* or *INTEGER* parent types: The values in the range *Lower* to *Upper*. *Lower* may be specified as *MIN*, the minimum value of the parent type, and *Upper* as *MAX*, the maximum value.
SIZE SizeConstraint	For *SET OF*, *SEQUENCE OF* or *STRING* parent types: Values where the number of elements lies in *SizeConstraint*, which may be any subtype of the non-negative integers.
FROM CharList	For character string parent types: strings restricted to characters in *CharList*.

Table 8.5 Classes and their scopes in ASN.1

Class	Used to tag:
UNIVERSAL	The types defined explicitly in [158].
APPLICATION	Types related to a specific application.
PRIVATE	Types related to a specific group of users.
(empty)	Local (context-specific) types.

Table 8.6 Universal class tag numbers (after [158])

1 BOOLEAN	11 – – –	21 VideotexString
2 INTEGER	12 – – –	22 IA5String
3 BITSTRING	13 – – –	23 UTCTime
4 OCTETSTRING	14 – – –	24 GeneralizedTime
5 NULL	15 – – –	25 GraphicString
6 OBJ.IDENTIFIER	16 SEQUENCE/SEQ. OF	26 ISO646String
7 OBJ.DESCRIPTOR	17 SET/SET OF	27 GeneralString
8 EXTERNAL	18 NumericString	28 – – –
9 REAL	19 PrintableString	29 – – –
10 ENUMERATED	20 T61String	30 – – –

8.3.2 ASN.1 Values

Values of the ASN.1 types are denoted in ASN.1 in an obvious way. For example, values of type *BOOLEAN* as TRUE or FALSE, values of type *INTEGER* as optionally signed decimal integers, values of type *BITSTRING* and *OCTETSTRING* as sequences of binary or hexadecimal digits in single quotes ('11010001'B or 'C23F81'H), character strings as sequences of characters from the designated set in double quotes ("John Q. Smith", "Smörgås") and values of *SET*, *SET OF*, *SEQUENCE* or *SEQUENCE OF* as lists of values of the component types in braces (for example: {1,3,5,7,11} for a value of type *SET OF INTEGER* or *SEQUENCE OF INTEGER*).

8.3.3 ASN.1 Encoding Rules

When a value expressible in ASN.1 is to be transmitted from one system to another, a set of rules is required for producing a standard external representation of the value concerned. The standard set of such rules is described in [159], often referred to as *BASN.1*. This uses a TLV encoding scheme, which in the case of structured types is applied recursively to the fields of the data structure. Some examples are given in Figure 8.1.

The coding of the type identifier is shown in more detail in Figure 8.2. For types with small tag numbers, a single octet is used of which the most significant two bits (marked bits 8 and 7 in the figure) give the tag class, bit 6 shows whether the value subfield contains a complete TLV encoding of a value of some type (a so-called *constructed encoding*), or directly gives the value of the current type (a so-called *primitive encoding*). In the latter case we have reached a 'terminal element' in the recursive application of the encoding rules. For tag numbers ≤30, the five least significant bits are an unsigned binary representation of the tag number. For larger numbers, the five least significant bits are all ones, and the number is encoded in one or more following octets, depending on its magnitude, as illustrated in Figure 8.2.

Type: BOOLEAN
Value: TRUE
Coding: *BOOLEAN Length Value*
          01_{16} 01_{16} FF_{16}

Type: SEQUENCE{name IA5String, ok BOOLEAN}
Value: {name "Smith", ok TRUE}
Coding: *SEQUENCE Length*
          30_{16} $0A_{16}$
              IA5String   Length Value
              16_{16} 05_{16} $536D697468_{16}$
              BOOLEAN Length Value
              01_{16} 01_{16} FF_{16}

Type: [PRIVATE 3] SEQUENCE{name IA5String, ok BOOLEAN}
Value: {name "Smith", ok TRUE}
Coding: *[PRIVATE 3] Length*
          $C3_{16}$ $0C_{16}$
              SEQUENCE Length
              30_{16} $0A_{16}$
                  IA5String   Length Value
                  16_{16} 05_{16} $536D697468_{16}$
                  BOOLEAN Length Value
                  01_{16} 01_{16} FF_{16}

Fig. 8.1 Examples of encoding in BASN.1

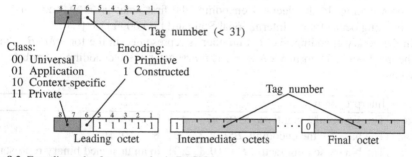

Fig. 8.2 Encoding rules for type codes in BASN.1

The length can be encoded in two ways. In the *definite* form, the length is given explicitly, encoded in a way rather like the tag number, using one or more octets depending on its magnitude, as shown in Figure 8.3. In the *indefinite* form, the length field consists of a single octet, 1000 0000, and the value field is terminated by two octets consisting entirely of 0-bits, known as the *end-of-contents octets*. All the examples in Figure 8.1 use the single-octet definite form.

For a primitive encoding, which will always correspond to a simple type, the value field is encoded directly in the obvious way, depending on its type, as follows:

BOOLEAN: false: 0000 0000, true: Any non-zero octet.

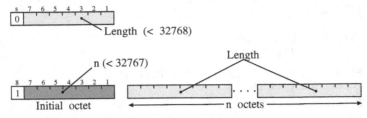

Fig. 8.3 Encoding rules for lengths in BASN.1

INTEGER: Twos-complement binary representation using the minimum number of octets for unambiguous representation, most significant bit first (in the most significant bit of the first octet).

ENUMERATED: The encoding of the integer associated with the name in the type definition. For example, given a type defined as:

```
ENUMERATED{ july(7), august(8), september(9) }
```

then august will be encoded by the encoding of 8.

REAL: For real value 0, the contents field is empty.

For real value $+\infty$, one octet: 0100 0000 and for $-\infty$, one octet: 0100 0001 is used.

For all other non-zero real values, there is a choice between a decimal and binary representation. In the decimal encoding, the first octet is 0000 00xx, and the remaining octets follow International Standard ISO 6093 [132][3].

In the binary encoding, the real number is represented in the form $M \cdot B^E$, with the mantissa in the form $S \times N \times 2^F$. The first octet of the encoding is 1sbb ffgg, where:

Bits	Interpretation
s	The sign of the mantissa, S: 0: $+1$, 1: -1
bb	The base for the encoding, B: 00: 2, 01: 8, 10: 16
ff	The binary scaling factor, $F \in \{0,1,2,3\}$, in an unsigned binary representation.
gg	The format for the exponent: 00: Single-octet (octet 2), 01: Two-octet (octets 2 and 3), 10: Three-octet (octets 2,3 and 4), 11: Length (say L) follows in octet 2 of the encoding, and exponent fills octets $3..(3+L-1)$. The exponent, E, is in all cases encoded in a 2-complement signed binary representation.

The modulus of the mantissa, N, is a non-negative integer value in an unsigned binary encoding, which follows the the octets of the exponent.

---

[3] The bits xx give the ISO 6093 number form: 01: Form NR1, 10: Form NR2, 11: Form NR3.

BIT STRING: For an n-bit bit string: An initial octet, followed by $(n+7)$ div 8 octets containing the n bits of the bit string, starting with the first bit of the string in the most significant bit of the first octet.

The initial octet contains an unsigned representation of $(8 - (n \bmod 8)) \bmod 8$, the number of unused bits in the last octet.

OCTET STRING: The octets of the string, in the order in which they appear in the string.

xxxString: For an n-character string: n octets, each of which contains an 8-bit encoding of a character of the string, in the order in which the characters appear in the string.

NULL: Empty. (The length is always 0.)

For a constructed encoding, which may correspond to a bitstring, octetstring or character string, or to a structured type, the value is encoded by a complete TLV encoding using the rules described above.

It should be evident that this style of encoding gives great flexibility, permitting the representation of the values of arbitrary non-recursive data structures. Recursive data structures, such as lists or trees, have to be represented in some appropriate manner in terms of the types of Table 8.4. Variants of the BASN.1 encoding which offer *data compression* [160] or for encoding ASN.1 using *XML* [161] (see Section 8.4.3 below) have also been proposed, but we will not discuss them here.

8.4 ASCII encodings

Whereas BASN.1 encoding is the encoding of choice for data structures in ISO and ITU-T protocols, and in some Internet Application Layer protocols with relation to these, such as SNMP [219] and LDAP [228], many other Internet Application Layer protocols use so-called *ASCII* encodings for PDUs to be transmitted between application processes. In an ASCII encoding, the type of the PDU and often the individual fields in the PDU are identified by plain text keywords, which – at least in the simplest cases – are made up of characters from the US-ASCII character set. This type of encoding is by no means space-efficient, but makes it possible for the human reader to understand at least the general content and purpose of the PDU without the use of a computer to interpret the encoding. The PDUs are also easy to produce by standard application programs, as they can be input and output as ordinary lines of text.

Examples of this style of encoding are found in the well-known Internet protocols FTP [215], SMTP [213], POP3 [222], IMAP4 [226], NNTP [216] and HTTP [43]. Figure 8.4 gives an example of a set of PDUs exchanged using SMTP, as would be the case when sending a mail message to a mail server for transmission to a named addressee. Like the other protocols mentioned here, SMTP uses *matched tag* encoding, in which commands start with an alphabetic keyword and responses start with a numeric response code; both commands and responses are terminated by a NL character.

```
HELO goofy.dtu.dk
```
$\boxed{\textit{250 design.dilbert.org}}$
```
MAIL FROM:<bones@goofy.dtu.dk>
```
$\boxed{\textit{250 OK}}$
```
RCPT TO:<snodgrass@design.dilbert.org>
```
$\boxed{\textit{250 OK}}$
```
DATA
```
$\boxed{\textit{354 Start mail input; end with <CRLF>.<CRLF>}}$
```
From: Alfred Bones <bones@goofy.dtu.dk>
To:   William Snodgrass <snodgrass@design.dilbert.org>
Date: 21 Aug 2000 13:31:02 +0200
Subject: Client exploder

Here are the secret plans for the client exploder
    etc. etc. etc.
    .
```
$\boxed{\textit{250 OK}}$
```
QUIT
```
$\boxed{\textit{221 design.dilbert.org}}$

Fig. 8.4 Exchange of messages in SMTP.
Commands from the client to the server are in `typewriter` font and replies from server to client
are boxed in $\boxed{\textit{italic typewriter}}$ font.

8.4.1 MIME encoding

A particularly interesting form of ASCII encoding is the *MIME* encoding used for
representing data in various formats for transmission between application processes.
MIME is an acronym for *Multipurpose Internet Mail Extensions*. Originally designed as a representation for non-ASCII data in Internet mail messages to be sent
by the SMTP protocol, it has subsequently also been exploited in other contexts. In
contrast to the very fine-grained style of encoding seen in ASN.1, MIME encoding
is intended for use with substantial chunks of data, such as documents or images.
Each such chunk is known as a *MIME entity* [224]. An entity is encoded as a *header*
followed by a *body*, where the header consists of a sequence of *fields* which specify:

1. The *content type* of the body.
2. The *encoding* of the body.
3. A *reference* (for example, a serial number or identifier) which can be used to
   refer to the body from other entities.
4. A *textual description* of the entity.
5. Possibly some *extension fields*, describing additional or non-standard attributes
   of the entity.

   The content type header field specifies a *type* and *subtype*, where the type
can be *discrete* or *composite*. An entity of a discrete type contains a single block
of data representing a text, image, audio stream, video stream or similar, while an

Table 8.7 Standard MIME entity types and subtypes [225]

Discrete type	Subtypes	Explanation
text	plain	Plain text, viewed as a sequence of characters, possibly with embedded line breaks or page breaks.
	enriched	Text with embedded formatting commands in a standard markup language.
image	jpeg	Images encoded in accordance with the JPEG standard using JFIF encoding [206].
audio	basic	Single channel audio encoded using 8-bit ISDN mu-law at a sample rate of 8000 Hz. [254]
video	mpeg	Video encoded in accordance with the MPEG standard [207].
application	octet-stream	Arbitrary binary data.
	postscript	Instructions for a PostScript™ interpreter.
	x-...	User-defined application subtype.

Composite type	Subtypes	Explanation
message	rfc822	A complete mail message in accordance with Internet RFC822.
	partial	A (numbered) fragment of a larger MIME entity.
	external-body	A reference to the body of a mail message which is not embedded in the current entity.
multipart	mixed	A sequence of independent body parts, each delimited by a unique sequence of characters.
	alternative	A sequence of body parts, each delimited by a unique sequence of characters, and each representing an alternative version of the same information.
	digest	A sequence of independent body parts, which by default are messages.
	parallel	A set of independent body parts, each delimited by a unique sequence of characters.

entity of a composite type is composed from smaller entities, which may themselves be of discrete or composite type. A number of standardised types and subtypes are pre-defined in the MIME standards, and others can be added either informally or via a formal registration process to the IANA. The standard types defined in Part 2 of the Internet MIME standard [225] can be seen in Table 8.7. The types currently registered with the IANA can be found listed on the IANA's website at:

`http://www.iana.org/assignments/media-types/`

For several of these types and subtypes, content type header fields may also include *parameters*, for example the actual character set used in a text/plain entity, the delimiter string in a multipart entity, the fragment number in a message/partial entity, the access type (FTP, ANON-FTP, LOCAL-FILE,...), expiration date, size and access rights (read, read-write) for a message/external-body entity, and so on.

The encoding header field describes the way in which the content has been encoded *in addition to* the encoding implied by the content type and subtype. An encoding which is not an identity transformation may be needed if the body of the entity contains data which for some reason cannot be passed transparently by the protocol in use. For example, basic SMTP can only be used to transfer sequences of ASCII characters in a 7-bit representation. The standard encodings are:

7bit   No transformation has been performed on the data, which consist entirely of lines of not more than 998 characters in a 7-bit representation, separated by a CRLF character pair.

8bit   No transformation has been performed on the data, which consist entirely of lines of not more than 998 characters in an 8-bit representation, separated by a CRLF character pair.

binary   No transformation has been performed on the data, which consist of a sequence of arbitrary octets.

quoted-printable   A transformation to quoted-printable form has taken place on the data, such that:

1.   non-graphic characters,
2.   characters which are not ASCII graphical characters,
3.   the equals sign character,
4.   white space (SP, TAB) characters at the end of a line

are replaced by a 3-character code "=XY", where X and Y are two hexadecimal digits which represent the code value of the character. US-ASCII graphical characters (apart from =) may optionally be represented in the same way or may appear literally. Lines longer than 76 characters are split by the insertion of 'soft line breaks' (represented by an equals sign followed by a CRLF character pair). Thus for example:

```
Les curieux =E9v=E9nements qui font le sujet de cette chron=
ique se sont produits en 194., =E0 Oran.
```

represents the text *Les curieux événements qui font le sujet de cette chronique se sont produits en 194., à Oran.* – the opening sentence of Albert Camus' novel "La Peste". Here E9 is the code value for é, E0 is the value for à, and the equals sign which ends the first line indicates a soft line break. This transformation is intended to allow text to pass through systems which are restrictive with respect to line length and character set.

base64   A transformation to base-64 coding has taken place.
Here, each 24 bit sequence of data is encoded as 4 characters from a 64-character subset of the US-ASCII set of graphical characters, where each character corresponds to 6 bits of the data, as shown in Table 8.8. For example:

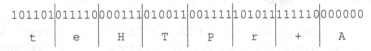

Data sequences which are not multiples of 6 bits are padded on the right with 0-bits to a multiple of 6 bits before conversion to characters as above; if they are then not a multiple of 4 characters, they are further padded on the right with the character "=". The characters are broken up into lines of not more than 76 characters, the lines being separated by CRLF (which has no significance for

Table 8.8 Base64 encoding of 6-bit binary sequences

Data	Character	Data	Character	Data	Character	Data	Character
000000	A	010000	Q	100000	g	110000	w
000001	B	010001	R	100001	h	110001	x
000010	C	010010	S	100010	i	110010	y
000011	D	010011	T	100011	j	110011	z
000100	E	010100	U	100100	k	110100	0
000101	F	010101	V	100101	l	110101	1
000110	G	010110	W	100110	m	110110	2
000111	H	010111	X	100111	n	110111	3
001000	I	011000	Y	101000	o	111000	4
001001	J	011001	Z	101001	p	111001	5
001010	K	011010	a	101010	q	111010	6
001011	L	011011	b	101011	r	111011	7
001100	M	011100	c	101100	s	111100	8
001101	N	011101	d	101101	t	111101	9
001110	O	011110	e	101110	u	111110	+
001111	P	011111	f	101111	v	111111	/

Table 8.9 MIME entity types and subtypes for S/MIME [245]

Type	Subtypes	Explanation
multipart	signed	A signed, cleartext message with two parts: the message itself and the signature.
application	pkcs7-mime	A signed or encrypted MIME entity or a set of one or more public-key certificates.
	pkcs7-signature	Signature from a signed multipart message.
	pkcs10-mime	A certificate registration request message.

the coding). This transformation is intended to allow binary data to pass through systems which are restrictive with respect to line length and character set.

The rather curious length restrictions on character sequences are historical relics from a time when mail handling systems had very limited buffer capacity. A complete example of a mail message, composed of a multipart entity in MIME encoding, and illustrating several of these features, is shown in Figure 8.5.

8.4.2 S/MIME encoding

S/MIME [245] is an enhancement to MIME which offers security facilities, so that documents can be digitally signed, encrypted or both. This involves the introduction of some new MIME content types, which are shown in Table 8.9. The pkcs7-mime subtype can be used for several purposes, and the way in which an entity with this subtype is to be understood is specified by a MIME parameter, smime-type, which can take on values as follows:

```
From: Ebenezer Snurd <ebes@bugeyed.monster>
To: Rod Akromats <rak@tundranet.ice>
Date: Wed, 09 Aug 2000 12:34:56 +0100 (CET)
Subject: Finalised material
MIME-Version: 1.0
Content-type: multipart/mixed; boundary=5c12g7YTurbl9zp4Ux
```

This is the MIME preamble, which is to be ignored by
mail readers that understand multipart format messages.

```
--5c12g7YTurbl9zp4Ux
Content-type: text/plain; charset=ISO-8859-1
Content-transfer-encoding: 8bit
```

Dear Rod,
  Here are some recent pictures, including the mail I told
you about from the Clones. Enjoy!
    Ebe.

```
--5c12g7YTurbl9zp4Ux
Content-type: image/jpeg; name="clopics.jpg"
Content-transfer-encoding: base64
```

/9j/4AAQSkZJRgABAQAAAQABAAD/Ap3u107+yacdfefe66menop4RorS8hach8tf3
...
```
--5c12g7YTurbl9zp4Ux
Content-type: message/external-body; access-type=local-file;
             name="/usr/home/ebes/pix/clo08.ps";
             site="drones.hive.co.uk"
Content-type: application/postscript
Content-id: <id003@woffly.speakers.com>
--5c12g7YTurbl9zp4Ux--
```

This is the MIME epilogue. Like the preamble, it is
to be ignored.

Fig. 8.5 MIME encoding of a mail message with three parts.
The parts are separated by a boundary marker starting with "--", followed by the boundary string
"5c12g7YTurbl9zp4Ux". Header fields are shown in typewriter font and bodies in *italic*
typewriter font.

signed-data   indicates a signed MIME entity. This is made up of a sequence of
   blocks, including the actual message, a message digest (MD5 or SHA) encrypted
   with the signer's private key, and information about the signer, such as its public
   key certificate(s).

enveloped-data   indicates an encrypted MIME entity. This is made up of a sequence of blocks, including the actual message content encrypted using a session key for an SKCS (3DES or RC2/40), the session key encrypted using the
   receiver's public RSA key, and information about the sender, such as its public
   key certificate(s).

```
From: Ebenezer Snurd <ebes@bugeyed.monster>
To: Rod Akromats <rak@tundranet.ice>
Date: Wed, 09 Aug 2002 12:34:56 +0100 (CET)
Subject: Greetings from Ebe.
MIME-Version: 1.0
Content-type: multipart/signed; micalg=md5;
   boundary=to5oman4y8sec2ret7s
--to5oman4y8sec2ret7s
Content-type: text/plain; charset=ISO-8859-1
Content-transfer-encoding: 8bit
```

> *Dear Rod,*
>   *Finally I made it to S. America with the documents I*
>   *promised to deliver. Hope to see you soon.*
>   *Ebe.*

```
--to5oman4y8sec2ret7s
Content-type: application/pkcs7-signature; name=smime.p7s
Content-transfer-encoding: base64
Content-disposition: attachment; filename=smime.p7s
```

ghyHhHUujhJhjH77n8HHGTrfvbnj756tbB9HG4VQpfyF467GhIGfHfYT6
4VQpfyF467GhIGfHfYT6jH77n8HHGghyHhHUujhJh756tbB9HGTrfvbnj
n8HHGTrfvhJhjH776tbB9HG4VQbnj7567GhIGfHfYT6ghyHhHUujpfyF4
7GhIGfHfYT64VQbnj756

```
--to5oman4y8sec2ret7s--
```

Fig. 8.6 MIME encoding of an S/MIME multipart/signed mail message

certs-only   indicates an entity containing only public key certificates or a certificate revocation list.

S/MIME uses public key certificates in accordance with the ITU-T recommendation X.509 [180]. In general, S/MIME entities contain binary information and are transferred using the base64 MIME transfer encoding; the only exception can be the plaintext message part of the multipart signed entity type, which can be transferred using any encoding which ensures that the message will not be altered during the transfer. Figure 8.6 shows an example of a mail message, which you should try to compare with Figure 8.5; the second part of the message is the signature, which is intended to be delivered to the receiver's mailer as an attachment.

8.4.3 XML encoding

The final ASCII encoding which we shall consider here is the encoding associated with the *Extensible Markup Language (XML)* [271]. XML is a notation originally developed for describing the structure and content of text documents, and is in fact a restricted form of the *Standard Generalized Markup Language (SGML)*,

```
document     ::= prolog element
prolog       ::= [XMLdecl] [doctypedecl]
XMLdecl      ::= "<?xml" VersionInfo [EncodingDecl] "?>"
VersionInfo  ::= "version" "=" """ VersionNum """
EncodingDecl ::= "encoding" "=" """ EncName """

element      ::= EmptyElemTag |
                 Stag content Etag
Stag         ::= "<" Name {Attribute}* ">"
Etag         ::= "</" Name ">"
EmptyElemTag ::= "<" Name {Attribute}* "/>"
content      ::= [CharData] { (element | Ref) [CharData] }*
Ref          ::= EntityRef | CharRef
EntityRef    ::= "&" Name ";"
CharRef      ::= "&#" { digit}+ ";" |
                 "&#x" {hexdig}+ ";"

Name         ::= ( letter | "_" | ":" ) {alfanumc}*
EncName      ::= letter {alfanum}*
Attribute    ::= Name "=" """ { (Ref | notmetac) }*
VersionNum   ::= {alfanumc}+
alfanum      ::= letter | digit | "." | "-" | "_"
alfanumc     ::= alfanum | ":"
letter       ::= "a" | ... | "z" | "A" | ... | "Z"
digit        ::= "0" | "1" | ... | "9"
hexdig       ::= digit | "a" | ... | "f" | "A" | ... | "F"
notmetac     ::= any character except < & or "
```

Fig. 8.7 Syntax of XML documents.
The syntax is given in EBNF, where [x] indicates an optional syntactic element x, while {x}*
indicates a repetition of 0 or more elements and {x}+ a repetition of 1 or more elements.

standardised by ISO [164]. However, XML is now more generally employed for describing hierarchically structured data of any kind, and is therefore convenient for use when exchanging such data between computer systems.

The basic text objects which are exchanged using XML are known as *XML documents*. A simplified syntax for XML documents is shown in Extended BNF (EBNF) notation in Figure 8.7. The full syntax allows a document to include comments, white space, processing instructions, parameterisations, optional sections and other information which we shall not consider here; the complete description can be found in [271].

A well-formed XML document starts with a prolog which identifies the *version* of XML being used and optionally specifies the *character encoding* employed in the document. The default encoding is the Unicode encoding UTF-8 [229], of which the standard US-ASCII encoding is a subset. The prolog is followed by an element, which is the body of the document and specifies its actual content.

The overall structure of the document is hierarchical, and is often described in the form of a tree whose root is the top-level element and whose nodes are the underlying elements. An element may have a content, made up of portions of text ("character data", CharData) or other elements, or it may be *empty*. XML uses *matched tag* encoding, and each element and sub-element is identified by a *tag* referring to the *name* of the element. Empty elements just consist of a tag, EmptyElemTag, possibly containing attributes:

```
<img href="pooh.gif"/>
```

Elements with content start with a *start tag*, Stag, which may also contain attributes, and are terminated by the corresponding *end tag*, Etag. For example:

```
<h1>Pooh's Poem</h1>
<stanza align="right">
    <line>Isn't it funny</line>
    <line>How a bear likes honey?</line>
    <line>Buzz! Buzz! Buzz!</line>
    <line>I wonder why he does?</line>
</stanza>
```

It follows from the requirement of hierarchy that sub-elements must not overlap but be properly nested, as in the case of the elements stanza and line in the example.

The name of an XML element may contain letters, decimal digits and the four special characters point, hyphen, underline and colon. The character colon (":") has a special significance, as it is used to construct names which are qualified by a *prefix* which indicates that the name is taken from a particular *namespace*, i.e. the set of names which are defined in a particular set of definitions. The namespace prefix is used to ensure that names are unambiguous within the scope of one or more XML documents, so that for example the start tags:

```
<goofy>
<loc:goofy>
<ohnonotagain:goofy>
```

refer to goofy elements defined in different contexts (assuming of course that the prefixes loc and ohnonotagain refer to different namespaces).

Generally, each namespace has two identifiers:

1. The *namespace prefix*, a short identifier which can be used as a convenient abbreviation for the full name of the namespace.
2. A long identifier, which is the full name of the namespace, and conventionally has the form of a *URI* (see Section 11.4.1), i.e. an identifier which specifies the name of a system and a path to a resource (typically a file) on that system. When a URI is used as a namespace identifier, it is in fact not necessary that it refer to a real system or to an existing resource. The only requirement is that it is unambiguous in all the contexts in which it will be used. To ensure this in practice, it will usually refer to a system under the control of the originator of the XML element and to a (possibly non-existent) file on this system.

A namespace definition defines the prefix and its equivalent full name. For example:

```
loc="http://phoney.com/fakefile1"
```

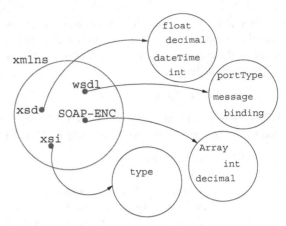

Fig. 8.8 Some common namespaces in XML. The namespace with prefix xmlns contains definitions of the other standard namespaces, which contain definitions of elements and types. Namespaces are here identified by their prefixes. Only a few examples are shown.

defines loc as a prefix which abbreviates "http://phoney.com/fakefile1". The definition is included as an *attribute* of an XML element and is valid throughout that element unless locally overwritten by inner namespace definitions in embedded sub-elements. A common practice is to define such a namespace for each document containing definitions of named XML elements or types. We shall later meet a number of standard namespaces referring to collections of standard types and other definitions for use in XML. For example, the namespace prefix xmlns refers to the namespace for the standard set of XML namespace definitions, and the prefix xmlns:xsd refers to the namespace which contains standard XML type definitions. This is illustrated in Figure 8.8. Since xmlns is the default namespace prefix for namespace definitions, xmlns:xsd can normally be reduced just to xsd. The full rules for disambiguating names with only a partial prefix or no prefix at all can be found in [272].

The desired structure for the document is usually (though not necessarily) specified by the use of a so-called *schema language*; if such a specification is given, the document is required to conform to it. There are many proposals for schema languages for XML, but we shall only consider two possibilities, namely to use:

1. A *Document Type Definition (DTD)*, as defined in the specification of XML version 1.0 [271].
2. An *XML Schema*, as defined in [267, 268].

If a DTD is used, a doctypedecl is included in the prolog of the XML document. The syntax of this is shown in Figure 8.9. Essentially, this offers two possibilities:

1. The DTD can be included locally in the document, as a markupdecl enclosed in square brackets.
2. The DTD (again as a markupdecl) can be in an external file, referred to via a *URI*, which specifies the system on which the file is found and the path to the file.

```
doctypedecl  ::= "<!DOCTYPE"  Name  [ExternalID]
                     [ "["  {markupdecl}*  "]" ] ">"
markupdecl   ::= elementdecl | AttListDecl | EntityDecl

elementdecl  ::= "<!ELEMENT"  Name  contentspec  ">"
contentspec  ::= "EMPTY" | "ANY" | Mixed | children
Mixed        ::= "("  "#PCDATA"  {"|" Name}* ")*" |
                 "("  "#PCDATA"  ")"
children     ::= ( choice | seq ) [repeater]
choice       ::= "(" cp { "|" cp }+ ")"
seq          ::= "(" cp { "," cp }* ")"
cp           ::= ( Name | choice | seq ) [repeater]
repeater     ::= "?" | "*" | "+"
AttListDecl  ::= "<!ATTLIST"  Name  {AttDef}*  ">"
AttDef       ::= Name  AttType  DefaultDecl
AttType      ::= StringType  | TokenizedType | EnumeratedType
DefaultDecl  ::= "#REQUIRED" | "#IMPLIED"    | ["#FIXED"] AttValue
EntityDecl   ::= "<!ENTITY"  Name  Entityvalue  ">"
AttValue     ::= literal
EntityValue  ::= literal
```

Fig. 8.9 Syntax of Document Type Definitions

The content of a DTD consists of a sequence of *markup declarations*, each of which specifies the structure, form or other properties of the elements which may appear in the body of the document. The content of elements may be defined in terms of choices between or sequences of other elements, which may be themselves be choices (indicated by "|"), sequences (indicated by "*" or "+") or optional elements (indicated by "?"). It is also possible to define elements which have no content (EMPTY) or arbitrary content (ANY).

Figure 8.10(a) shows an example of a DTD, as it might appear in a separate file. It describes the structure of documents for use as business cards: Each card contains a description of a person, one or more lines of address, one or more phone numbers and an optional e-mail address. The description of a person is itself a sequence of elements, which specify the person's name, optionally his or her position in the company, and the name of the division of the company in which he or she works. Each of the "terminal" items is here just described as #PCDATA, which essentially just means it is a legal XML character sequence. The hierarchical structure of such business cards is shown in Figure 8.10(b).

The person's name (pname) is associated with two *attributes*: The person's title and professional qualifications, which are optional. In general, an attribute value can be defined as being:

- #IMPLIED: Giving a value for the attribute is optional, and no default is defined.
- #REQUIRED: Giving a value for the attribute is mandatory, and no default is defined.
- A specific value. Giving a value for the attribute is optional, and the specific value is used as default.

(a)   (b)

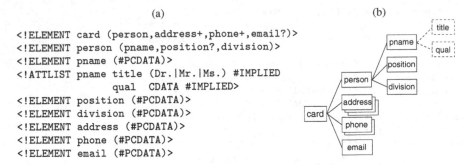

```
<!ELEMENT card (person,address+,phone+,email?)>
<!ELEMENT person (pname,position?,division)>
<!ELEMENT pname (#PCDATA)>
<!ATTLIST pname title (Dr.|Mr.|Ms.) #IMPLIED
                qual  CDATA #IMPLIED>
<!ELEMENT position (#PCDATA)>
<!ELEMENT division (#PCDATA)>
<!ELEMENT address (#PCDATA)>
<!ELEMENT phone (#PCDATA)>
<!ELEMENT email (#PCDATA)>
```

Fig. 8.10 (**a**) A DTD describing the structure of business cards and (**b**) the corresponding structural hierarchy

```
<?xml version="1.0" encoding="UTF-8" ?>
<!DOCTYPE card SYSTEM "card.dtd">
<card>
  <person>
     <pname title="Dr." qual="M.A.,Ph.D.">Phil Anderer</pname>
     <position>Director of Product Enhancement</position>
     <division>Design &amp; Technology</division>
  </person>
  <address>PhoneySpecs Inc.</address>
  <address>28751B Beach Avenue</address>
  <address>Georgetown, Grand Cayman</address>
  <phone>(+1-809)9876-5432</phone>
  <phone>(+1-809)2345-6789</phone>
  <email>phil@phoney.com</email>
</card>
```

Fig. 8.11 A document which conforms to the DTD for business cards

- #FIXED value: Giving a value for the attribute is optional, but if one is given it must be the specific value, which is the default value.

In the case of the title attribute, an explicit choice of allowed values is given. In the case of the qual attribute, any sequence of characters will do. An instance of an XML document which conforms to this DTD is shown in Figure 8.11.

The DTD notation is by now considered a rather outdated schema language, as it does not enable the designer to specify very much about what is allowed and what is not allowed in documents which conform to a given definition. For example, in the case of the business card DTD, it is not possible to specify that the phone number actually has the correct syntax for an international phone number – it just has to be a sequence of characters. Similarly, it is not possible to specify relationships which have to be preserved *between* various parts of the document, for example that a particular element may only appear if another one is also present. The more modern *XML Schema* language is one attempt at rectifying these deficiencies.

A schema in the XML Schema notation describes the structure and type of the elements which make up the document. This can be done at a much greater level of detail than by using a DTD, as the notation permits the definition of types which very precisely describe the values which are allowed to appear in the elements of the document. A *schema* for the business card documents might, for example, be as shown in Figure 8.12. Note that the attributes of the schema element show that this set of type and element definitions is associated with a namespace with prefix xmlns:c and full name "http://phoney.com". This namespace, referred to by the abbreviated prefix c, is used to ensure that references to locally defined type and element names are unambiguous. An XML document which uses this definition to describe an instance of a business card could then look as in Figure 8.13. In the figure, it is assumed that the schema is located in a file cards.xsd as referred to in the schemaLocation attribute in the start tag of the card element.

8.4.4 XML types

The types which may be used to specify entities in XML are described in reference [268], which also explains how new types can be defined in terms of already defined ones. XML types fall into two categories:

1. **Simple types**, whose elements are essentially unstructured values, which can be used as the values of attributes or as "character data".
2. **Complex types**, whose elements may contain attributes or be composed of subelements.

The type name anySimpleType is used to denote the union of all possible simple types, and anyType the union of all possible simple and complex types.

XML Simple Types

A simple type may be:

- An *atomic type*. An element of an atomic type describes a value without distinguishable inner parts, such as an integer, a real, or a string.
- A *list type*. An element of a list type describes a sequence of items of an atomic type.
- A *union type*, composed from two or more atomic or list types. An element of a union type can belong to any of the types included in the union.

Some of the standard simple types available in version 1.0 of XML are summarised in Table 8.10. All the examples in the table are in fact atomic types. The namespace xsd referred to in the type names is the XML standard namespace which contains the definitions of XML Schema Data types.

In XML, types are all defined in terms of a set of basic pre-defined types which are considered *primitive*. Of the simple types given in Table 8.10, those above the

```
<schema xmlns="http://www.w3.org/2001/XMLSchema"
        xmlns:c="http://phoney.com"
        targetNameSpace="http://phoney.com"
        elementFormDefault="qualified">

  <element name="card">
    <complexType>
      <sequence>
        <element ref="c:person"/>
        <element name="address" minOccurs="1" maxOccurs="3" type="xsd:string"/>
        <element ref="c:phone"  minOccurs="1" maxOccurs="2"/>
        <element name="email" type="xsd:string"/>
      </sequence>
    </complexType>
  </element>

  <element name="person">
    <complexType>
      <sequence>
        <element ref="c:pname"/>
        <element name="position" minOccurs="0" maxOccurs="1" type="xsd:string"/>
        <element name="division" type="xsd:string"/>
      </sequence>
    </complexType>
  </element>

  <element name="pname">
    <complexType>
      <element name="personname" type="xsd:string"/>
      <attribute name="title" type="c:titles"    use="optional"/>
      <attribute name="qual"   type="xsd:string" use="optional"/>
    </complexType>
  </element>

  <element name="phone">
    <complexType>
      <sequence>
        <element name="ccode" type="c:countrycode"/>
        <element name="subno" type="c:subscriberno"/>
      </sequence>
    </complexType>
  </element>

  ┌─────────────────┐
  │ Type definitions │
  └─────────────────┘
</schema>
```

Fig. 8.12 An XML Schema description of the structure of business cards.
Definitions of the types titles, countrycode and subscriberno can be found in Figure 8.14.

```
<?xml version="1.0" encoding="UTF-8" ?>
<card xmlns="http://phoney.com"
      xmlns:xsi="http://www.w3.org/2001/XMLSchema-instance"
      xsi:schemaLocation="http://phoney.com   cards.xsd">
  <person>
      <pname title="Dr." qual="M.A.,Ph.D.">Phil Anderer</pname>
      <position>Director of Product Enhancement</position>
      <division>Design &amp; Technology</division>
  </person>
  <address>PhoneySpecs Inc.</address>
  <address>28751B Beach Avenue</address>
  <address>Georgetown, Grand Cayman</address>
  <phone>
    <ccode>(+1809)</ccode>
    <subno>9876-5432</subno>
  </phone>
  <phone>
    <ccode>(+1809)</ccode>
    <subno>2345-6789</subno>
  </phone>
  <email>phil@phoney.com</email>
</card>
```

Fig. 8.13 A document which conforms to the XML Schema schema for business cards

line are primitive. Types such as int, short and negativeInteger are examples of *derived* simple types. In general, an XML type may be derived from one or more other XML types (known as its *base types*) by:

- **Restriction**.
- **List** construction, to give a list type.
- **Union** construction, to give a union type.

The examples in the table are all defined by applying various forms of *restriction* to the primitive type decimal or string: For example, int is derived by selecting those decimal numbers which have zero fractional part and whose integral parts lie in the interval $[-2^{31}.. + 2^{31} - 1]$. Similarly, enumerated types can be defined by selecting a subset of some base type. The required restrictions are defined by specifying the values for one or more *facets* of the base type from which the restricted type is to be derived. Table 8.11 lists the facets available for this purpose.

For example, a type 20Century whose values include the years of the 20th century (1901–2000) could be defined from the base type decimal as shown in Figure 8.14(a). Similarly, a type digraph whose values include all combinations of pairs of (lower or upper case) English letters could be defined as in Figure 8.14(b), and the types required for completing the XML Schema definition in Figure 8.12 could be defined as shown in Figure 8.14(c), (d) and (e). These state that exactly the strings "Dr.", "Mr." and "Ms." can be used as titles, that a country code consists of a plus sign followed by a sequence of decimal digits starting with a non-zero digit, all enclosed in parentheses (for example "(+358)"), and that a subscriber number

Table 8.10 Some built-in simple XML types. The types above the line are *primitive types*, and those below the line are *derived types*, in this case derived from the type decimal or string by various forms of *restriction*.

Type name	Set of values in type	Value examples
xsd:decimal	Decimal fractions, $\mathbb{Q}$	12.345678, -1.23, 10.00
xsd:float	Signed single precision floating point numbers, $\{m \cdot 2^e \mid m \in \{-2^{24}..2^{24}\} \wedge e \in \{-149..104\}\}$	-12.345E3
xsd:double	Signed double precision floating point numbers, $\{m \cdot 2^e \mid m \in \{-2^{53}..2^{53}\} \wedge e \in \{-1075..970\}\}$	-12.3456789E3
xsd:boolean	Boolean values, $\{\text{true}, \text{false}\}$	true
xsd:string	Strings of characters	`"good morning"`
xsd:dateTime	Date/times	2004-04-01T04:05:06
xsd:base64Binary	Base64 encoded binary	GWalP2A=
xsd:hexBinary	Hexadecimal integer	0FB7
xsd:integer	Integers, $\mathbb{Z}$	1256734982471524, -1
xsd:negativeInteger	Negative integers, $\{i \in \mathbb{Z} \mid i < 0\}$	-32768
xsd:nonNegativeInteger	Non-negative integers, $\{i \in \mathbb{Z} \mid i \geq 0\}$	0, 12345671826381
xsd:long	64-bit signed integers, $\{-2^{63}..2^{63}-1\}$	-1, 1234567890
xsd:unsignedLong	64-bit unsigned integers, $\{0..2^{64}-1\}$	0, 1, 1234567890
xsd:int	32-bit signed integers, $\{-2^{31}..2^{31}-1\}$	-1, 1234567
xsd:unsignedInt	32-bit unsigned integers, $\{0..2^{32}-1\}$	0, 123456
xsd:short	16-bit signed integers, $\{-2^{15}..2^{15}-1\}$	-1234, 456, 0
xsd:unsignedShort	16-bit unsigned integers, $\{0..2^{16}-1\}$	1234, 456, 0
xsd:normalizedString	Strings with TAB, CR, LF replaced by SP.	`"  Who   is this?  "`
xsd:token	Strings with leading and trailing space removed and adjacent space characters replaced by single space.	`"Who is this?"`

Table 8.11 Facets for restriction of simple types in XML

Facet	Explanation
length	The number of units of length occupied by values of the type: measured in characters for a string or URI, in octets for a hexBinary or base64Binary value, and in the number of elements for a list type.
minLength	The minimum permitted number of units of length.
maxLength	The maximum permitted number of units of length.
pattern	A Perl-like regular expression constraining the pattern of characters in the lexical representation of the values.
enumeration	An enumerated subset of the base type.
whiteSpace	A rule for handling white space characters in types derived from the string base type: **preserve:** No transformation of white space. **replace:** Replace TAB, CR and LF by SP. **collapse:** After replace, remove leading and trailing space and collapse contiguous sequences of spaces to a single SP.
maxInclusive	Inclusive upper bound of value space.
maxExclusive	Exclusive upper bound of value space.
minInclusive	Inclusive lower bound of value space.
minExclusive	Exclusive lower bound of value space.
totalDigits	Maximum total number of digits.
fractionDigits	Maximum number of digits in fractional part of number.

```
(a)  <xsd:simpleType name="20Century">
       <xsd:restriction base="xsd:decimal">
         <xsd:fractionDigits="0"/>
         <xsd:minExclusive value="1900"/>
         <xsd:maxInclusive value="2000"/>
       </xsd:restriction>
     </xsd:simpleType>

(b)  <xsd:simpleType name="digraph">
       <xsd:restriction base="xsd:string">
         <xsd:length value="2"/>
         <xsd:pattern value="[a-zA-Z]+"/>
       </xsd:restriction>
     </xsd:simpleType>

(c)  <xsd:simpleType name="titles">
       <xsd:restriction base="xsd:string">
         <xsd:enumeration value="Dr."/>
         <xsd:enumeration value="Mr."/>
         <xsd:enumeration value="Ms."/>
       </xsd:restriction>
     </xsd:simpleType>

(d)  <xsd:simpleType name="countrycode">
       <xsd:restriction base="xsd:string">
         <xsd:whiteSpace="collapse"/>
         <xsd:pattern value="\(\+[1-9][0-9]*\)"/>
       </xsd:restriction>
     </xsd:simpleType>

(e)  <xsd:simpleType name="subscriberno">
       <xsd:restriction base="xsd:string">
         <xsd:whiteSpace="collapse"/>
         <xsd:pattern value="[0-9]+(\-[0-9]+)*"/>
       </restriction>
     </simpleType>
```

Fig. 8.14 Simple XML types defined by restriction.
(a) A type including the years from the 20th century. (b) A type including all digraphs of letters from the English alphabet. (c), (d) and (e): Types required for the XML Schema definition of Figure 8.12.

consists of one or more non-empty sequences of decimal digits separated by minus signs (for example "123-4567-22")[4].

---

[4] Note than in patterns, the backslash character is used as an *escape character*, to indicate that the following character is to appear literally in the string, instead of having its usual significance for specifying the pattern. This is necessary if any of the pattern metacharacters \|.-^?*+{}() [] are to be used literally.

XML Complex Types

In contrast to elements of simple types, which contain a single value and no attributes, an element of a complex type may contain attributes and possibly also a
content, which may be made up of one or more individually identifiable sub-parts.
This makes it possible to define complex *structures* in XML and to describe the
content and other properties of instances of these structures.

Figure 8.12 contains a number of examples of definitions of complex types in the
XML Schema notation. *Attribute declarations* specify the name of the attribute, the
type of the value of the atribute, and possibly a usage requirement, which specifies
whether a value for the attribute must be provided. The usage requirement can be
optional (the default), required or prohibited. Attributes can only have simple
types.

The actual content of elements of a complex type is described by a *content model*,
which may be:

- **Empty:** No content can be provided. This is the default.
- **Simple:** Only character data is allowed.
- Defined by a **regular expression:** as a combination of sequences of or choices
  between elements. The elements may be of different types, and may be fully
  defined by name and type or by reference to another element definition. Each of
  them may be qualified by the attributes minOccurs and/or maxOccurs to specify
  respectively the minimum and maximum number of times that they may appear.

The type person in Figure 8.12 is an example of a complex type defined by a
regular expression, in this case a sequence of three elements, of which the first is
defined by reference to the definition of the element pname, and the two others are
defined by name and type. Furthermore, the second one is optional (minOccurs=0
and maxOccurs=1).

A content model which uses sequences can be used to describe structures such
as records (where the elements may have different types or be optional) and arrays. Including choices makes it possible also to describe variant records. No standard schemas for such structures are, however, defined in the specification of XML
Schema [267]. New complex types can, as in the case of simple types, also be derived from already defined complex types by restriction. We shall not go into details
here, but refer you to [267].

Large number of schemas defining complex types have been published, both for
general purposes and in connection with specific applications. We shall in Section 10.6.5 see some examples of the use of XML in connection with access to
distributed objects, and in Section 11.5 how it is used for describing general web
services.

```
(a) <?xml version="1.0">
    <PaymentInfo xmlns="http://clearing.org/payment">
      <Name>Alice Malice</Name>
      <CreditCard>
        <Number>9900 1357 9111 3151</Number>
        <Issuer>Financial Disservices Inc.</Issuer>
        <Expiry>11/07</Expiry>
      </CreditCard>
    </PaymentInfo>

(b) <?xml version="1.0">
    <PaymentInfo xmlns="http://clearing.org/payment">
      <Name>Alice Malice</Name>
      <EncryptedData>
        <EncryptionMethod
            Algorithm="http://www.w3.org/2001/04/xmlenc#aes128-cbc"/>
        <ds:KeyInfo xmlns:ds="http://www.w3.org/2000/09/xmldsig#">
          <ds:Keyname>Alice Malice</ds:Keyname>
        </ds:KeyInfo>
        <CipherData>
          <CipherValue>6tbB9HG4VQbnj7567Gh...</Ciphervalue>
        </CipherData>
      </EncryptedData>
    </PaymentInfo>
```

Fig. 8.15 XML encryption.
(a) The original XML document; (b) The document with the CreditCard element encrypted. Only part of the CipherValue element is shown here.

8.4.5 XML Security

Just as S/MIME offers a set of extensions to MIME which make it possible to ensure security of MIME-encoded data by encryption or by adding digital signatures, so a set of extensions for similar purposes have been defined for XML. XML encryption is described in reference [269], and XML signatures in [270].

Encryption can be applied to entire XML documents or individual elements within these documents. The element to be encrypted is replaced by an EncryptedData element, as illustrated in Figure 8.15(b), where the original document is as shown in Figure 8.15(a). The EncryptedData element contains:

- A CipherData element whose content is the value of the encrypted element in base64 encoding or a reference to an external document containing the encrypted data. Optionally, a reference to the source of the original cleartext, such as the name of the element in the cleartext document or a URI referring to the document, may also be included.
- An optional EncryptionMethod element, containing details of the encryption algorithm used, such as the identity of the algorithm, the size of the keys and so on. The identity of the algorithm is given by referring to a standard URI, as

defined in [269]. For example, the URI in Figure 8.15 is associated with AES using a 128-bit key and CBC encoding of consecutive blocks of data.

• An optional ds:KeyInfo element giving details of the encryption key(s) used. Keys may be specified by referring to the name of a key agreed with the recipient of the document, by passing an encrypted version of the key or by specifying a technique for key agreement, such as the Diffie-Hellman protocol discussed in Section 6.5.

• An optional EncryptionProperties element, giving other properties of the encrypted data, such as a timestamp.

If the optional pieces of information are not included, the recipient is assumed to have pre-knowledge of them.

The application of digital signatures to XML documents is complicated by the need to bring the document into a standard form which is used by both the sender when applying the signature and the recipient when checking it. This is not entirely trivial, since the namespaces used in an XML document may change as the document passes through the network. The process of bringing the document into a standard form is known as *canonicalisation*. The actual signature may envelop the element to be signed, be enveloped within the element or refer to a sibling element in the same document or elsewhere via a URI. An example can be seen in Figure 8.16. As in the case of encryption, the algorithms used for producing the signature, producing the message digest, performing canonicalisation and so on are described by reference to a standard URI, specified in [270]. This example uses an RSA-based signature with SHA-1 message digest (often known as a *PKCS #1* signature [248]), and uses the standard C14N canonicalisation algorithm which is described in [266]. The public key used for the RSA algorithm is here explicitly included. A large number of alternative algorithms and techniques for key transport are described in [270].

Further Reading

There is very little general literature on the principles of protocol encoding, but there are innumerable specific examples of PDU encodings which you might like to study – or which you will need to study if you want to implement a particular protocol. Consult the list of protocols in the references at the end of this book!

In this book we have not considered the Physical layer of the OSI Reference Model in any detail. However, the question of how to code data in the Physical layer is an important one, and there is a large body of literature on the subject, under the general headings of Data Transmission and Coding Theory. This covers areas such as analogue and digital representations of data and their sensitivity to errors. Books on transmission technologies and media, such as radio-, cable- and fibre optic-based systems, often deal with Physical layer encoding as well. Some good general reviews can be found in references [87, 108].

```
<SignatureId="AliceSig"xmlns="http://www.w3.org/2000/09/xmldsig#"/>
  <SignedInfo>
    <CanonicalisationMethod
        Algorithm="http://www.w3.org/TR/2001/REC-xml-c14n-20010315"/>
    <SignatureMethod Algorithm="http://www.w3.org/2000/09/xmldsig#rsa-sha1"/>
    <Reference URI="http://www.maliceworks.org/alice/pay23.xml">
      <Transforms>
        <Transform Algorithm="http://www.w3.org/TR/2001/REC-xml-c14n-20010315"/>
      </Transforms>
      <DigestMethod Algorithm=http://www.w3.org/2000/09/xmldsig#sha1"/>
      <DigestValue>jkI3yzskruB5af2u2Aiaklp4RTo=</DigestValue>
    </Reference>
  </SignedInfo>
  <SignatureValue>MOOcow34AAptathiR=...</SignatureValue>
  <KeyInfo>
    <KeyValue>
      <RSAKeyValue>
        <Modulus>xa7SEU+...</Modulus>
        <Exponent>AQAB</Exponent>
      </RSAKeyValue>
    </KeyValue>
  </KeyInfo>
</Signature>
```

Fig. 8.16 A detached XML signature

Exercises

8.1. Write a computer program which can perform bit stuffing and unstuffing on
HDLC frames. (An alternative exercise would be to design a VLSI chip which could
perform the same functions.) Try to make your implementation as efficient as possible. When you have completed it, measure how fast it runs, in terms of the number
of bits of data which can be stuffed or unstuffed per second.

8.2. The following two bit sequences are received (after removal of bit stuffing)
by a system which uses the HDLC protocol with the standard 8-bit encodings for
the address and control fields, and the 16-bit CRC-CCITT frame checksum. The
leftmost bit in each sequence is the first bit to be received. The individual octets of
the frame have been transmitted according to the usual HDLC convention, with the
least significant bit first.

```
01111110 11000000 01010001 01011100 10000000 01111110

01111110 11000000 00111110 11000010 11001010 00001010
11000011 00101001 01111110
```

What HDLC PDUs have been received?

8.3. A certain computer system represents data in the form of binary trees, which are
represented by a structure with pointers, such that each element in the tree contains a

value, a pointer to the left sub-tree below this element, and a pointer to the right sub-tree below this element. If the relevant sub-tree is not present, the pointer nil is used. Propose a definition in ASN.1 of the type of such trees, if each value is a composite value composed of a natural number, a string (not exceeding 20 characters in length) of characters from the IA5 alphabet, and an optional sequence (of arbitrary length) of signed integers.

8.4. Some computer networks can experience a security problem due to *password sniffing* – listening to the passing traffic until a recognisable login sequence containing a password is transmitted from one system to another. Consider how encryption could be introduced into the system to combat this problem:

1. In the Data Link Layer, if the HDLC protocol is to be used.
2. In the Presentation Layer, if traffic between the users and the remote computers is to be transmitted by use of an Application Layer protocol which describes the data in ASN.1.

Note: To solve this problem, you will need to consider carefully exactly how much of each PDU needs to be encrypted, if encryption takes place in the layer considered, and what effect the alternatives have on the speed and efficiency of the protocol.

8.5. The following data structures described in ASN.1 are a simplified version of some of those used in the ISO/ITU-T directory, whose functions have been introduced in Chapter 7:

Name	*::= RDNSequence*
RDNSequence	*::= SEQUENCE OF RelativeDistinguishedName*
RelativeDistinguishedName	*::= SET OF AttributeValueAssertion*
AttributeValueAssertion	*::= SEQUENCE {AttributeType,AttributeValue}*
AttributeType	*::= OBJECT IDENTIFIER*
AttributeValue	*::= ANY*

These definitions are supplemented with the following association between the actual *OBJECT IDENTIFIER*s used to identify the *AttributeType*s and the actual types of the corresponding *AttributeValue*s:

Attribute	OBJECT IDENTIFIER	Type of AttributeValue
commonName	ds attributeType 3	*caseIgnoreString SIZE(1..64)*
surname	ds attributeType 4	*caseIgnoreString SIZE(1..64)*
countryName	ds attributeType 6	*PrintableString SIZE(2)*
localityName	ds attributeType 7	*caseIgnoreString SIZE(1..128)*
stateOrProvinceName	ds attributeType 8	*caseIgnoreString SIZE(1..128)*
streetAddress	ds attributeType 9	*caseIgnoreString SIZE(1..128)*
organizationName	ds attributeType 10	*caseIgnoreString SIZE(1..64)*
organizationalUnitName	ds attributeType 11	*caseIgnoreString SIZE(1..64)*
title	ds attributeType 12	*caseIgnoreString SIZE(1..64)*
description	ds attributeType 13	*caseIgnoreString SIZE(1..1024)*
telephoneNumber	ds attributeType 20	*caseIgnoreString SIZE(1..32)*
seeAlso	ds attributeType 34	*RDNSequence*

The type *caseIgnoreString* is defined as *CHOICE{T61String, PrintableString}*. The T61 character set is the one used for Teletex transmission, and includes most of the non-Cyrillic characters used in European languages. The Printable character set is the set of upper and lower case letters of the English alphabet, together with the decimal digits, punctuation marks (' ()+,-./:=?) and the character Space.

A person is identified by a *Name* which defines relevant attributes of the person concerned. This must contain the attributes *commonName* and *surname*, and may optionally contain the attributes *description*, *seeAlso*, and *telephoneNumber*. An organizationalPerson is identified by the same attributes as a person, possibly with the addition of the attributes *localityName*, *stateOrProvinceName*, *streetAddress*, *organizationalUnitName* and *title*.

Give an example of an ASN.1 value which could be used as a *Name* for a person. Then give an example for an organizationalPerson.

8.6. In the text, it is stated that the plaintext message part of a `multipart signed` S/MIME entity must be transferred using an encoding which ensures that the message will not be altered during the transfer. Explain why this requirement is necessary. Under which circumstances would `quoted-printable` be a suitable transfer encoding for such messages?

8.7. With the rapidly increasing use of the Internet, there is a good deal of concern that it will soon run out of bandwidth. One factor which affects this is the *efficiency* of the protocols used to transfer information, where by efficiency we here understand the number of bits of useful information transferred divided by the total number of bits transferred.

In this exercise, you are to consider the efficiency of the SMTP protocol, based on the example shown in Figure 8.4. First, work out the efficiency taking only the exchanges at the application level into account, assuming that the entire text of Alfred Bones' message to William Snodgrass (starting "Here are the secret plans...") contains 192 ASCII characters, and that the addresses, embedded mail headers and other details are exactly as shown in the figure. Then repeat the exercise assuming the message contains 4192 characters.

How few bits are required to represent English texts of respectively 192 and 4192 characters? How few bits are required to express the command (HELO, MAIL, RCPT,...) and response (250, 354, 221,...) codes used in the protocol? How many bits are in fact used for these purposes?

Now consider what is going on in the layers below the application layer, and include the effect of these layers in your calculation. Suppose the protocol stack uses TCP in the Transport layer, IPv4 in the Network layer and 100 Mbit/s Ethernet in the Data Link and Physical layers. You may assume that TCP is used as follows:

1. that the TCP connection between the client and server is already set up when the messages shown in the figure are sent.
2. that the receiving TCP entity sends an acknowledgment in response to each data PDU received.
3. that each message from client to server or *vice versa* is sent in a single TCP PDU. (This also means that the actual text message is sent as a single PDU.)

4. that no errors occur, so retransmission is unnecessary.

At the IP level, you may assume that each TCP PDU is dealt with separately, that segmentation is used to ensure that each IP PDU can fit into the payload of a 100 Mbit/s Ethernet PDU, and that the IP header consists of the basic header, together with segmentation information if segmentation is used. You will need to look up the details of the header sizes and maximum payload sizes, if you do not know them.

With all these assumptions, how many bits have to be transmitted in order to complete transmission of Alfred Bones' mail in the two cases considered previously, where the body of the mail contains 192 characters and 4192 characters respectively?

8.8. Harry the Hacker & Co. want their business cards to include both the home address and the business address of their employees. Suggest how the XML schema defined in Figure 8.12 should be modified to describe buisness cards of this type.

8.9. The IT department of the Royal Library of the Kingdom of Wom (which you will know about from Exercise 7.4) stores information about library books in the form of XML documents. Each book is identified by a title, one or more authors, (optionally) one or more editors, a publisher, a publication year and an ISBN number.

Suggest an XML Schema description of the structure of such a document, and give an example of an XML document which conforms to this schema.

Chapter 9
Protocols in the OSI Lower Layers

"I lay the deep Foundations of a Wall ... "
"Æneid"
John Dryden.

Up to now in this book we have taken an abstract view of protocols. The time has now come to look at some more concrete examples. We shall do this by presenting a series of protocols which are in common use for data communication, and by giving an analysis of the protocol mechanisms which they make use of. This presentation will be related to the layers in the OSI Reference Model [133] in which the protocols belong, and will therefore also illustrate typical features and mechanisms in each layer. In this chapter, we shall look at the lowest four layers of the Reference Model, collectively often known as the OSI Lower Layers. These provide services for data transmission, i.e. transport of data between systems without any consideration for the meaning of these data. The top three layers, often designated the OSI Upper Layers, which provide services more oriented towards actual applications of various kinds, will be considered in the next chapter.

The *OSI Lower Layers* comprise the Physical, Data Link, Network and Transport layers of the OSI Reference Model. The aim in all these layers is to provide data transmission services of increasing reliability and scope:

Physical Layer: Bit transmission between systems which are directly connected via a medium.

Data Link: Block transmission between systems which are directly connected via a medium.

Network: Block transmission between systems connected via arbitrary networks, possibly composed from sub-networks.

Transport: Block transmission on an end-to-end basis, such that the properties of the underlying network(s) are hidden.

The Physical Layer protocols are largely concerned with signalling in physical media, and therefore lie outside the scope of this book. The interested reader is referred to one of the many excellent texts on data transmission which are available. We shall consider the remaining layers in turn, taking typical examples of protocols from the layer concerned and using a standard scheme for describing each of them.

9.1 Data Link Layer

9.1.1 Connection-mode

Connection-mode services are favoured within public networks, where the historical influence of the telephone system is very obvious. Thus the typical connection-mode protocols found at this level are link protocols for use over point-to-point links of the type found in the digital or analogue telephone system. In the latter case, suitable modems must be used in the physical layer so that digital data can be sent in analogue form over the physical link.

In fact, although we here speak of point-to-point links, the physical link may well have several parties attached to it, in a so-called *multi-drop* configuration, but in the connection-mode protocols in common use a given instance of communication usually only involves one sender and one receiver. Thus the general requirement is for the data link protocol to offer multiplexing of the physical link. As we have seen in Section 4.5.1, multiplexing may be based on

Centralised control, where one of the parties has responsibility for allocating the shared service to the participating senders.
Distributed control, where all parties are placed on an equal footing.

In the context of connection-mode data link protocols, the party who initiated establishment of the connection is often known as the *primary* part, while the other party (or parties, in the case of a multi-drop configuration) are known as *secondaries*. If the protocol has centralised control, the primary part is the party which exercises the control; it is allowed to initiate data transmission and control functions, whereas the secondary can only respond to the primary.

The example which we shall consider is the ISO High-level Data Link Control (HDLC) protocol. This has one of the widest ranges of applicability, as it can be operated in three *modes*, reflecting different styles of operation of the link:

1. **Normal response mode**, for communication between a primary and one or more secondaries, where the primary has the full responsibility for control of the link, and a secondary may only send to the primary in *response* to being polled by a *command* sent by the primary. This is a typical example of a multiplexing protocol with centralised control.
2. **Asynchronous balanced mode**, for communication between two parties, a primary and a single secondary, who may both initiate data transmission and control functions on an equal footing. Thus both primary and secondary may send commands and responses, and the protocol has distributed control.

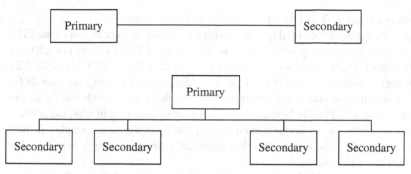

Fig. 9.1 Data link configurations.
Above: Simple point-to-point data link; **Below:** Multi-drop configuration with several secondaries.

3. **Asynchronous response mode**, for communication between a primary and one
   or more secondaries, where only the primary may perform control functions such
   as error recovery and disconnection, but where the secondary may transmit data
   DPDUs as responses without being explicitly polled by a command from the
   primary.

Several other closely-related protocols are also in common use. For example, the
ANSI standard ADCCP is more or less identical to HDLC, while ITU-T's Balanced Link Access Protocol (LAP-B) (used at the data link level of X.25) and
the commercial Synchronous Data Link Control (SDLC) protocol are both more
or less subsets of HDLC. The connection-mode LAN Logical Link Control protocol, ISO/IEEE LLC Type 2 [151], is also very similar to the asynchronous balanced
mode of HDLC.

Protocol example: HDLC (ISO4335) [131].
Service provided: Connection-mode point-to-point full- or half-duplex code
   transparent sequence preserving data transmission.
Assumed underlying service: Physical service permitting full- or half-duplex
   synchronous transmission of bits.
Connection phase: Two-way exchange connection establishment.
Data transfer phase: Two-way simultaneous (in balanced mode) or alternating
   (in other modes) window protocol, using sequence numbers counted *modulo*
   8 (optionally, *modulo 128*). Positive acknowledgments separate (RR or RNR
   DPDU) or piggy-backed on data DPDUs in reverse direction. Go-back-n retransmission initiated by negative acknowledge (REJ DPDU). Selective retransmission initiated by optional selective reject mechanism (SREJ DPDU). Broadcast
   from primary to all secondaries.
Disconnection phase: Two-way exchange protocol for explicit disconnection initiated by primary part. Abort if secondary part becomes inoperative, causing
   emission of Disconnect Mode (DM) DPDU.
Other features: Two-way exchange XID (eXchange IDentifier) sub-protocol for
   discovery of other station addresses and properties.

Two-way exchange TEST sub-protocol for test of stations.

Coding: PDUs delimited by flag fields, with bit stuffing of the content of the PDU to give code transparency with respect to flags. CRC-CCITT (16 bit) or CRC-32 (32 bit) block checksum. *Ad hoc* binary coding of all fields in DPDU (Table 8.2).

Addressing: n-octet address (default: $n = 1$) identifying the party who sends (or is requested to send) the *response*, regardless of which party sends the frame under consideration. Thus in Normal or Asynchronous response modes, the address always identifies the *secondary*, even if the primary is the actual sender. In Balanced mode, the address identifies the (intended) responder, which may be either the primary or secondary.

In each octet, only the 7 most significant bits represent the actual address; a least significant bit with value 1 indicates the last octet in the address. Address 1111111 indicates broadcast from primary to all secondaries, intended for transmitting status messages not requiring a response[1].

Fault tolerance: Corruption of all types of PDU. Loss or duplication of data PDUs. Not tolerant to floating corpses, but these are unlikely since no alternative routes are available between the communicating parties.

9.1.2 Connectionless-mode

Connectionless-mode data link protocols are typically preferred in private systems, such as local area networks, and the principal examples of this type of protocol are LAN protocols for use on a bus or ring LAN. Technically speaking, the Data Link layer in LANs is made up from two sub-layers:

1. The **Medium Access (MAC)** sub-layer, which offers multiplexed access to the Physical layer transmission facilities of the LAN, in general via a multiplexing protocol with distributed control.
2. The **Logical Link Control (LLC)** sub-layer, which, on the basis of an arbitrary MAC sub-layer service, offers a traditional connectionless-mode or connection-mode Data Link service between arbitrary systems attached to the LAN.

Here we shall concentrate our attention on the MAC sub-layer. The standard connectionless-mode LLC protocol, known as the ISO/IEEE LLC Type 1 protocol [151], offers no extra functionality, in relation to the standardised LAN MAC sub-layer services, except an extra level of multiplexing to allow multiple streams of data between the same physical systems. As mentioned above, the corresponding connection-mode LLC protocol, ISO/IEEE LLC Type 2, also described in [151], is very similar to the asynchronous balanced mode of HDLC.

Protocol example: CSMA/CD Local Area Network (ISO8802.3) [152].

---

[1] Multicast addresses are in principle also allowed, but the protocol does not explain how their use is supported.

Table 9.1 IEEE and ISO standardised LAN technologies

IEEE	ISO	Technology
802.3	8802-3	Carrier Sense Multiple Access/Collision Detect (CSMA/CD)
802.5	8802-5	Token Ring
—	8802-6	Distributed Queue Dual Bus (DQDB)
802.9	8802-9	Integrated Services (IS) LAN
802.11	8802-11	Wireless LAN
802.12	8802-12	Demand-priority Access
802.15	—	Wireless Personal Area Networks (WPAN)
802.16	—	Fixed Broadband Wireless Access (FBWA)

Service provided: Connectionless-mode point-to-point or multicast full duplex code transparent data transmission.

Assumed underlying service: CSMA/CD LAN Physical Layer (ISO8802.3).

Connection phase: None.

Data transfer phase: Unacknowledged data transfer.

Disconnection phase: None.

Other features: Statistical time-division multiplexing with distributed control. Collision resolution by random wait with truncated binary exponential backoff.

Coding: Start of DPDU marked by delimiter field. CRC-32 block checksum. *Ad hoc* binary coding of all fields in DPDU.

Addressing: 16-bit or 48-bit flat addressing. Single-station or group addressing.

Fault tolerance: Corruption of data PDUs.

A number of other LAN MAC protocols, which are described in other parts of the ISO8802/IEEE 802 family of standards, are listed in Table 9.1. Notice that several numbers are missing in the table. Some of the missing items cover general topics, such as LAN architecture (802.1), Logical Link Control (802.2) and security (802.10); others have just never become standards or have been withdrawn as obsolete. Many of the standards also come in several variants, for different Physical Layer data rates or different physical media (or both). This is particularly noticeable for the CSMA/CD [152] and the Wireless LAN [155] technologies.

The Token Ring protocol [154] the FDDI (Fibre Distributed Data Interface) protocol [171] and the now obsolete Token Bus protocol [153] use token-based control of access to send on the medium, following the general principles sketched in Exercise 4.10. The differences largely reflect the different physical media used in these types of LAN:

Token Bus: Coaxial cable bus, carrying data at 1, 5 or 10 Mbit/s. The token is in this case passed round a logical ring connecting each station with its logical successor – not necessarily its physical neighbour.

Token Ring: Physical ring based on point-to-point connections between successive stations, using twisted-pair or other cables carrying data at 1, 4 or 20 Mbit/s.

FDDI: Physical ring based on point-to-point connections between successive stations, using fibre optic technology to carry data at 100 Mbit/s.

9.2 Network Layer

9.2.1 Connection-mode

Connection-mode network services are, as in the case of the Data Link layer, preferred in public networks. In addition to having the basic routing functionality required by the OSI Reference Model, they offer a high degree of reliability. This is essentially achieved by duplicating some of the functions, such as the window mechanism for sequence and flow control, which are found in the Data Link layer, so that the same functionality is made available on a network-wide basis rather than just on a neighbour-system basis.

Protocol example: ITU-T X.25 PLP (Packet-level Protocol) [129].

Service provided: Connection-mode point-to-point full duplex code transparent sequence preserving data transmission, with facilities for network reset (resetting a single connection) and restart (clearing all non-permanent connections and resetting permanent connections).

Assumed underlying service: Service provided by ITU-T X.25 LLP (Link-level Protocol), essentially the same as the asynchronous balanced mode of HDLC.

Connection phase: Two-way exchange connection establishment. Multiplexing of several network connections onto a single data link connection and corresponding demultiplexing. Selection of Network Quality of Service (NQOS), sequence number space, maximum NPDU size.

Data transfer phase: Normal data: Two-way simultaneous window protocol, using sequence numbers counted *modulo 8* (optionally, *modulo 128*). Positive acknowledgments separate (RR or RNR NPDU) or piggy-backed on data NPDUs in reverse direction. Optionally, go-back-n retransmission initiated by negative acknowledge (REJ NPDU). Segmentation and reassembly.

Interrupt data: Two-way exchange protocol for data transfer independent of flow control (RR/RNR/REJ) for normal data.

Disconnection phase: Two-way exchange protocol for explicit disconnection initiated by either party. Automatic disconnection after data link exception.

Other features: Two-way exchange Reset sub-protocol for resetting a single connection. Two-way exchange Restart sub-protocol for clearing all non-permanent connections and resetting all permanent connections.

Coding: *Ad hoc* binary coding of all fields in NPDU.

Addressing: Partitioned addressing in accordance with ISO8348 [141]. Single-station addressing only.

Fault tolerance: Loss or duplication of data NPDUs.

9.2.2 Connectionless-mode

Connectionless-mode network protocols are used to give the necessary routing functionality required in the Network layer without the overhead required by connection-mode protocols. There are two well-known protocols of this type, with identical functionality but with different encodings of the NPDU: The Internet/DoD *Internet Protocol (IP)* [210], which is the dominant network protocol in the Internet community, and the ISO *Internet Protocol* [142]. As the use of the term *internet* implies[2], these protocols are specifically designed for data transfer through a system of interconnected networks, which may have different properties with respect to maximum PDU size, security, reliability and so on. Thus the protocols contain features which allow for this, such as *(re-)segmentation*, *route recording* and *source routing*.

Protocol example: Internet Protocol (IP), version 4 [210].

Service provided: Connectionless-mode point-to-point or multicast full duplex code transparent data transmission.

Assumed underlying service: Connection-mode or connectionless-mode Data Link service.

Connection phase: None.

Data transfer phase: Unacknowledged data transfer. Segmentation and reassembly. Optional checksum for PCI fields of NPDU.

Disconnection phase: None.

Other features: NPDU lifetime control via "Time-to-live" counter in PDU. Traffic priority (16 levels). Optional route recording. Optional source routing. Error reporting via separate ICMP protocol if data NPDU is discarded. Optional specification of security requirements.

Coding: *Ad hoc* binary coding of fixed fields in NPDUs, with TLV encoding of optional fields.

Addressing: Partitioned addressing. Single-station or group addressing.

Fault tolerance: Corruption of PCI of NPDUs if optional checksum is used.

Note that, in contrast to the ISO Internet protocol, where error reporting after discard of NPDUs is an integral (though optional) part of the protocol, it is in IP mediated by the *Internet Control Message Protocol (ICMP)* [211]. This is a separate protocol which also provides a number of other administrative functions, including indication of network congestion, exchange of timestamp information, automatic echo to check for liveness of a given destination system, and facilities to collect information about given destinations.

---

[2] Don't get confused: *internet* is a general term used for systems of interconnected networks, as well as being the common name for a specific network system, the Internet, and its associated suite of protocols.

9.2.3 Network Layer Security

After several attempts to introduce security in the Network layer in an *ad hoc* manner, a rapidly increasing number of security failures in the Internet at the start of the 1990s led to the development of more integrated solutions to the problem. In the Network layer, traffic passing through the network is exposed to a number of threats which can be exploited by intruders, including:

- Eavesdropping (at this level often called *packet sniffing*), which may expose logon information, passwords, database contents or other sensitive information to be used by applications.
- Address spoofing, in which intruders create PDUs with false IP addresses (typically false source addresses). This can be used to fool applications into accepting messages in the belief that they come from an authorised source rather than from an intruder.

To counteract these threats, it is necessary to ensure that the Network Service offers *confidentiality* and *authentication*.

A series of Internet standards [233–241] describe how these facilities can be added to the service provided by the Internet Protocol, IP, either in version 4 or version 6. Collectively, these standards are commonly known as *IPsec*. Three basic protocols are defined:

Authentication Header (AH) Protocol: [234] Adds a header containing a sequence number and a MD5 or SHA-1 MAC, in order to ensure authentication and integrity of the IP payload. The MAC is calculated over the IP payload (see below), the Auhentication Header itself, and all the IP header fields which do not change in transit through the network.

Encapsulation Security Payload (ESP) Protocol: [238] Encrypts the IP payload and adds a header containing a description of the selected encryption algorithm, together with optional authentication information. The encryption covers the IP payload (see below) and any padding information used to pad the payload in order (partially) to hide information about traffic flow which could be deduced from the size of the IP PDU.

Internet Security Association and Key Management Protocol (ISAKMP): [240] Used to exchange information about encryption and MAC algorithms, cryptographic keys and other security parameters used in the AH and ESP protocols. IPsec introduces the concept of a *Security Association (SA)*, which is an agreement between two parties, say A and B, about which security parameters to use for traffic in one direction between them. For two-way traffic, an SA is required for each direction. ISAKMP includes facilities for negotiating the parameters of such SAs, including:

- **Key agreement** using a variety of key agreement protocols, including Diffie-Hellman [30], an authenticated version of Diffie-Hellman known as *Oakley* [242], and RSA-based key exchange.
- **Key transport** using X.509 public key certificates [180].

- **Transform specification** to define the desired encryption function and its parameters.
- **Digital signature** to ensure the integrity and guarantee the origin of the ISAKMP information.

IPsec offers two basically different modes of operation, known as *transport mode* and *tunnel mode* respectively. A given SA will work in one of these modes, which is selected when the parameters of the SA are agreed upon. The choice of mode dictates the nature of the payload which is protected by the AH or ESP protocol:

Transport mode: The payload is essentially the Transport layer PDU carried as data in the IP PDU. When IPsec is used together with IPv4, the payload includes all the data which follow the IP header. With IPv6, it also includes any IPv6 extension headers which are present.

Tunnel mode: The payload is an entire IP PDU which is *embedded* as data within an outer IP PDU for transfer through the network. Thus if AH is used, the entire inner IP PDU (including all its header fields) is authenticated; if ESP is used, the entire inner IP PDU is encrypted and optionally authenticated. Typically, the inner PDU is embedded when it reaches a firewall or secure router at the boundary of the (supposedly secure) originating network or sub-network. The entire (inner+outer) PDU is then sent to a corresponding firewall at the boundary of the destination network, where the inner PDU is extracted and sent on to its final destination. The 'tunnel' through which the inner PDU is passed is the link between the two networks, on which the IPsec protocols are used to protect the PDU from manipulation by intruders. This is illustrated in Figure 9.2.

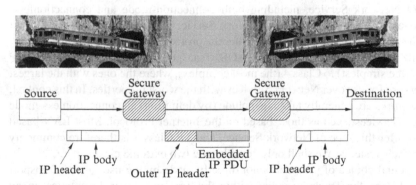

Fig. 9.2 IPsec tunnel mode. Just as the train is protected from view when it is in the tunnel, so the inner PDU is protected by the ESP or AH header when it is embedded in the outer PDU for transfer between two secure systems over an insecure link.

Table 9.2 ISO Transport Quality of Service.

Class	Component(s)
Speed	Delay in establishing connection.
	Throughput (octets/unit time).
	End-to-end transit delay for a TSDU.
	Delay in releasing connection.
Accuracy	Probability of failure in establishing connection, due to misconnection, refusal or excessive delay.
	Residual Error Rate (Section 3.2.4).
	Resilience of connection (probability of unrequested disconnection).
	Probability of transfer failure, i.e. failure to meet the specified throughput, transfer delay or Residual Error Rate values.
	Probability of failure in releasing connection.
Protection	Protection against passive monitoring.
	Protection against modification, replay, addition or deletion.
Priority	Priority for maintaining the requested QOS if the service provider has to degrade the service for some users.

9.3 Transport Layer

9.3.1 Connection-mode

The OSI connection-mode Transport Service (COTS) [137] is intended to offer reliable data transfer (and the associated control) on an end-to-end basis, thus in principle completely hiding the topology, reliability and other properties of the network from the users of the Service. Since it also intended to work over most common types of Network Service, including both connection-mode and connectionless-mode ones, the task of hiding the Network Service's properties is quite a difficult one. The ISO/OSI solution is to use different protocols, depending on the properties of the network. There are in fact five OSI Transport Protocols, known as ISO TP Class 0 (the simplest) to Class 4 (the most complex), where the ones with the largest numbers are for use over Network Services with the worst properties. In this context, poor networks are generally taken to include (by definition) all connectionless-mode Network Services, such as those based on the Internet Protocol. Most LAN-based systems offer this type of Network Service, and TP Class 4 is therefore commonly used in such systems. We shall only consider the two extreme classes here.

The actual choice of protocol is not directly made by the user of the Transport Service, but by the Transport entity within the Transport layer. In practice, many Transport entities only have an implementation of one of the classes, but in cases where there are several classes available, the choice is made on the basis of the Quality of Service (QOS) agreed by the service users when the Transport connection is established, in relation to the QOS of the underlying Network Service. The Transport QOS describes a variety of aspects of the service required, as shown in Table 9.2. Although the figure specifically refers to the Transport layer, a similar set of components is used to describe the QOS in other OSI layers.

Table 9.3 Timers in ISO Class 4 Transport Protocol.

Time	Timer name	Significance
T1	Local retransmission	Maximum time the local T-entity will wait for acknowledgement before retransmitting a TPDU.
R	Persistence	Maximum time the local T-entity will continue to retransmit a TPDU that requires acknowledgement.
L	PDU lifetime	Maximum time between initial transmission of a TPDU and receipt of any acknowledgement concerning it.
W	Window	Maximum time a T-entity will wait before retransmitting up-to-date information about receive window size and position.
I	Inactivity	Maximum time that a T-entity will permit inactivity. If no TPDUs are received within this time, the connection will be broken.

Protocol example: ISO TP0 (ISO8073, Class 0) [138].

Service provided: Connection-mode point-to-point full duplex code transparent sequence preserving data transmission.

Assumed underlying service: Network service in 'Class A': acceptable error rates for both indicated network errors (signalled by the network service by N-RESET indication or similar) and residual (non-indicated) errors.

Connection phase: Two-way exchange connection establishment. Negotiation of Transport Quality of Service (TQOS), sequence number space, maximum TPDU size.

Data transfer phase: Two-way simultaneous window protocol, using sequence numbers counted *modulo 128* (optionally, *modulo 2^{31}*). Positive acknowledgments separately (AK TPDU) or piggy-backed on data (DT TPDU) in reverse direction. Segmentation and reassembly.

Disconnection phase: Automatic disconnection following detection of network disconnection (N-DISCONNECT.ind) or network reset (N-RESET.ind)[3].

Other features: —

Coding: *Ad hoc* binary coding of fixed fields in TPDUs, with TLV encoding of optional fields ('parameters') (Table 8.3).

Addressing: Hierarchical addressing. T-address formed by concatenating *T-selector* onto N-address.

Fault tolerance: Loss or duplication of data (DT TPDUs) or acknowledgments (AK TPDUs).

Whereas the ISO Class 0 protocol provides minimal functionality, and is therefore only suitable for use when the underlying network is comparatively reliable, the Class 4 protocol is designed to be resilient to a large range of potential disasters, including the arrival of spurious PDUs, PDU loss and PDU corruption. To ensure this degree of fault tolerance, the protocol uses a large number of timers, whose identifications and functions are summarised in Table 9.3. The persistence timer is

---

[3] Network restart is assumed to give rise to N-DISCONNECT.ind on all connections.

only conceptual, as R is equal to $T1 \cdot (N-1)$, where N is the maximum number of attempts to retransmit a PDU, as illustrated in Figure 4.9. The significance of $T1$, the local retransmission time, and L, the maximum PDU lifetime, have been discussed in Chapter 4. The window timer is used to ensure that at least some kind of PDU (usually an AK TPDU) is sent every W time units, even if no 'real' traffic is being generated. If no PDUs at all arrive within an interval I, the Network connection is assumed to be broken. Thus the inactivity timer protects against unindicated failures of the network.

Protocol example: ISO TP4 (ISO8073, Class 4) [138].

Service provided: Connection-mode point-to-point full duplex code transparent sequence preserving normal data transmission, together with expedited data transmission without guarantee of sequence preservation.

Assumed underlying service: Network service of arbitrary quality, even 'Class C': unacceptable error rates both for indicated network errors and residual (non-indicated) errors.

Connection phase: Three-way handshake connection establishment. Multiplexing of several transport connections onto a single network connection and corresponding demultiplexing; identification of individual connections by unique pairs of references. Splitting of a transport connection over several network connections and corresponding recombining. Negotiation of Transport Quality of Service (TQOS), sequence number space, maximum TPDU size, use of checksum.

Data transfer phase: Normal data: Two-way simultaneous window protocol, using sequence numbers counted *modulo 128* (optionally, *modulo* 2^{31}). Positive acknowledgments separately (AK TPDU) or piggy-backed on data (DT TPDU) in reverse direction. Dynamic window sizing by credit mechanism on each connection independently of the others, with credit information passed in AK TPDUs. Segmentation and reassembly. Concatenation and separation.

Expedited data: Two-way simultaneous window protocol, using sequence numbers counted *modulo 128* (optionally, *modulo* 2^{31}). Positive acknowledgments separately (EA TPDU) or piggy-backed on expedited data (ED TPDU) in reverse direction. Segmentation and reassembly.

Checksum in all TPDU types if agreed during connection establishment. Recovery after network failure (N-DISCONNECT or N-RESET).

Disconnection phase: Two-way exchange protocol for explicit disconnection initiated by either party.

Other features: Use of timers as indicated in Table 9.3.

Coding: *Ad hoc* binary coding of fixed fields in TPDUs, with TLV encoding of optional fields ('parameters') (Table 8.3).

Addressing: Hierarchical addressing. T-address formed by concatenating *T-selector* onto N-address.

Fault tolerance: Loss, duplication or spurious arrival of data or control TPDUs. Corruption of TPDUs if optional checksum is used. Network service failure (N-DISCONNECT or N-RESET) during any phase[4].

A similar functionality to ISO TP4 is offered by the Internet/DoD *Transmission Control Protocol (TCP)* [212]. Two important differences are that TCP supports a stream oriented service, so window size and credit are measured in *octets* rather than in TPDUs, and that the ISO Expedited data concept, using separate high priority TPDUs, is replaced by a concept of *urgent data*, which can be included as part of ordinary TPDUs. TCP does not have separate types of TPDU for control and data traffic, but incorporates control functions such as connection establishment and release in the form of flags which can be set in the TPDU.

Protocol example: Internet Transmission Control Protocol (TCP) [212].

Service provided: Connection-mode point-to-point full duplex code transparent sequence preserving stream oriented data transmission for normal and urgent classes of data.

Assumed underlying service: Connectionless-mode network service.

Connection phase: Three-way handshake connection establishment.

Data transfer phase: Normal data: Two-way simultaneous stream oriented window protocol, with octets identified by sequence numbers counted *modulo* 2^{32}. Positive acknowledgments piggy-backed on data TPDU in reverse direction. Dynamic window sizing with window size up to 2^{16} by credit mechanism on each connection independently of the others, with credit information (measured in octets) passed in TPDUs. Segmentation and reassembly.

Urgent data: Up to 2^{16} octets passed in separate field at head of data area of TPDU.

1's-complement checksum in all TPDUs covers TPDU header and data.

Disconnection phase: Two-way exchange protocol for explicit termination of data flow in one direction; complete disconnection when flow in both directions is terminated.

Other features: Use of timers for Local Retransmission, PDU Lifetime and Persistence (denoted 'User Timeout'), as in Table 9.3. Time-Wait timer is used to ensure that opposite party receives acknowledgment when closing connection.

Coding: *Ad hoc* binary coding of fixed fields in TPDUs, with TLV encoding of optional fields.

Addressing: Hierarchical addressing. T-address formed by concatenating 16-bit *port number* onto N-address.

Fault tolerance: Loss, duplication or spurious arrival of TPDUs. Corruption of TPDUs.

---

[4] Network restart is assumed to give rise to N-DISCONNECT.ind on all connections.

9.3.2 Connectionless-mode

Connectionless-mode Transport Protocols are favoured for certain styles of application, where there is no requirement for long sequences of data transfers between the
same two parties. For example, the application might involve simple transactions in
which one party sends an enquiry and the other replies to it, but where no single pair
of parties exchange much data. For such purposes, connection-mode protocols will
in general use unnecessarily many resources, and a connectionless-mode protocol is
often preferred.

Protocol example: ISO Connectionless-mode Transport Protocol (ISO8602) [148].
Service provided: Connectionless-mode point-to-point or multicast full duplex
   code transparent data transmission.
Connection phase: None.
Data transfer phase: Unacknowledged data transfer. Optional checksum for TP-
   DUs.
Disconnection phase: None.
Other features: —
Coding: *Ad hoc* binary coding of fixed fields in TPDUs, with TLV encoding of
   optional fields.
Addressing: Hierarchical addressing. T-address formed by concatenating
   T-selector onto N-address.
Fault tolerance: Corruption of data PDUs if optional checksum is used.

The corresponding Internet connectionless-mode transport protocol is known as the
User Datagram Protocol (UDP) [209]. It has the same functionality but a different
encoding.

Further Reading

To find more information about the protocols discussed in this chapter, you should
really look at the original descriptions in the standards, which include full details of
the protocol procedure and encoding. Some information about how to get hold of
the standards can be found in appendix B.

   As remarked previously, it lies outside the scope of this book to deal with protocols in the Physical layer, which are intended to give a service for transmitting
individual bits over a physical medium. However, to get the most out of the literature which exists on the subject, you should be aware of certain basic ideas.
In practical systems, especially public networks, transmission in the physical layer
is very often divided into two parts: Actual transmission on the medium, between
pieces of equipment known as *Data Circuit-terminating Equipment (DCE)s*, and
transmission to the DCE from user equipment, known in this context as *Data Terminal Equipment (DTE)*, or the reverse. The DTE-DCE transmission is generally

described in terms of an *interface*, which has four sets of characteristics: mechanical (the physical arrangement of signal and control leads), electrical (the coding of the bits in terms of voltage changes), functional (the purpose of the various signals which are exchanged) and procedural (the sequence of events for transmitting data). Well-known interface standards include RS-232C, RS-449/RS-422, X.21 and the S- and T-interfaces for the Integrated Services Data Network (ISDN).

Most general texts on data transmission and data networks, deal with the Physical layer protocols in detail. Good general sources on the lower layers are [58] and [120]. More specialised texts are available describing particular types of network, such as local area networks (LANs) [121] and ISDN [55].

Chapter 10
Application Support Protocols

> *"For the fashion of Minas Tirith was such that it was built on seven levels,*
> *each delved into the hill, and about each was set a wall, and in each wall*
> *was a gate.... Up it rose, even to the level of the topmost circle, and there*
> *was crowned by a battlement".*
>
> "The Return of the King"
J. R. R. Tolkien.

The OSI Upper Layers comprise the Session, Presentation and Application layers
of the OSI Reference Model. These rely on the Transport Service to give suitably
reliable end-to-end data transfer, where the degree of reliability is specified by the
Transport Quality of Service demanded by the Transport Service user. With this in
mind, the accent in the protocols within the upper layers is less on fault tolerant data
transfer, and more on providing facilities for supporting a wide range of applications. The layers have the following functionalities:

Session Layer: Dialogue control within a group of two or more application
   processes, including the setting of synchronisation marks in the data streams,
   and roll-back to these marks.

Presentation Layer: Conversion of data structures into representations acceptable to the individual application processes on possibly heterogeneous systems.

Application Layer: Direct support for various types of distributed application.

The OSI protocol suite provides protocols which implement all these layers separately. The Internet protocol suite, on the other hand, has no separate Session and
Presentation protocols, and their functionality is incorporated to the extent necessary
in the Internet Application Layer protocols.

10.1 Session Layer

The OSI Session Service offers dialogue control in a very general sense. Firstly,
it offers its users (and thus ultimately the applications) the possibility of running
several consecutive dialogues with other parties over the same or different Transport

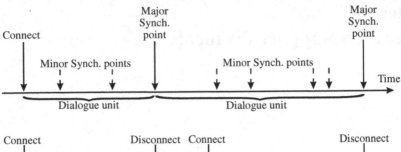

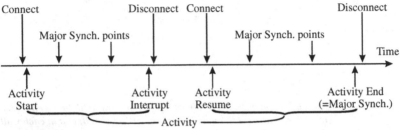

Fig. 10.1 Dialogue units and activities in the OSI Session service.
Above: Dialogue units with major and minor synchronisation points; **Below:** An activity consisting of several dialogue units.

connections, of controlling whether half or full duplex transmission should be used, of dividing the dialogue up into logically separate units, known as *dialogue units* and *activities*, and of setting marks in the data streams associated with such units, so that the users can *resynchronise* the dialogue to one of these marks and have it repeated from there. Two types of mark are distinguished:

1. **Major synchronisation points:** which are set by a confirmed service, as discussed in Section 4.3.2, and which logically separate the data stream 'before' the mark completely from the stream 'after' the mark.
2. **Minor synchronisation points:** which are set by an optionally confirmed service. This does not give the complete separation offered by a major synchronisation point, but usually gives the non-initiator enough information for it to be able to control resynchronisation if required.

In the OSI Session layer, a *dialogue unit* is a part of a two-party dialogue such that all communication within it is completely separated from all communication before and after it. Thus, except in the trivial case where it starts at the establishment of a connection or ends when the connection is broken, a dialogue unit corresponds to the period of activity between consecutive Major Synchronisation points. An *activity* is an even larger unit, composed of one or more dialogue units. These do not have to be consecutive, as an activity may be suspended and subsequently resumed on the same or on another connection. Starting an activity starts a dialogue unit; ending an activity ends a dialogue unit and sets a major synchronisation point. These concepts are illustrated in Figure 10.1.

Table 10.1 OSI Session Service tokens

Token	Effect if available	Effect if unavailable
Data	Owner may send data (half duplex), and be initiator for other services.	Always full duplex, No limitations on other services.
Major/Activity	Owner may be initiator for Major Synch. point or Activity.	No Major Synch. points or Activities.
Synch-minor	Owner may be initiator for Minor Synch. point.	No Minor Synch. points.
Release	Owner may propose disconnection. Non-owner may refuse. *(Negotiated release)*	Both parties may propose disconnection. No negotiated release.

Secondly, as already mentioned in Section 4.4.3, the service uses a mechanism with *tokens* to control the two users' access to various facilities. There are four tokens, each of which may be agreed by the users to be *available* or *unavailable* for the connection when this is set up. The users also agree where the available tokens are initially to be placed, but may subsequently send them to and fro in order to give one another access to the facilities concerned. The meaning of the tokens depends on whether they are available or not, as explained in Table 10.1.

Finally, the service offers several types of data transfer in addition to ordinary data, with a view to allowing small amounts of data to be sent independently of the ordinary data, possibly 'against the rules' which apply to ordinary data. These extra data streams are known as:

1. **Expedited data:** which as usual means data that is guaranteed to arrive not later than ordinary data sent at the same time.
2. **Typed data:** which go against the flow dictated by the half-duplex discipline, if this is used.
3. **Capability data:** which, unlike ordinary data, can be sent when there is no current activity, if activities are used.

The OSI Session Service offers a wealth of facilities, and since all this complexity is often unnecessary (and expensive to implement), the user is given the possibility of selecting which types of facility are wanted: The facilities are grouped into *functional units*, each of which is related to a particular concept in the service, such as the use of resynchronisation, the use of activities or whatever. These functional units are summarised in Table 10.2. Only the *Kernel Functional Unit*, which offers the most basic facilities, is obligatory, while the remaining functional units can be selected as required.

Protocol example: ISO Connection-mode Session Protocol (ISO8327) [140].
Service provided: Connection-mode point-to-point full- or half-duplex code transparent normal and expedited data transmission.

Optional facilities for division of data exchanges on a connection into *dialogue units*, each of which is logically separated from preceding and succeeding dialogue units on the same connection by a major synchronisation point.

Table 10.2 Services and Functional Units in ISO Session Service (after [139]).

Functional Unit	Services
Kernel	Connection establishment
	Normal data transfer
	Orderly release
	User Abort
	Provider Abort
Negotiated release	Orderly release
	Give tokens
	Please tokens
Half-duplex	Give tokens
	Please tokens
Duplex	(No additional service)
Expedited data	Expedited data transfer
Typed data	Typed data transfer
Capability data exchange	Capability data exchange
Minor synchronise	Minor synchronisation point
	Give tokens
	Please tokens
Major synchronise	Major synchronisation point
	Give tokens
	Please tokens
Resynchronise	Resynchronise
Exceptions	Provider exception reporting
	User exception reporting
Activity management	Activity start
	Activity resume
	Activity interrupt
	Activity discard
	Activity end
	Give tokens
	Please tokens
	Give control

Optional facilities for division of data exchanges into *activities*, which can be suspended and restarted on the same or a different connection, or can be abandoned (thus discarding all transmitted data).

Optional facilities for insertion of marks *(synchronisation points)* into the data stream, and rollback *(resynchronisation)* to previously set marks.

Token-based control of right to send data (if half-duplex service is chosen), to set marks, to start new dialogue units or activities and to refuse to clear the connection even though the other party proposes this.

Connection phase: Two-way exchange connection establishment. Negotiation of Session QOS, maximum SPDU size, available functional units, availability of tokens and initial placing of available tokens.

Data transfer phase: Normal data: Two-way simultaneous unacknowledged data transfer if duplex service is chosen; two-way alternating unacknowledged data transfer if half-duplex service is chosen.

Expedited data: Two-way simultaneous unacknowledged data transfer.

Typed data: Two-way simultaneous unacknowledged data transfer.

Capability data: Two-way simultaneous unacknowledged data transfer if duplex service is chosen; two-way alternating unacknowledged data transfer if half-duplex service is chosen.

Disconnection phase: Two-way exchange protocol for explicit disconnection initiated by either party.

Other features: Two-way exchange protocol for major synchronisation points. Unacknowledged or two-way exchange protocol for minor synchronisation points. Two way exchange protocol for resynchronisation.

Unacknowledged protocols for start and resumption of activities. Two-way exchange protocols for interrupting, discarding or termination of activities.

Unacknowledged protocols for transfer of tokens. Unacknowledged or two-way exchange protocol for requesting tokens from the current owner.

Coding: TLV coding of all SPDUs.

Addressing: Hierarchical addressing. S-address formed by concatenating *S-selector* onto T-address.

Fault tolerance: —

10.2 Presentation Layer

The Presentation Layer is responsible for the conversion of data structures into representations which can be used by the application processes on the various systems in a distributed system. A trivial example of this is the conversion of text strings from one character code (say ISO649) to another (say EBCDIC), but in OSI systems, all data structures which can be specified in ASN.1 can be converted into appropriate locally valid representations.

To reduce the number of conversion functions required in a large heterogeneous system, the OSI Presentation Layer is based on the use of a common, machine-independent representation, known as a *transfer syntax*, for representing data which are being transferred between systems. This is illustrated in Figure 10.2. This way of doing things means that, if there are m different types of system, with different local representations, then each of them only needs to have one conversion function (to/from transfer syntax) instead of $(m-1)$. However, it also means that each two parties who wish to communicate must agree on a suitable transfer syntax, which must be capable of expressing all the data structures in the *universe of discourse* used by the application. The structures in this universe are expected to be described by an abstract syntax, and the mapping between this abstract syntax and the transfer syntax is known as the *presentation context*. In OSI examples, the abstract syntax will of course normally be given in ASN.1, and the transfer syntax used will usually be BASN.1.

Protocol example: ISO Connection-mode Presentation Protocol (ISO8823) [157].

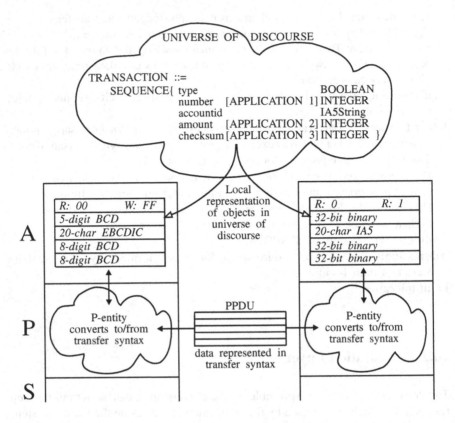

Fig. 10.2 Functioning of the OSI Presentation Layer. The data structures here are specified by an abstract syntax in ASN.1.

Service provided: Connection-mode point-to-point full- or half-duplex code transparent normal and expedited data transmission.

Selection of *presentation context*.

Use of Session layer Activity, Synchronisation point, Resynchronisation, Token passing, Capability Data, Typed Data and Exception sub-services, whose primitives are *passed through* the Presentation layer to (or from) the Session layer.

Connection phase: Two-way exchange connection establishment.

Data transfer phase: Normal data: Two-way simultaneous unacknowledged data transfer if duplex service is chosen; two-way alternating unacknowledged data transfer if half-duplex service is chosen.

Expedited data: Two-way simultaneous unacknowledged data transfer.

Disconnection phase: Two-way exchange protocol for explicit disconnection initiated by either party.

Other features: Two way exchange protocol for selection of new presentation context.

Coding: BASN.1 encoding of all PPDUs.

Addressing: Hierarchical addressing. P-address formed by concatenating *P-selector* onto S-address.

Fault tolerance: —

10.3 Application Layer

The OSI Application layer provides direct support for a variety of common applications in distributed systems. Since it is envisaged that an almost unlimited number of different applications could be of interest within OSI, and that they would have widely differing combinations of requirements, the service offered by the Application layer is put together from a set of modules, known as *Application Service Elements (ASEs)*. This structure is illustrated in Figure 10.3. Formally speaking [172],

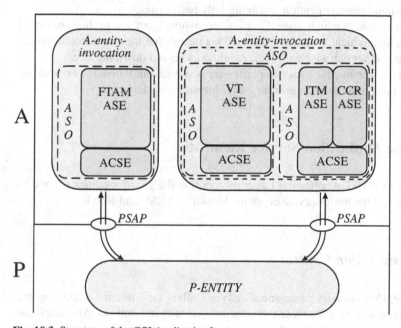

Fig. 10.3 Structure of the OSI Application Layer.

both an ASE and an Application Entity made up of a particular combination of ASEs are considered as *types* of object. Each instance of an ASE type is known as an *ASE-invocation* and each instance of an Application Entity as an *Application-entity-invocation* or *AE-invocation*. Each AE-invocation is made up of one or more *Application Service Objects, ASOs*, each of which is itself composed of one or more smaller ASOs and/or ASE-invocations.

Currently, there are two basic ASEs (Association Control Service Element, ACSE [149], and Remote Operations Service Element, ROSE [169]), and several more specific ones for useful tasks, such as control of commitment, concurrency and recovery (CCR), file transfer (FTAM), virtual terminals (VT), job transfer (JTM), electronic mail (MOTIS/MHS), transaction processing (TP) and so on. Overall management of OSI systems is also based on the use of application layer protocols.

In the figure, two AE-invocations have been activated. One of these is comparatively simple, consisting of a single ASO which is composed of an invocation of ACSE, together with an invocation of one application-specific ASE for file transfer, FTAM. The second AE-invocation is more complex, with an ASO made up of two smaller ASOs, one of them composed of three ASE-invocations and the other of two ASE-invocations.

We shall not consider all Application Layer protocols in detail here, but will concentrate on examples which illustrate various communication patterns in distributed applications. Roughly speaking, we can divide application protocols up into ones which support:

1. Point-to-point communication involving only two parties.
2. Communication in which several parties are involved, but where they are organised in a hierarchical, tree-like manner. This means that they only communicate with one another pairwise with their neighbours up and down the tree.
3. Communication in which several parties are involved, but where they communicate with one another in an arbitrary, non-hierarchical manner.

10.4 Basic Application Service Elements

Most OSI and ITU-T Application Layer protocols make use of facilities offered by one (or both) of the basic service elements known as ACSE and ROSE.

10.4.1 Association Control

ACSE [149, 150] (usually pronounced *'aksee'*) offers facilities for setting up and maintaining *associations* between two application entity invocations. An association corresponds to a connection in the other layers, but for technical reasons[1] another term has to be used. The facilities are very simple, permitting the user of ACSE to set up an association and to release it again. No facilities for data transfer are provided – they are assumed to be supplied by the other ASEs which are used together with ACSE. The service and its protocol can be summarised as follows:

---

[1] In the OSI Reference Model, an (N)-connection is defined as being between two (N)-users in the (N+1)-layer. Since the Application layer is the uppermost layer, there is by definition no '(N+1)-layer' for its users to be in.

Protocol example: ISO ACSE Protocol (ISO8650) [150].

Service provided: Connection-mode pairwise point-to-point facilities for establishment and release of associations.

Selection of *application context*.

Abnormal release initiated by service provider or either user.

Connection phase: Two-way exchange protocol for establishment of association.

Data transfer phase: None

Disconnection phase: Two-way exchange protocol for normal release of association.

Other features: —

Coding: BASN.1 encoding of all APDUs.

Addressing: A-titles for calling and called entities, together with the P-addresses derived from these via a suitable directory, are exchanged in the connection phase.

Fault tolerance: —

10.4.2 Remote Operations

The other basic ISO/ITU-T ASE, ROSE [169], supplements ACSE by offering a toolkit from which various more complex application protocols can be constructed. This makes it radically different from most of the other services discussed here, which offer fixed facilities for specific purposes. Even more radically, whereas most of our other examples are based on peer-to-peer protocols which consider the participants to be equals, ROSE is based on a *Client-Server* model of a distributed system, where there is an asymmetric relationship between the participants: The Client can request the Server to perform some operation, and the Server can send the Client some result (perhaps merely status information), but not *vice-versa*.

By suitably combining these two basic elements in ROSE, almost any Application Layer protocol can be built up. This includes both synchronous protocols, where the initiator waits for a response before issuing a new request, and asynchronous protocols, where it is not necessary to wait. As a simple example, let us consider how ROSE can be used for describing synchronous Remote Procedure Call (RPC) facilities, of the type introduced in Section 4.3.2. These consist just exactly of exchanges in which the Client makes a request and the Server sends a response to this. This is illustrated in Figure 10.4, which shows both a successful and an unsuccessful Remote Procedure Call interaction between a Client and a Server. The actions in the Client and Server in the figure can be considered as elements of the RPC service. These give rise to activation of the ROSE service for sending Client requests and Server responses, leading to the protocol elements shown in the central column of the figure.

In general, the ROSE service allows the Client in its request to *INVOKE* three types of operation, known as:

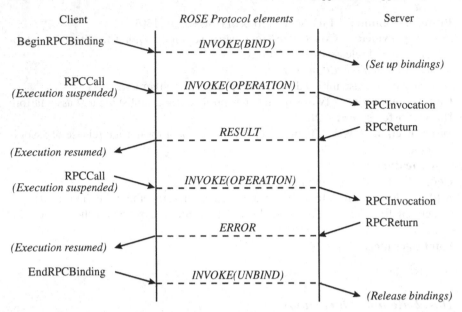

Fig. 10.4 Using ISO/ITU-T ROSE to implement RPC facilities.

BIND,   in which it tells the Server which objects and operations will be referred
to in subsequent invocations.
UNBIND,   in which the most recently performed binding operation is annulled.
OPERATION,   which is to be understood as meaning any other operation mentioned in the currently valid binding.

The Server can give a positive (*RESULT*) or a negative (*ERROR*) response to a previous request from the Client. Finally, either party can *REJECT* the other's request
or response, giving a reason for this rejection. All these service elements are uncon-
firmed.

The protocol used by ROSE [170] is trivial: An unacknowledged APDU bearing
suitable BASN.1-encoded data which describe the request or response is sent from
the Client's to the Server's side or *vice-versa*. Since there is a one-to-one mapping
between ROSE service elements and APDUs, the protocol elements (and their corresponding APDUs) have the same names as the service elements: RO-INVOKE,
RO-RESULT and so on. This has at times caused some confusion between the service and protocol aspects of ROSE, which – it must be admitted – does not fit very
neatly into the usual ISO/OSI pattern of things. We shall refrain from further discussion of this somewhat philosophical point here.

10.5 Commitment, Concurrency and Recovery

Many distributed applications have, like the kind of file manipulation supported by FTAM, a need to ensure reliable access to data from several parallel activities. Simultaneous access to the same data structures, be they files or whatever, can easily give the users inconsistent views of the situation.

A classical example is the case of two simultaneous transactions on the same bank accounts, as illustrated in Figure 10.5. Here, Jones transfers £100 to Smith's account and Evans transfers £50 to Jones' account. An accountant seeing this ex-

Fig. 10.5 Simultaneous transactions on the same accounts. Initially: Smith = £1000, Jones = £2000, Evans = £1500.
What is the final balance on Jones' account?

Transaction A	Transaction B
Smith:= Smith + 100;	Jones := Jones + 50;
Jones := Jones − 100;	Evans:= Evans − 50;

ample would presumably imagine that Jones finishes up with £1950 on his account. However, if you know anything about parallel programming, you probably realise that there are at least two other possible results, depending on the order in which the operations are dealt with. The problem is that, for example, to add or subtract £x from Jones' account, it is necessary first to read the current balance, then evaluate the new balance and update the balance stored in the account. Consistent results will only be obtained if Transaction B is prevented from reading Jones' balance until Transaction A has *completely* finished its update of Jones' account, or *vice versa*.

In such a situation, we therefore require the individual changes on the stored balance to be *atomic actions*. These are actions which are carried out as a whole or not at all, and which exclude other simultaneous actions which read or modify the same data, the so-called *bound data* for the atomic action. This requirement of mutual exclusion, which is often defined by saying that partial results of a sequence of operations are not accessible outside the atomic action, is commonly known as *isolation*. Evidently, isolation implies a need for *serialisation* of atomic actions, so that concurrent actions are in fact performed sequentially.

In the case of bank transactions, we would also want each entire transaction to be atomic. Otherwise we might, for example, debit Jones' account for £100, but (due to some system fault) fail to credit this amount to Smith's account. This is the kind of thing which banks try *very* hard to avoid!

The two examples of atomicity here give rise to three distinct requirements in a distributed system:

Concurrency control is needed to ensure that simultaneous actions on the *same* data (such as Jones' account) take place in a well-ordered and consistent manner, ensuring isolation.

Commitment is needed to ensure that groups of related actions (such as entire transactions) take place as a whole or not at all.

Recovery   is needed to ensure that, if some failure occurs during an atomic action, then the atomic action will be able to progress correctly (to completion or annullment) after the failure has been corrected.

The ISO Commitment, Concurrency and Recovery (CCR) Service Element and its associated protocol [189, 190] are intended to supply this functionality. They are based on the idea that a distributed application involves one or more Application Entities, which initiate atomic actions among one another. These atomic actions may be hierarchically nested, forming a so-called *atomic action tree*, as in Figure 10.6. The figure illustrates a transaction where entity A initiates an atomic action which

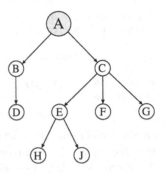

Fig. 10.6 An atomic action tree

involves B and C. In CCR, A is said to be the (immediate) *superior* for B and C, while B and C are said to be A's (immediate) *subordinates*. Similarly, B is the superior for D, C the superior for E, F and G, and E the superior for H and J. The 'top-level' superior in the atomic action tree, here A, is known as the *master*. A superior initiates an atomic action involving its subordinates and is also responsible for initiating commitment when the action is assumed to be complete. Note that, since CCR is basically a point-to-point service, a superior wishing to set up an action tree with several subordinates (such as B and C for A) must set up the branches one at a time.

In CCR, the basic commitment mechanism uses a centralised two-phase commit algorithm. This is supplemented by a mechanism for recovery after failure in the superior or one of the subordinates during commitment of an atomic action, as discussed in connection with **Protocol 16** in Chapter 5. A superior which wishes to initiate recovery after a failure tells all its subordinates that it has previously ordered commitment, and waits for the subordinates to tell it how far they got with the process of commitment. In the CCR protocol, each subordinate may reply DONE, indicating that it has completed commitment, or RETRY-LATER, indicating that it is not yet able to reply, for example because it has lost contact with one of *its* subordinates. Correspondingly, a subordinate which wishes to initiate recovery tells its superior that it had offered to commit, and waits for a reply; the superior can then reply RETRY-LATER or UNKNOWN, where the latter means that no atomic action exists, so that the subordinate should perform rollback.

Protocol example: ISO CCR Protocol (ISO9805) [190].

Service provided: Connection-mode pairwise point-to-point facilities for initiating an atomic action.

Pairwise point-to-point facilities for commitment of an atomic action, including facilities for positive (*READY*) or negative (*ROLLBACK*) response to commitment request from superior, and for recovery after a failure in the superior or subordinate.

Connection phase: None (see below).

Data transfer phase: None (see below).

Disconnection phase: None (see below).

Other features: Two-way exchange protocol for starting new branch, involving two service users, in an atomic action tree at the start of a new atomic action.

Centralised two-phase commit protocol for terminating atomic action by commitment or causing rollback if commitment is unattainable.

Two-way exchange protocol for recovery after a failure during the commitment procedure.

Coding: BASN.1 encoding of all APDUs.

Addressing: A-titles for the master and for the superior of the current branch of the action tree are passed to the subordinate during initiation of an atomic action.

Fault tolerance: Failure of any subordinate before commitment. Communication failure or fail-stop failure of superior or subordinate during commitment procedure.

Note that there are no connection or disconnection phases in the CCR protocol, which relies on the ACSE to establish and break associations between a superior and its subordinates. Moreover, CCR does not itself include data transfer or concurrency control; the application using the CCR service is supposed to know which data are to be bound during a particular atomic action and is supposed to apply some suitable method of concurrency control, such as locking, to ensure exclusive access if required. The ISO CCR service merely offers facilities for ensuring that data *transmitted* between the start of an atomic action and its completion by commitment or abort (rollback) are treated appropriately.

10.6 Client-server Systems

A popular paradigm for the construction of distributed systems is to base them on Client-Server architectures, in which processes acting as *Servers* offer to perform services for other processes acting as *Clients*. We have already seen several simple examples of this style of operation, such the name servers and process servers discussed in Chapter 7, and the SMTP example shown on page 252 in Chapter 8, and we will see several more in the next chapter.

Technically speaking, a server gives its clients the ability to perform a set of operations on an *shared abstract datatype (SADT)*. It is an *abstract* datatype in the sense that the client does not need to concern itself with the way in which the data structures and procedures are implemented. The client merely sees an abstract *interface* to the data structure, giving the procedures which are available. Thus the client-server paradigm is a distributed analogue of the well-known Object Oriented programming paradigm, where the server is an object. This observation leads naturally to the idea that systems can be constructed from hierarchies of servers, as in OO programming. Entire operating systems and large distributed systems have been constructed according to this principle – for example TABS [118], Argus [83] and Camelot.

10.6.1 Remote Procedure Call

An essential element in distributed systems based on the Client-Server paradigm is the *Remote Procedure Call (RPC)* abstraction. This offers an interface which appears to be identical with an ordinary procedure call, but where the called procedure may be in another process in the same machine or on a remote system. RPC was originally defined by Birrell and Nelson [14] as *"the synchronous language-level transfer of control between programs in disjoint address spaces, whose primary communication medium is a narrow channel"*, a definition which stresses three important properties of RPC:

1. The participants are in different address spaces.
2. There is a (logical) channel which permits transfer of data between the participants.
3. Transfer of data is associated with transfer of control, as in activation of ordinary procedures in classical programming languages.

Subsequent work on RPC mechanisms has occasionally deviated from the definition on other points, for example by providing *asynchronous* (non-blocking) rather than *synchronous* (blocking) transfer of control, while the narrowness of the channel depends on the technology used, and can obviously be debated.

   The semantics of actually executing the procedure may in fact deviate from what would be expected with a traditional procedure call, since after a failure in a remote machine it may be impossible to tell whether a message requesting execution of a procedure has been received and acted upon. Repeating the message may cause the procedure to be executed more than once; on the other hand, failing to repeat the message may result in the procedure not being executed at all. It has become conventional to refer to RPC mechanisms as having different *call semantics*, depending on what is guaranteed, as follows:

Exactly-once: The system guarantees that the procedure will return a result after being executed once, just as in a traditional local procedure call.

At-most-once: The system guarantees that the procedure will return a result after being executed not more than once.

At-least-once: The system guarantees that the procedure will return a result after being executed one or more times.

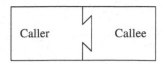

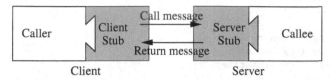

Fig. 10.7 Procedure call (above) and Remote Procedure Call (below)

Maybe: The system makes no guarantees about execution of the procedure or the return of results after a failure.

Exactly-once semantics is unfortunately extremely costly, if not impossible, to achieve in a distributed system; this may make it difficult to ensure that local and remote RPC work in the same way. On the other hand, with at-most-once or maybe semantics there is a risk that the procedure will not be executed at all, while a system with at-least-once semantics will possibly execute the procedure several times. This can be tolerated if the procedure is *idempotent*, i.e. leads to the same result regardless of how many times execution is repeated, whereas it is a problem if the procedure has side effects.

The standard view of a system which uses RPC is shown in Figure 10.7. Both the calling process (the *caller*) and the called procedure (the *callee*) see an interface just as if it were a local procedure being activated. To make this possible when the caller and callee reside in different address spaces, each is extended with a *stub*, which passes the parameters and results to the underlying communication system for transfer between the processes. The caller and its associated stub make up the *client* and the callee and its stub make up the *server*[2].

Stubs perform an activity known as *marshalling* to get parameters and results into a form suitable for transfer as a message via the communication system. This involves transforming data values to an appropriate transfer representation, including the serialisation of complex data structures and (as far as possible) the substitution of pointers by actual values. Correspondingly, the stub at the receiving end *unmarshals* the contents of incoming messages and passes the parameters or results on across the procedure interface.

Stubs are nowadays compiled from descriptions of the interfaces for the procedures to be called, written in an *Interface Definition Language (IDL)*. These descriptions typically have the form of procedure headers or function prototypes, usually tagged with additional information about whether the parameters are to be passed to, from, or both to and from the procedure. An example, in the IDL for CORBA [101],

---

[2] In some RPC-based systems, servers are known as *objects*, to underline the similarity between client-server systems and the caller/object structure characteristic of object oriented systems.

```
typedef unsigned long ACNumber;
typedef unsigned long PINcode;
typedef string        Date;

exception UnknownAC;
exception InvalidPIN;
exception NotEnoughFunds;

interface AC
  struct ACdetails string    owner;
                   long long balance;
                   Date      lasttrans;
                   ;
  void Credit(in  long long Amount);
  void Debit (in  long long Amount) raises( NotEnoughFunds );
  void When  (out Date      latest);
  void Show  (out ACdetails AClist);
;


interface Control
  AC   Access(in  ACNumber  acno,
              in  PINcode   pin  ) raises (UnknownAC, InvalidPIN);
;
```

Fig. 10.8 CORBA IDL description for banking interface

can be seen in Figure 10.8. The CORBA IDL has a syntax based on C++; other IDLs are based on Java, C or other languages. The example shows two interfaces:

- AC, which offers procedures for performing operations on a bank account. The details of this account are described by the structure ACdetails, which contains information about the owner, the current balance and the date of the latest transaction on the account. Operations are provided for crediting the account, debiting the account, finding the date of the latest transaction and returning all the stored account details.
- Control, which offers a single procedure, Access. Given an account number and a personal identification number (PIN code), this returns a reference to an object of type AC which describes the corresponding account.

From the IDL description, the stub compiler generates code in some convenient implementation language, which will marshal and unmarshal arguments and results of the appropriate types in an efficient manner. If a type cannot be dealt with automatically by the compiler, for example because it exploits pointers in some way which the compiler cannot analyse, the user may have to supply a suitable portion of code. Details of this compilation are not really a topic which has much to do with protocol design, however, and the interested reader is referred to the literature elsewhere [51].

10.6.2 Binding

In a system which supports remote operations, clients must be able to find servers offering the interfaces in which they are interested. As discussed in Chapter 7, the client may be provided with the name of the server as an item of 'common knowledge', or may find an appropriate server via a *registry* or *trader*, which maintains a database of available interfaces and the servers which provide them. A registry is itself a kind of specialised server, which typically offers at least four operations to its clients (which are of course the "ordinary" servers and their clients):

bind: Registers a service interface and associates it with a network name or URI.

rebind: Associates a new service interface with an already registered network name or URI.

unbind: Removes information about a service interface with a given network name or URI.

lookup: Obtains a reference to a service interface with a given network name or URI.

bind, **rebind** and **unbind** are used by (ordinary) servers to register their services, while **lookup** is used by (ordinary) clients to find a desired service. In some Client-Server systems, such as ones based on CORBA, a further database known as an *interface repository* is used for storing the interfaces available in the system, including descriptions of the datatypes defined in the IDL for use in the interface.

In many practical RPC systems, the lookup function will also deal with importing the necessary stub code, identifying the client to the server and so on. Sometimes this activity is (rather confusingly) denoted *client binding*, as it sets up a relationship between the client and the server. This is especially important in secure systems, where the server needs to have convincing information about the identity of the client, before it will allow actual RPC calls to be executed. The identity may be supplied in various ways, for example (with increasing security):

- As a *process identifier*.
- As a previously agreed *(identifier,password) pair*.
- As a *digital signature*.

In a secure system, the server will check the identity of the client during client binding, and may also require identity information to be supplied together with each call of a remote procedure.

10.6.3 Asynchronous RPC

The normal, synchronous form of RPC exhibits the traditional flow of control of local procedure calls, and the blocking which this involves in fact makes it easier to implement the necessary inter-process communication, since the client and the called procedure in the server cannot be active at the same time. Nevertheless, the

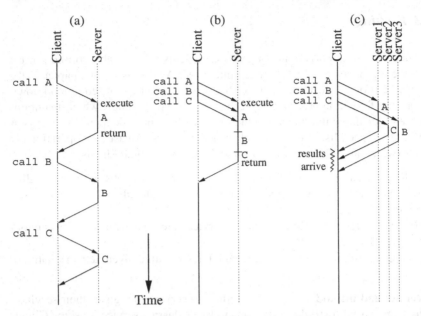

Fig. 10.9 Synchronous and Asynchronous Remote Procedure Call.
(a) Synchronous RPC. Client is blocked (dotted line) during call.
(b) Asynchronous RPC to a single server without return of results. Calls of A, B and C can be
overlapped. The final call of C is synchronous; arrival of the results from C tells the client that all
calls have been dealt with.
(c) Asynchronous RPC to three servers with return of results. Calls can be overlapped. Client data
structures are needed for checking progress and saving results.

lack of parallelism inherent in this form of control has led to a certain interest in
asynchronous RPC, where the client is allowed to continue immediately after sending off a request for execution of a procedure. This is a particular advantage when
the server is on a remote machine, as the time for exchange of call and return messages will then normally be considerable and it often becomes worthwhile to set
several RPC requests going instead of just waiting for them to execute sequentially.
Even more parallelism can be exploited if calls can go to several servers on several
remote machines, as illustrated in Figure 10.9. If both client and processor run on
the same processor, on the other hand, asynchronous RPC is rarely of interest, for
the obvious reason that if the client continues execution after a call, then the CPU is
not available for the server to execute the call.

Asynchronous RPC systems can roughly be divided into systems which return
results and systems which do not. If no results are to be returned, the client must
marshal the parameters and transmit the call message, and can then continue with
whatever it is busy doing. In some systems, to give the client at least a certain possibility of keeping track of what has happened, a sequence of asynchronous RPC
requests to a particular server must be terminated by a normal, synchronous RPC request which 'flushes' the channel to the server. When the result of this synchronous

call is received, the client knows that all the asynchronous requests have been dealt with – though of course the type of call semantics offered by the system will determine the extent to which the called procedures have in fact been executed.

10.6.4 Object Services and Middleware

Systems which support generalised Client-Server architectures, such as the industry standard CORBA or Microsoft DCOM, often offer a number of general purpose services which can be used to support the construction of complex system components. In the case of CORBA, these general purpose services include the previously mentioned trader service, together with services to support concurrency control, security, naming, handling events, handling of persistent objects, transactions and providing a reliable time source. Most of these topics have already been covered in other contexts in this book, and we shall not go into more details here.

Transactions are an especially important topic in object oriented systems [119], as it is necessary to have a strategy for dealing correctly with *nested transactions*. For example, it may make sense for a child transaction to be allowed to abort without forcing the parent transaction to abort. Careful consideration also has to be given to concurrency control if several children may be started at the same time, so that the objects support parallelism. Nested transactions are discussed in [3, 41, 127].

System architectures which involve the use of general purpose services to support applications are often denoted *middleware* architectures. Typically, such systems consist of three elements:

1. A *communication* element, involving layers up to the OSI Transport layer, and providing a reliable service for transfer of messages between systems.
2. A *middleware* element, which offers general support services to applications.
3. An *application* element, which involves the actual application and its user interface.

The purpose of the middleware is to allow applications to be implemented in a platform-independent manner. Thus the middleware is in most cases used to hide not only the network but also the details of the local operating system from the application.

RPC is itself a simple example of middleware. It hides from the application all the details of the messages which have to be sent between the client and server, the way in which these have to be marshalled and unmarshalled and the security mechanisms which are used. More advanced styles of middleware include support for particular application programming paradigms:

Remote Object Invocation (ROI): Offers facilities for activation of methods on objects located on remote systems.
Message Oriented Middleware (MOM): Offers facilities for asynchronous exchange of messages.

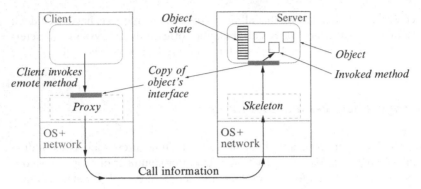

Fig. 10.10 Architecture of a system with Remote Object Invocation

Stream-oriented Communication: Offers facilities for supporting the exchange
of continuous media, such as audio and video, for example in distributed multi-
media applications.

ROI systems, such as *Java RMI* (Remote Method Invocation) are more complex
than plain RPC systems because of the need to pass references to *remote objects*
through a distributed system. The object itself, including all its state, continues to
reside on the server side of the system. On the client side, a so-called *(object) proxy*
is imported from the server. This is illustrated in Figure 10.10. The proxy is the
object-oriented version of the *client-side stub* used in simple RPC systems, and –
like the stub – it offers the same interface to the client as the remote object would.
The server-side stub is in ROI systems often known as the *skeleton*. As in the case
of RPC, it may not be possible to find a suitable marshalling algorithm for *all* types
of object; the type must be *serializable*. Typically, the proxy is set up when *binding*
takes place, and contains code for marshalling, unmarshalling, handling security
and so on. This code is imported from the server, and many ROI systems simply
represent remote object references by network references, which specify the server
name or address and a path to the file on the server containing the proxy code.
For example, the *URIs* used in HTTP and other systems (to be discussed in the next
chapter) are suitable for this purpose. Apart from these differences in representation,
the protocols used in ROI systems are essentially the same as with RPC.

MOM systems, such as IBM's *MQSeries*, offer support for distributed applications which rely on message passing via networks of message queues. Applications
do not need to know about the structure of the underlying communication network
or the addresses of the systems involved, but just see the queues, which are identified
by logical names. The underlying middleware looks after functions such as routing
between queues, translation to appropriate local syntax for data and so on.

Finally, Stream-oriented middleware systems offer functionality for ensuring the
transfer of continuous streams of data, as required in distributed multimedia applications. So-called continuous media, such as video and audio, typically have
isochronous timing requirements. This means that the individual frames or audio

samples must be transferred with an end-to-end delay which lies within a certain *interval*: $[d_{min}, d_{max}]$. This requirement is often called *bounded jitter*. At the same time, the streams have particular bandwidth requirements, which must be fulfilled in order to achieve a given quality of presentation. Middleware to support this type of application needs to ensure that the network and operating system can meet these *Quality of Service (QOS)* requirements in a platform independent manner. This requires the systems involved to exchange information about the currently available bandwidth and the currently achieved QOS, so that resources can be allocated to ensure that the QOS requirements are met.

10.6.5 SOAP

A rather different approach to creating a platform-independent mechanism for supporting remote access to services is to use the *Simple Object Access Protocol*, usually just known as *SOAP*. In simple cases, a remote procedure on a server or a method on a remote object can be activated by sending a *SOAP request* to the object, specifying the procedure or method and its arguments, and the results are returned in a *SOAP response*. In more general cases, information can be passed through several intermediate systems (in SOAP known as *nodes*), which can play different *roles* in processing the information. Two important standard roles are:

- **ultimateReceiver**, where the node is to act as the ultimate destination for the information, as in the case of an RPC server.
- **next**, where the node is to act as an source or relay, which passes on the information to another node, as in the case of an RPC client.

SOAP requests and responses are both examples of *SOAP messages*, and are encoded in the fully platform-independent *Extensible Markup Language (XML)* [271], which has been described in Section 8.4.3. Each SOAP message is syntactically an *XML document*, made up of a *SOAP envelope*, which contains an optional *SOAP header*, typically specifying instructions intended for the various nodes which handle the message, and a mandatory *SOAP body*, intended for the ultimate receiver of the message. The header and body may each contain one or more child elements. The child elements of the header are known as *header blocks*. This hierarchical structure is illustrated in Figure 10.11.

A simple example of a SOAP request is shown in Figure 10.12 on page 313. In this example, we imagine that the method to be activated returns the temperature observed in a named city at a given date and time. The SOAP request is an XML document following the syntax given in Figure 8.7 on page 258, where the body of the document is a SOAP Envelope. A SOAP message must *not* include a DTD, but uses *XML Schema* to describe its structure and content. Both the body and header must (if present) be XML elements. Thus the SOAP Envelope starts with a `<env:Envelope>` start tag and finishes with a `</env:Envelope>` end tag, and

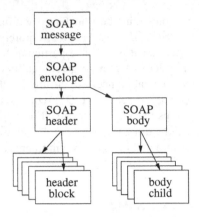

Fig. 10.11 Hierarchical structure of a SOAP message

similarly for the other elements which appear. In version 1.2 of SOAP, messages use two basic namespaces, which by tradition are given the namespace prefixes:

- **env:** which abbreviates the full namespace identifier:

    http://www.w3.org/2003/05/soap-envelope

  This namespace includes definitions for SOAP envelopes and the standard elements within these, such as SOAP headers, bodies and faults.
- **enc:** which abbreviates the full namespace identifier:

    http://www.w3.org/2003/05/soap-encoding

  This namespace includes schemas defining the types used in SOAP and the rules for serialising them.

Further standard namespaces are defined for specific ways of using SOAP, for example for RPC-like applications.

   The basic SOAP types in enc: include all the simple types of XML and a number of SOAP-specific definitions of complex types such as structs and arrays. In SOAP, a *struct* is an XML element with named sub-elements, which themselves can be of any types. Structs are used to model the *structure* or *record* types found in many conventional programming languages. The names of the sub-elements in a struct are significant; their order is not significant. For example:

```
<e:Bibentry>
  <author>Alfons Aaberg</author>
  <title>My life as a latchkey child</title>
  <pubyear>2015</pubyear>
</e:Bibentry>
```

is an instance of a struct type with three elements, two strings and an integer.

   An *array* in SOAP is an ordered sequence of elements. Thus the order of the elements is significant, but the names of the elements are not. The elements may be of the same type, as in:

```
<?xml version="1.0"?>
<env:Envelope xmlns:env="http://www.w3.org/2003/05/soap-envelope">
  <env:Header>
    <t:query xmlns:t="http://www.picopayment.com/query"
             env:encodingStyle="http://www.picopayment.com/encoding"
             env:mustUnderstand="true">   3   </t:query>
  </env:Header>
  <env:Body>
    <m:getTemp xmlns:m="http://www.weathermax.com/">
    <city>Kyoto</city>
    <time>2004-04-01T07:35</time>
    </m:getTemp>
  </env:Body>
</env:Envelope>
```

Fig. 10.12 A SOAP request to invoke a method getTemp with two arguments: *city* and *time*.

```
<Primes enc:itemType="xs:int" enc:arraySize="5">
  <number>2</number>
  <number>3</number>
  <number>5</number>
  <number>7</number>
  <number>11</number>
</Primes>
```

which is an instance of an array with five elements of int type (i.e. an array of type int [5]). Or they may be of different types, as in:

```
<Notes enc:itemType="xs:ur-type" enc:arraySize="4">
  <item xsi:type="xsd:decimal">11.3</item>
  <item xsi:type="xsd:float">-27.517E03</item>
  <item xsi:type="xsd:string">Monday morning</item>
  <item xsi:type="xsd:string">Friday after 3.00pm</item>
</Notes>
```

which is an instance of an array with four elements of mixed types: a decimal fraction, a floating point number and two strings. Note that the type of the array elements is given as xs:ur-type, which denotes *the union of all types* (i.e. "any type").

The SOAP Header, if any, within the Envelope of the request is used to provide information about how the SOAP message is to be handled by the various nodes through which it passes. This may include instructions for how SOAP nodes playing various roles should deal with the message, or contain general information related to the application involved. There can be several header blocks in the header, for example giving instructions for nodes with different roles. In Figure 10.12, the header contains a single block with information related to an accounting mechanism for the weather service: the price in "picounits". The definitions which explain this can be found in the namespace with the t: prefix, specified by the namespace definition:

```
xmlns:t="http://www.picopayment.com/query"
```

SOAP header blocks may have a mustUnderstand attribute with a Boolean value. If the value is true, as in Figure 10.12, then all nodes which are intended to process that header block[3] must understand and process *all* the items specified within the block. Otherwise they must discard the message and cause a fault. Such header blocks are said to be *mandatory*. If the mustUnderstand attribute is absent or has the value false, it is optional whether the relevant nodes can process the block.

The SOAP Body within the Envelope of the request specifies the *method* to be invoked and the *argument values* to be used. This information is described by a single struct or array delimited by tags identified by the name of the method, which is traditionally defined within the namespace with the m: prefix. The full definition of this namespace is typically included in the attributes of the struct or array. In Figure 10.12, a struct with the tag <m:getTemp> is used, and the namespace m: is specified by the namespace definition:

```
xmlns:m="http://www.weathermax.com/"
```

The sub-elements within this struct describe the method's arguments. In the example, getTemp has two arguments, city of type string and time of type dateTime, whose actual values are Kyoto and 2004-04-01T07:35 (i.e. 7:35 in the morning on 1 April 2004) respectively. Note that the types are not given explicitly within the instance of the struct – they are defined by an XML schema in the namespace.

SOAP response messages correspondingly convey return information to the calling system. Responses fall into two categories:

1. **Normal responses**, carrying return values such as function values.
2. **Fault responses**, indicating that the method invocation has failed.

Examples in the case of the getTemp method are shown in Figure 10.13. In the case of a normal response, the SOAP Body contains a single XML struct or array whose tag name is conventionally derived from the name of the invoked method by appending the character sequence Response, here giving the tag <m:getTempResponse>. This element contains sub-elements which describe the values returned from the invocation. The principal return value, if any, of the invoked method is given by an rpc:result sub-element, which refers to the sub-element which actually carries the value: in this example, the temperature sub-element, carrying the value 6.2 of type float. As in the case of the call information, the types of the return values do not appear explicitly in the instance of the struct, but are defined by a schema in the namespace with prefix m:. If the principal return value is void, then the rpc:result sub-element can be omitted.

In the case of a fault response, the SOAP body contains a single XML struct with the tag <env:Fault>, which contains a description of the fault. This description contains at least two XML elements:

1. A Code element specifying a *fault code* which describes the general class of fault;
2. A Reason element containing explanatory text.

In version 1.2 of SOAP, there are five standard fault codes (which are, in fact, the elements of the env:faultCodeEnum enumeration type). These are listed in Table 10.3. Fault elements may optionally contain further information:

[3] Remember that a header block can have an attribute which specifies that it should only be handled by nodes playing a specific role.

```
(a) <?xml version="1.0"?>
    <env:Envelope xmlns:env="http://www.w3.org/2003/05/soap-envelope">
       <env:Header>
          <t:query xmlns:t="http://www.picopayment.com/query"
                   env:encodingStyle="http://www.picopayment.com/encoding"
                   env:mustUnderstand="true">   3    </t:query>
       </env:Header>
          <env:Body>
             <m:getTempResponse
                   env:encodingStyle="http://www.w3.org/2003/05/soap-encoding"
                   xmlns:m="http://www.weathermax.com/"
                   xmlns:rpc="http://www.w3.org/2003/05/soap.rpc">
                <rpc:result>m:temperature</rpc:result>
                <m:temperature>6.2</m:temperature>
             </m:getTempResponse>
          </env:Body>
    </env:Envelope>
```

```
(b) <?xml version="1.0"?>
    <env:Envelope xmlns:env="http://www.w3.org/2003/05/soap-envelope">
          <env:Body>
             <env:Fault>
                <env:Code>
                   <env:Value>env:Sender</env:Value>
                </env:Code>
                <env:Reason>
                   <env:Text xml:lang="en">
                        Too many parameters in call of "getTemp"</env:Text>
                   <env:Text xml:lang="da">
                        For mange parametre i kald af "getTemp"</env:Text>
                </env:Reason>
             </env:Fault>
          </env:Body>
    </env:Envelope>
```

Fig. 10.13 SOAP responses to an invocation of the getTemp method.
(a) Normal response with return value; (b) Fault response due to an error on the caller's side.

Table 10.3 Standard faultcodes in SOAP

Fault Code	Explanation
VersionMismatch	An invalid namespace was referred to in the SOAP Envelope element.
MustUnderstand	A SOAP header block contained a *mustUnderstand* attribute with value true, but could not be understood by the node which should handle it.
DataEncodingUnknown	A SOAP header block or body child element is scoped with a data encoding that the node which should handle it did not support.
Sender	The SOAP request was incorrectly formed or contained insufficient information to enable it to be processed.
Receiver	The SOAP request could not be processed (even though it was correctly formed).

3. A Node element containing a URI which identifies the node on which the fault was detected.
4. A Role element which describes the *SOAP role* of the system where the fault was detected.
5. A Detail element which carries application specific error information.

This additional information is particularly helpful in cases where SOAP is used to support more complex patterns of message passing than simple RPC.

To ensure the security of SOAP messages, digital signatures and/or encryption can be applied to the XML elements which make up the SOAP requests and responses. We have seen in Section 8.4.5 some examples of how this can be done; further details can be found in references [269, 270]. In a SOAP document, it is standard practice to include the security information within the SOAP Header as an XML Security element. This is defined in the XML namespace wsse and includes the signature and/or ciphertext for all or part of the SOAP Body, together with one or more *security tokens* in the form of user ids, X.509 certificates or other forms of authentication which can prove the sender's identity and right to perform the requested operations. Further details can be found in [261, 263, 264].

We shall return in the next chapter to a number of contexts in which SOAP is used in combination with HTTP to offer services through the Internet.

10.7 Security Middleware

Middleware is also a useful solution when security has to be dealt with in applications. General middleware schemes such as CORBA and DCOM have their own security services, but within the Internet protocol suite, a specific suite of support protocols for providing application security has been developed. This is known as *Transport Layer Security (TLS)* [227], and is a further development of version 3.0 of the *Secure Socket Layer (SSL)* protocol suite developed by Netscape Corporation for supporting security in Web-based applications.

There are four elements in the TLS protocol suite, which are positioned in the Internet layered architecture is shown in Figure 10.14. The four elements fall into two groups:

TLS Record Protocol: This is a genuine middleware protocol, inserted between the Transport Layer and the Application Layer, so as to provide a service offering basic *encryption* and *data integrity* services to applications.

TLS Application Protocols: These are three Application Layer protocols which are used to control the operation of the Record Protocol.

Handshake Protocol: Used for client/server *authentication*, and to agree on the desired encryption algorithms and keys for use in the Record Protocol.

Change Cipher Spec Protocol: Used to select the agreed encryption algorithm and keys for use until further notice.

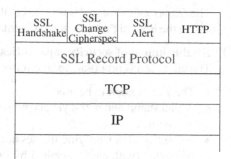

Fig. 10.14 The TLS protocol suite's relation to the OSI layers.

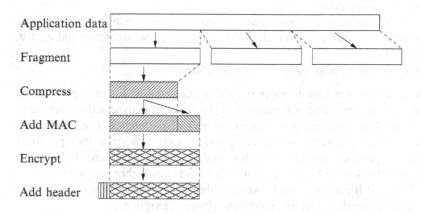

Fig. 10.15 Features of the TLS Record Protocol.

Alert Protocol: Used to transfer information about failures or unexpected events in the operation of the Record and Handshake Protocols.

The *Record Protocol* offers general security facilities which can be applied to Application Layer PDUs. Each APDU to be transmitted is processed by execution of the following steps:

1. *Fragmentation* into blocks of size not greater than 2^{14} bytes.
2. (Optional) *lossless compression.*
3. Addition of a *MAC*, using a shared secret MAC key.
4. *Encryption*, using a shared secret encryption key.
5. Addition of a *header*, which indicates the Application protocol in use: Hand-shake, Change Cipher Spec, Alert or "other application".

This process is illustrated in Figure 10.15. The MAC algorithms currently allowed in TLS are MD5 and SHA-1. The encryption algorithms allowed are all SKCS algorithms, including the block ciphers AES, IDEA with 128-bit keys, RC2 with 40-bit keys, DES with 40- or 56-bit keys, 3DES, and Fortezza with 80-bit keys, and the stream cipher RC4 with 40- or 128-bit keys.

The *Handshake Protocol* is used to establish parameters of the secure connection for use in the Record Protocol. It is a Client/Server protocol with 4 phases as follows:

1. **Establishment of security capabilities:**
   The client sends proposals for the following parameters:

   - The *TLS version* to be used.
   - A timestamp and a 28-byte cryptographically secure random number, for use as a *nonce*.
   - A *Session ID* identifying the session. If the ID is empty, a new session will be started (with an ID supplied by the server in its response). If the ID is not empty, it must identify a session for which cryptographic algorithms and keys have been agreed previously.
   - A list of one or more *CipherSuites*, where each CipherSuite specifies a combination of a *Key exchange* algorithm, an encryption algorithm and a MAC algorithm[4].
   - A list of one or more *compression algorithms*.

   Where the client is able to support several possibilities, for example with respect to the CipherSuite or compression algorithm, it is expected to include all the possibilities in its proposal, listed in order of preference. If a new session is to be started, the server selects one possibility and sends it in its reply to the client. If a previous session is to be resumed, the server is expected to be able to recognise the Session ID and select the CipherSuite and other parameters as used previously; if it cannot do so, it executes the Alert protocol to transfer an error message to the client, and the Handshake Protocol terminates.

2. **Server authentication and key exchange:**
   The server performs the selected key exchange protocol. If an anonymous key exchange protocol, such as the original Diffie-Hellman key agreement protocol described in Section 6.5 on page 184, has been selected, then authentication is omitted. Otherwise the server will first authenticate itself to the client, typically by sending a X.509 certificate. If this does not itself include enough information to establish a shared secret, the server assumes that the client will respond with the necessary information in the next phase of the Handshake Protocol.

3. **Client authentication and key exchange:**
   The client performs the selected key exchange protocol in an analogous manner to the server. If unauthenticated key exchange by the Diffie-Hellman protocol is to be used, the client just replies to the server with Diffie-Hellman parameters in the usual way. If authentication is required, the client sends a certificate. If the certificate does not include sufficient information for the server to determine the shared secret, a suitable key exchange protocol is then performed. This is commonly just a *key transport* protocol, in which the client encrypts the secret using the public key provided in the server's certificate, and sends the encrypted secret to the server. The secret established in this phase of the Handshake Protocol is in

---

[4] In SSL, the combination of the encryption algorithm, MAC algorithm and the necessary keys is known as a CipherSpec. This term is not used in TLS.

fact a *shared pre-secret*, from which the true *master secret* is evaluated by both parties for use in the cryptographic algorithms.

4. **Finish:**

The basic exchange of cryptographic parameters is terminated, and the Change Cipher Spec protocol is executed in order to bring the CipherSuite and keys which have been agreed upon into use.

Using the selected CipherSuite and keys, a final *Finished* message is then sent from the server to the client, including a summary of all the information exchanged during execution of the Handshake Protocol. Since the CipherSuite has now come into force, this summary is encrypted and protected by a MAC. The client is expected to verify that the content of this message agrees with what has in fact been exchanged during the execution of the previous steps of the protocol. The client then sends a similar Finished message to the server, which the server must verify. If the verification succeeds at both sides, the Handshake Protocol terminates; if not, the Alert protocol is used to inform the opposite party that the protocol has failed, and the session is abandoned.

The two other TLS Application Protocols are trivial. The Change Cipher Spec protocol merely involves transmission of a single message from one party to the other, indicating that the agreed CipherSuite and keys are to be taken into use. The Alert protocol involves transmission of a status, information or error message between the two parties.

Further Reading

The Upper Layer protocols described in this chapter are intended to support applications, and a good way to understand them better is to extend your knowledge of distributed applications in general. Distributed databases are an area which it is particularly rewarding to study, since they combine elements of many other application types. In fact, almost all the concepts of Commitment, Concurrency and Recovery and of the more general Transaction Processing originated in one way or another in distributed databases.

An important topic in this connection is *concurrency control*, which we have not gone into in any detail in this book, partly because most of the techniques used originate in centralised systems and have no bearing on protocol mechanisms. There are in fact several styles of concurrency control. The simplest and best known one is to use locks [39] to ensure exclusive access for write operations on data. A typical example of this style is the use of *semaphores* in centralised systems; passing a semaphore by executing a **wait** or **P** operation is equivalent to locking the associated resource. A well-known problem in this style of concurrency control is that deadlock may arise if two transactions are waiting for one another's locks to be freed. Deadlock can be avoided, for example by locking objects in a canonical order, but this usually reduces concurrency severely. The alternative cure is deadlock detection, which may be based on timeouts or on building a *wait-for graph* to discover which transactions are waiting for one another in a mutually cyclic manner. Examples of algorithms for deadlock detection in distributed systems can be found in [22, 23, 88].

A second style of concurrency control is *optimistic control*, as introduced by Kung and Robinson [74]. This exploits the fact that genuine locking conflicts are in fact quite rare, so locking (which in practice gives a substantial administrative overhead) is in most cases superfluous. In optimistic control, no locks are used, but each transaction is checked when it is about to commit, to see whether its read or write operations have conflicted with other transactions. Yet another method is to use *timestamps* on transactions [10]. In rough terms, a write request is only valid if the data item was last read and written by an older transaction; a read request is valid only if the data item was last written by an older transaction. A general review of many of these methods for use in distributed databases can be found in [9].

Chapter 11
Application Protocols

"You know my methods. Apply them.
"The Sign of Four"
Arthur Conan Doyle.

On the basis of the general basic facilities described in the previous chapter, large number of protocols for use in specific applications have been devised, and in this chapter we shall consider some typical ones. The examples will be taken from both the OSI and the Internet protocol suites, and will illustrate various ways in which specific application requirements can be taken into account.

When considering how a protocol for a particular type of distributed application is to be organised, an important factor to take into account is the *pattern of communication* required. There are several basic possibilities:

- **Peer-to-peer** communication. Here, the application makes use of exchanges of information between two parties with equal status (peers).
- **Client-server** communication. Here, two parties are involved, but all initiative comes from the client, and the server merely responds to the client's queries or instructions.
- **Hierarchical** communication. Many parties are involved, but are organised in a tree-like hierarchy, so that all communication takes place between them pairwise, along the branches of the tree.
- **Multi-peer** communication. Many parties are involved, but are all considered peers, so communication can take place between any subset of them.
- **Agent-based** communication. Many parties are involved, and communicate with one another in an adaptive, intelligent manner in an effort to solve a common problem.

We shall see examples of applications which illustrate all these architectures.

11.1 File Transfer

The current generation of file transfer protocols are typical examples of protocols which support point-to-point communication of data at the application program level. The data are in this case files, or portions of files – records, blocks or the like. The aim of this is generally speaking to give an application program on one system the impression that the files on a remote file system can be directly manipulated in the same way as local files can.

In its full generality, this aim is very difficult to achieve, since the range of file systems which exist on different types of machine under diferent operating systems is enormous. Not only do file systems differ markedly in the naming conventions for files, they also offer widely differing ranges of file management operations (for creation, deletion, renaming and so on), and widely differing file structures (sequential, index sequential, blocked, spanned and so on), for which different access methods are required. Thus operations intended for the local file system will in general need to be mapped onto other operations in the remote file system.

11.1.1 ISO File Transfer and Management

A good solution to a major part of this problem is offered by the ISO File Transfer and Management (FTAM) service and its associated protocol [144–147]. Here, all operations on files are expressed in terms of a *Virtual File Store (VFS)*, which is an abstract data type – i.e. a set of data structures and operations on them – which models an idealised file system. The data structures describe:

- The organisation of the data within the file, in terms of a possibly hierarchical structure of individually manipulable *File Access Data Units (FADUs)*,
- The *file attributes* of the file, which describe more or less static properties, such as its name, size, date of creation, accounting information, access control information and so on,
- The *activity attributes* of the file, which describe aspects of the current access to the file, such as the current position for file access, and the currently permitted forms of file access (read, insert, replace, extend or erase), concurrency control restrictions (exclusive, shared or no access), and the size of the units which are to be locked when exclusive access is required – the *locking granularity* (file or FADU).

To perform a file operation on a remote system, the operation must be expressed in terms of operations on the VFS, and a suitable representation of these operations is then transferred to the remote system, where they are interpreted on the real file system there. This is illustrated in Figure 11.1. An obvious advantage of this way of doing things is that only one mapping (between the local operations on the real file system and operations on the VFS) and its inverse are required in each system, instead of one mapping *for each type of remote system.*

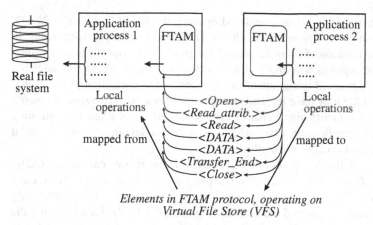

Elements in FTAM protocol, operating on
Virtual File Store (VFS)

Fig. 11.1 Principle of operation of ISO FTAM

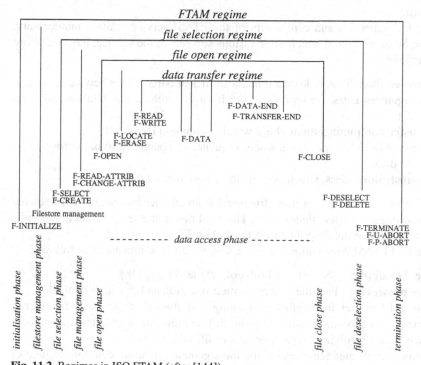

Fig. 11.2 Regimes in ISO FTAM (after [144])

Operations on files in general involve specifying which file is to be used, what kind of access (read/write/...) is required, the position in the file at which access is required and so on. To avoid duplicating all this information in every operation, ISO FTAM works with a scheme of nested *regimes* for setting up the environment within which an operation will be performed. This is illustrated in Figure 11.2. For example, the *file selection regime* is entered by using the *F-SELECT* or *F-CREATE* services in the so-called *file selection phase*. These services respectively result in the selection and creation of a unique named file, to which the operations performed in the embedded regimes will apply. The selection is valid until the file selection regime is left as a result of using one of the services of the deselection phase. While it is selected, the file may have its attributes changed (in a *file management phase*), it may be opened for particular forms of access (in a *file open phase*), positioning and data transfer operations may be performed on it (in a *data access phase*), and it may be closed again (in a *file close phase*).

Likewise, during the data access phase, a data transfer regime can be entered by using the *F-READ* or *F-WRITE* services. The party who initiates entry to this regime then becomes the *initiator* for the data transfer, and can transfer data respectively from or to the currently selected file until the regime is left by the initiator using the *F-TRANSFER-END* service. The actual transfer takes place via a sequence of zero or more *F-DATA* primitives, which bear the data, and is terminated by an *F-DATA-END* primitive.

The full generality and complexity of the FTAM service is often unnecessary, and five *Service Classes*, which offer various sub-sets of the service, have therefore been defined:

1. **Transfer class**, for simple data transfer of files or parts of files between systems.
2. **Management class**, for control of the filestore, without any facilities for data transfer.
3. **Transfer and management class**, which combines (1) and (2).
4. **Access class**, which permits a whole sequence of operations to be performed on remote data.
5. **Unconstrained class**, which permits the whole service to be used.

These service classes are in turn structured from smaller combinations of related facilities, grouped as *functional units*. The facilities in the various functional units and service classes are described in detail in [146].

The ISO FTAM Application Service Element can be summarised as follows:

Protocol example: ISO FTAM Protocol, (ISO8571-3) [146].
Service provided: Facilities for confirmed selection and deselection of files.
    Optional facilities for confirmed opening and closing of files, and for unconfirmed connection-mode point-to-point full- or half-duplex code transparent data transmission involving files or portions of files (FADUs).
    Optional confirmed facilities for file management (creation, deletion, change of attributes).
    Optional facilities for locking at the level of individual FADUs.
Connection phase: None (see below).
Initialisation phase   Two-way exchange protocol for establishment of FTAM regime. Negotiation of FTAM QOS, service class, available functional units, Application and Presentation contexts. Transfer of initiator's identity, accounting information, password.

File selection phase Two-way exchange protocols for selection of an existing file or creation and selection of a new named file. Selection of forms of access (read, insert, replace, extend, erase, read attribute, change attribute, delete) required in the selection regime, and of password control for any or all of these. Selection of form of concurrency control (not required, shared access, exclusive access, no access).

File management phase Two way exchange protocol for reading or making confirmed changes to named file attributes.

File open phase Two-way exchange protocol for opening a file, possibly with selection of new Presentation context (reflecting a new *contents type* for the file), concurrency control, forms of access, recovery mode or locking granularity.

Data access phase: Unacknowledged transfer for initiating a sequence of read or write transfers respectively from or to a remote file. Unacknowledged data transfer. Unacknowledged transfer for terminating a sequence of read or write transfers. Two-way exchange for terminating a read or write sequence.

Two-way exchange protocol for cancelling transfer of a data unit.

If File Access FU is selected, two-way exchange protocols for positioning of file for subsequent access and for deleting portions of a file.

Optional error recovery protocol, using Session layer minor synchronisation point and resynchronisation facilities.

File close phase Two-way exchange protocol for closing currently selected file.

File deselection phase Two-way exchange protocol for deselection of the currently selected file.

Two-way exchange protocol for deletion of currently selected file.

Termination phase Two-way exchange protocol for orderly termination of FTAM regime.

Disconnection phase: None (see below).

Other features: Concurrency control, possibly via use of the CCR ASE (see below). Concatenation and separation of APDUs into PSDU.

Coding: BASN.1 encoding of all APDUs.

Addressing: A-titles for calling and called entities, together with the P-addresses derived from these via a suitable directory, are exchanged in the initialisation phase.

Fault tolerance: Resistance to errors which cause the supporting communication system or the end systems to fail, if the error recovery protocol is used.

Note that FTAM does not itself offer facilities for connection and disconnection. In the OSI Application layer, as discussed above, such facilities are part of the Association Control Service Element (ACSE), which is common for almost all other service elements. The APDUs of the FTAM initialisation phase are exchanged via the ACSE service primitives used to establish the association between the two application processes, and the PDUs of the termination phase are exchanged via the ACSE primitives used to release this association.

11.1.2 Internet FTP

Because it is intended to deal with files of arbitrary structure and content, ISO FTAM is a complex protocol. For use in distributed systems where the file systems are known to be more or less the same in all nodes, simpler protocols are available and are often preferred. The Internet/DoD File Transfer Protocol (FTP) [215] assumes, for example, that a file can be structured:

1. As an unbroken sequence of data bytes (**File** structure).
2. As a sequence of sequential records, separated by newline or carriage return line feed characters (**Record** structure).
3. As a set of independently identifiable pages (**Page** structure).

and that the content of the file can be of one of four types:

ASCII: Characters, which for transfer will be converted to an 8-bit ASCII representation.

EBCDIC: Characters, which for transfer will be converted to an 8-bit EBCDIC representation.

Image or Binary: Contiguous sequences of bits, which for transfer will be packed into 8-bit bytes.

Local: 'Logical bytes' of an arbitrary size specified by the user, each of which for transfer will be sent in a sequence of one or more 8-bit bytes, with padding to fill the last byte of the sequence.

The current structure is selected by using the STRU command, and the type by using the TYPE command. The ASCII and EBCDIC types are particularly intended for efficient transmission of text files between systems which use ASCII and EDCDIC character codes respectively, as no conversion is then actually required. For these two types, three sub-types are also defined, which indicate whether the file is intended to be sent to a printer and, if so, what sort of printer control characters it contains:

Non Print: The file does not contain characters intended for controlling a printer.

TELNET: The file contains ASCII/EBCDIC vertical format controls (CR, LF, NL, VT, FF) which a printer should interpret.

Carriage Control: The file contains ASA Fortran vertical format control characters in the first character of each line.

The protocol enables the user to perform read, write, append, create, delete and rename operations on files and directories – a repertoire which is suitable for many simple applications.

The actual protocol is extremely simple: It consists of a sequence of two-way exchanges between a party acting as a Client and the system containing the file system, which acts as a Server. In each exchange, a *command* identified by a 3- or 4-letter code goes from Client to Server, and an *acknowledgment* containing a 3-digit return code indicating the success or failure of the command is sent back in the other direction. These exchanges take place on a *control channel*; data transfer

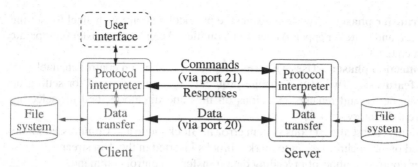

Fig. 11.3 Default configuration of Internet FTP

takes place over a separate *data channel*, which may potentially be connected to a system other than the server. As default, TCP port 21 is used for the control channel and port 20 for the data channel, but the PORT command can be used to select an alternative IP address and/or port number for the data channel. The default system organisation is shown in Figure 11.3.

Data transfer may take place in one of three *modes*, selected by using the MODE command:

Stream mode: This is the default mode. Data are transferred as a stream of octets, which is broken up into convenient sized blocks for transmission via TCP.

Block mode: The file is transferred as a series of data blocks, each of which is preceded by a header giving the type and length of the block. The types are bit encoded, where the individual bits can indicate that the block is the last in a record, the block is the last in the file, the block may contain errors, or the block is a marker block for possible resynchronisation of the data stream after errors.

Compressed mode: The file is transferred as a series of data blocks, where sequences of repeated octets are compressed using replication count compression.

The choice of mode is independent of the structure of the file (File, Record or Page), although it is obviously easier to send, say, a Page structured file in Block mode than in Stream mode.

FTP is, despite everything, a relatively complex protocol, and not all FTP clients or servers offer implementations of all its features. As a minimum, a server *must* offer to transfer files with the ASCII Non-print type, the File and Record file structures, and the Stream mode. As an exercise, you might like to investigate what some of the FTP servers which you have access to can offer.

The Internet FTP protocol can be summarised as follows:

Protocol example: Internet File Transfer Protocol (Internet Standard STD9, RFC959) [215].

Service provided: Connection-mode facilities for file system manipulation and code transparent file transfer between systems.

Other ASEs required: —

Connection phase: Uses TELNET Login procedure on control channel.

Data transfer phase: Two-way exchange protocol on control channel for setting up read and write (or append) operations on files. Actual data transfer on separate data channel.

Disconnection phase: Uses TELNET Logout procedure on control channel.

Other features: Two-way exchange protocol on control channel for setting up create, delete and rename operations on files and directories and for selecting current directory.

Optional restart after serious system error in Block mode and Compressed mode, based on resynchronisation to marker blocks inserted in the data stream.

User-controlled abort of preceding data transfer or control command.

Coding: ASCII encoding of Control-APDUs. Data-APDUs as headerless octet sequences in Stream mode, TLV encoded blocks in Block mode, and TLV encoded blocks with replication compression in Compressed mode.

Addressing: —

Fault tolerance: Resistance to errors which cause one of the participating FTP processes to fail, if the optional restart facilities are used.

Note that FTP, like other Internet Application Layer protocols, incorporates facilities which in an OSI protocol would be provided by the Session Layer (marker blocks, resynchronisation) or Presentation Layer (character set translation, data compression).

11.1.3 Network File System

Somewhat more generality than FTP is offered by the Network File System (NFS™) protocol, which is particularly common in UNIX™ systems. This uses the same basic idea as FTAM, expressing all file operations in terms of operations on an abstract file system, which in this case is merely an idealisation of all *UNIX* file systems, and therefore considerably less general than the VFS used in FTAM. Much of the remaining functionality of FTAM is available in NFS, including facilities for reading and setting file attributes, and for ensuring tolerance to network and file system faults. Important technical differences are that:

1. The actual protocol is based on the use of remote procedure calls.
2. The protocol is *stateless*. This makes it easier to recover from faults, but means that concepts such as the current regime and the currently selected file are absent. Thus each operation on a file must specify all relevant details, such as the file's name, the position for access and so on.
3. Locking and concurrency control are not part of the protocol, but are assumed to be dealt with, if necessary, by the underlying UNIX operating system.
4. Instead of BASN.1, XDR encoding, which does not contain explicit type information, is used for data elements to be transferred.

Some of these differences make the protocol more efficient, while others make it less so, or merely avoid a problem, which then has to be solved by some other means.

However, they do illustrate that there are in general many ways of offering more or less the same functionality to the user.

11.2 Distributed Transaction Processing

Given a suitable foundation, such as the facilities for Commitment, Concurrency and Recovery provided by the ISO CCR ASE, it is possible to build up more general systems to support the use of *transactions*. In this context, a transaction is a set of related operations which enjoys the so-called *ACID* properties:

Atomicity: Each transaction is carried out as a whole or not at all.

Consistency: Each transaction transforms its bound data from one consistent state to another.

Isolation: A transaction does not make partial results of its operations available to parts of the system which are not taking part in the transaction.

Durability: Failures do not affect the result of an already completed set of operations.

As we have seen in the case of CCR, the Isolation rule implies a need for some kind of *concurrency control* which can *serialise* concurrent update operations on the same bound data.

The ISO Distributed Transaction Processing (OSI TP) service and its corresponding protocol [195–197] offer general facilities for fulfilling these requirements. The basic element in OSI TP is the *dialogue*, which involves two users of the service. Thus OSI TP, like CCR, is based on point-to-point communication. If many parties are involved in a transaction, their communication is organised in a hierarchical manner, known as a *dialogue tree*. In the dialogue tree, each branch is a dialogue. The user who initiated this dialogue is known as the *superior* and the other user as the *subordinate*.

A dialogue offers its two participants the basic possibilities of *transferring data* from one to the other, of notifying one another of *errors*, of *terminating* the dialogue in an orderly manner, and of *aborting* the dialogue. Other facilities can be agreed between the participants when the dialogue is set up. For instance, the participants may agree that the dialogue is to have *polarised control*, in which case a token mechanism is used to give one of the participants at a time control over the dialogue, or *shared control*, in which case the two participants have the same capabilities. Likewise, by choosing an appropriate *handshake level*, they may request that a *handshake service* for *synchronising* their activities to mutually agreed processing points be made available.

More importantly, perhaps, the participants can choose whether or not they should be able to use OSI TP's facilities for initiation, commitment and rollback of *transactions* in which they take part. If they do not request access to these facilities, then it is up to the individual *users* of the OSI TP service to provide the functionality needed to achieve the ACID properties for their transactions. Such transactions are known as *application-supported transactions*. This style of transaction might, for example, be used if the application is a database system which already has the appropriate commitment, concurrency and recovery mechanisms incorporated into its DBMS. Transactions which use OSI TP's facilities for transaction support are correspondingly known as *provider-supported transactions*.

If OSI TP's facilities for transaction support are available in a dialogue, the superior for that dialogue can dynamically select whether to use them by choosing an appropriate *coordination level*. A coordination level of COMMIT selects the facilities, and NONE deselects them.

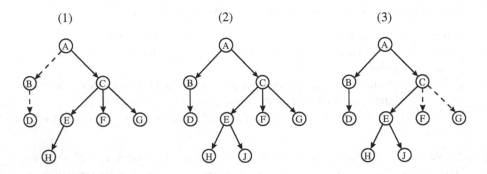

Fig. 11.4 Transaction trees in a dialogue tree. The figure shows a chained sequence of three transactions involving participants A, B,...,J. Dialogues in use for provider-supported transactions are indicated by *full lines* and those not in use by *dashed lines*.

At any one time, a dialogue with coordination level COMMIT can support activities associated with a single transaction in which its participants are involved. These activities are associated with a branch in a *transaction tree*, which describes the hierarchical relationship between all the participants in the transaction, and is in all important respects the same as the atomic action tree used in CCR (Figure 10.6). When a transaction branch is 'pruned' from the transaction tree (normally due to termination of the relevant transaction), the dialogue becomes available for use in another transaction involving the same two participants. Thus in general the transaction tree for a given transaction will be a sub-graph of the current dialogue tree, and there may be several disjoint transaction trees within the same dialogue tree.

In many applications, it is necessary not only to have individual atomic transactions, but sequences of related transactions, perhaps involving different groups of participants. Such sequences are in OSI TP known as *chained sequences* of transactions. Each of the transactions corresponds to a transaction tree in the current dialogue tree, and as the sequence is executed these transaction trees succeed one another in the dialogue tree. These concepts are illustrated in Figure 11.4. Note that the dialogue tree does not need to be static during this process; it may need to grow (by the addition of new dialogues) to accomodate a succession of transactions of increasing size. For example, in order to perform Transaction 2 in Figure 11.4, participant E must extend the dialogue tree by initiating the dialogue between E and J.

For a particular dialogue, a chained sequence is in OSI TP characterised by a succession of transaction branches throughout which the coordination level remains at COMMIT. Separation of chained sequences is achieved by interpolating a period where the coordination level is NONE. This can only be done in OSI TP if facilities for dealing with unchained transaction sequences have been selected for use over the dialogue.

As in the case of FTAM, the full generality of OSI TP is not always needed, and useful sub-sets of the full service can be put together from *functional units*. These sub-sets are intended to support:

1. **Application**-supported transactions.
2. **Chained** provider-supported transactions.
3. **Unchained** provider-supported transactions.

Details of the functional units required for these classes of support can be found in [196].

Protocol example: ISO Distributed Transaction Processing Protocol (ISO10026–3) [197].

Service provided: Connection-mode pairwise point-to-point facilities for distributed transaction processing.

Token-based right to control dialogue operations (except rollback, error reporting and abrupt termination (abort)) via Session layer token mechanism, if Polarised Control FU is selected.

Optional facilities for commitment, using CCR services.

Optional facilities for synchronisation of the activity of two participants by handshake mechanism.

Optional facilities for performing unchained DTP-supported transactions.

Other ASEs required: ACSE and CCR ASE.

Connection phase: None.

Data transfer phase: —

Disconnection phase: None

Other features: Two-way exchange protocol for implementing handshake mechanism for synchronisation.

Coding: BASN.1 encoding of all APDUs.

Addressing: A-titles for initiating and recipient Application entities, and for the corresponding TP users, are exchanged during dialogue establishment.

Fault tolerance: —

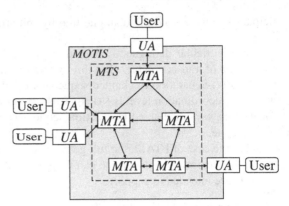

Fig. 11.5 The logical structure of a MOTIS (after [191]). UA are User Agents, which handle the interaction with the users. MTA are Message Transfer Agents in the Message Transfer System (MTS).

11.3 Message Handling

Message handling is the term used to cover various forms of distribution of messages, together with the associated operations of accumulating replies, returning receipts for delivery or indications of non-delivery, and so on. This includes point-to-point electronic mail as a special case.

The general requirement, not always fulfilled in practical systems, is for a reliable distribution system which is resilient to failures, both in the orginal sender, the ultimate addressee and the intervening systems, if any. This may sound like the requirements for any other data communication system, but message handling also involves presentation of the transmitted data in a manner which can be understood by the human reader, and may involve features such as dealing with the names and addresses of registered users of the service or delivery with absolute timing requirements. This means that the protocols involved belong in the Application layer, where such concepts can be handled.

A message handling system is within ISO known as a *Message Oriented Text Interchange System (MOTIS)* [191] and within ITU-T as a *Message Handling System (MHS)*. The abstract architecture for such a system according to ISO and ITU-T is shown in Figure 11.5. The architecture is based on the so-called *User-Agent* model of a distributed system, in which a set of *agents* cooperate to perform some task in a distributed manner. Note that this is substantially different from the architectures on which the previous examples of this chapter have been based, since it is not hierarchical. In the case of a MOTIS, the agents fall into two groups:

User Agents, UA,   which mediate the interaction between the users of the message system and the sub-system which actually transfers the messages.

Message Transfer Agents, MTA,   which cooperate to provide the message transfer service offered by the Message Transfer System, MTS.

In relation to the OSI Reference Model, these agents are all Application Entity invocations.

It should perhaps be pointed out that there are many possible practical realisations of this architecture, ranging from simple systems where the User Agents and Message Transfer Agents are processes within the same physical system, and the users are human beings sitting at dumb terminals, through systems where each UA is built into an intelligent terminal, for example based on a PC, to systems where a powerful front-end contains multiple UAs. Likewise, the MTS may be anything from local interprocess communication to a large public network.

11.3.1 The MOTIS Message Transfer Sub-layer

In relation to the layered OSI Reference Model, the MTS can be regarded as forming a Message Transfer Sub-layer within the Application layer. The service offered by this sub-layer to the User Agents includes all the basic facilities for exchange of messages. Each message is identified by a unique *message identification*, supplied by the MTS. Messages can have various types of contents, for example text, graphics or encoded speech, and the various types may be encoded in various ways. The *content type, encoded information types*, and any conversions performed on the encoding as the message passes through the system, are all passed along with the message. A message will only be passed on to a UA if the UA is registered as being capable of dealing with messages of the given type and encoding. The originating UA may, if necessary, forbid conversion of encodings. The originating and receiving UA may also agree on some form of *access management* to maintain the security of the information exchanged between them.

Messages are time-stamped by the MTS as they pass through the system, and the time that the originating UA submitted the message and the time when it was delivered to the receiving UA are indicated to the recipient. The time taken can be controlled to a certain extent by giving the message a *priority* (known as the *grade of delivery*), which can specify that the message is *urgent* (needing faster delivery than normal) or *non-urgent* (able to tolerate slower delivery than normal). Optionally, the MTS may be asked by the originating UA to *defer delivery* until after a certain date and time, or to cancel the message if it cannot be delivered after a certain *latest delivery time*. The originator may also ask the MTS to cancel a previous message marked for deferred delivery, although this may not always work, as in a distributed system the message may already have been delivered by the time the order to cancel it arrives.

The originating UA can also specify what kind of information about the delivery or non-delivery of the message is required. The default is for the originating UA to be notified of *non-delivery*, and the apparent reason for it. Optionally, this notification can be suppressed, or confirmation of delivery to the destination UA can be supplied. The originator may also request having the contents of any undeliverable message returned to him, and may request each message to be marked with an *audit trail*, which records all the intermediate MTAs through which the message passes.

There are various ways in which distribution of the message may be controlled. Thus the originating UA may specify that the message is to be delivered to several destination UAs, that a named *distribution list* is to be used to specify the destination UAs, or that a given *alternative recipient* may be chosen if delivery to the specified destination UA is not possible. A recipient UA may tell the MTS that messages intended for it are to be *redirected*, and the originator can tell the MTS that a particular message is *not* to be redirected, even if the intended recipient is not at the expected location.

A recipient UA may also tell the MTS that messages, or messages with certain content types or priorities, are to be *held for delivery* until some later time, and may subsequently tell the MTS that it can now accept any held messages.

Finally, an originating UA may use various mechanisms for getting information about the state of the MTS and the other UAs. For example, it can use a *probe* to discover whether a message potentially could be delivered, and it can obtain information about the ability of a remote UA to deal with messages with particular content types or in particular encodings.

An MTA is composed of invocations of three ASEs: A Message Transfer ASE (MTSE) is responsible for the actual message handling, and makes use of facilities offered by an ACSE and a Reliable Transfer ASE (RTSE [167, 168]). MTAs (or, strictly speaking, MTSEs) communicate with one another by the so-called *p1 protocol*. This is illustrated in Figure 11.6. The p1 protocol is a very simple protocol,

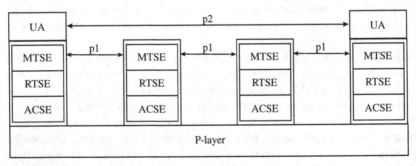

Fig. 11.6 Peer-to-peer protocols in MOTIS/MHS.
p1 is used for communication between MTAs and p2 for communication between UAs. MOTIS/MHS uses two other protocols, which are not strictly peer-to-peer protocols: p3, for communication between a UA and an MTA, and p7, for communication between a UA and a Message Store. These are usually realised as internal interface protocols.

similar in style to the ROSE protocol. It uses the reliable transfer (RT-TRANSFER) facilities of the RTSE to transfer three types of MTS APDU:

1. **Message** APDUs, which carry submitted user messages and all the necessary descriptive information and delivery instructions, as discussed above.
2. **Report** APDUs, which carry information about previously submitted user messages.

3. **Probe** APDUs, which are used to test whether it would be possible to transfer a message of a particular type to a particular recipient, thus implementing the probe facility mentioned above.

Additionally, the RT-OPEN and RT-CLOSE facilities are used to set up the initial bindings when users sign on to the service, and the RT-TURN-PLEASE and RT-TURN-GIVE facilities to control the direction of daa flow by a token mechanism. The RTSE in turn makes use of the underlying facilities in the Presentation and Session layers for token control, activity control and the setting of synchronisation points.

We can summarise the protocol as follows:

Protocol example: ISO MOTIS Message Transfer (p1) Protocol (ISO10021-6, ITU-T X.419) [193].

Service provided: Connection-mode facilities for reliable distribution of messages within an MTS.

Other ASEs required: ACSE and Reliable Transfer ASE.

Connection phase: None.

Data transfer phase: One-way alternating data transfer protocol based on token control of dataflow.

Disconnection phase: None

Other features: Unacknowledged protocol for transfer of token. Application layer routing.

Coding: BASN.1 encoding of all APDUs.

Addressing: A-titles (here known as MTA names) for the calling and responding MTA are exchanged when the initial bindings are set up via the RT-OPEN operation, which is embedded in the operation of establishing the association.

Fault tolerance: —

Note that the p1 protocol does not itself offer any facilities for fault tolerance. These are assumed to be supplied by the Reliable Transfer protocol on which the p1 protocol depends. Note also that the p1 protocol implements facilities for *routing* in the Application layer. This very unusual feature follows from an assumption that the mail system is divided into domains at the user level, and that the names and/or addresses reflect this domain structure, which does not necessarily follow the corresponding structure in the Network layer. For administrative reasons it is desirable to use the mail domains as the basis for routing mail; in fact in many cases this will be obligatory because transfers from one mail domain to another can only take place via specific gateways between domains. Thus mail routing needs to be performed in the Application layer rather than in the Network layer.

11.3.2 The MOTIS Interpersonal Messaging Service

Using the Message Transfer Service, the User Agents can cooperate to offer the users an *Interpersonal Messaging Service, IPMS*, which supplements the Message

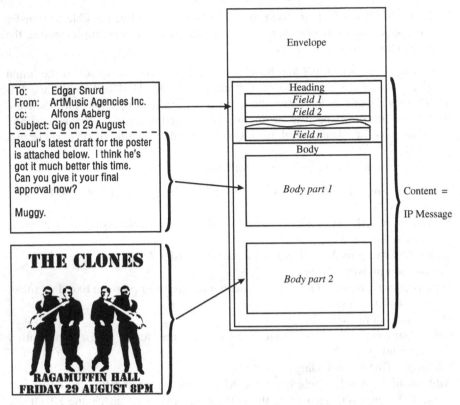

Fig. 11.7 The structure of an Interpersonal Message.

Transfer Service with facilities of a more user-oriented nature. The general form of
an interpersonal message (IPM) is illustrated by the example in Figure 11.7. The
message consists of a *body*, composed of one or more *body parts*, which contain the
actual information to be sent, together with a *heading*, composed of a sequence of
fields in which the originating user supplies information such as his own identification and that of the intended recipient or recipients, the subject of the message, the
priority and security requirements and so on. The body parts may, as in the example
in the figure, be of different types and/or in different encodings, such as ordinary
text in various character sets, encoded speech, or pictures in various graphical representations, such as Group 3 telefax or Videotex. They may also themselves be
interpersonal messages; this facility is used when *forwarding* received messages to
another user.

Replies indicating receipt or non-receipt of interpersonal messages are sent in
interpersonal notifications (IPNs), which are constructed by the IPMS itself, rather
than the users. Each notification consists of a number of *common fields* analogous
to the fields in the IPM heading, together with a set of *receipt fields* indicating the
time of receipt and so on, if the message was received, or a set of *non-receipt fields*

indicating the reason for non-receipt and possibly returning the unreceived message, if the message was not received.

The protocol, known as p2 (Figure 11.6), is very simple. Each interpersonal message is enclosed in an *envelope*, which contains information about the intended recipients, content types, encodings, delivery instructions and so on required by the MTS, and is transmitted to the recipient UA in a MTS Message APDU. Each interpersonal notification is likewise transmitted to its recipient (the originating UA of the message of which it notifies the receipt or non-receipt) in a Report APDU.

Protocol example: ISO MOTIS Interpersonal Messaging (p2) Protocol (ISO 10021-7, ITU-T X.420) [194].

Service provided: Connection-mode facilities for reliable distribution of messages between end-users.

Other ASEs required: MTSE, ACSE and Reliable Transfer ASE.

Connection phase: None.

Data transfer phase: —

Disconnection phase: None

Other features: —

Coding: BASN.1 encoding of all APDUs.

Addressing: A-titles (here known as O/R names) for the originator and intended recipient(s) of each IPM are included in the heading of the IPM and the common fields of the IPN. These O/R names are assumed to follow the X.500 attribute-based naming scheme described in Section 7.1.1. The corresponding O/R addresses (Section 7.2.3) are assumed to be available via an appropriate directory.

Fault tolerance: —

11.3.3 Internet Mail Protocols

Internet mail is based on a slightly different strategy from that seen in MOTIS/MHS, but provides many of the same functions. The strategic difference is that the basic mail distribution protocol transfers mail from the sender's User Agent to a server acting as destination MTA. This server places the mail in a *mailbox* associated with the intended recipient, and a further protocol is used by the recipient's User Agent to extract arriving mail from the mailbox. The architecture of the system is illustrated in Figure 11.8.

The basic protocol for mail distribution is the Internet Simple Mail Transfer Protocol (SMTP) [213], which is designed (like FTP) for use directly over TCP/IP. As in the case of FTP, the protocol is very simple, and consists of a sequence of two-way exchanges between the parties involved in the mail transfer, one of which acts as Client and the other as Server. In each exchange, a *command* identified by a 4-letter code goes in one direction, and an *acknowledgment* containing a 3-digit reply code indicating the success or failure of the command is sent back in the other

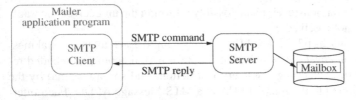

Fig. 11.8 Typical internet SMTP client-server architecture

direction. In the basic SMTP protocol described in [213], commands were provided which enable the user to:

- Sign on as Client to initiate a mail transfer dialogue (HELO).
- Give the address to which replies are to be sent (MAIL).
- Verify a user name (VRFY). The recipient replies with the full name and mailbox address of the given user.
- Expand distribution lists (EXPN). The recipient replies with a list of user names and mailbox addresses.
- Specify a destination address for a message (RCPT); several RCPT commands may be given for the same message, making it is possible to send it to several recipients.
- Send the text of a message (DATA); this message can only be a portion of text in the US ASCII character set, in a 7-bit representation.
- Terminate the current dialogue (QUIT).

Reply codes between 200 and 299 indicate that the requested action has been successfully completed; 300–399 indicate that the command was accepted, but more information is needed to complete the action; 400–499 indicate a temporary error condition, where it may be meaningful to try to send the command again, and 500–599 indicate a permanent error condition, such as a missing mailbox, where it currently makes no sense to send the command again.

An example of the exchanges involved in the use of basic SMTP has been shown in Figure 8.4. As in the case of the MOTIS/MHS Interpersonal Messaging Service, the actual message (sent after the DATA command) consists of a *header*, made up of a sequence of *header fields*, followed by a *body*, containing the actual information to be sent. The header fields may include such information as the time of submission of the message, the identification of the sender, the intended recipient(s) for the message and for any replies generated, the subject of the message, and references to previous messages which are in some way related to this one. The originating MTA is expected automatically to add a header field with a unique reference number to identify the message, and any MTA which receives the message is expected to add a further field which states where the message was received from.

Subsequently, a substantial set of *extensions* have been defined for SMTP. Clients wishing to use the basic extensions must start their dialogue with a command EHLO (instead of HELO) and a server which implements the extensions must recognise this new command. The EHLO command carries information about which extensions are required. An important example of when this is necessary is when characters are to be transmitted in an *8-bit* representation. An important group of more advanced extensions are the group known as *Multipurpose Internet Mail Extensions (MIME)*, which enable messages to contain more complex data than simple ASCII texts, by allowing:

1. Message bodies containing text in character sets other than US ASCII.
2. A series of formats for non-text message bodies, such as images, audio and video.
3. Multi-part message bodies.
4. Message headers in character sets and encodings other than US ASCII.
5. Authenticated and encrypted message bodies.

MIME encoding has been described in Section 8.4.1, and an example of a complete message, with header fields and several body parts using MIME encoding, can be seen in Figure 8.5. Other SMTP extensions allow for more informative error codes, return of delivery status, transfer of information about message sizes and command pipelining.

The SMTP protocol can be summarised as follows:

Protocol example: Internet Simple Mail Transfer Protocol, SMTP (Internet Standard 10, RFC821) [213], with extensions described in RFC1869, RFC1870, RFC1891, RFC2034, RFC2045–2049 and RFC2197.

Service provided: Connection-mode facilities for distribution of messages between an end-user and a mailbox associated with another end-user.

Other ASEs required: —

Connection phase: Two-way exchange protocol (HELO or EHLO).

Data transfer phase: Sequence of two-way exchanges to specify recipient (or recipients), address for replies, subject, and actual data.

Disconnection phase: Two-way exchange protocol (QUIT).

Other features: Timestamping of messages. Return of delivery status, return of enhanced error codes, transfer of information about message sizes, command pipelining, if the use of appropriate SMTP extensions has been agreed in connection phase.

Coding: ASCII encoding of all PDUs, possibly with MIME encoding (see Section 8.4.1) if use of appropriate SMTP extensions has been agreed in connection phase.

Addressing: Internet address identifies destination system and user name identifies a mailbox which is unique for the addressee.

Fault tolerance: —

Since SMTP only provides for transfer of messages from an end-user to a *mailbox* belonging to another end-user, the addressee's User Agent needs to provide facilities for extracting messages from this mailbox and presenting them to the addressee. As stated above, this requires an additional protocol for communication between the recipient's User Agent and the destination MTA. Commonly used protocols for this purpose are POP [222] and IMAP [226]. Both these are simple

Client-Server protocols, where the User Agent acts as Client and the MTA mailbox system as Server. We shall not describe them in detail here.

While basic SMTP only offers a small subset of the facilities found in MO-TIS/MHS, SMTP with MIME offers a substantial subset of these facilities. However, SMTP does not itself contain mechanisms which give fault tolerance, so unlike MOTIS/MHS the reliability of the protocol is essentially based on the fact that the underlying Transport service makes use of the comparatively fault-tolerant TCP protocol. Obviously the user has to decide to a certain extent whether simplicity and cheapness outweigh lack of facilities and potential loss of messages.

11.4 Hypertext and the World Wide Web

The World Wide Web is a distributed system which offers global access to information. The basic architecture follows a Client-Server model, with a very large number of servers, on which the information is stored, offering uniform access to the clients. The unit of information generally corresponds to a file on the server, and is known as a *(Web) resource*.

11.4.1 Uniform Resource Identifiers

Uniform access is assured by the use of a unified, global naming scheme in which each resource is identified by a *Uniform Resource Identifier (URI)* which specifies a so-called *scheme* identifying the access protocol to be used, the *server* (with optional *user information* and information about the *port* to be accessed), and the *path* to the file. In addition, the URI may provide a *query* to be interpreted by the resource and/or specify a *fragment* which identifies a part of the resource. A slightly simplified syntax (in Extended BNF notation) for URIs is given in Figure 11.9; a more complete description can be found in [250].

Some examples of URIs are as follows:

http://www.usenix.org/membership/renew.html
  Refers to the resource to be found via path /membership/renew.html on the server with hostname www.usenix.org, to be accessed using the HTTP protocol.
http://abc.com/˜smith/index.html
  Refers to the resource to be found via the path ˜smith/index.html on the server with hostname abc.com, to be accessed using the HTTP protocol.
http://abc.com:80/˜smith/index.html
  Refers explicitly to port 80 (the default port number for the HTTP protocol), but is otherwise identical to the second example.
http://www.bahn.de/bin/query?text=Berlin&maxresults=10
  Refers to the resource to be found via path /bin/query on the server with host-

```
absoluteURI ::= scheme  "://"  server  path ["?" query] ["#" fragment]
server      ::= [userinfo "@"] hostport
hostport    ::= host [":" port]
host        ::= hostname | IPv4address | IPv6address
port        ::= { digit }*
path        ::= "/" { segment "/" }*
userinfo    ::= { uchar }*
segment     ::= { pchar }*
query       ::= { uric }*
fragment    ::= { uric }*
hostname    ::= { domainlabel "." }* toplabel
domainlabel ::= alphanum | alphanum { (alphanum | "-") }* alphanum
toplabel    ::= alpha    | alpha   { (alphanum | "-") }* alphanum
alphanum    ::= alpha | digit
nchar       ::= alpha | digit | "-" | "_" | "." | "!" |
                "~" | "*" | "'" | "(" | ")" | ":" |
                "&" | "=" | "+" | "$" | ","
uchar       ::= nchar | ";"
pchar       ::= nchar | "@"
uric        ::= nchar | ";" | "@" | "/" | "?"
alpha       ::= "A" | "B" |...| "Z" | "a" | "b" |...| "z"
digit       ::= "0" | "1" |...| "9"
```

Fig. 11.9 Syntax of Uniform Resource Identifiers. The syntax is given in EBNF, where [x] indicates an optional syntactic element x, and {x}* a repetition of 0 or more elements.

name www.bahn.de, to be accessed using the HTTP protocol.

The query text=Berlin&maxresults=10 will be passed on to the resource.

ftp://ftp.isi.edu/in-notes/rfc2396.txt

Refers to the resource to be found via the path /in-notes/rfc2396.txt on the server with hostname ftp.isi.edu, to be accessed using the FTP protocol.

telnet://ratbert.comfy.com/

Refers to the resource to be found via the path / on the server with hostname ratbert.comfy.com, to be accessed using the TELNET protocol.

Hostnames are expressed using the standard Internet naming convention presented in Chapter 7. Paths are expressed relative to some base defined within the server. User information, userinfo, is typically a user identifier, possibly with security-related parameters required to gain access to the resource.

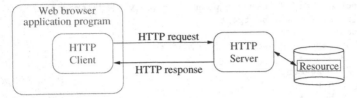

Fig. 11.10 Typical Internet HTTP client-server architecture

11.4.2 Hypertext Transfer Protocols

Hypertext is a generic term for the content of documents which potentially may involve various types of information, such as:

- **Static elements** of various types, such as text, images and sounds.
- **Dynamic elements**, which are to be created 'on the fly' by the execution of programs.
- **Embedded links** to resources containing further information. This information may be intended to be accessed automatically when the document containing the link is accessed, or it may require some action on the part of a human user in order to activate the link.

The task of a hypertext transfer protocol is to offer a service for storing and re-trieving hypertext documents. The classic example is currently the Internet/DoD Hypertext Transfer Protocol (HTTP) [43]. This makes use of a series of two-way exchanges between a Client, which is typically integrated into a Web browser, and one or more Servers, in this context usually known as Web servers. In each ex-change, the Client sends a *request* which identifies a *resource* by giving its URI, specifies an action (known as a *method*) to be performed on the resource, and op-tionally gives parameters describing the action in more detail. The Server replies with a *Response* which gives a status code for execution of the action, and possi-bly includes further information about the resource. This information may include the content of the resource and/or other parameters. The overall architecture of the system is illustrated in Figure 11.10.

A very simple example of an HTTP exchange is shown in Figure 11.11. The GET request specifies the URI from which the resource is to be retrieved and the protocol version to be used (here version 1.1). The response is a code (200 OK) indicating success, followed by further PCI in the form of *header fields* associated with the response and the actual content of the resource, which in the example is a document in *Hypertext Markup Language (HTML)*. The header fields are terminated by a blank line. The document contains an embedded link to a further resource, in this case containing an image at URI http://www.wpooh.org/pooh.img. It is the client's task to fetch this further resource when required. Normally, the Web browser or other program in which the client is embedded will determine when this will take place, possibly after consulting the user. In more complex cases, documents may also contain references to programs to be executed by the client (as so-called

```
GET http://www.wpooh.org/~pooh/index.html  HTTP/1.1
Host: www.wpooh.org
```

```
HTTP/1.1 200 OK
Date: Thu, 8 Aug 2002 08:12:31 EST
Content-Length: 332

<html>
<head>
  <title>Pooh's Homepage</title>
</head>
<body>
  <h1 align=center>Winnie the Pooh</h1>
  <img src="http://www.wpooh.org/pooh.gif",alt="Pooh">
  <p>
   Our little bear is short and fat
   Which is not to be wondered at.

   He gets what exercise he can
   By falling off the ottoman.
  </p>
</body>
</html>
```

Fig. 11.11 Simple exchange of messages in HTTP.
The request from the client to the server is in `typewriter` font and the reply from server to client is boxed in `typewriter` font. The actual content of the resource within the box is in *italic typewriter* font.

applets) or the server (as so-called *active server pages* or *server scripts*), in order to produce parts of the content of the resource dynamically.

The standard methods available via HTTP and their functions are:

GET   Retrieve content of resource.

PUT   Store new content in resource.

DELETE   Delete resource.

OPTIONS Request information about resource or server.

HEAD   Get headers (but not actual content) of resource.

POST   Transfer information to an application, for example for transmission as mail, processing as a Web form, etc.

TRACE   Trace route to server via loop-back connection.

Obviously, these methods are only available on a given server if the user on the client has suitable authorisation from the server.

The numerical response codes 100–199 indicate an informational response, 200–299 indicate that the requested action was successfully completed, and 300–399 that further action is needed to complete the request. Codes 400–499 indicate a client error, such as faulty request syntax or missing authentication, while codes 500–599 indicate situations where the server could not fulfil an apparently valid request.

```
GET pub/WWW/xy.html  HTTP/1.1
Host: www.w3.org
Accept: text/html, text/x-dvi;q=0.8
Accept-Charset: iso-8859-1, unicode-1-1;q=0.5
Accept-Encoding: gzip, identity;q=0.5, *;q=0
Accept-Language: da, en-gb;q=0.8, en;q=0
Range: bytes=500-999
Cache-control: max-age=600
```

Fig. 11.12 A more complex HTTP Get request

More complex forms of request allow the client to specify more closely what is required or to describe its own abilities. This is done by following the main request with further PCI in the form of header fields, as in the conventions for using MIME. It is possible, for example, for the client to:

- Define acceptable media types (header field `Accept`), i.e. media types which the client-side system can deal with. These are described using a notation similar to that for MIME content-types, for example as `text/html`, `text/x-dvi`, `video/mpeg` and so on.
- Define acceptable character sets (header field `Accept-Charset`, specifying a list of one or more character sets).
- Define acceptable natural languages in which the document may be written (header field `Accept-Language`, specifying a list or one or more language codes).
- Define acceptable forms of compression or encoding, such as `gzip` or the use of Unix `compress` (header field `Accept-Encoding`, specifying a list of one or more encodings). The encoding `identity` means that no compression takes place.
- Specify that only part of the document is to be transferred (header field `Range`, specifying a range in bytes).
- Restrict the operation to resources which obey given restrictions with respect to their date of modification (header fields `If-Modified-Since` and `If-Unmodified-Since`, specifying a date and time).
- Control caching of the document (header field `Cache-Control`, specifying rules such as the maximum age for which a cached document is valid (`max-age`), or giving directions not to store a document (`no-store`) or always to retrieve it from the original server rather than a cache (`no-cache`)).
- Provide information for authorisation purposes (see Section 11.4.4 below).

An complete example of a more complex GET request is shown in Figure 11.12. This specifies that the resource at URI `http://www.w3.org/pub/WWW/xy.html` should be retrieved using HTTP version 1.1. The further header fields are to be understood as follows:

- The client can accept contents in HTML or DVI syntax. The q-parameter, here `q=0.8`, associated with the DVI media type means that the client will only give

```
HTTP/1.1 200 OK
Date: Thu, 8 Aug 2002 08:12:31 EST
Content-Length: 332
Content-Type: text/html; charset=iso-8859-1
Content-Encoding: identity
Content-Language: en
Content-MD5: ohazEqjF+PGOc7B5xumdgQ==
Last-Modified: Mon, 29 Jul 2002 23:54:01 EST
Age: 243

<html>
  ...
</html>
```

Fig. 11.13 A more complex response to a GET request in HTTP.
The actual content of the document (in *italic typewriter* font) has been abbreviated in the figure.

files of this type a relative preference of 0.8. Absence of a q-parameter implies q=1.0.

- The client will accept character sets iso-8859-1 and unicode-1-1, but will only give the latter a relative preference of 0.5.
- The client will accept gzip compression with preference 1.0, while the identity transformation has preference 0.5 and all other forms of compression (denoted by *) should be avoided (q=0).
- The client will accept documents in Danish (da) with preference 1.0, British English (en-gb) with preference 0.8, and all other forms of English should be avoided (q=0).
- Bytes 500 to 999 (inclusive) of the document are to be retrieved.
- The document can be taken from a cache unless the cached copy has an age which exceeds 600 seconds.

More complex *responses* than in Figure 11.11 can be used to inform the client about the content or encoding of the document, give the reasons for an error response, or provide information about the server itself. As in the case of requests, this information is provided in the form of header fields. The response shown in Figure 11.11 is in fact the minimum one, with header fields giving only the obligatory information: The *length* of the document retrieved and the *date* (and time) at which retrieval took place. Figure 11.13 shows a more complex response which could have been received after the same request, if the server had included some of the optional header fields. The Content-Type, Content-Encoding and Content-Language give the actual values of these parameters and should be expected to correspond to the acceptable values, if any, specified in the request. The Content-MD5 field gives a base64 encoded MD5 checksum for the content. The Age field is included if the content has been taken from a cache, and gives the length of time in seconds that the content has been stored in the cache. The Last-Modified field gives the date and time at which – to the server's best knowledge – the content of the resource was last modified. Such complex responses are, of course, essential when the request is OPTIONS, where the purpose is to obtain information about the capabilities of the server, such as which content types or encodings it is able to handle.

The Internet HTTP protocol can be summarised as follows:

Protocol example: Internet Hypertext Transfer Protocol, version 1.1 (RFC2616) [43].

Service provided: Connection-mode facilities for information storage and retrieval.

Other ASEs required: —

Connection phase: —

Data transfer phase: Two-way exchange protocol for read and write operations on named resources.

Disconnection phase: —

Other features: Two-way exchange protocol for deletion of resources. Two-way exchange protocol for querying properties of resources and/or systems on which resources are stored. Two-way exchange protocol for transfer of documents for processing.

Timestamping of messages. Control of caching. Specification of acceptable message types, languages, content encodings, character sets. Challenge-response mechanism for authentication of client (see Section 11.4.4).

Coding: ASCII encoding of all PDUs.

Addressing: Uniform Resource Identifier (URI) identifies destination system and path to resource.

Fault tolerance: Resistance to corruption via optional MD5 checksumming of resource content during transfer.

11.4.3 Web Caching

Since most distributed information retrieval applications involve transfer of considerable amounts of data through the network, caching is commonly used in order to reduce the amount of network traffic and reduce response times. HTTP, which is intended to support such applications, therefore includes explicit mechanisms for controlling the operation of caching. Since these illustrate a number of ideas which are important in several application areas, they will be described in some detail here.

In general, caching mechanisms in information systems attempt to achieve *semantic transparency* for the cache. A cache is said to be semantically transparent when its operation affects neither the requesting client nor the server from which the resource originates, except with respect to improving performance. In other words, the client receives exactly the same response (ignoring possible differences in hop-by-hop headers) as it would have received if the request had been handled directly by the server which holds the definitive copy of the resource – the so-called *origin server*. If transparency is – for whatever reason – not required by the client, or cannot be achieved by the cache or the server, then HTTP requires the application user to be warned.

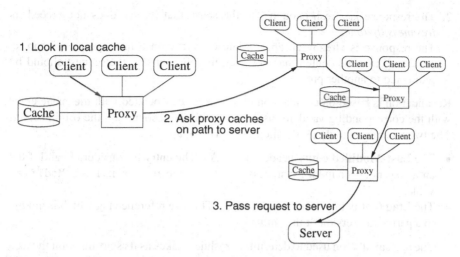

Fig. 11.14 Caching of Web resources by proxies

HTTP allows for several caches to be in use on the path from the client to the origin server. Although this will be unnecessary in simple cases, it will typically be useful when the request is passed to the server via a series of intermediate systems. Such an intermediate system may for example be a:

Proxy: which collects up requests from (and distributes responses to) one or more clients, and makes a new request by acting as client for a further server. A *transparent proxy* just passes on the request (and the returning response) unaltered, whereas a non-transparent proxy creates a modified request, typically in order to provide some added value.

Gateway: which acts as an intermediary for another server, but (unlike a proxy) appears to the client to be the desired origin server.

Tunnel: which acts as a blind relay between two connections.

A scenario in which several proxies, each serving several clients, and each containing a cache, are involved in responding to a request, is illustrated in Figure 11.14. A request from one of the clients will in the first instance be collected up by the proxy to this client. If a proxy has no fresh copy of the requested resource in its cache, it attempts to pass the request on to another proxy on the path to the origin server. If all of these attempts fail to locate a fresh copy of the document, the origin server itself is ultimately contacted. The response returns to the original client by the reverse route.

A cache must respond to a request with the most up-to-date response that is appropriate to the request and which meets at least one of the following conditions:

1. The response has been checked for equivalence with what the origin server would have responded. This check is performed by using the *revalidation* mechanism described below.

2. The response is "fresh enough", in the sense that its *age* does not exceed its *freshness lifetime*.
3. The response is already an appropriate error response message or a response indicating that the content has not been modified or that the request should be redirected to another proxy.

Revalidation is based on comparison of a *validator* associated with the cache entry with the corresponding validator associated with the resource on the origin server. The two most commonly used validators in HTTP are:

- The **Last-Modified** entity-header value. A cache entry is considered valid if the entity has not been modified since the date and time given by its `Last-Modified` value.
- The **Etag** (entity tag) entity-header value. This is a reference tag which is unique to a particular version of the entity.

The age calculation used to determine freshness takes as its starting point the `Age` header field included in all responses taken from a cache, and the `Date` header field which gives the time at which the origin server generated the original response. The `Age` field gives the cache's estimate of how much time has passed since the response was generated or revalidated by the origin server. When HTTP/1.1 is in use, this estimate, say a, is essentially the sum of the time that the response has been stored in each of the caches along the path from the origin server, plus the time spent in transit through the network between caches. An independent estimate of the age can be evaluated as the difference between the local time when the response arrives, say t_{resp}, and the `Date` value, d. Thus a conservative estimate of the age is:

$$a_r = \max(t_{resp} - d, a)$$

Now if the network can impose delays, there may be a discrepancy between the value d supplied by the server and the time at which the response arrives at the first cache. This *response delay* can be estimated by the cache as $(t_{resp} - t_{req})$, where t_{req} is the time at which the request was issued by the system containing the cache. So a corrected estimate of the age at the time when the response arrived is:

$$a_c = a_r + (t_{resp} - t_{req})$$

Finally, the cache's age estimate must be corrected for the *residence time*, which is the time which has passed efter the arrival of the response, until the cache has to retrieve the entity in order to send it to a client. At local time t_{loc}, the cache's final estimate of the age is therefore:

$$age = a_c + (t_{loc} - t_{resp}) = a_r + (t_{loc} - t_{req})$$

To ensure that all these time estimates are reliable, it is assumed that the systems concerned all use a clock synchronisation protocol, such as NTP.

To decide whether a give cache entry is valid, it is necessary to compare the age, evaluated as above, with an estimate of the *freshness lifetime*, f_{lim}, for the response.

There are three basic ways in which this can be evaluated, which are used in the following order of priority:

1. If the `Cache-Control` header field of the response includes a *max-age* value, a_{max}, then this value is taken as the limit for acceptable age:

$$f_{lim} = a_{max}$$

2. If an `Expires` header field appears in the response, then the age limit is taken as the difference between the date and time specified in the Expires field, t_{exp}, and the current, local date and time, t_{loc}.

$$f_{lim} = t_{exp} - t_{loc}$$

3. A heuristic method can be used to estimate f_{lim}.

The basic criterion for validity of a cache entry is then that $(age < f_{lim})$. However, the cache control mechanisms offered in HTTP/1.1 are very general, and allow the *client* to deviate from this simple criterion in various ways by specifying, for example, that:

- The cached value must be valid for at least a given further period of n seconds (`min-fresh=n`).
- The cached value is acceptable even if it is outdated, as long as its freshness lifetime has not been exceeded by more than n seconds (`max-stale=n`).
- Cached values are not to be returned. Instead, values are always to be retrieved from the origin server (`no-cache`). This strategy is commonly known as *end-to-end reload*.
- Values are to be taken from the cache and *not* from the origin server (`only-if-cached`). This strategy is useful at times when the network suffers from poor connectivity or similar unreliability.
- Cached values are always to be revalidated with the next cache or the server (`max-age=0`). This strategy is commonly known as *end-to-end revalidation*.

Similarly, the protocol allows the *origin server* to insist that each cache should always revalidate any copy of a response before returning it to the client. This is done by including a `must-revalidate` directive in the response from the server. Likewise, a `proxy-revalidate` directive can be used by the server to ensure that proxies will always revalidate a cache entry for each of the clients serviced by the proxy.

The discussion above mostly applies to responses generated by use of the GET or HEAD methods, which are used to *retrieve* information. Methods such as PUT, DELETE and POST, which are intended to *modify* or *delete* information, must cause all cache entries for the relevant entity to be *invalidated*, either by removing them from the cache or by marking them as invalid (and thus forcing revalidation to take place next time the entity is to be retrieved). All methods other than GET and HEAD must also cause any changes in the actual Web resource to be *written through* to the origin server, so that this always contains updated values for the content of the resource. Other styles of cache, such as the *write-back* or *copy-back* caches used in some types of application, in which it is possible to delay updates until some convenient later moment, are *not* permitted in systems which use HTTP.

11.4.4 HTTP Authentication

In order to protect the server against unauthorised access to its resources, and to protect the client against fake servers, HTTP includes a *challenge-response* mechanism for authenticating the client to the server and (optionally) vice versa [49]. This can be used with all the HTTP methods, but is of course especially important when the client uses methods such as PUT, POST or DELETE which can change the state of the resources.

The basic mechanism for use between a client and server is:

- The **Challenge** is sent by the server in a `WWW-Authenticate` header field of an HTTP *response* with error code "`401 Unauthorized`", in response to a client HTTP request which refers to a protected resource.
- The **Response** is sent in an `Authorization` header field of an HTTP *request* from the client. This request is in other respects just a repeat of the original client request.
- If the **Response** is satisfactory, the server sends a positive HTTP response; if not, it again responds with error code "`401 Unauthorized`". If mutual authentication is required, the server includes an `Authentication-Info` header field, including a **MutualResponse** in the positive HTTP response.

Two challenge-response schemes are defined:

Basic: The Challenge consists of a string which identifies the *realm* of the protected resource. The Response sent by the client consists of a *userid* and *password* encoded in a base64 encoding. The entire exchange is illustrated in Figure 11.15(a). In this figure, the authorisation code `dGJvbmVzOkFscGgwMm5VbT8=` is the base64 encoding of the string `tbones:Alph02nUm?`, where the user name is `tbones` and the password is `Alph02nUm?`.

Digest: The Challenge consists of a string identifying the *realm* of the protected resource, a *nonce* and possibly details of the message digest algorithm to be used in creating the Response. The default message digest algorithm is MD5 . In its simplest form, the Response sent by the client contains the realm, nonce, username, and the message digest of a suitable secret known to the client. A standard choice for the secret is the user password concatenated with the realm and userid. The nonce and message digest can be given in base64 encoding or as a sequence of hexadecimal digits. The server will check that the value of the digest corresponds to the expected value for the named user. The entire exchange is illustrated in Figure 11.15(b).

If mutual authentication is required, the MutualResponse finally sent by the server to the client will include a message digest of some second secret shared by

Step	Direction	Request or response

(a) 1.	request	`PUT /groggy/gnu.html HTTP/1.1`
		`Host www.goofy.dtu.dk`
		
		[New content of resource]

2.	response	`HTTP/1.1 401 Unauthorized`
		`Date: Thu, 29 Nov 2007 06:31:59 EST`
		`WWW-Authenticate: Basic realm="GnuProtect"`

3.	request	`PUT /groggy/gnu.html HTTP/1.1`
		`Host www.goofy.dtu.dk`
		`Authorization: Basic dGJvbmVzOkFscCGgwMm5VbT8=`
		
		[New content of resource]

4.	response	`HTTP/1.1 200 OK` `Date: Thu, 29 Nov 2007 06:32:05 EST`

(b) 1.	request	`PUT /groggy/gnu.html HTTP/1.1`
		`Host www.goofy.dtu.dk`
		
		[New content of resource]

2.	response	`HTTP/1.1 401 Unauthorized`
		`Date: Thu, 29 Nov 2007 06:35:01 EST`
		`WWW-Authenticate: Digest realm="GnuProtect" algorithm=MD5`
		`                  nonce="Jap3Zyh75Mmbl+w..."`

3.	request	`POST /groggy/gnu.html HTTP/1.1`
		`Host www.goofy.dtu.dk`
		`Authorization: Digest realm="GnuProtect" algorithm=MD5`
		`               nonce="Jap3Zyh75Mmbl+w..."`
		`               response="2629fae49393a...c591"`
		`               uri="/groggy/gnu.html" username="tbones"`
		
		[New content of resource]

4.	response	`HTTP/1.1 200 OK` `Date: Thu, 29 Nov 2007 06:35:18 EST`

Fig. 11.15 HTTP authentication: **(a)** Basic scheme; **(b)** Digest scheme. Only selected header fields are shown

the client and server. This demonstrates that the server knows the client's secret, in accordance with the general principles for mutual authentication discussed in Section 6.4. More details can be found in [49].

It should be noted that neither of these schemes of challenge-response is very secure. In the Basic scheme, the userid and password are essentially sent in cleartext through the network. The Digest scheme is stronger, since an intruder – instead of obtaining the user's full credentials – can in general only repeat the current transaction. However, this is still dangerous if the transaction involves the PUT, POST or DELETE method. Neither of the schemes ensures confidentiality of the transaction. Techniques for achieving a higher level of security are discussed in Section 11.4.6.

The discussion above applies to authentication between a client and the origin server. As we have discussed in Section 11.4.3, there may also be one or more *proxies* on the path to the server which may attempt to respond to the client's request. These proxies may also demand that the client authenticate itself. The mechanism for this is very similar to that used with servers, except that a proxy will include its Challenge in a `Proxy-Authentication` header field in a `"407 Proxy Authentication Required"` error response, and the client must then send its Response in a `Proxy-Authorization` header field in the renewed client request.

11.4.5 Stateful HTTP and Cookies

In the basic form of HTTP described in [43], successive request/response exchanges between a client and a server are assumed to be independent of one another, and the protocol does not assist the client or server to build up a memory of what information has been exchanged. The protocol is said to be *stateless*. However, many Web-based applications rely on the use of a sequence of related requests and responses, which make up a *session*. For instance, in a commercial transaction a customer using an HTTP client will often need to provide information via a series of Web forms, which are successively sent to the server in POST requests, with responses being returned from the server to the client. The application dealing with these forms needs to be sure that they all belong to the same customer's transaction. For this to be possible with a stateless protocol, the client would have to repeat information about the customer and other details of the transaction in each request sent to the server during a session. This can be very inefficient.

The concept of *cookies* was introduced to deal with this problem. The original proposal for a cookie mechanism was developed by Netscape, and has subsequently been refined for use with HTTP/1.1 [247]. As we have seen in Chapter 4, it is in general necessary for the communicating parties to include more PCI in their PDUs in order to inform one another about their respective states. In HTTP, this is done by including additional *header fields* in the requests and responses. The cookie mechanism utilises two new header fields, in order to enable the client and server to exchange information about the state of a session:

Cookie: included in a request sent by the client, in order to inform the server about all cookies relevant to the current session.

Set-Cookie2:   included in a response sent by the server, in order to request the client to store more state information, in the form of one or more (new or modified) cookies described in the header field.

An example of a complete session involving a customer purchase can be seen in Figure 11.16. During this session, the server sends the client three cookies, named `Customer`, `Catitem` and `Delivery`, and the client uses these in subsequent requests to the server. Each cookie is described by a name and a list of attributes, each specified by a name and (in most cases) a value. When setting a cookie, the server can, for example, include the attributes:

Step	Direction	Request or response
1.	request	POST /bigbuy/login HTTP/1.1
		[data in form to identify customer]
2.	response	HTTP/1.1 200 OK
		Set-Cookie2: Customer="Fred-Snooks-261";
		Version="1"; Path="/bigbuy"
3.	request	POST /bigbuy/catalog HTTP/1.1
		Cookie: $Version="1";
		Customer="Fred-Snooks-261"; $Path="/bigbuy"
		[data in form for items selected by customer]
4.	response	HTTP/1.1 200 OK
		Set-Cookie2: Catitem="Catfood-053";
		Version="1"; Path="/bigbuy"
5.	request	POST /bigbuy/delivery HTTP/1.1
		Cookie: $Version="1";
		Customer="Fred-Snooks-261"; $Path="/bigbuy"
		Catitem="Catfood-053"; $Path="/bigbuy"
		[data in form to select delivery method]
6.	response	HTTP/1.1 200 OK
		Set-Cookie2: Delivery="Bike-001";
		Version="1"; Path="/bigbuy"
7.	request	POST /bigbuy/checkout HTTP/1.1
		Cookie: $Version="1";
		Customer="Fred-Snooks-261"; $Path="/bigbuy"
		Catitem="Catfood-053"; $Path="/bigbuy"
		Delivery="Bike-001"; $Path="/bigbuy"
		[data in form to complete purchase]
8.	response	HTTP/1.1 200 OK

Fig. 11.16 An HTTP session with cookies. Only cookie-related header fields are shown

- `Version`, specifying the version of the cookie specification in use. This attribute is mandatory.
- `Domain`, specifying the domain for which the cookie is valid.
- `Path`, specifying the subset of URLs on the origin server to which the cookie applies.
- `Port`, specifying a list of one or more ports to which the client may return the cookie in a request header. If this attribute is omitted, any port can be used.
- `Max-age`, specifying the time for which the cookie is valid, defined and evaluated as for HTTP caching.
- `Comment`, giving information about how the server intends to use the cookie. Alternatively, the `CommentURL` attribute can be used to refer to a URL where this "cookie policy" is described.

Since information held in cookies may include personal user data or confidential material, it is important to be able to control the security aspects of the handling of cookies. The `Comment` and `CommentURL` attributes are intended to provide the client application with information which can be used to decide whether or not to accept the cookie. In addition, the server may specify that the cookie should be discarded as soon as the session terminates (atttribute `Discard`), or that the client application should send the cookie to the server in a secure manner (attribute `Secure`), in order to ensure confidentiality and integrity. The Internet cookie specification [247] does not say how this is to be done; some suitable methods for achieving HTTP security in general are discussed in Section 11.4.6 below.

When the client sends information to the server during a session which uses cookies, it can similarly include the `Version`, `Path`, `Domain` and `Port` attributes in the `Cookie` header field of its HTTP request. When sent from the client, these must match the values which the server specified should be set in the cookie, and the server will check that this is the case, in order to ensure that the client is referring to a cookie which was in fact supplied by the server. Cookies for which the server has specified `Discard` will, of course, be discarded when the user session ends, but cookies can in general have a much longer lifetime, and can then be re-used from session to session.

For security reasons, the client will correspondingly check all cookie descriptions arriving from a server in HTTP responses. It is required to reject (i.e. refuse to store) any cookie whose description in the `Set-Cookie2` header field of the HTTP response fails to meet all of the following conditions:

- The `Path` attribute must be a prefix of the URI in the corresponding HTTP request.
- The `Domain` attribute must contain embedded dots (or be `.local`).
- The `Domain` attribute must domain-match the hostname of the host which generated the request.
- The port to which the request was sent must be one of those in the `Port` attribute.

Caching can in principle also introduce a security risk by causing copies of cookies to be left in caches round and about in the Internet. This effect cannot be controlled via the cookie-related header fields, but requires the client and server to use appropriate `Cache-control` header fields, such as:

- `Cache-control: no-cache` which forbids caching.
- `Cache-control: private`   which forbids caching of requests or responses in shared caches.
- `Cache-control: no-cache="set-cookie2"` which forbids caching of the `Set-Cookie2` header field

11.4.6 Secure HTTP

The basic Hypertext Transfer protocol only supports a very limited form of security, in the form of *credentials* which may be supplied by the client in order to *authenticate* itself to a server, and a *challenge* mechanism which the server may use in order to force the client to authenticate itself. Two strategies are currently available for achieving additional security in Web transactions:

1. Use the *TLS protocol suite* described in Section 10.7 in order to offer a secure Transport service on which to base the operation of HTTP. Web servers which use this strategy are identified by URIs in which the protocol scheme is `https`, and use port 443 as the default TCP port, so that secure and insecure traffic can be handled separately.
2. Use *Secure HTTP* (S-HTTP [246]) in order to introduce security functions within the Application layer itself. Web servers which use this strategy are identified by URIs in which the protocol scheme is `shttp`. They continue to use default port 80, but use a different syntax for requests and responses, so that secure and insecure traffic can be handled separately.

Both TLS and S-HTTP offer transaction confidentiality, authentication, integrity and non-repudiation of origin. This makes them suitable for use in information systems in which confidential information is exchanged. A typical example is a system in which personal information, such as credit card numbers, bank information, social security numbers or the like have to supplied to or retrieved from a Web site.

S-HTTP makes use of a new method, denoted `Secure`, for handling information in a secure manner, and uses the protocol designator `Secure-HTTP/1.4` in both requests and responses for this method. Typically, the method is used to transfer encapsulated requests and responses for standard HTTP methods, such as GET, PUT, POST and so on. A number of additional header fields are defined for use with the Secure method, in order to specify the capabilities of the client and server with respect to security functions. These include the ability for the client to:

- Define acceptable ways of adding encryption and authentication (header field `Content-Privacy-Domain`). There are two current possibilities: to use Cryptographic Message Syntax (CMS [244], a further development of PKCS-7 [230]) and to use MOSS (essentially part of S/MIME).
- Define the type of the encapsulated content (header field `Content-Type`), which in most cases will be `message/http`.
- Supply a MAC for the encapsulated content (header field `MAC-Info`).
- Specify which algorithms may be used for:

  - Signing (`SHTTP-Signature-Algorithms`).
  - Forming message digests (`SHTTP-Message-Digest-Algorithms`).
  - Encrypting message content (`SHTTP-Symmetric-Content-Algorithms`).
  - Encrypting header fields (`SHTTP-Symmetric-Header-Algorithms`).
  - Forming MACs (`SHTTP-MAC-Algorithms`).

- Specify which forms of security to apply (`SHTTP-Privacy-enhancements`), where the possibilities are signing, encryption and authentication.
- Specify which types of certificate may be used (`SHTTP-Certificate-Types`), where the possibilties are X.509 and X.509/v3.
- Specify which key exchange algorithms may be used (`SHTTP-Key-Exchange-Algorithms`), where the possibilities are Diffie-Hellman, RSA, Inband (key transport within the encapsulated HTTP message) and Outband (agreed by means lying outside the protocol).

```
(a)  GET secret.html HTTP/1.1
     Host: www.e-trade.dk
     Date: Thu, 8 Aug 2002 08:12:31 EST
     Security-Scheme: S-HTTP/1.4
     Accept: text/html
     Accept-Charset: iso-8859-1
     Accept-Language: *

(b)  Secure * Secure-HTTP/1.4
     Content-Type: message/http
     MAC-Info: 31ff8122,rsa-md5,b3ca4575b841b5fc7553e69b0896c416,outband
     Content-Privacy-Domain: CMS
     MIAGCS.....
          .....goAAAA
```

Fig. 11.17 An HTTP GET request and its embedding in a S-HTTP Secure request.
(b) The original GET request. (b) The GET request encapsulated in a Secure request. After the
Secure-specific header fields, the authenticated and encrypted GET request in CMS syntax appears
in base64 encoding (in *italic typewriter* font). Only a portion of the encoding is included in
the figure.

As in standard HTTP, the server's reply includes corresponding fields which, if the
client offers several possibilities, may select one of them.

In addition, further header fields are defined for use with the standard HTTP
methods, in order to specify information relevant to the security functions, such as
which security scheme is being used (with S-HTTP, this will of course currently
be S-HTTP/1.4), which encryption and MAC algorithms are to be used, signatures,
MAC values and information about keys. It is assumed that this type of information
is confidential and it is therefore to be supplied within the encapsulated body of the
SHTTP message. A typical HTTP request from a client intended for a secure server
could for example be as shown in Figure 11.17 (a). For transmission this would be
encapsulated within a S-HTTP request as shown in Figure 11.17 (b). Note that the
Secure request also hides the URI for the resource to be accessed, supplying only a
*, while the real URI is encapsulated in the embedded GET request.

11.5 Web Services

The Web Services paradigm for construction of distributed systems offers applications the possibility of using remote services via standard Internet application layer
protocols such as HTTP. A typical approach is to use a Web server to pass input
information to an object on the server, and to pass output information back from
the object to the service user, which acts as a client of the Web service. The most
direct way to do this is to transmit arguments in an HTTP GET or POST request
(see page 343) from a Web client to the Web server, which passes them on to the

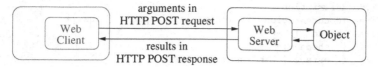

Fig. 11.18 Object access in simple Web services

```
POST   /Weather   HTTP/1.1
Host: www.weathermax.com
Content-type: application/soap+xml; charset="utf-8"
Content-length: 482
```

<?xml version="1.0"?>
<env:Envelope xmlns:env="http://www.w3.org/2003/05/soap-envelope">
 <env:Header>
  ...
 </env:Header>
 <env:Body>
  ...
 </env:Body>
</env:Envelope>

Fig. 11.19 An HTTP request to invoke the getTemp method from Figure 10.12.
The HTTP request header is in typewriter font and the request body is in *italic typewriter* font. This body has the form of an XML encoded SOAP message.

object whose method is to be invoked; the results are passed back the opposite way in a GET or POST response. This is illustrated in Figure 11.18.

A simple protocol for this purpose is *SOAP*, which we have described in Section 10.6.5. The most recent version of SOAP is version 1.2, defined in [274, 275]. To indicate that the body of the HTTP request or reponse is to be handled as a SOAP request or reponse, the media type, given by the Content-type or Accept header fields in the HTTP request or response, should be application/soap+xml and the charset attribute should be the default XML character set, utf-8. The resource which should handle the SOAP message will be specified by the URI given in the HTTP request.

An example of a SOAP request embedded in an HTTP POST request is shown in Figure 11.19; details of the headr and body of the SOAP request have been omitted. This request will be dealt with by the resource http://www.weathermax.com/ Weather. The SOAP specification [273] recommends that when SOAP is used over HTTP, then the HTTP GET method is used (for efficiency reasons) for so-called *idempotent* operations, i.e. operations which do not change the state of the resource being accessed, while the PUT method should be used for operations which potentially change the state of this resource.

```
document      ::=  description
description   ::=  [documentation]  { insert }*  [types]  { ibs }*
insert        ::=  include | import
types         ::=  { schema }*
ibs           ::=  interface | binding | service
interface     ::=  { opfault }*
opfault       ::=  {operation}*  { fault}*
binding       ::=  { opfault }*
service       ::=  {endpoint }+
operation     ::=  { input }*  {output}*  {infault}*  {outfault}*
```

Fig. 11.20 Syntax of WSDL documents. Each of the syntactic elements is an XML element.
The syntax is given in EBNF, where [x] indicates an optional syntactic element x, {x}* indicates
a repetition of 0 or more elements and {x}+ a repetition of 1 or more elements.

11.5.1 Web Service Description Language

To make use of a web service in a practical application a description of the service
must be produced in a standard format and made available to potential users of
the service. This description is encoded as an XML document, which is structured
according to the rules of the *Web Service Description Language (WSDL)* [277], and
includes:

- A definition of the *service interface*;
- A definition of the *service implementation*;
- If it is a concrete implementation rather than an abstract service description
  which is being described, a description of the *service endpoint* (typically the
  URL used for contacting the service).

The syntax of WSDL documents is given in Extended BNF in Figure 11.20. A
document consists of a description XML element, which is made up of a number
of smaller elements:

1. An optional documentation element, used to provide user-readable documentation.
2. Zero or more insert elements, each of which can be either an include element
   or an import element. These are used to include external definitions in the current WSDL document. An include element refers to a definition of a component
   in the same namespace as the current description, while an import element
   refers to a definition of a Web Service component in another namespace. The
   effect of inclusion is cumulative, so if a document A includes B which includes
   C, then the components defined by A include all the components defined in A, B
   and C.
3. An optional types element, used to define the datatypes of the messages used
   by the service, expressed in terms of a scheme in some XML schema language.
4. Zero or more ibs elements, each of which can be:

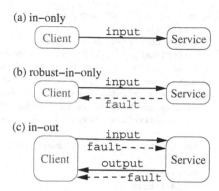

Fig. 11.21 Basic message exchange patterns in WSDL operations

a. An `interface` element, which describes an abstract interface to the Web Service as a set of abstract operations involving transfer of messages, together with a set of fault messages to be used in case of errors.
b. A `binding` element, which describes the concrete message format and protocol to be used to exchange the messages required by an interface.
c. A `service` element, which specifies where the service can be accessed.

Each `interface` element contains one or more `operation` elements, which describe the pattern of communication used by the operation and the messages to be passed over the interface in the inward and outward directions during normal operation, and the fault messages to be used in case of errors. Three basic *message exchange patterns (MEPs)* are defined:

in-only: A single message is passed across the interface in the inward direction (towards the server). No fault messages are propagated. This is typically used to send parameters for methods which are to be invoked with *maybe* semantics.

robust-in-only: A single message is passed across the interface in the inward direction. Fault messages are propagated in the opposite direction.

in-out: A single message is passed across the interface in the inward direction, after which a single message is passed across the interface in the outward direction. Fault messages caused by the inward-going message also propagate in the inward direction, while those caused by the outward-going message also propagate in the outward direction.

These basic patterns are illustrated in Figure 11.21. Further MEPs can be defined if required. A WSDL specification for a typical RPC-like SOAP-based service, which (amongst other things) offers the `getTemp` method described in Figures 10.12 and 10.13, is shown in Figure 11.22. You could imagine, for example, that this is part of a service offered by a company who make weather information available to their customers, where `getTemp` is used to get temperature data for a given city at a given date and time. As can be seen in this example, the elements typically have a name attribute, which identifies them and may be used as a reference by other elements. The namespaces used to ensure uniqueness of names are specified as attributes of the `description` element. Most of these are typically standard XML namespaces,

```
<?xml version="1.0" encoding="utf-8"?>
<description
  xmlns="http://www.w3.org/ns/wsdl"
  targetNameSpace="http://www.weathermax.com/2004/wsdl/wthSvc"
  xmlns:tns="http://www.weathermax.com/2004/wsdl/wthSvc"
  xmlns:wmns="http://www.weathermax.com/2004/wsdl/schemas/wthSvc"
  xmlns:wsoap="http://www.w3.org/ns/wsdl/soap"
  xmlns:soap="http://www.w3.org/2003/05/soap-envelope"
  xmlns:wsdlx="http://www.w3.org/ns/wsdl-extensions">

  <documentation> This document describes the ... service </documentation>

  <types>
    <xs:schema ... >
      <xs:element name="getTempRequest" type="tgetTempRequest"/>
      <xs:complexType name="tgetTempRequest">
        <xs:sequence>
          <xs:element name="city" type="xs:string"/>
          <xs:element name="time" type="xs:dateTime"/>
        </xs:sequence>
      </xs:complexType>
      <xs:element name="getTempResponse" type="xs:float"/>
      <xs:element name="invalidReqError" type="xs:string"/>
    </xs:schema>
  </types>

  <interface name="weatherInterface">
    <fault name="invalidReqFault" element="wmns:invalidReqError"/>
    <operation name ="getTemp"   pattern="http://www.w3.org/ns/wsdl/in-out"
               style="http://www.w3.org/ns/wsdl/style/iri"   wsdlx:safe="true">
      <input  messageLabel="In"  element="wmns:getTempRequest"/>
      <output messageLabel="Out" element="wmns:getTempResponse"/>
      <outfault ref="tns:invalidReqFault" messageLabel="Out"/>
    </operation>
       ...
  </interface>

  <binding name="weatherBinding"  interface="tns:weatherInterface"
           type="http://www.w3.org/ns/wsdl/soap"
           wsoap:protocol="http://www.w3.org/2003/05/soap/bindings/HTTP/">
    <operation ref="tns:getTemp"
               wsoap:mep="http://www.w3.org/2003/05/soap/mep/soap-response"/>
    <fault ref="tns:invalidReqFault"  wsoap:code="soap:Sender"/>
       ...
  </binding>

  <service name="weatherService"  interface="tns:weatherInterface">
    <endpoint name  ="weatherEndpoint"  binding="tns:weatherBinding"
              address="http://www.weathermax.com/WeatherService"/>
  </service>
</description>
```

Fig. 11.22 A WSDL 2.0 specification for a service offering the `getTemp` method from Figure 10.12

but the `targetNameSpace` and `tns` namespaces are used specifically in WSDL definitions in order to ensure that *locally* defined names are unambiguous with respect to definitions imported (via `import` elements or by other means) from other files. These two namespaces are conventionally chosen to refer to the same URI, which is unique for the service being defined. Thus in Figure 11.22 they are both associated with the URI:

> `http://www.weathermax.com/2004/wsdl/wthSvc`

and the name `tns:getTempRequest`, for example, refers to the locally defined name `getTempRequest` associated with one of the messages. Similarly, a further namespace (in this example `wmns`) is introduced in order to refer to schemas defined in the description.

The `binding` element, which specifies how the service's operations are invoked, essentially describes an `interface` implemented using a particular protocol. WSDL is independent of the underlying protocol, and bindings are available for SOAP, CORBA, DCOM, .NET and other standard object access protocols. In this particular example the binding is for SOAP, used for RPC-like access to the service with HTTP as the underlying "transport protocol", as indicated by the `type` and `wsoap:protocol` attributes of the `binding` element. However, just as SOAP is not the only possible object access protocol for use in connection with Web Services, so HTTP is not the only possible underlying protocol; alternatives include the Internet protocols FTP and SMTP, together with a number of proprietary protocols.

11.5.2 Publication and Discovery of Web services

As in the cases of RMI and CORBA, the service description must be propagated to a *service registry* as part of the process of *publication* of the service. A protocol known as the *Universal Description, Discovery and Integration (UDDI)* protocol is used by service providers for registering the description and by service requestors (i.e. Clients) for discovering the service. The basic model for the registry is business-oriented, so in general the registry contains information not only about services, but also about the *businesses* which offer services and the relationships between such businesses.

UDDI [262] makes use of SOAP over HTTP (or HTTPS) to contact the registry, using XML elements in the body of the SOAP messages to carry the required information. These elements can be thought of as representing different types of PDU for UDDI. They fall into six groups, which in the context of UDDI are usually known as *API sets*, since they correspond to sets of functions which the user might wish to exploit in an application:

Inquiry API set: Defines XML elements for finding information about services, businesses, relationships between businesses and bindings between services.
Publication API set: Defines XML elements for inserting, updating or deleting information about services, businesses or bindings.

```
(a) <uddi:find_service xmlns="urn:uddi-org:api_v3">
       <findQualifiers>
          <findQualifier>approximateMatch</findQualifier>
       </findQualifiers>
       <name>Weather%</name>
    </uddi:find_service>

(b) <uddi:serviceList xmlns="urn:uddi-org:api_v3">
       <serviceInfos>
          <serviceInfo serviceKey="8abc0123-0136-c12f-d098-801eed654321"
                       businessKey="8765faee-0188-c12f-d09a-801eed654321">
             <name>WeatherService</name>
          </serviceInfo>
          <serviceInfo serviceKey="b3e1be80-affe-119f-80a8-0050fc331c1b"
                       businessKey="a90d047e-affe-119f-83d4-0050fc331c1b">
             <name>Weather4you</name>
          </serviceInfo>
       </serviceInfos>
    </uddi:serviceList>
```

Fig. 11.23 A UDDI find_service inquiry and the corresponding response from the registry

Security Policy API set: Defines XML elements for fetching or discarding security tokens used for entity authentication.

Custody and Ownership Transfer API set: Defines XML elements for transferring ownership or other rights for information in the UDDI registry.

Subscription API set: Defines XML elements which enable clients to register (or cancel) their interest in receiving information about changes to given items in the UDDI registry.

Value Set API set: Defines XML elements which enable clients to validate UDDI references by checking that the objects referred to have values within a given value set.

A very simple example is shown in Figure 11.23, which shows a service inquiry and the corresponding response. Both enquiry and response are enclosed in the body of a SOAP message for transport.

In this example, the client requests information about services whose names start with the string Weather (% is a wildcard character indicating "any sequence of characters"). Searching is here by name, using approximate matching, but a large number of other criteria can be used, such as search by category, by identifier or by matching to a specification given in WSDL. The response is a list of serviceInfo elements, each containing the name of a service matching the given search criterion. In addition, each serviceInfo element specifies a serviceKey and businessKey as attributes which respectively identify the service and the business which offers it. Each of these keys is a *Universal Unique Identifier (UUID)*, as defined in ISO Standard 11578 [208]. UUIDs are intended to be globally unique, and are constructed by concatenating the current time, the local MAC and IP addresses and a random number to get a 128-bit unique identifier. In UDDI, UUIDs are associated with

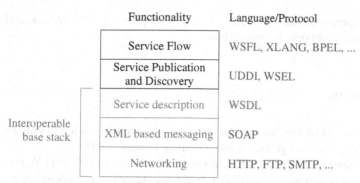

Fig. 11.24 Web Services Architecture conceptual stack

businesses, services, bindings and so-called *tModels* which describe the technical properties of a service, typically in terms of a WSDL specification.

Once the name and business and service keys for a service have been found, further details of the business and service can be found in the registry by using further UDDI inquiries. For example, an inquiry including a get_serviceDetail element would retrieve details about the service, get_businessDetail details about the business, and so on. Publication is somewhat more complicated because of the need to supply authentication information to the registry, so that for example only the business which is responsible for a given service can insert or delete information about that service. Authentication makes use of the XML Signature and XML Encryption facilities described in Section 8.4.5. Full details of the XML elements which have been defined for use in UDDI requests and responses can be found in [262].

11.5.3 Web Service Architectures

It should be clear by now that the Web service architecture is considerably more complex than the simple description at the start of Section 11.5 might get you to imagine. In fact it consists of several layers which are added on to the chosen data transfer protocol, which in full generality does not even need to be HTTP. The complete architecture of the Web Services protocol stack is illustrated conceptually in Figure 11.24. The function of the uppermost layer, associated with Service Flow, is to make it possible to *compose* simpler web services into more complex ones. A major aim of this is to be able to provide services for performing complete business processes, in which documents from various sources are passed round and processed in some way. One of the main candidates for use in this layer, *Business Process Execution Language (BPEL)*, of which the latest version is known as WS-BPEL [265], focusses directly on this issue. However, the way in which this layer works is

currently not completely standardised among various suppliers of Web services, and
we shall not go into more details about it here.

Further Reading

There is a huge amount of literature on the topics of this chapter, and it will only be
possible to give you a few rough indications of where to start looking.

The area of *distributed information systems*, of which the World Wide Web is
just one example, has become enormously important in recent years. There is conceptually no limit to the types of information available in such systems: bibliogra-
phies, reference works, catalogues, books and reports, software, still or moving pictures, sounds,.... Special protocols have been developed for some of these areas, for
example for searching library catalogues [202, 203] and for multi-media transfers.
These latter are especially interesting to study because transfer of sound or moving
pictures places strict real-time requirements on the protocol, and because the identification of contexts in a sequence of sounds or pictures is a special challenge. Search
engines for finding relevant items in huge information bases are still a problem area,
and continue to be a topic for research.

Systems based on the use of cooperating agents are currently a subject of intensive research, and many practical areas of application have been considered. The
simple example which we have seen in this chapter is an example of a system of
static agents. Many interesting systems instead use *mobile agents*, which can move
between systems. Mobile agents have been proposed for use in many areas, such as
collecting up information from the Internet, controlling communication networks,
and in artificial intelligence applications such as robotics. The way in which a group
of agents exchange information in order to achieve their common goal is often described by a so-called *coordination language*, and a study of this area is a very useful
introduction to some aspects of agent systems. A good review of coordination languages and the protocols used to implement them can be found in the monograph
edited by Omicini et al. [103], while Baumann [6] gives a good overview of the
technologies behind mobile agents. The proceedings of the two series of international workshops on *"Intelligent Agents for Telecommunication Applications"*, and
on *"Cooperative Information Agents"* are good places to search for the results of recent research into both theory and applications of agents in the telecommunications
and information retrieval areas.

A new trend in the construction of very large distributed systems is to base them
on *Grid technology*. This is a technology for coordinating the activities of a potentially huge number of computers, in order to supply users with computer power, in
the form of CPU power, storage and other resources. The analogy is to the electric
grid, which provides users with electric power without their having to think about
exactly where it comes from. Foster and Kesselman's book simply entitled "The
Grid" [47] describes many of the ideas and the protocols involved.

The standardised protocols dealt with in this chapter have been rather basic ones, which illustrated particular patterns of communication. Among ISO/ITU-T Application layer protocols, notable omissions have been protocols to support:

1. **Virtual terminals**, which follow the same general principles as FTAM, expressing all operations in terms of an abstract data structure [165, 166].
2. **Directories**, which permit lookup of addresses from names, following the *X.500* principles discussed in Chapter 7. These are described in the multi-part ISO 9594 standard [173]– [180].
3. **System Management**, which in OSI is an Application layer function, based on a general Management Information Service (CMIS [181]) and Protocol(CMIP [182]). More detailed individual aspects of management are described in the multi-part ISO 10164 standard [204]– [205].

There are also a large number of specialised areas for which standardised protocols have been developed, such as office automation, graphics, industrial automation, electronic data interchange for trade purposes (EDI), banking and so on. The area of e-commerce and e-government has spawned a whole series of protocols, which are good examples of how to achieve a high degree of security to maintain user confidence.

Web Services are a hot topic seen from a commercial perspective, since there is a widespread belief that they are the key to offering Internet-based services to the general public. As you might suppose, from the very nature of things much of the literature on Web Services is available via the Web. Organisations such as SoapWare, which acts as a forum for SOAP developers, have produced a number of specialised tutorials on the use of version 1.1 of SOAP, which can be found on SoapWare's website at www.soapware.org. Further developments, including the specification of SOAP 1.2 and WSDL 2.0, have taken place under the auspices of the organisation W3C, whose main web site is at www.w3c.org. A tutorial on SOAP 1.2 forms "Part 0" of the SOAP specification [273], and a tutorial on WSDL forms "Part 0" of the WSDL specification [276].

Different commercial actors in the area of Web Services unfortunately continue to have rather different views on the overall architecture of Web Service systems. However, in recent years there has been a significant effort towards agreeing on a common standard for the application-oriented Service Flow layer of the architecture. The first move in this direction was an agreement between several important players (BEA, IBM, Microsoft, SAP and Siebel Systems) to define a common standard, *BPEL4WS* [7], to replace IBM's *BPEL* and Microsoft's *XLANG*. Subsequent work within the OASIS organisation, has refined BPEL4WS, and led to the development of *WS-BPEL* [265]. A good deal of information on this activity can be found via OASIS' website at www.open-oasis.org. Hull and Su [66] give a good general review of the challenges to be dealt with in this layer.

Appendix A
Notation

A.1 Data Types and Variables

The notation used to denote data types closely follows that of the specification language VDM [72]:

Type	Denoted set of values
$\mathbb{B}$	The Boolean values: $\{\text{true}, \text{false}\}$.
$\mathbb{N}_0$	The non-negative integers: $\{0, 1, 2, \ldots\}$.
$\mathbb{N}_1$	The positive integers: $\{1, 2, \ldots\}$.
$\mathbb{Z}_n$	The integers modulo n: $\{0, 1, \ldots, (n-1)\}$.
bit	Bits: the integers $\{0, 1\}$.
char	The characters of some convenient character set.
tok	A countable set of tokens, i.e. distinguishable values whose structure does not concern us.
T-set	The finite subsets of the type T.
$*^{*}T$	The finite sequences of zero or more values of type T.
$S \times T \times \ldots$	The tuples whose first elements are of type S, second elements of type T, etc.
$S\|T$	Objects which are either of type S or of type T.
$S \rightarrow T$	The functions from S to T.

A variable x of type T is denoted by $x : T$, while a tuple with elements $x, y, \ldots$ of types $S, T, \ldots$ is denoted by $(x : S, y : T, \ldots)$.

A.2 Data Values and Expressions

In addition to the standard notations of set theory and arithmetic, the following notations are used:

$\{\}$	The empty set.

card s	The cardinality of set s: the number of elements in s.
[]	The empty sequence.
hd q	The first (head) element of sequence q.
tl q	The tail of sequence q: the elements remaining after removal of hd q.
len q	The length of sequence q: the number of elements in q.
$[x, y, \ldots]$	The sequence whose first element is x, second element is y, etc.
$q(i)$	The i'th element of sequence q, where $1 \le i \le \text{len } q$ (and $q(1) = \text{hd } q$).
$q \dagger [i \mapsto x, j \mapsto y, \ldots]$	The sequence q in which the i'th element has been replaced by x, the j'th element by y, etc.
$q \frown r$	The concatenation of the sequences q and r: the sequence consisting of the elements of q followed by the elements of r.
$(x, y, \ldots)$	The tuple whose first element is x, second element is y, etc.
$x \oplus y$	$(x + y) \bmod 2$; for Boolean values x, y: the exclusive or of x with y.
$x \ominus y$	$(x - y) \bmod 2$. (For $x, y \in \text{bit}$, the same as $x \oplus y$.)
$succ(i)$	The successor of i in a finite subset of the integers, $\mathbb{Z}_N$: $(i + 1) \bmod N$.

A.3 Processes and Process Expressions

αP	The alphabet of process P.
$\alpha_c P$	The channel alphabet of process P.
$STOP_A$	Deadlock: a process which refuses to take part in any events in the event set A, or in communications over the channel set A.
$(a \rightarrow P)$	Prefixing: a process which initially takes part in the event a and then behaves like process P.

a can be an event from a finite alphabet of elementary events, or can be an input or output event over a channel, where:

$c!e$	denotes output of value e on channel c.
$c?x : T$	denotes input of a value for variable x of type T on channel c.
$\bigsqcup_{i \in D} c[i]!x$	denotes multiple offers of output via the channels $c[i]$ for all $i \in D$.
$c[i \in D]?a : T$	denotes input of a value for the variable a of type T on any of the channels $c[i]$ for $i \in D$.

$P \sqcap Q$	Internal non-deterministic choice between processes P and Q.
$P \mathbin{\|\!\|} Q$	External non-deterministic choice between processes P and Q.
$P \parallel_A Q$	Parallel composition of processes P and Q with synchronisation over events in the set A.
$P \parallel Q$	Parallel composition of processes P and Q with synchronisation over all events in their common alphabet.
$P \parallel\!\parallel Q$	Parallel composition of processes P and Q without synchronisation (pure interleaving).

$P[d/c]$ Renaming, with all occurrences of event c in process P replaced by event d, or all occurrences of channel c replaced by channel d.

$P \setminus A$ Hiding of all events in the event set or channel set A in process P.

(**if** b **then** P **else** Q)   Conditional behaviour: the process which behaves like P if the Boolean expression b is true, and otherwise behaves like Q.

A.4 Traces, Failures and Transitions

$\langle \rangle$ The empty trace.

$\langle s_1, s_2, \ldots \rangle$ The trace with events $s_1, s_2, \ldots$.

$s \frown t$ Trace concatenation: the trace whose first elements are those of s and whose remaining elements are those of t.

$\#s$ Trace length: The number of events in the trace s.

$(s \leq t)$ Trace prefix: true if the first events of trace t are the events of trace s.

$s \upharpoonright L$ Trace restriction: The trace s restricted to the events in the event set L or the communication events over the channel set L.

$past(c)$ The channel history for channel c.

$initials(P)$ The set of initial events of P.

$traces(P)$ The set of traces of P.

$refusals(P)$ The set of all refusal sets of P.

$failures(P)$ The set of all failures of P.

$P \xrightarrow{a} Q$ Process P can take part in event a and will then behave like process Q.

$P \xRightarrow{s} Q$ Process P can take part in the trace s and will then behave like process Q.

A.5 Inference Rules for Process Specifications

P **sat** R Process P satisfies the specification R. (Predicate R is an invariant of P).

$\Gamma \vdash \Delta$ An inference: all predicates in Δ can validly be inferred from those in Γ.

$\frac{\Gamma 1 \vdash \Delta 1}{\Gamma 2 \vdash \Delta 2}$ An inference rule: if $\Gamma 1 \vdash \Delta 1$ is valid, then so is $\Gamma 2 \vdash \Delta 2$.

A.6 Security

PK_A The public key for user A in a PKCS.

SK_A The secret (private) key for user A in a PKCS.

SK_{AB} The secret key for communication between users A and B in a SKCS.

$P \models X$ P believes X to be true.

$P \mid\sim X$ P once said X (and therefore believed X at the time).

$P \longmapsto X$ P has jurisdiction over X (and therefore should be trusted on matters concerning X.)

$P \xleftrightarrow{K} Q$ P and Q may properly communicate using the good key K.

$\{X\}_K$ X is encrypted using the key K.

$P \triangleright X$ P sees X.

$\sharp X$ X is fresh.

$P \to Q : X$ P has sent X to Q.

Appendix B
Standardisation of Protocols

B.1 Standards Organisations

Many organisations define standard protocols for use in data communication or other telecommunication systems. Among the most important official organisations are:

ISO The International Organisation for Standardization, which produces international standards in many technical areas, including data communication.

ITU-T The International Telecommunication Union, Telecommunication Standardization Sector (formerly known as CCITT), a UN organisation which produces standards (so-called *Recommendations*) for telecommunication. Telecommunication is here to be understood in a broad sense, and thus covers some forms of data communication, namely those forms which go via public telephone or data networks.

IEC The International Electrotechnical Commission, which produces standards for (amongst other things) electrical equipment, including process equipment and communication equipment.

IEEE The Institute of Electrical and Electronics Engineers, an organisation in the USA which produces standards in many areas of electrical engineering, including computers and data communication, and which has been especially active in standardisation of local area networks (LANs).

ECMA The European Computer Manufacturers Association, a European organisation for the computer industry, which has published standards covering many areas of data communication.

ISO, ITU-T and IEC are true international organisations, in the sense that their members represent individual nations. For ISO, the members are the various national standardisation bodies; for ITU-T, the members are the national tele-administrations.

At one time, all these organisations, as well as various national bodies, produced competing standards. This was obviously unsatisfactory, and in recent years extensive collaboration has been the order of the day. ISO and IEC have a joint committee (known as JTC1 – Joint Technical Committee 1) for standardisation in the general area of information processing. ITU-T and ISO have an agreement to coordinate their efforts to standardise OSI-related standards, so that standards on the same subject from these two organisations have the same technical content (and preferably also exactly the same text). Several examples of this can be seen in the list of references following this appendix, where ITU-T recommendations corresponding to given ISO standards are listed. IEEE and ISO have a similar arrangement for standards related to local area networks, so that IEEE standards from the '802-series' (all of which are related to LANs) are published by ISO as parts of ISO Standard 8802.

A completely different style of standardisation can be found in the so-called Internet standards. Although many of these have been standardised by the U.S. Department of Defense (DoD), which issues standards for military systems of all kinds, they in fact originate within the Internet community – the people and institutions who use the ARPA Internet system. This is not in itself an organisation, but more a distributed forum for discussion. However, there is a central committee, the Internet Architecture Board (IAB), which publishes the results of the discussion so that others may make use of them.

B.2 Standards Documents

When you start to look into standards, you may wonder about the system used to identify them. For the uninitiated, it can also be confusing that the same 'standard' appears in different versions, with slightly different identifications, as it passes through the process of reaching final approval in the organisation concerned.

B.2.1 ISO standards

ISO standards documents are identified by a set of letters, which give the type and current status of the document, together with a number which identifies the topic, and possibly a date identifying the version. For example: ISO8072 (1984) denotes the 1984 version of ISO standard 8072.

The letters can, for basic standards, be:

ISO: The final, accepted version of an international standard.

DIS: Draft International Standard. The (supposedly) final draft before formal acceptance by ISO. The contents of such a document have reached a technically stable state, and are not expected to be altered substantially as a result of further discussions. At this stage the document is in most countries published for public criticism, so that interested parties can be aware of what is on the way.

CD: Committee Draft. The contents of such a document are of a more preliminary nature, and may be subject to substantial change before the final version is accepted. Committee drafts are not usually available to the general public.

Modifications to existing ISO standards are published in the form of *addenda* or *amendments*. The final version of an addendum bears the letters **AD**, and an amendment **AM**. Final drafts (corresponding to DIS) are denoted by **DAM** and preliminary drafts (corresponding to CD) by **PDAM**. ISO also publishes technical commentaries and other documents of a similar nature, which do not have the same status as standards. These are known as *technical reports*, identified by the letters **TR**, with final drafts denoted **DTR** and preliminary drafts **PDTR**.

Standards are numbered in the order in which they originate (as CDs, PDAMs or PDTRs); the various drafts and the final version all have the same number. However, since ISO standardises an awful lot of things, you cannot in general deduce much about the topic by looking at the number. The final versions of ISO standards are published as they appear. They can be purchased from the standardisation organisation which represents ISO in the country where you live.

B.2.2 ITU-T recommendations

ITU-T recommendations are identified by a letter, which gives the approximate area to which the recommendation relates, together with a number, which more precisely identifies the topic, and a date identifying the version. For example: X.214 (1988) denotes the 1988 version of ITU-T Recommendation X.214.

The letters for the areas most relevant to data communication are:

G   Digital networks.
I   Integrated Services Digital Network (ISDN).
T   Telematic services.
V   Data communication over the telephone network.
X   Data communication networks.
Z   Formal description techniques.

Within most areas, the recommendations are numbered in the order in which they have been introduced. But in the X-series, from X.200 upwards, a more informative numbering scheme is followed:

200–229	OSI service and protocol standards.
290–299	OSI conformance testing.
400–420	Message handling systems.
500–521	Directories.
700–745	Management

Among the OSI service and protocol standards, number $21x$ identifies the standard for the service in OSI layer x, and $22x$ the standard for the corresponding protocol.

Drafts of ITU-T recommendations are not published outside the technical groups which consider them. About every four years, the latest approved versions are published in a compendium, which in the hard copy version currently consists of more than 60 volumes. Many of them are now available without charge from ITU-T's web site at:

```
http://www.itu.int/
```

The others can be purchased via the website or by contacting ITU-T.

B.2.3 Internet standards

Internet standards are so-called *RFCs* – Requests for Comments – which are available via the Internet itself. Each RFC has a number which identifies the topic. For example: RFC793, which describes TCP.

Numbers are allocated in the order in which the RFCs appear, and so do not say anything significant about what sort of topic the RFC deals with, or about the status of the document. The procedure for approval is somewhat similar to ISO's: an initial proposal is discussed as a *Proposed Standard*. After a minimum of six months it may be accepted as a *Draft Standard*. Finally, after at least a further four months, it may be accepted as a *Standard Protocol* for Internet use. An Internet standard protocol is given an extra number which identifies it in the series of full standards (STD). For example, RFC793 is Internet Standard STD7. If a modified version of the protocol is subsequently developed, it gets a new RFC number. The current status of all RFCs is published at regular intervals in a general catalogue, which – of course – is itself an RFC, denoted STD1, and entitled *"Internet Official Protocol Standards"*.

As in the case of ISO, the Internet publication process also operates with other categories of document, apart from what one might consider actual standards. For example, an RFC may be categorised as *Informational*, if it gives generally useful information (about which consensus has not necessarily been achieved), *Experimental*, if it describes interesting but relatively untested new ideas, or *Historical*, if it describes a now outdated technique. Finally, some RFCs may be categorised as describing *Best Current Practice* in some area; these are also given an extra number, which in this case identifies the document in the series of best current practices (BCP). For example, RFC2026 is BCP9.

The form of publication is, as you might suppose, quite different from that used by the more official international organs such as ISO and ITU-T. Generally speaking, the RFCs and all comments on them are published via the Internet itself. The IAB (strictly, the Internet Engineering Steering Group, IESG) coordinates the results of the discussion and looks after the formalities of promoting RFCs from proposed standard to draft standard to full standard. Full details of the current procedure can be found in reference [223].

RFCs can be easily obtained via the Internet. The RFC Editor maintains a Website:

```
http://www.rfc-editor.org/rfcsearch.html
```

which gives access to RFCs by various criteria, such as the number of the RFC, the status of the RFC (proposed standard, draft standard, etc.), or by keyword-based search.

Although the original standards for HTTP were developed as Internet RFCs, more recent development of Web-based technologies, such as HTML, XML, SOAP, and WSDL, takes place under the auspices of a separate organisation, the World Wide Web Consortium (W3C). Standards agreed by the W3C can be found on their web site:

    `http://www.w3.org/`

Finally, the OASIS consortium coordinates further work on web services, including UDDI and BPEL. The results of their work can be found via their web site at:

    `http://www.oasis-open.org/`

References

1. Adiseshu, H., Parulkar, G., Varghese, G.: A reliable and scalable striping protocol. In: Proc. ACM SIGCOMM'96, pp. 131–141. ACM (1996)
2. Ahamad, M., Neiger, G., Burns, J.E., Kohli, P., Hutto, P.W.: Causal memory: Definitions, implementation and programming. Distrib. Comput. **9**, 37–49 (1995)
3. Aspnes, J., Fekete, A., Lynch, N., Merritt, M., Weihl, W.: A theory of timestamp-based concurrency control for nested transactions. In: Proc. 14th. Int. Conf. on Very Large Data Bases, pp. 431–434 (1988)
4. Baran, P.: On distributed communication networks. IEEE Trans. on Communications **CS-12**, 1–9 (1964)
5. Bartlett, K.A., Scantelbury, R.A., Wilkinson, P.T.: A note on reliable full-duplex transmission over half-duplex links. Commun. ACM **12**(5), 260–261 (1969)
6. Baumann, J.: Mobile Agents: Control Algorithms, *Lecture Notes in Computer Science*, vol. 1658. Springer-Verlag (2000)
7. BEA, IBM, Microsoft, SAP AG, Siebel Systems: Business Process Execution Language for Web Services Version 1.1 (2003)
8. Bellovin, S.: Internet RFC 1948: Defending Against Sequence Number Attacks (1996)
9. Bernstein, P.A., Goodman, N.: Concurrency control in distributed database systems. ACM Comput. Surv. **13**(2), 185–221 (1981)
10. Bernstein, P.A., Shipman, D.W., Rothnie, J.B.: Concurrency control in a system for distributed databases (SDD-1). ACM Trans. Database Syst. **5**(1), 18–51 (1980)
11. Bertsekas, D., Gallager, R.: Data Networks. Prentice-Hall International (1987)
12. Bertsekas, D.P., Özveren, C., Stamoulis, G.D., Tseng, P., Tsitsiklis, J.N.: Optimal communication algorithm for hypercubes. J. Parallel and Distrib. Comput. **11**, 263–275 (1991)
13. Birman, K.P., Joseph, T.A.: Reliable communication in the presence of failures. ACM Trans. Comput. Syst. **5**(1), 47–76 (1987)
14. Birrell, A.D., Nelson, B.J.: Implementing remote procedure calls. ACM Trans. Comput. Syst. **2**(1), 29–59 (1984)
15. Bishop, M.: Computer Security: Art and Science. Addison-Wesley (2002). ISBN 0-20-144099-7
16. von Bochmann, G.: Finite state descriptions of communication protocols. Comp. Networks **2**, 361–372 (1978)
17. Bolognesi, T., Brinksma, E.: Introduction to the ISO specification language LOTOS. Comp. Networks and ISDN Syst. **14**, 25–59 (1987)
18. Brassard, G.: Modern Cryptology, *Lecture Notes in Computer Science*, vol. 325. Springer-Verlag (1988)
19. Brookes, S.D., Hoare, C.A.R., Roscoe, A.W.: A theory of communicating sequential processes. J. ACM **31**(3), 560–599 (1984)

20. Burns, J.: A formal model for message passing systems. Tech. Report TR–91, Comp. Science Dept., Indiana University (1980)
21. Burrows, M., Abadi, M., Needham, R.M.: Authentication: A practical study in belief and action. In: Proc. 2nd. Conf. on Theoretical Aspects of Reasoning about Knowledge, pp. 325–342 (1988)
22. Chandy, K., Lamport, L.: Distributed snapshots: Determining global states of distributed systems. ACM Trans. Comput. Syst. **3**(2), 63–75 (1985)
23. Chandy, K.M., Misra, J., Haas, L.M.: Distributed deadlock detection. ACM Trans. Comput. Syst. **1**(2), 144–156 (1983)
24. Chang, E.G., Roberts, R.: An improved algorithm for decentralized extrema-finding in circular configurations of processors. Commun. ACM **22**(5), 281–283 (1979)
25. Chiu, D.M., Jain, R.: Analysis of increase and decrease algorithms for congestion avoidance in computer networks. Comp. Networks and ISDN Syst. **17**(1), 1–14 (1989)
26. Cristian, F.: Probabilistic clock synchronization. Distrib. Comput. **3**, 146–158 (1989)
27. Daemen, J., Rijmen, V.: AES Proposal: Rijndael (1999). Available via URL `http://csrc.nist.gov/encryption/aes/rijndael/`. Selected as the NIST Advanced Encryption Standard algorithm.
28. Dally, W.J., Seitz, C.L.: Deadlock-free message routing in multiprocessor interconnection networks. IEEE Trans. Comput. **C-36**(5), 547–553 (1987)
29. Davies, D.W.: The control of congestion in packet switching networks. IEEE Trans. on Communications **COM-20**(3), 546–550 (1972)
30. Diffie, W., Hellman, M.E.: New directions in cryptography. IEEE Trans. on Inf. Theory **IT-22**(6), 644–654 (1976)
31. Diffie, W., van Oorschot, P.C., Wiener, M.J.: Authentication and authenticated key exchanges. Designs, Codes and Cryptography **2**, 107–125 (1992)
32. Dijsktra, E.W.: A note on two problems in connexion with graphs. Num. Matematik **1**, 269–271 (1959)
33. Dijsktra, E.W., Scholten, C.S.: Termination detection for diffusing computations. Inf. Proc. Letters **11**(1), 1–4 (1980)
34. Dolev, D., Klawe, M., Rodeh, M.: An $O(n \ln n)$ unidirectional distributed algorithm for extrema finding in a circle. J. Algorithms **3**, 245–260 (1982)
35. Dolev, D., Strong, H.R.: Polynomial algorithms for multiple processor agreement. In: Proc. 14th ACM Symp. on Theory of Comput., pp. 401–407 (1982)
36. Dolev, D., Strong, H.R.: Authenticated algorithms for Byzantine agreement. SIAM J. Comput. **12**(4), 656–666 (1983)
37. Duato, J.: A new theory of deadlock-free adaptive routing in wormhole networks. IEEE Trans. on Parallel and Distrib. Syst. **4**(12), 1320–1331 (1993)
38. Dwork, C., Skeen, D.: The inherent cost of nonblocking commitment. In: Proc. 2nd ACM SIGACT/SIGOPS Symp. on Principles of Distrib. Comput., Montreal, Canada, pp. 1–11 (1983)
39. Eswaran, K.P., Gray, J.N., Lorie, R.A., Traiger, L.L.: The notions of consistency and predicate locks in a database system. Commun. ACM **19**(11), 624–633 (1976)
40. European Computer Manufacturers' Association: Tech. Report ECMA TR/20. Layer 4 to 1 Addressing (1984)
41. Fekete, A., Lynch, N., Merritt, M., Weihl, W.: Nested transactions and read/write locking. In: Proc. 6th. Symp. on Principles of Database Syst., pp. 97–111 (1987)
42. Fidge, C.: Logical time in distributed computing systems. IEEE Computer **24**, 28–33 (1991)
43. Fielding, R., Mogul, J.C., Frystyk, H., Masinter, L., Leach, P., Berners-Lee, T.: Internet RFC 2616: Hypertext Transfer Protocol – HTTP/1.1 (1999)
44. Fischer, M.J.: The consensus problem in unreliable distributed systems. In: Foundations of Computation Theory, *Lecture Notes in Computer Science*, vol. 158, pp. 127–140. Springer-Verlag (1983)
45. Fischer, M.J., Lynch, N.A., Merritt, M.: Easy impossibility proofs for distributed consensus problems. Distrib. Comput. **1**, 26–39 (1986)

46. Fischer, M.J., Lynch, N.A., Paterson, M.S.: Impossibility of byzantine consensus with one faulty process. In: Proc. 2nd ACM Symp. on Principles of Database Syst., pp. 1–7 (1983)

47. Foster, I., Kesselman, C. (eds.): The Grid: Blueprint for a New Computing Infrastructure, second edn. Morgan Kaufmann (2003). ISBN 1-55860-933-4

48. Francez, N.: Distributed termination. ACM Trans. Progr. Lang. Syst. **2**(1), 42–55 (1980)

49. Franks, J., Hallam-Baker, P., Hostetler, J., Lawrence, S., Leach, P., Luotonen, A., Stewart, L.: Internet RFC 2617: HTTP Authentication: Basic and Digest Access Authentication (1999)

50. Frey, D., Adams, R.: !%@:: A Directory of Electronic Mail Addressing and Networks. O'Reilly and Associates (1990)

51. Gibbons, P.B.: A stub generator for multilanguage RPC in heterogeneous environments. IEEE Trans. Software Eng. **SE-13**(1), 77–87 (1987)

52. Gligor, V.D., Shattuck, S.H.: Deadlock detection in distributed systems. IEEE Trans. on Software Engineering **SE-6**(5), 435–440 (1980)

53. Gordon, J.: Strong RSA keys. Electronics Letters **20**(5), 514–516 (1984)

54. Gray, J.: Notes on data base operating systems. In: R. Bayer, et al. (eds.) Operating Systems – An Advanced Course, *Lecture Notes in Computer Science*, vol. 60, pp. 393–481. Springer-Verlag (1978)

55. Griffiths, J.M.: ISDN Explained, second edn. John Wiley & Sons (1992)

56. Günther, K.D.: Prevention of deadlocks in packet-switched data transport systems. IEEE Trans. on Communications **COM-29**(4), 512–524 (1981)

57. Hailpern, B.: Verifying Concurrent Processes Using Temporal Logic, *Lecture Notes in Computer Science*, vol. 129. Springer-Verlag (1982)

58. Halsall, F.: Computer Networking and the Internet, fifth edn. Addison-Wesley (2005). ISBN 0-321-26358-8

59. Hayes, J.P., Mudge, T.: Hypercube supercomputers. Proc. IEEE **77**(12), 1829–1841 (1989)

60. Henshall, J., Shaw, S.: OSI Explained: End-to-end Computer Communication Standards. Ellis Horwood (1990)

61. Hirschberg, D.S., Sinclair, J.B.: Decentralized extrema-finding in circular configurations of processors. Commun. ACM **23**(11), 627–628 (1980)

62. Hoare, C.A.R.: Communicating sequential processes. Commun. ACM **8**(21), 666–677 (1978)

63. Hoare, C.A.R.: A calculus of total correctness for communicating processes. Sci. Comput. Program. **1**, 49–72 (1981)

64. Hoare, C.A.R.: Communicating Sequential Processes. Prentice-Hall International (1985)

65. Holzmann, G.: Design and Validation of Computer Protocols. Prentice-Hall International (1991)

66. Hull, R., Su, J.: Tools for composite web services: A short overview. SIGMOD Record **34**(2), 86–95 (2005)

67. Irland, M.I.: Buffer management in a packet switch. IEEE Trans. on Communications **COM-26**(3), 328–327 (1978)

68. Jacobsen, V.: Congestion avoidance and control. In: Proc. ACM SIGCOMM'88, Stanford, California, pp. 314–329. ACM (1988)

69. Jain, R.: Congestion control in computer networks: Issues and trends. IEEE Network Magazine pp. 24–30 (1990)

70. Jain, R.: Congestion control and traffic management in ATM networks: Recent advances and a survey. Comp. Networks and ISDN Syst. **28**(13), 1723–1738 (1996)

71. Johnson, D.B., Maltz, D.A., Broch, J.: Dsr: The dynamic source routing protocol for multihop wireless ad hoc networks. In: C.E. Perkins (ed.) Ad Hoc Networking, chap. 5, pp. 139–172. Addison-Wesley (2001)

72. Jones, C.B.: Systematic Software Development Using VDM, second edn. Prentice Hall International (1990)

73. King, P.J.B.: Computer and Communication Systems Performance Modelling. Prentice-Hall International (1990)

74. Kung, H.T., Robinson, J.T.: Optimistic methods for concurrency control. ACM Trans. Database Syst. **6**(2), 213–226 (1981)

75. Lamport, L.: Time, clocks and the ordering of events in a distributed system. Commun. ACM **21**(7), 558–565 (1978)

76. Lamport, L.: Specifying concurrent program modules. ACM Trans. Progr. Lang. Syst. **5**(2), 190–222 (1983)

77. Lamport, L.: The weak Byzantine Generals problem. J. ACM **30**(3), 668–676 (1983)

78. Lamport, L., Melliar-Smith, P.M.: Byzantine clock synchronization. In: Proc. 3rd ACM Symp. on Principles of Distrib. Comput., pp. 68–74 (1984)

79. Lamport, L., Melliar-Smith, P.M.: Synchronizing clocks in the presence of faults. J. ACM **32**(1), 52–78 (1985)

80. Lamport, L., Shostak, R., Pease, M.: The Byzantine Generals problem. ACM Trans. Progr. Lang. Syst. **4**(3), 382–401 (1982)

81. Lampson, B.W.: Atomic transactions. In: B.W. Lampson, et al. (eds.) Distributed Systems – Architecture and Implementation, *Lecture Notes in Computer Science*, vol. 105, pp. 246–265. Springer-Verlag (1980)

82. Lindsay, B., Selinger, P., Galtieri, C., Gray, J., Lorie, R., Putzolu, F., Traiger, I., Wade, B.: Single and multi-site recovery facilities. In: I.W.Draffan, F. Poole (eds.) Distributed Data Bases. Cambridge University Press (1980)

83. Liskov, B.: The Argus language and system. In: M. Paul, H.J. Siegert (eds.) Distributed Systems – Methods and Tools for Specification, *Lecture Notes in Computer Science*, vol. 190, pp. 123–132. Springer-Verlag (1985)

84. Lynch, N.A.: A hundred impossibility proofs for distributed computing. In: Proc. 8th ACM Symp. on Principles of Distrib. Comput., pp. 1–27 (1989)

85. Majithia, J., Irland, M., Grangé, J.L., Cohen, N., O'Donnell, C.: Experiments in congestion control techniques. In: J.L. Grangé, M. Gien (eds.) Flow Control in Computer Networks. North-Holland (1979)

86. Mattern, F.: Virtual time and global states of distributed systems. In: M. Cosnard, P. Quinton (eds.) Parallel and Distributed Algorithms, pp. 215–226. Elsevier Science Publishers (1989)

87. McEliece, R.: The Theory of Information and Coding. Addison-Wesley (1977)

88. Menasce, D., Muntz, R.: Locking and deadlock detection in distributed databases. IEEE Trans. Software Eng. **SE-5**(3), 195–202 (1979)

89. Menezes, A.J., van Oorschot, P.C., Vanstone, S.A.: Handbook of Applied Cryptography. CRC Press (1997). ISBN 0-8493-8523-7

90. Merkle, R.C., Hellman, M.E.: On the security of multiple encryption. Commun. ACM **24**, 465–467 (1981)

91. Merlin, P.M., Schweitzer, P.J.: Deadlock avoidance in store-and-forward networks – i: Store-and-forward deadlock. IEEE Trans. on Communications **COM-28**(3), 345–354 (1980)

92. Mills, D.L.: Internet time synchronization: The Network Time Protocol. IEEE Trans. on Communications **39**(10), 1482–1493 (1991)

93. Mills, D.L.: Improved algorithms for synchronizing computer network clocks. IEEE/ACM Trans. on Networking **3**(3), 245–254 (1995)

94. Milner, R.: A Calculus of Communicating Systems, *Lecture Notes in Computer Science*, vol. 92. Springer-Verlag (1980) ISBN 0-13-114984-9

95. Milner, R.: Communication and Concurrency. Prentice-Hall International (1989)

96. Mohan, C., Lindsay, B.: Efficient commit protocols for the tree of processes model of distributed transactions. In: Proc. 2nd ACM SIGACT/SIGOPS Symp. on Principles of Distrib. Comput., Montreal, Canada, pp. 76–88 (1983)

97. Mohan, C., Strong, R., Finkelstein, S.: Method for distributed transaction commit and recovery using Byzantine agreement within clusters of processors. In: Proc. 2nd ACM Symp. on Principles of Distrib. Comput., pp. 29–43 (1983)

98. Mullender, S. (ed.): Distributed Systems. Addison-Wesley (1989)

99. Needham, R.M., Schroeder, M.D.: Using encryption for authentication in large networks of computers. Commun. ACM **21**(12), 993–999 (1978)

100. Needham, R.M., Schroeder, M.D.: Authentication revisited. ACM Op. Syst. Review **21**(1), 7 (1987)

101. Object Management Group, Inc.: Common Object Request Broker Architecture, V2.3.1 (1999)
102. Olderog, E.R., Hoare, C.A.R.: Specification-oriented semantics for communicating processes. Acta Inf. **23**(9), 9–66 (1986)
103. Omicini, A., Zambonelli, F., Klusch, M., Tolksdorf, R. (eds.): Coordination of Internet Agents: Models, Technologies, and Applications. Springer-Verlag (2001). ISBN 3-540-41613-7
104. Pachl, J., Korach, E., Rotem, D.: Lower bounds for distributed maximum-finding algorithms. J. ACM **31**(4), 905–919 (1984)
105. Pease, M., Shostak, R., Lamport, L.: Reaching agreement in the presence of faults. J. ACM **27**(2), 228–234 (1980)
106. Pfleeger, C.P., Pfleeger, S.L.: Security in Computing, fourth edn. Prentice Hall (2006). ISBN 0-13-239077-4
107. Pitt, D.A., Sy, K.K., Donnan, R.A.: Source routing for bridged local area networks. In: K. Kümmerle, J. Limb, F. Tobagi (eds.) Advances in Local Area Networks, pp. 517–530. IEEE, IEEE Press (1987)
108. Proakis, J.G.: Digital Communications, third edn. McGraw-Hill (1995). ISBN 0-070-51726-6
109. Ramakrishnan, K., Floyd, S.: Internet RFC 2481: A Proposal to Add Explicit Congestion Notification (ECN) to IP (1999)
110. Rivest, R.L., Shamir, A., Adelman, L.: A method for obtaining digital signatures and public-key cryptosystems. Commun. ACM **21**(2), 120–126 (1978)
111. Roscoe, A.W.: The Theory and Practice of Concurrency. Prentice Hall (1998). ISBN 0-13-674409-5
112. Schneider, F.B., Gries, D., Schlichting, R.D.: Fault-tolerant broadcasts. Sci. Comput. Program. **4**(1), 1–15 (1984)
113. Schneier, B.: Applied Cryptography, second edn. John Wiley & Sons (1996). ISBN 0-471-12845-7
114. Shannon, C.E.: Communication theory of secrecy systems. Bell System Tech. J. **27**, 657–715 (1949)
115. Shoch, J.: Inter-network naming, addressing and routing. In: Proc. COMPCON'78, pp. 72–79 (1978)
116. Shreedhar, M., Varghese, G.: Efficient fair queuing using deficit round-robin. IEEE/ACM Trans. on Networking **4**(3), 375–385 (1996)
117. Skeen, D.: Nonblocking commit protocols. In: Proc. ACM/SIGMOD Conf. on Manag. of Data, Ann Arbor, USA, pp. 133–142 (1981)
118. Spector, A.Z., Daniels, D.S., Duchamp, D.J., Eppinger, J.L., Pausch, R.: Distributed transactions for reliable systems. In: Proc. 10th. ACM Symp. on Op. Syst. Principles, pp. 127–146 (1985)
119. Spector, A.Z., Schwartz, P.M.: Transactions: A construct for reliable distributed computing. ACM Op. Syst. Review **17**(2), 18–35 (1983)
120. Stallings, W.: Data and Computer Communications, eighth edn. Prentice Hall (2007). ISBN 0-13-243310-9
121. Stallings, W.: Local and Metropolitan Area Networks, sixth edn. Prentice Hall (2000). ISBN 0-13-012939-9
122. Stallings, W.: Cryptography and Network Security, fourth edn. Prentice Hall (2006). ISBN 0-13-187316-4
123. Tomlinson, R.S.: Selecting sequence numbers. In: Proc. ACM SIGCOMM/SIGOPS Interprocess Communication Workshop, pp. 11–23. ACM (1975)
124. Waite, W.M., Goos, G.: Compiler Construction. Springer-Verlag (1985)
125. Walrand, J.: Communication Networks: A first course. Irwin (1991)
126. Watson, R.W.: Identifiers (naming) in distributed systems. In: B.W. Lampson, et al. (eds.) Distributed Systems – Architecture and Implementation, *Lecture Notes in Computer Science*, vol. 105, pp. 191–210. Springer-Verlag (1980)

127. Weihl, W.E.: Theory of nested transactions. In: S. Mullender (ed.) Distributed Systems. Addison-Wesley (1989)
128. Zhou, C., Hoare, C.A.R.: Partial correctness of communicating processes and protocols. Tech. Monograph PRG-20, Oxford University Computing Laboratory, Programming Research Group (1981)

Standards

129. CCITT: Recommendation X.25: Interface between Data Terminal Equipment (DTE) and Data Circuit Equipment (DCE) for Terminals Operating in the Packet Mode and Connected to Public Data Networks by Dedicated Circuit (1988)
130. CCITT: Recommendation X.121: International Numbering Plan for Public Data Networks (1988)
131. International Standards Organisation: International Standard ISO4335: Data Communication: HDLC – Elements of Procedure (1979)
132. International Standards Organisation: International Standard ISO6093: Information Processing – Representation of Numerical Values in Character Strings for Information Interchange (1985)
133. International Standards Organisation: International Standard ISO7498: Information technology – Open Systems Interconnection – Basic Reference Model (1984). This is identical to CCITT Recommendation X.200
134. International Standards Organisation: International Standard ISO7498-2: Information technology – Open Systems Interconnection – Basic Reference Model – Part 2: Security Architecture (1989). This is identical to CCITT Recommendation X.800
135. International Standards Organisation: International Standard ISO7498-3: Information technology – Open Systems Interconnection – Basic Reference Model – Part 3: Naming and Addressing (1997). This is identical to CCITT Recommendation X.650
136. International Standards Organisation: International Standard ISO7498-4: Information technology – Open Systems Interconnection – Basic Reference Model – Part 4: Management Framework (1989). This is identical to CCITT Recommendation X.700
137. International Standards Organisation: International Standard ISO8072: Information technology – Open Systems Interconnection – Transport Service Definition (1996). This is identical to CCITT Recommendation X.214
138. International Standards Organisation: International Standard ISO8073: Information technology – Open Systems Interconnection – Connection Oriented Transport Protocol Specification (1997). This is identical to CCITT Recommendation X.224
139. International Standards Organisation: International Standard ISO8326: Information technology – Open Systems Interconnection – Basic Connection Oriented Session Service Definition (1996). This is identical to CCITT Recommendation X.215
140. International Standards Organisation: International Standard ISO8327: Information technology – Open Systems Interconnection – Basic Connection Oriented Session Protocol Specification (1996). This is identical to CCITT Recommendation X.225
141. International Standards Organisation: International Standard ISO8348: Data Communications – Network Service Definition (2002)
142. International Standards Organisation: International Standard ISO8473-1: Data Communications – Protocol for Providing the Connectionless-mode Network Service (1998)
143. International Standards Organisation: International Standard ISO8473-3: Data Communications – Protocol for providing the Connectionless-mode Network Service: Provision of the underlying service by an X.25 subnetwork (1995)
144. International Standards Organisation: International Standard ISO8571-1: Information technology – Open Systems Interconnection – File Transfer, Access and Management – Part 1: General introduction (1988)

145. International Standards Organisation: International Standard ISO8571-2: Information technology – Open Systems Interconnection – File Transfer, Access and Management – Part 2: Virtual Filestore Definition (1988)

146. International Standards Organisation: International Standard ISO8571-3: Information technology – Open Systems Interconnection – File Transfer, Access and Management – Part 3: File Service Definition (1988)

147. International Standards Organisation: International Standard ISO8571-4: Information technology – Open Systems Interconnection – File Transfer, Access and Management – Part 4: File Protocol Specification (1988)

148. International Standards Organisation: International Standard ISO8602: Information technology – Protocol for providing the OSI Connectionless-mode Transport Service (1995)

149. International Standards Organisation: International Standard ISO8649: Information technology – Open Systems Interconnection – Service definition for the Association Control Service Element (1996)

150. International Standards Organisation: International Standard ISO8650–1: Information technology – Open Systems Interconnection – Connection-oriented protocol for the Association Control Service Element: Protocol specification (1996)

151. International Standards Organisation: International Standard ISO8802-2: Information technology – Telecommunications and information exchange between systems – Local and metropolitan area networks – Specific requirements – Part 2: Logical link control (1998). This is identical to IEEE Standard 802.2

152. International Standards Organisation: International Standard ISO8802-3: Information technology – Telecommunications and information exchange between systems – Local and metropolitan area networks – Specific requirements – Part 3: Carrier sense multiple access with collision detection (CSMA/CD) access method and physical layer specifications (2000). This is identical to IEEE Standard 802.3

153. International Standards Organisation: International Standard ISO8802-4: Information technology – Telecommunications and information exchange between systems – Local and metropolitan area networks – Specific requirements – Part 4: Token bus access method and physical layer specifications (1990). This is identical to IEEE Standard 802.4

154. International Standards Organisation: International Standard ISO8802-5: Information technology – Telecommunications and information exchange between systems – Local and metropolitan area networks – Specific requirements – Part 5: Token ring access method and physical layer specifications (1998). This is identical to IEEE Standard 802.5

155. International Standards Organisation: International Standard ISO8802-11: Information technology – Telecommunications and information exchange between systems – Local and metropolitan area networks – Specific requirements – Part 11: Wireless LAN Medium Access Control (MAC) and Physical Layer (PHY) specifications (1999). This is identical to IEEE Standard 802.11

156. International Standards Organisation: International Standard ISO8807: Information technology – Open Systems Interconnection – LOTOS: A Formal Description Technique based on the Temporal Ordering of Observational Behaviour (1988)

157. International Standards Organisation: International Standard ISO8823: Information technology – Open Systems Interconnection – Connection Oriented Presentation Protocol: Protocol specification (1994). This is identical to CCITT Recommendation X.226

158. International Standards Organisation: International Standard ISO8824-1: Information technology – Abstract Syntax Notation One (ASN.1): Specification of basic notation (2002). This is identical to CCITT Recommendation X.208

159. International Standards Organisation: International Standard ISO8825-1: Information technology – ASN.1 encoding rules: Specification of Basic Encoding Rules (BER), Canonical Encoding Rules (CER) and Distinguished Encoding Rules (DER) (2002). This is identical to CCITT Recommendation X.209

160. International Standards Organisation: International Standard ISO8825-2: Information technology – ASN.1 encoding rules: Specification of Packed Encoding Rules (PER) (2002)

161. International Standards Organisation: International Standard ISO8825-4: Information technology – ASN.1 encoding rules: XML Encoding Rules (XER) (2002)
162. International Standards Organisation: International Standard ISO8831: Information technology – Open Systems Interconnection – Job Transfer and Manipulation concepts and services (1989)
163. International Standards Organisation: International Standard ISO8832: Information technology – Open Systems Interconnection – Specification of the Basic Class Protocol for Job Transfer and Manipulation (1989)
164. International Standards Organisation: International Standard ISO8879: Information Processing – Text and Office Systems – Standard General Markup Language (SGML) (1986)
165. International Standards Organisation: International Standard ISO9040: Information technology – Open Systems Interconnection – Virtual Terminal Basic Class Service (1997)
166. International Standards Organisation: International Standard ISO9041–1: Information technology – Open Systems Interconnection – Virtual Terminal Basic Class Protocol – Part1: Specification (1997)
167. International Standards Organisation: International Standard ISO9066-1: Information technology – Text Communication – Reliable Transfer, Part 1: Model and Service Definition (1989). This is identical to CCITT Recommendation X.218
168. International Standards Organisation: International Standard ISO9066-2: Information technology – Text Communication – Reliable Transfer, Part 2: Protocol Specification (1989). This is identical to CCITT Recommendation X.228
169. International Standards Organisation: International Standard ISO9072-1: Information technology – Text Communication – Remote Operations, Part 1: Model, Notation and Service Definition (1989). This is identical to CCITT Recommendation X.219
170. International Standards Organisation: International Standard ISO9072-2: Information technology – Text Communication – Remote Operations, Part 2: Protocol Specification (1989). This is identical to CCITT Recommendation X.229
171. International Standards Organisation: International Standard ISO9314-2: Information technology – Fiber Distributed Data Interface (FDDI) – Part 2: Token Ring Media Access Control (MAC) (1989)
172. International Standards Organisation: International Standard ISO9545: Information technology – Open Systems Interconnection – Application Layer structure (1994)
173. International Standards Organisation: International Standard ISO9594-1: Information technology – Open Systems Interconnection – The Directory – Part 1: Overview of concepts, models and service (1998). This is identical to CCITT Recommendation X.500
174. International Standards Organisation: International Standard ISO9594-2: Information technology – Open Systems Interconnection – The Directory – Part 2: Models (1998). This is identical to CCITT Recommendation X.501
175. International Standards Organisation: International Standard ISO9594-3: Information technology – Open Systems Interconnection – The Directory – Part 3: Abstract service definition (1998). This is identical to CCITT Recommendation X.511
176. International Standards Organisation: International Standard ISO9594-4: Information technology – Open Systems Interconnection – The Directory – Part 4: Procedures for distributed operation (1998). This is identical to CCITT Recommendation X.518
177. International Standards Organisation: International Standard ISO9594-5: Information technology – Open Systems Interconnection – The Directory – Part 5: Protocol specifications (1998). This is identical to CCITT Recommendation X.519
178. International Standards Organisation: International Standard ISO9594-6: Information technology – Open Systems Interconnection – The Directory – Part 6: Selected attribute types (1998). This is identical to CCITT Recommendation X.520
179. International Standards Organisation: International Standard ISO9594-7: Information technology – Open Systems Interconnection – The Directory – Part 7: Selected object classes (1998). This is identical to CCITT Recommendation X.521

180. International Standards Organisation: International Standard ISO9594-8: Information technology – Open Systems Interconnection – The Directory – Part 8: Authentication framework (1998). This is identical to CCITT Recommendation X.509

181. International Standards Organisation: International Standard ISO9595: Information technology – Open Systems Interconnection – Common Management Information Service (CMIS) (1991). This is identical to CCITT Recommendation X.710

182. International Standards Organisation: International Standard ISO9596-1: Information technology – Open Systems Interconnection – Common Management Information Protocol – Part 1: Specification (1991). This is identical to CCITT Recommendation X.711

183. International Standards Organisation: International Standard ISO9796-2: Information technology – Security techniques – Digital signature schemes giving message recovery – Part 2: Integer factorization based mechanisms (2002)

184. International Standards Organisation: International Standard ISO9796-3: Information technology – Security techniques – Digital signature schemes giving message recovery – Part 3: Discrete logarithm based mechanisms (2000)

185. International Standards Organisation: International Standard ISO9797-1: Information technology – Security techniques – Message Authentication Codes (MACs) – Part 1: Mechanisms using a block cipher (1999)

186. International Standards Organisation: International Standard ISO9797-2: Information technology – Security techniques – Message Authentication Codes (MACs) – Part 2: Mechanisms using a dedicated hash function (2002)

187. International Standards Organisation: International Standard ISO9798-2: Information technology – Security techniques – Entity authentication – Part 2: Mechanisms using symmetric encipherment algorithms (1999)

188. International Standards Organisation: International Standard ISO9798-3: Information technology – Security techniques – Entity authentication – Part 3: Mechanisms using digital signature techniques (1998)

189. International Standards Organisation: International Standard ISO9804: Information technology – Open Systems Interconnection – Service definition for the Commitment, Concurrency and Recovery service element (1998). This is identical to CCITT Recommendation X.851

190. International Standards Organisation: International Standard ISO9805-1: Information technology – Open Systems Interconnection – Protocol for the Commitment, Concurrency and Recovery service element: Protocol specification (1998). This is identical to CCITT Recommendation X.852

191. International Standards Organisation: International Standard ISO10021-1: Information technology – Open Systems Interconnection – Message Oriented Text Interchange Systems (MOTIS) – Part 1: System and service overview (1992). This is identical to CCITT Recommendation X.400

192. International Standards Organisation: International Standard ISO10021-2: Information technology – Open Systems Interconnection – Message Oriented Text Interchange Systems (MOTIS) – Part 2: Overall Architecture (1992). This is identical to CCITT Recommendation X.402

193. International Standards Organisation: International Standard ISO10021-6: Information technology – Open Systems Interconnection – Message Oriented Text Interchange Systems (MOTIS) – Part 6: Protocol Specifications (1992). This is identical to CCITT Recommendation X.419

194. International Standards Organisation: International Standard ISO10021-7: Information technology – Open Systems Interconnection – Message Oriented Text Interchange Systems (MOTIS) – Part 7: Interpersonal Messaging System (1992). This is identical to CCITT Recommendation X.420

195. International Standards Organisation: International Standard ISO10026-1: Information technology – Open Systems Interconnection – Distributed Transaction Processing – Part 1: OSI TP Model (1998)

196. International Standards Organisation: International Standard ISO10026-2: Information technology – Open Systems Interconnection – Distributed Transaction Processing – Part 2: OSI TP Service (1998)

197. International Standards Organisation: International Standard ISO10026-3: Information technology – Open Systems Interconnection – Distributed Transaction Processing – Part 3: Protocol specification (1998)

198. International Standards Organisation: International Standard ISO10038: Information technology – Local area Networks – MAC sublayer interconnection (MAC bridging) (1992)

199. International Standards Organisation: International Standard ISO10038/AM2: Information technology – Local area Networks – MAC sublayer interconnection – Amendment 2: MAC bridging – Source routing supplement (1992)

200. International Standards Organisation: International Standard ISO10118-2: Information technology – Security techniques – Hash-functions – Part 2: Hash-functions using an n-bit block cipher (2000)

201. International Standards Organisation: International Standard ISO10118-3: Information technology – Security techniques – Hash-functions – Part 3: Dedicated hash-functions (2004)

202. International Standards Organisation: International Standard ISO10162: Information technology – Documentation – Application Service for Information Systems – Bibliographic Search, Retrieval and Update Service (1993)

203. International Standards Organisation: International Standard ISO10163: Information technology – Documentation – Application Protocol for Information Systems – Bibliographic Search, Retrieval and Update Protocol (1993)

204. International Standards Organisation: International Standard ISO10164-1: Information technology – Open Systems Interconnection – Systems Management: Object Management Function (1993). This is identical to CCITT Recommendation X.730

205. International Standards Organisation: International Standard ISO10164-13: Information technology – Open Systems Interconnection – Systems Management: Summarization Function (1995). This is identical to CCITT Recommendation X.738

206. International Standards Organisation: International Standard ISO10918-1: Information Technology – Digital compression and coding of continuous-tone still images – Part 1: Requirements and guidelines (1994)

207. International Standards Organisation: International Standard ISO11172-2: Information Technology – Coding of Moving Pictures and Associated Audio for Digital Storage Media at up to about 1,5 Mbit/s – Part 2: Video (1993)

208. International Standards Organisation: International Standard ISO11578: Information technology – Open Systems Interconnection – Remote Procedure Call (RPC) (1996)

209. Internet: RFC 768: User Datagram Protocol (UDP) (1980)

210. Internet: RFC 791: Internet Protocol (1981). Identical to U.S. Department of Defense: MIL-STD 1777: *Military Standard Internet Protocol*

211. Internet: RFC 792: Internet Control Message Protocol (1981)

212. Internet: RFC 793: Transmission Control Protocol (1981). Identical to U.S. Department of Defense: MIL-STD 1778: *Military Standard Transmission Control Protocol*

213. Internet: RFC 821: Simple Mail Transfer Protocol (SMTP) (1982)

214. Internet: RFC 826: Ethernet Address Resolution Protocol: Or converting network protocol addresses to 48-bit Ethernet address for transmission on Ethernet hardware (1982)

215. Internet: RFC 959: File Transfer Protocol (FTP) (1985)

216. Internet: RFC 977: Network News Transfer Protocol (1986)

217. Internet: RFC 1034: Domain Names – Concepts and Facilities (1987)

218. Internet: RFC 1035: Domain Names – Implementation and Specification (1987)

219. Internet: RFC 1157: Simple Network Management Protocol (SNMP) (1990)

220. Internet: RFC 1321: The MD5 Message-Digest Algorithm (1992)

221. Internet: RFC 1591: Domain Name System Structure and Delegation (1994)

222. Internet: RFC 1939: Post Office Protocol – Version 3 (1996)

223. Internet: RFC 2026: The Internet Standards Process – Revision 3 (1996)

224. Internet: RFC 2045: Multipurpose Internet Mail Extensions (MIME) Part One: Format of Internet Message Bodies (1996)
225. Internet: RFC 2046: Multipurpose Internet Mail Extensions (MIME) Part Two: Media Types (1996)
226. Internet: RFC 2060: Internet Message Access Protocol, Version 4, rev.1 (1996)
227. Internet: RFC 2246: The TLS Protocol, Version 1.0 (1999)
228. Internet: RFC 2251: Lightweight Directory Access Protocol, Version 3 (1997)
229. Internet: RFC 2279: UTF-8, A Transformation Format of ISO 10646 (1998)
230. Internet: RFC 2315: PKCS #7: Cryptographic Message Syntax, Version 1.5 (1998)
231. Internet: RFC 2328: OSPF Version 2 (1998)
232. Internet: RFC 2373: IP Version 6 Addressing Architecture (1998)
233. Internet: RFC 2401: Security Architecture for the Internet Protocol (1998)
234. Internet: RFC 2402: IP Authentication Header (1998)
235. Internet: RFC 2403: The Use of HMAC-MD5-96 within ESP and AH (1998)
236. Internet: RFC 2404: The Use of HMAC-SHA-1-96 within ESP and AH (1998)
237. Internet: RFC 2405: The ESP DES-CBC Cipher Algorithm with Explicit IV (1998)
238. Internet: RFC 2406: IP Encapsulating Security Payload (1998)
239. Internet: RFC 2407: The Internet IP Security Domain of Interpretation for ISAKMP (1998)
240. Internet: RFC 2408: Internet Security Association and Key Management Protocol (ISAKMP) (1998)
241. Internet: RFC 2409: The Internet Key Exchange (IKE) (1998)
242. Internet: RFC 2412: The Oakley Key Determination Protocol (1998)
243. Internet: RFC 2453: Routing Information Protocol, Version 2 (1998)
244. Internet: RFC 2630: Cryptographic Message Syntax (1999)
245. Internet: RFC 2633: S/MIME Version 3 Message Specification (1999)
246. Internet: RFC 2660: The Secure Hypertext Transfer Protocol (1999)
247. Internet: RFC 2965: HTTP State Management Mechanism (2000)
248. Internet: RFC 3447: Public Key Cryptography Standards (PKCS) #1: RSA Cryptography Specifications, Version 2.1 (2003)
249. Internet: RFC 3561: Ad hoc On-Demand Distance Vector (AODV) Routing (2003)
250. Internet: RFC 3986: Uniform Resource Identifier (URI): Generic Syntax (2005)
251. Internet: RFC 4271: A Border Gateway Protocol 4 (BGP-4) (2006)
252. Internet: RFC 4632: Class Inter-Domain Routing (CIDR): The Internet Address Assignment and Aggregation Plan (2006)
253. ITU-T: Recommendation G.709/Y.1331: Interfaces for the Optical Transport Network (2003)
254. ITU-T: Recommendation G.711: Pulse Code Modulation (PCM) of Voice Frequencies (1972)
255. ITU-T: Recommendation I.321: B-ISDN Protocol Reference Model (1972)
256. National Bureau of Standards: Federal Information Processing Standard Publication 46: Digital Encryption Standard (1977)
257. National Bureau of Standards: Federal Information Processing Standard Publication 81: DES Modes of Operation (1980)
258. National Institute of Standards and Technology: Federal Information Processing Standard Publication 186: Digital Signature Standard (1994)
259. National Institute of Standards and Technology: Federal Information Processing Standard Publication 197: Advanced Encryption Standard (2001)
260. National Institute of Standards and Technology: Federal Information Processing Standard Publication 180-2: Secure Hash Standard (2002)
261. OASIS: Web Services Security: Username Token Profile 1.0 (2003)
262. OASIS: UDDI Spec Technical Committee Specification: UDDI Version 3.0.2 (2004)
263. OASIS: Web Services Security: SOAP Message Security 1.0 (2004)
264. OASIS: Web Services Security: X.509 Certificate Token Profile (2004)
265. OASIS: Web Services Business Process Execution Language Version 2.0 (2007)
266. W3C: Canonical XML (2001). This is identical to Internet RFC3076
267. W3C: XML Schema Part 1: Structures (2001)

268. W3C: XML Schema Part 2: Datatypes (2001)
269. W3C: XML Encryption Syntax and Processing (2002)
270. W3C: XML-Signature Syntax and Processing (2002). This is identical to Internet RFC3275
271. W3C: Extensible Markup Language (XML) 1.0, third edn. (2004)
272. W3C: Namespaces in XML 1.1 (2004)
273. W3C: SOAP Version 1.2 Part 0: Primer (Second Edition) (2007)
274. W3C: SOAP Version 1.2 Part 1: Messaging Framework (Second Edition) (2007)
275. W3C: SOAP Version 1.2 Part 2: Adjuncts (Second Edition) (2007)
276. W3C: Web Services Description Language (WSDL) Version 2.0. Part 0: Primer (2007)
277. W3C: Web Services Description Language (WSDL) Version 2.0. Part 1: Core Language (2007)

Index